ANNA Plus

D1519839

toExcel
San Jose New York Lincoln Shanghai

Anna Plus: Tales from a Town Called Wells

Published by toExcel
an imprint of iUniverse.com, Inc.

For information address:
iUniverse.com, Inc.
620 North 48th Street
Suite 201
Lincoln, NE 68504-3467
www.iuniverse.com

ISBN: 0-595-08941-0

Printed in the United States of America

Dedications
and
Acknowledgements

This book is dedicated to my late husband, Jesse Ivan Kitch, who died of cancer just two months after our trip back to Kansas from Craig, Colorado, to the Wells Centennial, August 27, 1987. I had lived in Craig for thirty-five years. Mr. K. and I made numerous trips back to our home state. He grew up in Southwest Kansas but loved my stories of my first thirty years in Ottawa Country and urged me to write them down.

The memories are mine, but I must confess that without the persistent encouragement, love and determination of my daughter, Judy Bryson, this book would not have become a reality. Many who have dreamed of writing it down have passed to their reward without having done so. That this book is an accomplished fact is due, largely, to her unceasing interest in my well-being and her ability to tackle the 'nuts and bolts' necessary to see my dream fulfilled.

Mr. K. would have been glad to share this page with my three children: Judy and her husband, Patrick Bryson; Terry and his wife, Stephanie Constable; Cheryl and her husband, Brian Coleman; and my first husband, James Constable, who now resides in Kentucky. Mr. K. also knew and loved my brother, Dale L. Allison, who has collaborated with me on many of the episodes in this book.

Others who must be included on this page of acknowledgments are Wayne Peck, my husband, who came to Colorado to see me in 1988 and asked me to marry him and return to my home community. His knowledge of Ottawa County spans four-score years, having spent his entire life here. In his words, "Where else is there?"

Avis Austin, my grade school classmate, then Avis Hanes, and her daughter, Eileen Comfort Adee, natives of Wells, have proof-read my stories over these six intervening years and helped me remember things I might have forgotten.

Darrel and Doll Comfort who moved to Yakima, Washington, with their son, Rex, in the fifties, have proof-read the book, answered my queries and followed my wanderings since childhood. They have been my life-long friends.

LeRoy and Maxine Windhorst have helped in countless ways to authenticate my recollections; Viv and Hazel Heald, natives of Wells, Marnece and the late John Schur, at home on the top of the hill west of Wells for eighty years, and their niece, Charlotte Crow, of the Sand Creek Community, have all confirmed or denied my recollections and patiently answered my calls.

Philip and Ruth Miller, who visit in our county each spring, have contributed to this book with their nostalgic memories of those years. Gene Peck, my brother-in-law, remembered Philip's burning gasoline

i

tank wagon and supplied the names of the section crew who helped him move it.

Edna Windhorst, the Community leader when I was a sewing leader for the Rockhill 4H Club is in Wells when I want to visit about those years.

Dave Comfort and his cousin Clayton have offered encouragement, read critically and convinced me that my recollections were important.

Leo and Javene Whitley, who now live in the house Dad built for us on Main Street beside the creamery have improved it so I'm proud to say my old home is still there.

Eugene Whitley and his mother, Viola and her sister, Grace Tucker still live in Wells. Viola and Grace both helped my mother when Dale and I were born.

Joe Grubham remembers Jim's field of hybrid corn he helped shuck for his sick neighbor.

The late Mrs. Glenna Heald, whose daughter found the Signature Quilt, furnished me with the fifty-six names of Wells people she found embroidered on it.

John Jagger produced the drawing of the Wells Post Office, made from the logo on my Centennial shirt.

I visited with Frank La Plant, Willis Darg, Joe Jagger and others about my mother's parents homestead, the Old Timers Day Parade in Bennington and the Coal Creek Crossing that Joe was searching for. I searched the Microfilm copies of the <u>Minneapolis Messenger</u> at the Minneapolis Library for the history of the Ottawa Country State Lake. Ruth Giesen told me about the old AAA office where she worked with the aerial photos when Jim Constable measured wheat ground for the government. Norline Hanes, the granddaughter of my mother's best friend and neighbor, Mrs. Bertha Brown, talked with me about our childhood. I am grateful for the way I was received by the people in my home community after more than forty years absence.

This book of recollections is my gift of thanks to all of them.

1918

> *Little drops of water,*
> *Little grains of sand*
> *Make the mighty ocean*
> *And the pleasant land......*

Anna stood at the window, her nose pressed flat to the glass, watching the drops of rain make little ships as they splashed into the puddles which had already formed in the sandy street that ran by her house. Her dark, somber eyes reflected her pensive mood this morning.

"Where is the mighty ocean?" she wondered. In her three-year old mind, the pleasant land consisted of the backyard where her papa had put up a swing for her and her brother Dale under the big maple tree...and the stretch of land to the east where the sun came up.

When the sun showed its face she would run out to that puddle in her bare feet and stomp up and down till she made the nicest "mud butter". It would squeeze up between her toes and up above her ankles. She could make mud pies in the sardine cans from the junk pile in the backyard. Of course she would have to wash her feet in the trough that led from the vat in the pump house out to the garden...before she could come back in the house...but the rain kept falling...

Last night she had heard her papa say as he sat on the old wooden front stoop that if the war was not so close to over he'd enlist. She had looked at her mama in alarm. But her face was calm - as though that would be just fine if it was what papa wanted to do! Anna had asked where the war was and was told that it was far away on the other side of the ocean.

Kansas was about as far from the ocean as one could be in the USA-- she knew that. They had gone to Minneapolis, down by the depot. The band was playing and everyone was dressed up with hair ribbons and ruffled skirts and parasols. The little boys had on their best pair of knickers, hair brushed back and shirt tails tucked in. Her mama and papa were very sober. They had come to see the soldiers march onto a flat car on the railroad tracks. The train would take them to Fort Riley where Company G would be trained and sent overseas to fight the Germans.

> *Kaiser Bill came up the hill*
> *To take a shot at France!*
> *Kaiser Bill came down the hill*
> *With Bullets in his pants!*

All the children were chanting and waving the little American flags. She and Dale each had a flag when they came home. She had heard her mama and papa discussing later that the soldiers did not get to go over

1

and fight together. When they got to Fort Riley they had split them up and sent them out with different companies. Papa explained that if a company got 'wiped out' they wouldn't all be from Minneapolis. Now her papa, the very center of her 'pleasant land' might enlist!......But, the rain had stopped. The sun was peeking through the clouds.

****

"I'll do it myself," said the little red hen,
And she did.

Anna watched as her Mama carefully tied a sun bonnet over her head.

"Where are you going Mama?" she asked.

"Today's the day I'm going to set the eggs under the brooder hens. Come, you can help," Mama said as she reached for Anna's bonnet, and tied it firmly under her chin. Anna didn't like the bonnet much, but little girls weren't supposed to be out in the sun without one.

It was a lovely spring morning. Mama pumped a bucket of water in the well house. As she came back outside she looked out towards the east.

"See Anna," she said as she pointed to the closest field. "That's where they're going to build a high school. You and Dale will be able to get a good education."

Mama explained how she went to high school in Concordia, but Papa stopped school after the sixth grade. There wasn't a junior high or high school near enough to his home for him to finish school and he had too many chores to do on the farm anyway. Mama described to Anna just what the school would be like.

Anna didn't really understand but she could tell that Mama's dream of the school was important to her. As Mama described it, Anna could almost see the big red brick building that would stand over there against the skyline.

She remembered the conversation on the porch. Did she dare ask Mama about it? Mama always backed up Papa and allowed no discussion of anything he told the children to do. Tentatively, Anna pulled at Mama's skirt," Mama, is Papa really going away to the war," she asked in a trembling voice.

Mama looked down at Anna and her eyes softened. "Don't you be worrying, Anna," she said. "There really isn't time for Papa to go now. The war's almost over. Come, there's lots to do today."

"Can I help you too?" asked Dale, coming up behind them. His bright blue eyes and eager face were almost obscured by a shock of light red hair.

"Run on out to the outhouse and when you come back, I'll button your rompers at the bottom, and we'll see," said Mama affectionately.

2

Anna watched as Dale ran on to the outhouse. She felt a little scornful of the way he always forgot to go. If he wasn't continually reminded, he'd have an accident, and then there would be another set of rompers to be washed. Anna wore the same clothes, and if Mamma wasn't careful there would be nothing for them to wear. What if Dale could count to 100 and was learning his multiplication tables? She knew what was really important!

Anna remembered when Mama's sister, Aunt Belva had come and stayed a week to help Mama sew the blue chambray rompers for her and Dale. Mama had cut out pair after pair, and then she and her sister had sewed and talked. Anna sat on a blanket on the floor and watched. At the end of the week, there were a dozen pairs. The trouble was, Dale could go through a half-dozen pairs a day. There was a tub full of wash soaking outside the back door right now that would have to be scrubbed on the board and hung out to dry this morning so they'd have something to put on tomorrow.

When Dale returned, trailing the back of his rompers, Mama smiled. buttoned him up and let him help them. She climbed up into the haymow and forked down a good supply of hay while Dale waited below and filled a basket. Papa had built such a nice brooder house, with six compartments for setting hens. Now there were at least six old hens in the chicken house that pecked Dale as he tried to get the eggs they had laid. Mama knew they were ready to brood, and she had saved up fifteen eggs to set under each of them.

They made nests in each compartment in the nice new brooder house. Papa had built it so cleverly. It had hinges on the long door in the roof so you could work on every nest and then close the door so the old hens couldn't run away and let their eggs get cold. Each compartment had its own run made from wire mesh so the baby chicks could run outside through a small trap door that the mother hen couldn't get through.

Mama looked proudly at the brooder house, and said, "If we have good luck with these hens, we may have sixty to seventy-five chicks in a few weeks."

Saving the eggs was a chore Anna and Dale had both helped with. They gathered eggs every day from the hen house. They knew the cross old rooster played a part too. He had been with the hens all spring and chased them and bit them on the head. When Anna and Dale saw him doing that they had run to the house for Mama.

"Mama, Mama, please come and stop the bad old rooster," Anna had pleaded. "He's biting the hens and hurting them."

Mama had smiled down at their worried faces. "I know it doesn't seem right, children," she had said. "But that's something the hens will have to put up with if we are to have little chicks in their eggs this spring.

Fifteen eggs in each nest--Dale counted them as he placed them in the nests. Anna double-checked his reckoning. Mama carried the broody old hens over from the chicken house and set each one carefully on the eggs. The watering cans and coffee cans for chicken feed were filled and the trap door in the roof was closed.

"No one else in town has such a fine brooder house," said Mama proudly. "Mrs. Brown says she's going to get an incubator to set on their enclosed back porch and that would be nice too. You can set 80 eggs in one of those Little Brown Hens and the big Bell City will take 100 eggs. But then you'd have the problem of being a mother hen yourself when the chicks got big enough to run out in the yard."

She looked down at Anna and Dale and smiled, "Right now I'd rather look after my own two little chicks."

Anna and Dale couldn't understand all of Mama's musing, but they were glad she cared more about them than the chickens!

"There will still be plenty to do," said Mama. We'll have to check the hens from time to time to see if the watering cans and feed cans are full and we'll also have to check if the old hens have pushed any of the eggs out of the nests. The hens have decided those eggs won't turn into chicks. They are rotten and will have to be thrown away."

"You mean, Mama," asked Anna breaking in, "Those are the ones where the old rooster didn't catch the hen?"

Mama just looked at Anna, and Anna knew that no further explanation would be forthcoming.

"And if we're really lucky," Mama continued briskly, "In three weeks, we'll have a perfect hatch."

Papa was working on a bridge. When he came home that evening, Mama, Dale and Anna were all three proud to tell him that they had started the spring crop of chickens that morning.

Mama said, "Dale counted out ninety eggs from the egg case and brought them out to the brooder house."

"And I helped," Anna broke in.

"Yeah, she can count to fifteen," Dale said.

"And Dale had to have clean rompers four times," Anna bragged, "And I wore the same pair all day."

****

Homesteadin' Ain't Easy

That evening, as they were finishing dinner and talking about the day, Dale changed the subject.

"Are you going to go to the war, Papa?" Dale's eyes were shining with excitement and not a little fear.

Papa glanced at Mama whose lips were set in a disapproving line despite her blank expression. Her folks were Quakers and she didn't approve of fighting. None of her people had served in any army, not in the Revolutionary War or the Civil War even though they were part of the Underground Railway.

4

"I don't think so, Dale," he said and both children let out a sigh of relief. "It's almost over, and I wouldn't get any further than training camp anyway."

"What would the war be like?" asked Dale, happy to probe further now that he knew his Papa wouldn't be there.

"It's hard to imagine Dale, without being there," Papa said with another glance at Mama. "It is very hard having to shoot at other people, and awful to be shot yourself. I know," he finished ruefully, rubbing his right hip.

"Really?" asked Dale excitedly. Both he and Anna begged to be told the story.

Papa looked at Mama again, but she didn't seem to mind. So he began. "I was out in Western Kansas, homesteading a farm with my cousin John. I was hoping to prove up the land, and then I would have been a farmer, rather than a master mason and a handyman, though I like this work well enough. Anyway we were loading a spring wagon, when somehow the gun Cousin John was holding discharged into my hip."

Anna and Dale winced at the thought. "Did he mean to?" asked Dale.

"I don't think so," said Papa, "But Cousin John really wanted that land for himself. Anyway, I heard later that he went to prison for something else so I guess he's paid for his crime if a crime it was," Papa paused, and shook his head, remembering.

"What did it feel like, what happened then? Please go on with the story," begged both of the children.

Papa laughed and said, "Hold your horses and let me get a word in edgeways. I can't remember much about how it felt. It was just a sharp pain at first, and after that I didn't feel much for awhile. I was bleeding a lot, and passed out. I can remember them taking me to a nearby sod shanty where a woman bound up my leg to stop the bleeding. The cloth she had was white, brand new and clean, but it had little black flowers on it. The ink in the print gave me blood poisoning. I had to travel for several days before they could get me to the doctors and the hospital in Topeka to take out the shot."

"They put me in a wagon and sent someone on a fast horse to tell my dad, your Grandpa Allison, about the accident, and telling him to meet us at the rails' end in Solomon. Dad was there when I arrived and we travelled together on the train to Topeka. But for Papa's being there, I wouldn't have a leg at all."

"Why's that, Papa," demanded Anna.

"Well, by that time I was in really bad shape. Most of the time I was dreaming, or talking nonsense to myself. I was burning up with fever from the blood poisoning. But one time when I was awake and making sense I talked to Papa. I told him if I was going to die I wanted to die in one piece, and I made him promise he wouldn't let them cut off my leg, no matter what. Papa promised me that, and he kept his word."

"But why would they cut off your leg, Papa?" asked Dale, his eyes round with alarm.

"To stop the poison in it from killing me. Anyway, a horse drawn ambulance met us when the train arrived in Topeka. I was placed in what looked like a wicker basket hanging from the ceiling. I can remember blacking out and waking up again as the basket swayed when the cart went over the railroad tracks. I wasn't awake for many days after that. The doctors told Papa that if he didn't let them cut off my leg, I would die. But Papa stood by his promise to me and I didn't die. I was only twenty-two and strong which helped and maybe God did too. It was six months before I could leave the hospital, and by then I was perfectly well."

Charlie didn't mention his continuing pain, his poor circulation, or that his friends affectionately called him "Old Step and a Half." The children didn't need to know everything.

"What happened then?" asked Anna.

"You children, and your questions," laughed Papa. "We could go on and on forever and you wouldn't be satisfied. Well let's see," and then his eyes flashed mischievously. "Before I was shot, I was going to marry a woman named Alta, but she didn't want to wait for a man who might not be able to walk. So she gave me the mitten and took up with someone else."

Dale and Anna looked at Mama whose lips were set in a very straight line. They could tell she didn't approve of this part of the conversation or of Alta, though Mama had only sniffed and tossed her head at the mention of Alta's name.

Quickly, Papa continued. "I guess that was the good thing about being shot. It's an ill wind that blows no good as they say. Alta left me free and then your mother and I got to know each other better and married. And of course, you two came along. I've a lot to be thankful for."

Anna and Dale nodded fervently in agreement, and even Mama smiled.

****

"Four and twenty turtle eggs baked in a pie..."

Anna couldn't wait to get out in the back yard. All through breakfast she looked through the window, watching the wind mill as it pumped water into the trough.

As Anna was finishing her breakfast, her Papa walked into the kitchen with a big bowl of white meat. "That big snapper John Windhorst brought us was full of eggs," he said. "Anna, I put them on top of the lid to the mash barrel. You can use them if you are making mud pies today. Where's Dale? I'm going to take him with me to work on the arch cave out at Claude and Minnie Winsetts."

"Thanks Papa," said Anna. "I think he's still in the bedroom getting dressed."

Anna ran outside to the well house and opened the door. There were the turtle eggs - covering the whole lid. They looked like ping-pong balls, round and white but they were soft-shelled. She would have to bake a lot of pies today or they would spoil sitting there in the sun and she had no ice-box in her playhouse in the grape arbor.

But she had plenty of water and nice soft dirt from the garden. She sifted her "flour" through an old piece of screen she had taken from the junk-pile along with the empty syrup pail she had found for her flour. Old sardine cans made very good pie tins and she had plenty of those stacked in her orange crate cupboard.

Anna watched as Dale and Papa harnessed up Punch and Judy, their mules, and loaded the cement forms in the spring wagon. She was glad Dale was going to get to go along with Papa today. Dale wouldn't like to have her cooking all day if he was home - he always wanted her to help him build something like a car and she'd have to run and get the hammer and the nails and hunt for tin cans for the head lamps and old baby buggy wheels so it would roll. She so much wanted to bake pies today.

It really didn't matter that her spoon was an ordinary stick or that her bowl was an old head lamp from a car. Anna set it down in the soft dirt by the trough, dipped the water with a cup that had been thrown away because it had lost its handle, poured the dirt from the syrup pail canister through the piece of screen. She mixed the ingredients together and then she tackled the magic eggs that were going to make her pies so very special. The eggs were soft shelled but the only way she could get into them was by putting them in the mixture and breaking them up with a stick. She stirred and stirred some more. Soon the dough was smooth and the batter looked as good to eat as her mother's chocolate cake dough.

She lifted the stick to her lips. Just a taste to see if the eggs had improved mud dough from what she remembered. Oh. No! The same gritty taste. Ah, well, she poured the dough into the sardine can pie tins, carefully smoothed out the dough, sifted a bit of "brown sugar" on top and set them out in the sun to bake.

Anna knew that they would bake hard as rocks and Dale and his friends would break them up and throw them at birds flying by, but for now they were going to be the most delicious pies she had ever baked. What was the rhyme? "fit for a king," they'd be.

So she wiped her hands on her rompers after carefully washing them in the trough and went in the house to eat some of the nice warm cookies she had smelled all the while she was baking...This had been a good morning.

When Dale and Papa came home, they all admired Anna's cakes.

Satisfied that her work had been properly appreciated, Anna asked, "What was it like, working on the arch cave?"

Anna didn't have to ask why they were building an arch cave. She knew they were to protect people from tornadoes, and to store potatoes and the like. But Papa had never built one for his own family - they stored cans of fruit and tomatoes in the cellar under the house. Papa never seemed to be afraid of tornadoes.

"Well, said Papa, "It's hot work preparing a great big square hole in the ground, even on a cool spring day with the mules doing most of the digging. And then we had to collect and place all the rocks for the arch in the roof."

"I worked hard," Dale broke in.

"Oh, yeah," said Anna somewhat jealously, "What did you do?"

"I helped pile up the dirt and the other boys and I threw rocks at the birds."

Anna didn't reply but she thought scornfully, "Some work, compared to making pies!"

****

"Hickory, dickory dock..
The mouse ran up the clock."

Dale sat under the table with the only clock in the house. Now he came crawling out, clutching the clock to make sure no one would take it away from him, as he had done every few minutes for the last hour.

"Now what time is it, Mama?" he asked.

"Dale, it is five minutes later than the last time you asked," said Mama with some impatience.

"But what time is that? What do you say?" he plead with such intensity that Mama looked at the clock once more and explained.

"See Dale, the big hand is on the three and the little hand is just past eleven. The little hand is the hour hand and the big hand is the minute hand, so it is eleven fifteen."

"But why do you call it fifteen when the little hand is pointing at three?"

"I declare Dale," said Mama shaking her head but with some pride, "I've never known a child to be so interested in numbers. None of the other children your age are going on and on about time."

"But why, Mama?" asked Dale persistently.

Stella sighed. She had lots of chores to do. She decided to explain again, hoping Dale would go back under the table and she could get on with her work.

"Dale, you remember that we have twenty-four hours in a day, and the clock measures twelve hours at a time, so the hour hand goes around the dial twice each day. We know it is either just after eleven o'clock in the morning or in the evening when we see the little hand like this." She looked at Dale and he nodded. Mama continued.

"There are sixty minutes in an hour. The clever thing about a clock is that we can measure both twelve hours and sixty minutes on the same dial. Can you guess why that is?"

"Is it because of these little lines between the numbers?" Dale asked.

"Very good," said Mama, pleased at his perception. "And also because sixty is equal to twelve times five. If you look closely at the little lines you will see that there are four lines between each number. If you count the lines off you will count to five when you are at the one on the dial or five times one, and to ten by the time you get up to the two, or five times two."

"And," said Dale excitedly, "I'll be at fifteen when I get to the three. That's five times three. So that's why you say fifteen when the big hand is on the three."

"Right," said Mama, delighted at how quickly he learned. "It's the same all the way around the dial. You can learn to tell time more easily if you learn your five times table better. Here, I'll write it out for you again."

Hurriedly, Mama took a sheet of paper and wrote out the five times table. Satisfied, Dale took the paper and the clock and crawled back under the table.

Anna was cutting paper dolls from the slick colored pages of last season's catalog. She had watched with interest as Mama explained how to tell time. However, she knew that Dale would learn to tell time, and then when it was necessary to know, he would always be there to say. No need for her to learn. She cut out a whole family. Just then she came to some grey sheets and started to cut those up too.

"No, Anna," Mama said. "We need all those gray flimsy sheets for out in the outhouse, but you can use all the slick bright colored sheets that you want. No one likes to use those."

Anna hunted in the catalog for all the slick sheets. She wished there were more. Busily, she cut away, and lined her paper families up in rows. Dale still sat under the table watching the hands moving ever so slowly around the face of the clock.

The children heard the back door shut softly, and Dale crawled out from under the table to find out where Mama was going. He went out the door and when he looked around the corner of the house, Mama was coming out of the tool shed with a spade in one hand and a bucket in the other. He crept up behind her, and watched as she dug a hole in the ground. As Mama poured the contents of the bucket out, Dale saw it was half full of dead chicks! Mama had found them when she had looked in on the old hens. The eggs were hatching and the hens had kicked the dead chicks out of the nest. Dale stared in horror as she began to cover the poor little chicks with dirt. Finally he could stand it no longer.

"Mama," he said pathetically, "When I die I don't want you to shovel dirt in my eyes."

Mama turned round quickly and saw Dale standing there, still holding the clock in his hand. He looked so stricken that she picked him up, clock and all, and carried him back to the house.

"Look at all the people, Mama. They're all dressed up to go to church," said Anna, still sitting in the floor with her paper dolls. Then she saw how sad they were.

"What wrong?" she asked jumping up in alarm.

Mama knelt down and gathered them both into her arms.

"Dale is sad because he saw me burying some of the little chicks in a hole in the ground. But that is the way it is, some little ones make it and some don't," Her voice broke there. It would be years before the children knew why. Stella had buried two little baby boys who were stillborn, one after the other before she had the two of them.

Mama went on and firmly changed the subject, "But the hens are so proud of those that do. Come let's go out in the yard and watch the little chicks strutting around."

Eagerly, Anna grabbed Mama's hand to lead her outside, but Dale grabbed the other hand, and said, holding up the clock, "Mama, what time is it now?"

****

"Whistling girls and crowing hens
Always come to some bad ends..."

The sputtering was deafening as the bright red airplane with big black numbers across its side swept low in the sky. Every eye in the town of Wells was fastened on the airplane as it continued to circle around the little village as though it was looking for a place to land. As the last sputter died in the air, it turned and quietly glided down and landed, out there in the open field to the east where Stella dreamed they would one day build the high school.

It was Sunday afternoon and Anna and Dale had company, Grandpa and Grandma Allison had driven over with Uncle Floyd and Uncle Jessie for Sunday dinner. It seemed that everyone in Wells had company as the crowd gathered, walking from all directions toward the great mechanical bird at the edge of their little town.

The man who flew in with it got out and produced a coal oil can from somewhere inside and started walking toward the collecting crowd. Some one was sent to fill that can and the pilot turned back to speak to people. His airplane had run out of gas. Anna and Dale were standing beside Grandma amongst the crowd making a big circle at a respectable distance around the airplane.

Grown men were talking to the pilot. He wore black leather leggings to his knees, a black helmet and goggles pushed up on his forehead. A black leather jacket and knee pants made him look like a man from the moon to the crowd dressed in overalls and long billowy dresses.

Anna noticed that the pilot had removed his black leather gloves - one was hanging over the edge of the cockpit and the other had fallen to the ground beside the airplane. She darted over and picked it up - she would just climb up and put it with the other one and look inside the place where the pilot sat. It was all black leather just like the clothes the man wore. And such a small seat that no one could ride with him.

Just then the pilot turned and saw Anna about to climb inside his airplane. He hurried over but not before Grandma had retrieved Anna. The pilot scolded Grandma for not keeping Anna in check - what if all the children had tried to look inside? They could break the airplane and it would not be able to fly when the gas arrived.

Later, as the little airplane started up its deafening engine and prepared to taxi through the crowd, Grandma scolded, "Anna, one might expect Dale to climb up on the side of that airplane or some other curious little boy - but a tiny little girl? Whatever possessed you? It's a wonder you didn't fall or tear your dress!"

Anna was strangely silent, still thinking about how it would feel to be up there in the sky in that little seat with nothing over your head. What if it rained?

Mother was standing in the yard - she could see as well from there. As Anna and Dale walked back toward the house, he asked, "What did it look like inside?"

"It was so small inside and all black leather like his coat. There were lots of circles in front of where he would sit - white circles with numbers on them." Anna explained. She could tell that Dale wished he could have seen for himself.

Anna's teen-age uncles teased her when she came in the yard. "I looked around and there was the seat of Anna's bloomers lookin' right at me from the side of the airplane," Uncle Jessie said. Everybody laughed and Anna felt her face turning red as she disappeared around the back of the house.

That night after the company had all gone home, Anna expected Mama and Papa to both scold her for 'being such a tomboy.' But the whole evening was spent talking about what Grandpa and Grandma had asked them to do. They wanted Mama and Papa to move out in the country and take care of their farm while they went to Montana for a year.

"Why do they want to go to Montana?" Anna asked.

"That's where Grandma's two daughters, your aunts, live with their families. They've been there for several years now ever since they married. Grandma is very homesick for them." Mama explained.

"But why do we have to go there?" asked Anna doubtfully, thinking of her grape arbor and all the other places she loved to play. "Uncle Jessie and Uncle Floyd live with them. Couldn't they look after the farm? Uncle Bert and Uncle Roy and Papa could come and help too, like we did last summer at the harvest."

"Your Uncle Jessie and Uncle Floyd are going along to Montana. And even though your Grandma has five sons, Papa is the oldest. So he must help when his Mama asks him to."

Papa was listening carefully to Mama's explanation and seemed pleased with her response. Dale had no doubts, he was all excited about getting to live on a farm.

"We can take old Ring and get the cows, Anna," he said enthusiastically. Ring was Grandpa's collie dog.

"You can do that and much more too, children. Your mother will need lots of help if I am to keep up with my cement work and the farm work too." Papa said.

"And maybe you will get tired of being such a tomboy, Anna. You may even want to sit quietly with your dress down over your knees and learn to embroider, or sweep the kitchen floor." said Mama, only half joking.

That night, Anna fell asleep thinking about that man up in the sky with just wings and a noisy engine with him.

****

"Old McDonald had a farm; ei, ei, oh!
And on this farm........." Author unknown

Punch and Judy were hitched to the wagon which was drawn up in front of the door to the little two-room house in Wells. All the groceries out of the kitchen, all the canned fruit, potatoes and onions out of the cellar, even the laying hens and their nests had to be moved to Grandpa's farm. Anna knew the farm was far away - it was six miles west of Wells, and south a mile past Johnnie Mossaway, and Elroy Stout's place. Anna and Dale were going to be gone from Wells for a year.

"Can I take the car I'm building?" Dale asked. Their neighbor, Clarence Brown had a car with a box on the back to carry the mail when the real mail carrier couldn't do it. It was a noisy sputtering thing that ran by itself, and Dale had been trying to build something like it for several days.

"Maybe next load, if we have room," said Papa, as he picked up a box and walked out to the wagon.

Anna thought, "But I can't move my playhouse - and there's no grape-arbor there...but there is a windmill and troughs where we can feed the pigs and the chickens..." Then she asked aloud, "Can I mix the mash with the sour milk for the pigs when we get to the farm, Mama?"

"Oh yes, honey, there will be lots you can do," Mama said in a tired voice.

Anna looked at her mother and felt she was not very happy to be going to the farm...Mama couldn't move her garden or fruit trees either.

Anna had heard her parents talking and knew her mother was worried about keeping the young trees watered after she moved so far away, especially as Anna's Papa was already working long hours on the roads for the township. Mama was also anxious that her laying hens would be upset by the move and might quit laying and go into a moult. But Mama had agreed with Papa that they had to help his mother. She missed her two daughters badly since they moved away off up there to Montana. Anna's family just had to go out to the farm so her grandparents could go and visit them.

"There's lots of work to do on a farm," Mama continued. "Your Papa and Grandmother had to run the farm after your Grandfather was injured and had to walk on crutches. That's why your Papa didn't finish school - there was always so much to do that he often couldn't go. But he finished his McGuffey's Reader anyway, and he's good with math," Mama finished proudly.

Papa came back into the house and said, "There's no way I can get those chicken crates on this load, Stella. I didn't know you had so much canned fruit and vegetables in the cellar. I think I'll just go on with this load. It will take four hours for the mules to cover the six miles to the farm and come back here, so we should be back by evening. I'll clean the chicken house at the farm while I'm there."

"Take both children with you. We don't have to do everything at once," Stella agreed. "It will take a week to make this move in an orderly fashion, and I need to collect my thoughts."

"That's a good idea, Stella," he said, and gave her a hug. "We'll catch up the chickens tonight after they've gone to roost."

Papa went back outside and got into the wagon. "Come on kids." he called, "Let's go." When Anna and Dale came running up, tumbling over each other in eagerness to scramble into the spring wagon, he laughed and said, "Come up on the seat beside me. I don't want you falling off the load."

When they arrived at the farm, Grandma and Grandpa were waiting to help the children with unloading all the canned fruit and vegetables. Papa set about cleaning the chicken house. When he came back in the house, Grandma was marveling at the amount of preserving Stella had done.

"Stella must have one hundred jars of tomatoes," Grandma told Charlie. "Anna and Dale have filled my whole pantry and half the cellar."

"Mother, I think you should make chicken and dumplings out of that big Buff Orpington rooster. Did you see him try to flog Anna when she came out to see what I was doing?" Papa asked. "Anna isn't as big as he is but she's a lot more useful to us! And I think he'll be mean to Stella's young laying hens - she has fifty of them that I'm going to have to mix in with your flock tomorrow."

"Well, I think he's served his purpose for this spring," agreed Grandma. "If you will catch him and put him in that crate out there, I'll have Port dress him for me and we'll have dinner for you when you come over tomorrow."

Dale and Anna liked to watch their Grandpa and the chickens - he had made pets of all the old hens. Their Grandpa would walk out in the middle of the flock, stand on one crutch, and lay the other one crosswise to make a perch. His old hens would fly up one at a time, walk across the crutch and eat shelled corn out of his pocket. But Grandpa didn't like that old rooster either.

"The other day," he said, "Old Buff tried to saw my crutch in two with his spurs; they're about an inch and a half long. He should have been in a stew-pot a year ago."

"Dale, run out toward the barn, and I'll catch that rooster when he starts after you," said Papa as he took the chicken hook off the wall of the porch.

"No," said Grandma. "Buff is too dangerous. Call the dog. Ring is afraid of him, but Ring will come, and that rooster will chase him right up to the door."

Papa caught old Buff and put him in the crate.

Grandpa said, "I'll feed him some sour milk and mash to tenderize his drumsticks and we'll dress him in the morning."

"Sounds like a fine idea to me," said Papa. He looked around for Dale and Anna and said, "Come on children, we still have a long ride home ahead of us."

As Papa was lifting Dale and Anna up to the wagon seat, Grandma came out on the porch with a long box of crackers and an orange for each of them.

"Where did you get the oranges?" Papa asked.

"At the Farmer's Store in Minneapolis. They got a crate of them in for Easter and Port bought a few after they cut the price. They said they were too expensive to start with and they would probably have no more in to sell until Christmas. But that's a long time for children to wait for an orange, isn't it, especially since we won't be here to see if Santa brings them one," Grandma said with a smile.

"Thank you, Grandma," said Anna. "We'll share with Papa as soon as he peels one - and we'll save some for Mama too."

They waved good-bye as Punch and Judy started off at a brisk pace with their empty wagon. Papa wrapped the reins over the dashboard as they turned out of the driveway and headed for Wells.

Both children were now very excited at the prospect of moving to the country. Dale asked, "Can we walk to the end of the pasture every evening and bring home the cows, Papa?"

"Oh yes," Papa answered. "But you'll have to have old Ring along with you. The old bull may not like two little children out in the pasture and he might chase you if you are alone. By evening they are usually clear down to the end of the pasture - past the trees and the creek. You can carry a bushel basket between you and pick up dry cow chips as you go. Your mother likes those to build a quick fire with in the morning."

14

"But how will we know if they are dry?" Anna asked.

Papa laughed, "Oh, you'll learn that fast enough, once you've tried to pick one or two up while they're still wet. There should be quite a few dry ones. I doubt if your Uncle Roy or Uncle Jessie have collected any since they could use a hatchet. They'd rather run out and chop an arm load of kindling."

"Maybe I could use a hatchet, too," Dale said.

"Well, maybe next year, son. Right now we don't want to do anything to worry your mother. You kids can do a lot to help if you just bring in a few cow chips and the cows every evening. When I'm working, Mama will have to milk the cows. You can gather the eggs and slop the hogs too."

They continued to plan what they would do, and then Anna and Dale dozed in the wagon. At last Papa turned the mules to go the last half-mile home, and finally there was Mama waiting for them in the door of their house. Anna and Dale went to bed without a murmur right after supper, but Mama and Papa had to wait for full darkness to catch the hens off the roosts and crate them for their trip in the morning.

****

*"Jack and Jill went up the hill
to fetch a pail of water..."*

Today Papa was helping with the threshing of the wheat crop and Dale and Anna were to go along to run errands and to help with some of the chores. The men would be needing lots to drink. The Kansas wheat fields were golden in the August sun after the wheat had been cut and shocked, and what breeze there was - was hot!

Mama called from the kitchen door, "Dale, you and Anna fill the water jug and take it to the field. Empty it and pump the well for a few minutes - enough to fill the trough for the little pigs. And then fill the jug with the coolest water in the well. And hurry! Anna, come and get your bonnet - you're getting as brown as an Indian."

Anna hated that bonnet except on Sunday morning - it was hot and the strings that tied under her chin hurt her neck. Dale and Anna trudged along to the field - barefoot, taking turns carrying the jug. It was heavy crockery and had only one handle to put your fingers through.

The closer they got to the field - the noisier and busier the place became. There were teams and wagons filled with bundles of ripe wheat. The bundle haulers were waiting their turn to toss the bundles into the threshing machine. It was a beehive of activity around that big steam engine and the thresher pouring out a small stream of grain on one side and a big mass of fluffy straw on the other side. The straw stack was huge - higher and bigger than the thresher, the steam engine and all the wagons put together. It looked so golden, beautiful and inviting in the morning sun.

15

Dale and Anna played in the loose, fluffy straw around the base of the stack and watched the straw being blown out - making the stack higher and bigger all the time. It was tempting to Anna, and she climbed higher and higher onto the stack - sliding back down - bonnet strings and long skirt blowing up - bare feet and arms outstretched like the wings of a airplane.

As she climbed back up to the top, Anna suddenly began to sink into the fluffy straw and the more flailing about that she did - the more she sank. Then the straw was all about her and she did not know which way was up. Anna's heart began to pound. She could hear it louder than the muffled roar of the threshing operation. What if she had to stay here forever and never could find her way out?

Anna tried once more to 'swim' to the top. It was hot and dusty and dark - no light shining through the straw! She realized she had lost her bonnet. Oh well, Anna thought, I don't need it now that I can't see the sun.

She continued to struggle without success. Then suddenly a big foot appeared in the straw and a big rough gloved hand. It was Papa! He dragged her out of the straw and down the side of the stack - it was hard going, even for Papa. He was holding her bonnet in his other hand by one string.

Dale was waiting at the bottom of the stack. Anna really didn't mind the scolding she got from her father or the teasing she got from her brother. And she didn't really mind the bonnet after that, with its string undone. That's how Papa had found her. It was lying on top of the stack where she had sunk!

That night when they got home, Papa told the whole story. Dale had come to call him off the 'thrashing machine' where Charlie was pitching bundles, to tell him Anna was in the stack and couldn't get out.

"Thank heaven's for the bonnet," Papa said, "I'd never have found her if I hadn't seen it in the stack."

Mama had tears in her eyes as she said, "Goodness, Anna! Why must you always be such a tomboy! It'll be a wonder if you live to grow up."

****

"To market, to market, to buy a fat pig
Home again, home again, dancing a jig."
- Old Nursery Rhyme

At last the harvest was over. The wheat was in the bin awaiting a day when there was time to load it in wagons and haul it to market.

"Today we will haul the wheat to Minneapolis," said Papa, as he sat down to the breakfast table. "Do you ladies think you can have a lunch packed by the time Dale and I get the horses harnessed?"

"Oh yes," said Stella, "We fried an extra chicken yesterday and baked bread and made cookies. We'll have peanut butter sandwiches, cold fried chicken, cookies and some of those little pear tomatoes off of that one plant in the garden. Dale, be sure to fill the water bags to hang on the wagon posts. We'll want something to drink ."

Anna ran out to the garden and brought in a syrup pail full of the little tomatoes to put in the picnic box, and filled the salt shaker to take along. Mama was cutting slices off the loaf of bread.

"Anna, you can spread the peanut butter on these slices to make sandwiches. And count out a dozen cookies from the jar." Mama was wrapping the chicken platter in a clean dishcloth which would serve as a tablecloth when they got to the park. Soon the lunch box was complete.

Mama tied her bonnet on firmly, placed a bonnet on Anna's head, and picked up the lunch box. "We'll keep this in our wagon so we can keep an eye on it. If we leave it with the men, it might be gone by noon."

Dale and Papa had the horses hitched to the wagons and Papa was waiting by the back wagon. "Up you go, Anna," he said as he tossed her up to the high seat on the spring wagon. Stella lifted her skirt so the hem would not trip her as Charlie helped her up to the step and on up to the high seat beside Anna. He handed the box of food up to Mama who placed it carefully in the corner of the wagon so it would not tip over or the cover blow off.

Anna loved riding along on the high seat behind the big team of horses. She and Mama could talk without Dale butting in, and there was the beauty of the Kansas landscape for them to enjoy. Dale and Papa were ahead of them in the other wagon, carrying on their own conversation. They passed the end of the pasture where their cows were grazing peacefully.

Across the road on the right and a bit closer to town was the Frakes place. Grandma Frakes lived there with her son. Papa often stopped in to see them, and he took Dale with him once. Anna remembered the cookies they brought home that time. Papa had said they would stop on their way home with the empty wagons so Mama and Anna could meet their nearest neighbor.

Closer to town, they passed by the house where the Cooper family lived. Anna was hoping to catch a glimpse of the Cooper twins who were about her age. She was very interested in them as the Coopers were black and she had never seen anyone who was black. Anna had heard Grandma tell Mama about going to see the twins when they were first born. Grandma said she went to see them as she had heard that the babies were black all over except for the palms of their hands and the bottoms of their feet. She found the babies to be very beautiful and the reports about their hands and feet were true.

"Mama, are the palms of those little kids' hands still white and the backs of their hands black?" asked Anna.

Mama knew Anna was referring to what Grandma had said, and she didn't really approve of such talk. "Honey, I don't know," said Mama hesitantly. "I don't think that's always so. And I don't think it's polite to be so curious about other people's appearance."

"But didn't people come to see Dale and me when we were babies?" Anna persisted.

"Oh, yes, your Uncle Roy and Aunt Blanche, Grandpa and Grandma, your Aunt Belva and all the close neighbors in Wells. Everyone brought cookies, fresh bread, jelly and fruit and vegetables they had canned. We had lots of company. And I'm sure your Grandma and the other people who went to see the Coopers took food and gifts for the babies, too. Twins are pretty special. I would have visited but we lived in Wells when they were born," Mama explained. "I don't think they have any relatives living around here."

"If they don't have any cousins or uncles or aunts, they must be pretty lonely," said Anna, watching their yard as they passed.

Soon they were at the edge of town and driving through the streets with buildings on either side.

"Will we get to go in the grocery store, Mama?" asked Anna.

"Oh, I think so," said Mama, "But we'll do that after we have sold our wheat and gone to the park to eat our lunch. It isn't good to go to a grocery store when you are hungry."

"Why is that, Mama?" asked Anna.

"Because, when you are hungry you will buy too much candy and spoil your appetite for our nice picnic lunch," Mama explained with a smile.

At last they arrived at the elevator. They drove the wagons onto a scale in front of the elevator and a man inside weighed the wagons full of wheat. Then the team pulled the wagons into the elevator, but they had to unhitch the horses before they could dump the wheat. A big hole opened up in the floor of the elevator and big hoists tipped the wagons. The wheat ran out of the end gates into the hole. Afterwards the teams were hitched up again and pulled the empty wagons back onto the scale. The man figured out how much the wheat weighed and paid Papa. Then they drove down to the Markley Grove to eat lunch.

Dale jumped out of the empty wagon before the wheels had stopped turning. "I'll beat you to the slide, Anna," he yelled as he raced over to the ladder and was flying down the long slide before Anna could be helped down from the empty wagon. Her skirt had caught on a wagon post.

"Aw, well, you don't mind," consoled Mama. "Run and swing while Papa and I get out the lunch. You'll have to watch that skirt on the slippery-slide and the teeter-totter and the monkey-bars anyway."

It was always cool under the big trees. They ate lunch and swung and slid and climbed till Papa said it was time to start home. "Come, children, we want to stop at the grocery store and it's four miles home," he said as he helped Stella up to her seat on the wagon. The empty

18

wagons were easy for the teams to pull as they left the Markley Grove and made their way up Main Street to the Farmer's Store.

Once inside, Dale and Anna stood quietly and looked about the store. The man behind the counter wrote on a pad of paper the items Mama wanted while they watched. Then he went about bringing them to the counter: twenty-five pounds of sugar, fifty pounds of flour, baking powder, soda, coffee, vanilla; the counter soon filled with groceries. When Papa ordered some meat, the man took a huge slab out of his cooler and sliced it on his big meat block. He weighed the meat on a scale and then carefully wrapped it using the rolls of string and paper which were right at hand.

Mama bought some yard goods and a dress for herself and Anna and some blue chambray for shirts for Dale and Papa. Finally both Dale and Anna were allowed to pick out a nickel sack of candy. Banana flavored marshmellow peanuts, lemon drops, peppermints, chocolate drops, and coconut kisses were all in glass jars. The grocery man could reach in and scoop out what you choose. Anna wanted a licorice pipe but she knew her mother wouldn't approve. 'Someday I'll have a penny and I'll come in here by myself and I'll buy one of those,' she thought to herself.

At last the boxes were full and the groceries were carried out to the wagons. They were ready to start home.

The big team of mules that Papa and Dale were driving set a much faster pace with the empty wagon. Soon the team of Grandpa's horses that Mama was driving broke out in a sweat trying to keep them in sight. Only a little more than an hour later, they were nearing the turn-in to Grandma Frakes' yard and Papa reined up till Mama drew along side. "Would you like to stop and meet Mrs. Frakes?" asked Papa, "These horses need some water and we won't stay long."

"Oh, yes," said Mama, "It will be nice to get in out of the heat for a few minutes, and I want to thank her for the cookies she's been sending every time you've stopped in."

Grandma Frakes smoked a corn-cob pipe and kept about a half-dozen bantam chickens in her little one-room house; two facts that Papa had neglected to tell Mama. However, Anna had no idea that Mama was shocked by this. Mama picked up a chicken off the arm of the rocking chair and sat, petting the friendly bird while she talked. The chickens each had a name and flew down off the corners of the cupboards to eat out of Anna and Dale's hands. Soon the horses were watered and they continued their journey home.

It had been a long and interesting day. Mama and Papa sat in the dining room visiting as Dale and Anna carried the bowls and spoons back to the kitchen.

Mama said, "Charlie, did you notice that Mrs. Frakes' chickens roosted on the side of the flour barrel?"

"Oh, I guess I didn't tell you about her pet chickens and her corn-cob pipe, did I?" laughed Papa. "I noticed that you thanked her and asked for her recipe for the molasses cookies."

"Well, they were good and stayed so soft and moist," defended Mama.

"And did you notice how well those banties were trained? They always landed on that flour barrel with their heads in and their tails out," laughed Papa as he kissed the children "Good Night" and carried the lamp to the kitchen.

****

Still sits the school house by the road,
a ragged beggar sleeping,
Around it still the sumacs grow,
and blackberry vines are creeping...
                    John Greenleaf Whittier

Dale was already six and Anna would be five in November. Stella wanted them to start to school. She visited the Concord school house a quarter of a mile away down the road, and met the teacher, Miss Williams, who was new that fall. The teacher assured Stella it would work out well to start both Dale and Anna at the same time. They would be fine if they just didn't catch cold right away.

Now, the big day had arrived. Anna and Dale were clean, dressed and ready to go.

"Here children," said Mama, "There's a new dinner pail for each of you and a tablet. And Dale, here is a box of crayons for both of you to share."

Dale and Anna set out proudly hand and hand, each carrying a shiny new dinner pail in their free hand. Slowly they walked down the road to the school house they could barely see in the distance.

Stella stood in doorway of the little weather beaten house and watched the two tiny figures until they reached the doorway of the school. Anna felt braver, seeing her there each time she glanced back. Stella hoped they would be all right. Dale and Anna had already had the whooping cough the previous spring, and pulled through even though several other children died in the epidemic. Dale was more frail than Anna, and had to be pulled out of bed several times by Charlie and held upside down while Stella pounded his back until he could breathe again.

Stella paused in her housework and chores a number of times that day to wonder how Anna and Dale were getting on. She and her sister Belva had been school teachers, and Stella knew well the problems of teaching fifteen to twenty children of all ages from five to twenty-one in a single room school house. But then the children were back, all smiles and enthusiasm. It would be all right.

One morning some weeks later Anna was looking at the little bows on either side of her head as Mama finished her braids. Anna already knew her ABCs. She could count to one hundred now, and she knew how to make her numbers too. She would have the crayons on her desk this morning. Anna liked to draw looking glasses, big ones, with a brown frame like the one she was seeing herself in right now.

Anna hopped up onto a chair and up on the sewing machine just under the mirror. Now she could see herself from top to bottom. Anna watched as her mother buttoned her shoes. Which foot was left and which foot was right? she wondered. That seemed so important to everybody. Ah, well, Dale knew.

It was cold now, and Anna had to wear stockings and a harness to keep them up. They were funny little rubber things that you put inside the tops of your stockings, and then put a metal thing on top and slid it up. She could do the ones in front but not the ones in back. Anna looked in the looking glass and reached back, but her hands did not go where she thought they would.

"Anna, you are trying to reach for your right leg with your left hand," said Mama. "Get down, you can't do that by looking in the looking glass anyway. And you could fall." Mama did up the harness in back, and handed Anna the pink chambray bloomers that matched her smock.

"Mama, why can't the looking glass tell left from right?" Anna asked.

"Honey, the looking glass can't tell you anything. It is just a reflection of you, and you have to think for yourself."

Mama gave her attention to putting Dale together. It wasn't that Dale didn't know how to dress himself. He just didn't think about it. Dale could even tie his shoes.

Anna watched them and said to her mother. "Dale could tie my shoes if I had some like his."

"Your shoes still fit you Anna, and as long as I can find the button-hook in the sewing-machine drawer where I put it, we'll stay with your pretty black patent slippers."

"Mama, it's my turn to have the crayons in my desk this morning. Dale keeps them hid in his desk all the time - he doesn't even use them when it is his turn."

Anna had her mind on the big looking-glass she was going to draw on her tablet. It would be as long as the paper. This morning she was going to draw a little girl in it - as tall as the mirror.

"The teacher doesn't want her to have the crayons in her desk until it's time to play with them, 'cause that's all Anna'll do is color when she has them," Dale explained as he picked up his dinner pail and set off.

"Button your coat and find your cap, Dale, it's chilly out this morning, and wear that cap when you're outside at recess. I don't want you catching cold again," Mama called after him. "Anna, remind him."

Anna pulled her coat tighter about her as she ran down the road after her brother. It was spitting snow from the gray sky and the school house seemed a long way off. It wouldn't be much fun today at recess. They always played 'Steal Sticks' and she was the smallest so she got to stand at the base and guard the sticks. Another girl a lot bigger than Dale had to guard the sticks at the other base. Dale always got to run around and tag anybody who crossed the center line. That looked a lot more exciting than just standing there getting colder and colder. Maybe Dale would change with her today. Anna ran harder to catch up with him.

"THE KITTY CAN MEW." The teacher had printed in big block letters across the blackboard for the morning's lesson. Dale sounded the words out right away. He and Anna got to go to the blackboard and practice making the letters while the children in the other classes came up to the recitation bench and took turns reading from their books.

"Dale and Anna, you may take your seats and print 'THE KITTY CAN MEW' across the top of a clean sheet of tablet paper. Then you are to fill the entire page on each line with the same words. Copying each letter carefully is the way to learn to print your alphabet," the teacher said.

Both Anna and Dale had learned to print their alphabet before they had started to school. Anna took a clean sheet of tablet paper and printed all the letters of the alphabet across the top. She would pick out the ones to make 'THE KITTY CAN MEW' later. She liked to listen as the big children stood up from the recitation bench at the front of the room and read from their books. Some of them could read almost as well as Mama. And some were so slow you couldn't tell what the story was about. When she got big, she would read right along.

Suddenly, it was time for recess. The teacher came to look at what she had printed.

"Anna, I didn't tell you to print the whole alphabet. Get a clean sheet of tablet paper."

Miss Williams quickly printed 'THE KITTY CAN MEW' across the top of it and said, "Now, Anna, you will have to stay in at recess and fill this page with these words. Do you understand?"

Anna was glad to stay in at recess. She quickly printed a few lines. This was so easy. Her mind wandered to the crayons in Dale's desk. While no one was in the schoolroom she would just get those crayons and have them in her desk for today.

She started on the picture that was still there in her mind. The frame for her looking glass always had to be brown but she could use any bright color for the reflection. She would color it very lightly and then she could draw a little girl looking at her from the looking glass.

Recess was over. Miss Williams came in and looked at what Anna had done. Her face was red and her hand was cold as she slapped Anna across the cheek.

"You must learn to mind what I tell you to do," she said angrily. "Now you have missed the whole recess and still haven't finished one page."

Anna sobbed uncontrollably as the teacher picked up the crayons and handed them back to Dale.

22

"It was her turn to have them," he said in Anna's defense.

"It will never be her turn till she learns to do her work first," Miss Williams told him firmly.

Anna kept sobbing. She had forgotten to put a handkerchief in her pocket that morning. She sniffled and swallowed her tears. 'THE KITTY CAN MEW' kept getting harder and harder to see. Anna knew she didn't need to practice the phrase anyway. She would never forget how to print 'THE KITTY CAN MEW.' Anna started to cough.

Mrs. Williams took Anna by the arm and led her outside. 'You must not vomit in the schoolhouse," she admonished.

Anna coughed and coughed. She began to cough and choke the way she had done when she had the whooping cough in the spring. At last the teacher went back in the school house to get Dale.

"Get your coats and dinner pails, Dale, you must take your little sister home. She is sick and I think she must be catching cold. She can't quit coughing."

The two dejected children stumbled into the kitchen sobbing out their story. Dale was nearly as tearful as Anna. He felt he should have let Anna have the crayons when they first got to school and she asked for them before the last bell rang.

"Maybe she would have hid them, and forgot about them long enough to do her work," he explained.

Mama didn't punish Anna, but she didn't sympathize with her either. "You should have done what Miss Williams told you to do."

Anna nodded. She knew the teacher was always right.

The next morning it was snowing, and Anna and Dale stayed home from school. It was Friday, anyway and Anna did seem to have a cold. Stella didn't blame Miss Williams for Anna's trouble, but this year was her first to teach. Maybe Anna was too young to get along there.

The next week Dale and Anna both had colds. Dale was sicker than Anna. He had croup and they had to put a tent over his bed. The fire was kept burning all night long to keep the tea kettle steaming under the tent flap. Miss Williams stopped by with cookies at the end of the week.

"We are practicing now for the Christmas program, Mrs. Allison, and I am hoping the children will be able to take part in it. They are both doing so well with their primary reader," Miss Williams said.

"Well, we'll see," said Mama. "They are both sick this week. Perhaps I will come and gather up their books and tablets so I can help them some at home."

Anna listened with satisfaction. She thought, 'I'll have my tablet and the crayons. I'll finish that picture of the little girl and the looking glass.'

Mama brought their things home and never mentioned school again that year. Anna colored lots of pictures, and Dale could read his primer from cover to cover by Christmas.

****

"Why do bells for Christmas ring?
Why do little children sing?....
                                        Eugene Field

Anna and Dale sat at the dining room table in Grandpa's house. The kerosene lamp cast long shadows on the wall behind Dale's chair. Dale was reading from Mama's old hymnal. He could read the whole song, "The Little Brown Church in the Vale." Anna didn't have to read all those little words - she had it memorized.

"Oh, come to the church in the wild wood, Oh, come to the church in the vale. No spot is so dear to my childhood as the little brown church in the vale. Oh, come, come, come, come, come, come, come, come, come to the church in the wild wood. Oh, come to the church in the vale."

Anna could read the word, 'come' wherever she saw it and could pick out the line that was nothing but 'comes.' "Mama, what is a wild wood? And what is a vale?" she asked as Mama came into the room.

"A vale is a valley that has grown up to trees and bushes all by themselves because God has planted them there - that's the wild wood," Mama explained.

"Did God put the little brown church there too?" asked Dale.

"No, the people who came to the valley built it there so they could come and thank God for the valley. And they sang, 'Oh come to the church in the wild wood' so other people would come there, once the church was built."

"We don't have a beautiful valley full of trees that God put there," said Anna wistfully.

"No, but we have the beautiful blue sky and the green pasture and the waving wheat fields that Pa says looks like buffalo running - the way they used to - in great herds before the people came to build the little towns and churches. We live in Kansas, and we have buffalo grass instead of wild wood."

"So what can we sing?" asked Anna.

"Oh, give me a home where the buffalo roam, where the deer and the antelope play, where seldom is heard a discouraging word, and the skies are not cloudy all day," Mama sang gaily. Anna and Dale listened in delight, and hummed along with her, trying to remember the words.

"So, Anna, don't be sad over our missing wild wood. We've lots else to thank God for, most of all right now for Christmas. Christmas was when God gave us the baby Jesus to teach us to love one another. When Jesus was born, God sent a bright star and people followed it to where the baby was lying in a manger and brought Him gifts. Ever since, on Christmas eve, old Santa Claus comes down from the North Pole to visit all the world and bring gifts to little children."

"Is he coming here?" Anna and Dale both asked at once. "When will he be here? How will he get here?"

24

Mama laughed at their eager questions. "We'll just have to leave all that to Santa," she said. "Remember that he is sent from God. How did the star just suddenly show up in the sky when Christ was born?" Mama smiled knowingly. "Maybe Santa is down in the cellar right now listening. Christmas Eve is tomorrow so you have to make a list of what you want for Christmas and he'll hear. I know a poem about it - it's called T'was the Night Before Christmas."

Mama knew so many things. She began to recite, "T'was the night before Christmas, and all through the house, not a creature was stirring, not even a mouse..."

Just as Mama finished, Papa arrived with the team and wagon. He was later than usual coming home. The milking was done, Anna, Dale and Mama had gathered the eggs and slopped the hogs and had wood in the wood box. They had already eaten supper too, and the rest of the stew was being kept warm for Papa on the back of the range. Dale and Anna had washed their faces and hands and put on their nightgowns, but they were allowed to stay up till they could kiss Papa good night.

"I put the horses in the barn - it feels like winter is coming," said Papa. "I'm going to take my heavier coat tomorrow and wear some gloves, too." Papa stood by the stove, rubbing his hands together and blowing on them to warm them up.

"Papa, did you know that Santa Claus is coming right here to bring Dale and me some presents?" asked Anna excitedly.

"Oh, I don't know. Did you write him a letter and tell him what you wanted?"

"We don't have time now," Dale said. "He's coming tomorrow night. But Mama thinks he might be downstairs where he can hear everything we say right now."

"Is that right?" asked Papa, casting a sidelong glance at Mama. "Well, in that case, what do you want?"

"Let's see, I need...Mama thinks I need a red stocking cap to pull over my ears when we go out after the cows and..." Dale started with his list.

"You'd better ask for a gray cap, Dale. That old bull out in the pasture doesn't like to see red on anybody," said Papa. "And, a brown one for Anna - to match her eyes."

"And I need a tablet and a new box of crayons too," said Anna.

"Could you think of something you just want,." asked Papa. "I'm sure you both need a lot of things, but if Santa Claus is listening right now, you might as well get in your order for what you really want."

"Charlie, you know that Santa's elves knit things like mittens that children need," Stella said. "And with all the little children looking for something in their stockings, they are bound to want the things they really need."

"And I really need mittens - brown ones to match the brown stocking cap we told Santa I want," said Anna. Mamma and Papa both looked pleased.

"Some story books for Mama to read to us would be nice," Dale said. "Do Santa's elves make books?"

"Well, if they don't, they'd better get started," Papa said, as he scooped up Anna and Dale, and carried them to bed in the front bedroom - off the cold parlor. He settled them down in the feather tick and pulled blankets and quilts around to tuck them in snugly.

"Papa." Anna said, "Mama's poem said, 'the stockings were hung by the chimney with care'- we don't have a chimney big enough for Santa to come down with a big sack of toys - and where can we hang our stockings?"

"Now children, you can decide all that tomorrow. Christmas eve isn't until tomorrow night. You're going to be busy helping your mother make cookies and pumpkin pies and stuffing for the duck. You'd better get off to sleep - morning will be here before you know it, and I've got to go finish that stew."

"Did the children say their prayers?" asked Stella as Charlie settled down at the kitchen table to his belated supper.

"I afraid I didn't remind them. They don't like that prayer about laying down to sleep and praying that the Lord will take their souls if they die before they wake. I don't blame them, who wants to die the day before Christmas?"

"I know," said Stella. "I've been teaching them a better one to go to bed on. It has the same first two lines, 'Now I lay me down to sleep, I pray the Lord my soul to keep,' but it ends differently. The last two lines are, 'And wake me with the morning light, to do what's right with all my might.' I'll go in and cover them again. They are almost too excited to sleep anyway, and I'll see if they remember the new prayer."

When Stella returned a few minutes later she said, "Would you believe, they were both sound asleep already?"

The day before Christmas flew by in a flurry of activities. The most important from the children's point of view was finding the best place to hang their stockings. A dozen places were decided upon and then discarded. At last Mama came up with the perfect solution. Dale and Anna hung their stockings on the chair-back at their own places at the dining room table.

"And," Mama concluded, "if old Santa has anything for you that is too big for a stocking - he can just lay it on the table at your place." Dale and Anna agreed it was a good idea.

It began to snow late in the afternoon but there was no way that Santa could travel on it with a sled. Anna and Dale were very concerned as they watched out the window.

"Don't worry," said Mama. "He'll make it somehow. Remember, he's been doing it ever since the birth of the Christ Child so many years ago, and in some places where he goes the children have never seen snow."

Papa got home before dark, put the horses in the barn, took off their harness and curried them before coming up to the house. He brought a little pail of fresh oysters in with him.

"They got in the barrel of fresh oysters at the Farmer's Store just in time for Christmas Eve, Stella," he said. "I got a sack of oyster crackers too, so we can have our Oyster Supper tonight."

"Did they have a crate of oranges too, Papa, like the big ones that Grandpa got after Easter?" asked Anna eagerly.

"Why, I never looked - Santa usually brings them at Christmas - that's how he stretches out the toe of your sock so it can hold more..."

Anna went to look at the sock she had chosen. It wasn't very big, she thought. But if it was hers then Santa would leave what was meant for her. Dale had a little sock, too...not much bigger than hers.

The oyster soup with the little round crackers floating on top was in a big bowl in the middle of the table, the big soup ladle beside it. Anna set the table with soup spoons beside the four small bowls, and Mama called them all to supper.

"Come children," she said. "The sooner we eat and the sooner you are fast asleep in bed, the sooner morning will come. Then you can get up and see what Santa has brought!"

The children flew through supper and then into bed. They were sure they'd never sleep that night.

Dale opened his eyes first. It was morning. "Anna," he cried, "We slept all night. I wanted to hear Santa - maybe he didn't come!"

They both raced out to the big dining room table. It was loaded with things too big for the little socks. The socks were both stretched to twice their size with oranges, candy, crayons, pencils and a little book for each of them rolled up and tied with a string so it would go in the sock. And there was a Big Chief tablet at each place, a gray stocking cap for Dale and a beautiful brown one for Anna - with two white buttons at each corner of the square top - she could tell it was meant for a little girl. And there were brown mittens for Anna and red ones for Dale.

Mama and Papa were sitting there laughing at all the excitement. "You'll have to keep your hands in your pockets when you go after the cows, Dale," said Papa with a twinkle in his eye. "But you can make snowballs in the yard today and break them in."

Dale ran to the window. There was snow on the ground, enough to make snowballs and there were tire marks in the snow, too.

"Anna, come and look!" he shouted excitedly. "Santa had to come in a car, see the marks?"

"And it must have been awful late. I stayed awake to listen almost all night," Anna said with awe.

And there were two presents neither one had asked for, a pop gun for Dale and the cutest set of little dishes for Anna. It was almost evening before Dale would no longer drink 'coffee' from Anna's little cups or stop to eat crumbs from his tiny plate on his way to shoot at the Indians with his pop gun. According to Dale, the Indians were lurking out behind the lilac bush by the porch.

"Mama, can't I just cock Dale's gun once and shoot it to watch the cork fly out of the end?" Anna asked plaintively.

"Put on your coats, caps and mittens and go out and make a snowman before the snow is all gone," Mama suggested.

Anna knew how her mother felt about guns - Mama didn't want her to play with the gun and there wasn't any point in arguing. Anna had often heard her mother complain about the way her papa's family used guns - she often said she wished she had half the money that those two teen-age brothers of Charlie's had burnt up in .22 shells - shooting at tin cans, rabbits, chickens and anything that moved, almost.

"Mama," said Anna thoughtfully, as she was pulling on the new mittens, "These are just like the mittens Aunt Belva was knitting. She had a whole stack of brown ones and some red ones too, like Dales's, in her knitting bag last summer."

Mama smiled down at Anna. "It's possible Aunt Belva has been helping Santa's elves. You could ask her about it next time she comes."

Anna nodded solemnly. As she went outside she thought to herself, If Aunt Belva is one of Santa's helpers, I bet Mama is too. How lucky for us!

****

"As I walked out one morning for pleasure,
I spied a cowpuncher a-ridin' alone..."
--from a cowboy song

It was a bright spring morning just right for calling on the neighbors. Dale and Anna ran out of the house to greet Johnnie Stout as he rode into the yard on his old nag. Johnnie was riding the horse bareback with only a bridle. She was so tame that she hung around his yard without any restraints.

Johnnie was one of Dale and Anna's favorite people. He always had something to say to them and he always took an interest in what they were doing. He had come over to speak to Papa this morning. Johnnie leaned over and picked Dale up and set him on the back of his horse, while he waited for Papa to come up from the barn.

"You too, Anna," said Johnnie as he reached down for her, intending to put her on the horse also.

Anna looked up there where Dale was and thought how far it would be to fall. "I think I'll just watch Dale," she said, backing up out of Johnnie's reach.

"This old mare will just stand here - she can't run fast enough to catch cold," laughed Johnnie as Anna still backed away, shaking her head.

Just then Papa walked up with old Ring, Grandpa's dog, along side. Ring knew he owned the whole farmyard - he always went with Dale and

Anna after the cows and barked at everyone who came to visit. So here was something for him to do right now. He started barking at Johnnie's horse. The old mare wheeled and jerked the reins out of Johnnie's hand.

She made one circle of the farmyard with Dale hanging onto her mane. His legs stuck out on each side of her back - much too short to fit into stirrups if there had been any but Johnnie always rode her bareback anyway. Old Ring kept barking and nipping at her heels. She gave one wild look at Johnnie as he tried unsuccessfully to catch the reins that were hooked to the bridle - and went racing out of the yard. His old mare was headed home with Dale still clinging desperately to her mane.

Mama ran out of the house as Johnnie and Papa were running down the driveway, "Anna, go in the house and wait there," she said as she rounded the corner of the house after Dale, clinging to the horse's mane, Papa, Johnnie and old Ring, still barking as they turned onto the road from the driveway headed north toward Johnnie's house a half a mile away.

Anna did as she was told, standing at the window crying in fear for her brother. She was there as Papa and Mama came back. Papa was carrying Dale. His face was a mass of blood and he was covered with blood and dirt from head to foot. But...he was crying...so he was alive!

Dale had hung onto that mane as long as he could and let loose to roll off into a deep ditch of hard-packed clay....but he had escaped the flying hoofs. He must have landed on his face - his lips were rolled back and split and his nose was skinned, his eyes were blacked and his hair was matted with weeds and dirt. Anna watched as Papa and Mama washed him off, put salve on his skinned places and put on his night clothes. He would have to stay in bed for a day or so but he had no broken bones. His eyes swelled shut and his mouth was so swollen that he couldn't eat for several days and he never did really care about horses after that.

That evening Johnnie Stout drove into the yard with his Ford car. He had been to Minneapolis and had brought back some big pink marshmallow peanuts for Dale and Anna. "My God, Charlie, I should have known better than to put Dale up on that old mare without even a saddle horn to hang onto. Even Anna knew better. I tried to put her up there too but she backed off and wouldn't let me," Anna heard him say from their bedroom off the living room.

Papa assured him that he felt it was old Ring's fault. "I should have shot that dog," he said, "But he belongs to Dad and Mother and they'll be home soon and we'll surely leave him here when we move back to Wells."

"Oh, did you hear from them recently?" asked Johnnie.

"Yes, we got a letter yesterday. They'll be home next week, sooner than they planned to but Mother hasn't been feeling good up there in Montana. She thinks she's homesick and says she'll feel better back here on the farm," Papa said.

"And I know I'll feel better back in Wells in our own house," Mama said. "We can plant the garden on time and set the hens in our own brooder house..."

"I'll surely miss you people when you do move back. Now, Charlie, if there's anything I can help you with, catching chickens, loading your wagons; anything. Just holler when you're ready and I'll be Johnnie on the spot," said Johnnie, sounding much relieved that Dale was on the mend, "Do you reckon those little shavers are still awake? I wanted them to know that I brought them some candy before they got off to sleep."

"I don't think they'll sleep much tonight," Mama said, "Anna was just out here asking for a drink for Dale. I think he'll keep her awake but she wanted to take care of him anyway".

Anna was sitting up beside Dale when Mama carried in the coal oil lamp so Johnnie could see them when he brought in the big sack of candy. Dale was lying there with a face so bruised that he could stand to have even a nice soft marshmallow peanut near it. Anna thought to herself that it was a mighty ill wind that blew nobody good - she'd get to eat that whole sack of marshmallow peanuts all by herself.

"Thank you, Johnnie," she said sadly.

****

"He leads me beside still waters;
He restores my soul.....
Psalms 23:2

"Grandma and Grandpa are coming home from Montana", announced Mama as she read their letter. "It has been a long hard winter for them and Grandma is homesick for her own kitchen. She wants to plant a garden." Mama was happy to tell Papa they'd have to move back to Wells when he came in from chores.

Papa also seemed happy to be plowing the garden in Wells and moving his little family back to their own little two-room house with the fruit trees all around it that would produce for sure this summer.

It always seemed that Papa should be two places at once since Grandpa walked on crutches. Uncle Roy and Aunt Blanche were young and had four children already and Uncle Floyd had married and moved and had a new baby and somebody had to help Grandma. Uncle Jesse, Papa's baby brother should have come home with Grandpa and Grandma. He was seventeen and big enough to help with the farming, but he stayed in Montana so Papa was back and forth every day that spring getting his folks settled back in their farm home. Papa had left half of Mama's laying hens on the farm so that Grandma would have eggs to fry for Port and the hired help that seemed to always be there to keep up with the farming.

Mama was still trying to save enough eggs to set the hens in the brooder house when Papa came home from his folks to say that Grandma was sick. "Dad had to do the cooking today because Mother was sick to her stomach," Papa said. "He made her so nervous movin about the kitchen on those crutches that I doubt if she'll be any better tomorrow".

"I will take the children and go over and cook for her tomorrow if you have more to do over there, Charlie," offered Mama. He looked so tired that she didn't mention that she hadn't got much planting done on her garden and had hoped he'd get home in time to help her finish with that.

Grandma did not get well - in fact, she seemed to get worse with each passing day. Doctor Winifred Vears came to see her and prescribed medicine for her to take after eating but no food would stay down.

Papa got Doctor Hinshaw from Bennington to come and see her but he did no better at prescribing medicine.

"I'd like to see her in my office," he said. "I have an X-ray machine that may show a tumor, although it's not likely, but we should give it a try. Stomach problems are hard to diagnose, so we should try everything that's available."

Papa went over in the car the next morning and took his mother to Bennington to Dr. Hinshaw's office. "They are sending the X-rays in to a specialist in reading such things," he told Mama when he came home to Wells that evening, "The doctor couldn't tell much about them, himself. He asked Mother how old she was. She told him, 'Sixty.' Then he asked her how many children she had and she answered: 'Eight, living - I've had fourteen altogether.' and the Doctor said, 'Well, Mrs. Allison, you go home and rest. We'll have these X-rays back in a few days and I'll bring them up. Maybe I'll know what to do for you.''

"Well, we will just have to wait till next week," Mama said. "Did he give her anything to stop those chills?"

"Yes, he gave her a whole handful of different pills to try and I told her we'd be over tomorrow and you could study the dosages and maybe she'd be well by the time the X-rays came back. Mother is so discouraged and she hates to have all of us waiting on her. She's used to waiting on everybody else," Papa sounded very discouraged, himself.

The X-rays came back and showed nothing. Grandma grew weaker and no medicine seemed to help. Papa decided she had given up her will to live. "Mother asked me today if I would see that they found out what ailed her after she was gone - she feels it may help some of us kids - maybe we're just like her, she said."

"Did she talk to the doctor about such a thing?" Mama asked.

"Not yet, but she said she was going to talk to Dr. Hinshaw about an autopsy - Dad just sat there and cried." As usual, it was Papa that his mother leaned on, not Grandpa. And Grandpa seemed to lean on him, too.

"Stella, do you remember when Howard Comfort had appendicitis and Dr. Cludas said he needed an operation at once. Cludas called Dr.

Outland from Kansas City and they operated on Howard on the kitchen table," Papa said. "Outland came out on the train as far as Minneapolis and someone brought him out to Bob Comfort's in a lumber wagon."

"That was just a miracle, he lived," Mama said. "They had to move fast, if that appendix had burst he would have died of peritonitis. They are doing a lot in the medical world now-a-days. I just wish they could come up with a miracle for your mother, Charlie."

That night in Wells was a busy one. The Allison's next-door neighbor, Mr. Richie knocked on their door to say that his wife was having a baby. Mama hurried over to help Mrs. Richie and her husband went to get Dr. Patterson.

The next morning they had a new baby girl and Mama came home to report that, "Mother and baby were doing fine."

"Stella, can you get away to go back over to the farm? Mother is worse today, Dad called and said she had been asking for you. I guess she had a very bad night," Papa explained as he flipped the pancakes and cut up Dale and Anna's pancakes for breakfast.

"The doctor prescribed Epsom salts for Mrs Richie and Mr. Richie is going down to the store to get it. He said a neighbor girl was going to come over for a few days, so I'll just run over with this chicken soup and tell them to get her today. She can give Mrs. Richie the salts." Mama talked as she ladled out the chicken into a syrup pail and got clothes for the children to wear for the day.

The next day Grandma was worse. Papa went back over to Wells to feed the chickens and the horses. "I think I'll stop and talk to Dr. Patterson, Stella, if I can catch him. If I can't I'll leave word for him to come over and see Mother. She's not keeping anything down, is she?" Papa's voice sounded so worried.

"She's sleeping a little right now. Take the children with you, Charlie. And be quiet, children. Will you pump a tub of water for me, Charlie, and fill the boiler on the range. Children, will each of you bring in an armload of wood and fill the woodbox quietly and don't slam the screen door. The least little sound and your grandma jumps and that wakes her. She needs to sleep."

Mama sounded worried too...Anna wished her grandma would get better...Mama washed sheets for her bed every day. The big galvanized tub out at the well curb was full of soiled nightgowns and sheets and the copper boiler was taking up half of the stove top every morning.

"Stella, I'm going to open a road so people can drive in the back yard from the north and come in the yard past the corral. Cars make such a noise. Then, when we leave, we'll drive around and string a wire across the front driveway. I'll need an old dishtowel to tie on it so no one will drive into it. Then visitors can either walk in from the road or go around the back way to drive in the yard," Papa said as he carried in the big pails of water to dump in the boiler.

Anna and Dale filled the woodbox quietly and they were ready to go back over to Wells and help Papa with the chores.

The little town of Wells was buzzing with the sad news about Mrs. Richie. It seemed that Mr. Richie had ordered Epsom salts from the grocery store with some other grocery items. He went to get the neighbor girl to stay with his young wife and new baby girl.

"She's fine this morning and we have a beautiful little girl. We've named her Berniece," Mr. Richie told everyone who asked as he went about running errands.

He dropped the young lady off at his door with the box of groceries. "You'll find some Epsom salts too," he said. "The doctor said she was to have a tablespoon in a glass of water this morning. Mrs. Allison brought over some chicken soup you can have for dinner. I'll be home before dark." The young father went to work, thinking all was well with his new family.

The "Epsom salts" that was given to the young mother was poison - an insecticide used to kill lice on chickens. It was in the same sized package as Epsom salts and, it was explained, had been mistakenly taken off the grocery shelf when Mr. Richie's grocery order was filled.

Papa explained the sad news to Mama as quietly as he could and Mama just put her hands over her face and disappeared out the back door. Anna and Dale sat down on the well-curb and cried. They could hear their mother crying out in the outhouse. Papa had said they were not to say anything about their young neighbor lady dying of poison and leaving a tiny baby without a mother. Grandma was too sick to hear about that. The clean white sheets were flapping in the breeze out at the clothes line. It was a nice sunny day but there was nothing anywhere on earth, it seemed, - to be happy about.

Aunt Florence Ayers came from Montana with her baby boy. Little Clifford was about 15 months old. The trip had been long on the train and he had summer complaint when they arrived. Uncle Jessie came home along with her this time.

"Now maybe we'll have a little help, Stella. I know you're getting very tired." Papa said. But Mama was busier than ever from that time on.

"Charlie, will you see if Jessie can't do something to keep the children out from under-foot and away from the house. There are seven of them all under six years old. If Jessie were a girl 17 years old, I'd know what to suggest she do with the children but I can't suggest anything to Jessie. Maybe you can think of something. They can't play in the house and they can't play in the shade of the house. They make too much noise. Florence is busy with little Clifford - he has diarrhea. Jennie's hands are full with the cooking and little Leota. Blanche is helping with the washing. Somebody is going to have to go to Minneapolis for groceries. I think Roy is going to do that and maybe he'll take little Kenneth with him. But that still leaves Leta, Lela, Lola, Dale and Anna. The doctor is coming and I have to bathe your mother and get her into a clean nightgown......" Mama's voice trailed off as she carried a basket of clothes to the clothesline.

Papa was emptying the tubs and the boiler, "Anna, you can help your mother hang up the washing; Dale, you can come with me. I have to feed the horses. You can fill the coffee cans with oats in the bin. Stella, I'll have Jessie fix up his little old wagon - it just needs a box. Then he can haul these little girls on the new road down by the corral. Come on girls, you can help Dale fill the oats buckets." Papa said.

Mama took the diapers as Anna straightened them and handed them to her. She found the corners of the sheets and handed them to her mother. It was almost peaceful out at the clothesline, "Is Grandma going to die, Mama?"

Mama looked down at her little girl and tears came to her eyes, "Honey we just don't know. She doesn't get any better and your grandpa wants all her children here to visit her. I don't know if that makes her better or worse. I know it's about twenty mouths to feed three meals a day. Your Aunt Jennie is a good cook and your Aunt Blanche helps with the wash. Since your Aunt Carrie couldn't come from Montana I'm really glad that your Aunt Florence did come...There, the washing is on the line. Thank you for helping me. And there's the doctor. Maybe Florence got your grandma's bed tidied up." Mama hurried in the house and Anna went down to the granary to see what Dale and the little cousins were doing.

They were all standing outside the granary door squealing because there were mice in the granary and every time they opened the door the mice ran up the upright two by fours. Dale was helping Papa feed the horses.

"I'll just go in there and catch those mice," Anna boasted. "Who's afraid of a little bitty mouse. I'll just go in there like Skippy does and grab 'em by the tail."

Skippy was a little rat terrier dog who caught rats and mice for Papa. He and Uncle Roy had plugged up all the holes in the foundation of the barn with rocks. Then they stationed Skippy at the one hole where the rats could come out, hooked a pipe onto the exhaust pipe of the Model T and stuck the other end under the barn and started the engine. As the rats came running out to get away from the exhaust fumes Skippy grabbed them by the back and hit their heads over a rock with a quick snap of his head. He had a pile of twenty-two rats when they quit coming out. Anna had no doubt she could do the same thing. She hopped into the granary and grabbed a mouse by the tail as he ran up a rafter. Snap! She hit his head on a two-by-four.

Leta, Lela and Lola squealed in admiration. Anna felt so brave she tried it again. She had killed three mice by the time Dale and Papa finished with the horses.

"Watch, Papa," she said as she jumped into the granary and caught a mouse by the tail. She looked around to see if Papa was watching and the mouse reached around and bit her on the back of the hand.

Anna screamed and threw the mouse and Papa scolded her all the way to the house to put peroxide on the bite. "Don't you know you could get hydrophobia from a mouse bite?" Papa asked. "We won't tell your mother what you did. She's got enough to worry about."

Anna decided he was right. Mama might scold them both and she really did have enough to worry about.

Uncle Jessie had built a new box for his little old wagon and he was giving wagon rides down by the barn. Three at a time could ride. They all took turns till supper time. Neighbors kept driving in to call on the sick and bring pies, cakes, chicken and dumplings and flowers from their gardens. Elizabeth had been a good neighbor and everyone wished her well.

Uncle Bert, Aunt Stella and their four daughters came over Sunday. That made twelve grown-ups to sit around the long table in the dining room. The twelve children could eat in the kitchen.

Mama said, "Charlie, I left my table boards over here when we moved the table back to Wells. They are out in the Well house with those empty jars stacked on them. I think those boards will fit your mother's table. Would you go get them, please?"

Papa came back from the well house empty-handed. "The jars are there but the boards are gone. Does anyone know what happened to the table boards?" Papa asked.

"Sure, I do," said Uncle Jessie. "You said for me to build a wagon-box for my wagon and haul the kids so I sawed them up."

Mama sniffed and looked down her nose as only Mama could when the occasion was just too disgusting to talk about. Papa also refrained from any further discussion of the table boards. Some of the women were out in the kitchen feeding the children or in with Grandma and no more than ten sat down at any one time anyway.

The terrible summer dragged on with the nights sometimes longer than the days, "Mama, where can I sleep?" Anna whispered. It was the middle of the night. Mama was lying on a cot outside the back door where it was cool. She and Aunt Florence were taking turns sitting up with Grandma.

"Honey, can't you find a blanket upstairs? Your Uncle Floyd and Aunt Jennie have a big one and only Leota is lying on it with them," Mama sounded so tired and Anna wished there was room for her on the narrow cot. She was tired too.

"Can't I lie here with you?" she whispered.

"No, honey, it's time for me to go in and sit with your grandma and your Aunt Florence will want this cot. Now go on back upstairs and find a spot on one of the blankets."

"When I woke up I was lying on the hard floor at the foot of Uncle Floyd's blanket," Anna whispered forlornly. "And Uncle Roy and Aunt Blanche have four children sleeping with them on their blanket and there is not a dry spot on it anywhere."

"Now, Anna, you will have to do the best you can to get through this night. If your Aunt Jennie and Uncle Floyd are asleep lie back down on the foot of their blanket quietly and go to sleep. If you wake up on the floor when morning comes you will have made it through the night anyway. Your grandmother is so sick she may be gone by morning so try to be patient with your problems," Mama spoke sternly but she hugged Anna as she went back into the living room quietly so Aunt Florence could get some sleep. Papa was sitting with Grandma, too. So Anna stole softly back upstairs, picked out the driest spot on Uncle Roy's blanket and managed to finish the night.

When Anna came down the stairs next morning she learned that Grandma had gone to heaven during the night. Mama was ironing a dress for her. Dale had come in from the barn with Uncle Jessie and they were eating pancakes.

"A nice neighbor lady is going to take you two children home with her, Anna, and your Uncle Ney is going to take you up to visit my mother today. Your Grandma Jordan wants to see how you've grown."

"Will we get to see my Grandma Allison again," Anna asked.

"Yes, your Uncle Ney and Aunt Ethel will bring you back tomorrow. Now hurry and dress and comb your hair and eat a bite. The neighbor lady is coming for you and we will see you tomorrow." Mama ushered them out the door and Anna noticed that everybody had gone somewhere, there were almost no cars around or buggies either.

"Where is everybody," asked Dale?

"They'll all be back tomorrow. They had to go home and get ready for the funeral. And I'll see you both tomorrow too. The children left with many questions still unanswered. They came back the next day.

The table in the dining room was spread with pies, cakes, deviled eggs, potato salad, fried chickens, and fresh baked rolls. The kitchen was scrubbed. All of Mama's family had come from Concordia, Glasco and Delphos. The parlor was closed off but friends and neighbors would go in silently and come out tearfully. People kept coming to 'pay their last respects' Mama said. At last the crowd thinned out. Leta and Lela, Dale and Anna were in the kitchen when someone in the living room said, "Do you want the children to see their grandmother?"

Anna heard her mother say, "I want Dale and Anna to." Aunt Blanche decided that Leta and Lela should also.

"Wash your hands and faces, children," said Mama. She combed their hair and explained as best she could that Grandma was laid out and that they should understand that she was not there. Her spirit had left her body and she was resting in peace.

The four children were brought into the living room to pay their last respects. Anna looked down and lined her feet up with the other three children as they stood in a formal row. Then she looked at the silent figure on the cot. Grandma's body was resting there in peace but Grandma had gone to heaven just as Mama said.

****

36

School days, school days,
Dear old Golden Rule days......
                                                    Old song

"Mama, can I have a big pink bow in my hair this morning?" asked Anna, her eyes alight with excitement. This was the first day of school - Anna would be six years old in November and Dale had turned seven in June. Anna remembered how Dale had bragged to Leta and Lela last summer over at Grandma's house - about how he was two years older than she was. But today she was catching up. Dale and she would both start even - in the first grade in Wells.

"Ow! You're pulling my hair," cried Dale, struggling to get away from his mother's firm grip.

"Dale, there's enough dirt in you ears to plant potatoes. Now you'll just have to stand still till I wash your ears - I have to hang on to your hair to keep you from jerking away," Mama explained. "Now, turn your head while I wash the other ear."

"Gee Whiz! I thought it was going to be fun to start to school. I hope I don't have to go through this every day!" wailed Dale. 'Ow, Ow, that hurt!"

'I hope we don't either,' Anna thought to herself as she tried to get her mother's attention. Dale's ears were always dirty! "Please button my smock in the back, Mama, and put this pink bow up here and I'm ready to go," she said aloud.

At last they were both ready to go. Each had a <u>Primer</u>, a new pencil and a Big Chief tablet. Of course, Dale was carrying their one box of crayons but they were both so happy to be starting to school again even that was no problem. Stella was pleased with the way things had worked out; there would be no problem with Anna being old enough and Dale was small for his age but he would be a strong first grader, having already mastered that <u>Primer</u> at Concord. There would be no lunches to pack - their big school, Wells Union II was just a stone's throw from her front door. They could come home for dinner, eat in fifteen minutes and go back to play in the school yard for a half an hour at noon. Yes, things were straightening out for her little family. Of course, Charlie was still spending a lot of time over at his folk's farm helping his dad get ready for a big farm sale. Port would take his son, Jessie, back with him to Montana where Florence and Carrie lived with their families. When Charlie's mother died. that was the end of farming for them. They wouldn't lease the farm for another year. She was thankful that Charlie could now get on with his own life for a change.

A week had gone by in the "Little Room" at Wells Union II. It was time for the First Grade Reading class to recite. Gladys Comfort was the teacher that year. All the children loved her. She said, "First Grade Reading; Turn. Rise. Pass".

Seated alphabetically from front to back of the school room were the four first graders: Anna Allison, Dale Allison, Avis Hanes and Averill Yonally. They had learned to line up on the sidewalk in that order in front of the other three grades and march in to take their assigned seats. The "Big Room" also lined up on the left hand side of the sidewalk and marched into the Big Room. First graders would be five years getting big enough to march into the Big Room and four years growing big enough and learning to read, write, and do arithmetic and spelling and music well enough to sit on the right hand side of the Little Room. Yes, indeed, they had a long way to go.

At the command, "First grade reading" the four first graders were to pick up their <u>Primer</u>. "Turn" meant to plant one's feet in the aisle. "Rise" meant, 'stand up.' At the call, "Pass," they filed up to the front of the room and stood in front of the recitation bench. "Be seated" was self-explanatory.

Averill Yonally was asked to read the first page in his Primer. With some hesitation he got through his recital. Next was Avis's turn. She read the page without a hitch. Then it was Dale's turn. He also had no problem, reading just as Avis had done - almost as though he'd been there before.

Miss Comfort said," Dale you read that perfectly. That's fine."

Anna spoke up with some pride, "Dale can read the whole Primer that way."

"Oh, he can?" asked Miss Comfort with surprise. Turning to Dale, she asked, "Can you, Dale?"

Dale lowered his long white eyelashes and said,"Yes," so softly one would have thought he was admitting to some high crime.

Miss Comfort turned to the back of the <u>Primer</u> and selected a page, handing her book to Dale to read. He read it as he had the first, without hesitation. "Dale, I should like you to take a note home to your mother after school," she said. "Anna, can you read the whole <u>Primer</u>, as well?

"No, just some of it," Anna answered, remembering about how well she liked coloring looking glasses.

So Mama had to talk to the teacher about Dale and Miss Comfort decided that since both Dale and Avis had already mastered the <u>Primer</u> the year before they could advance at once to the <u>First Grade Reader</u> while Averill and Anna could read the <u>Primer</u> and <u>First Grade Reader</u> their first year.

Fairview School where the Hanes children went to school had burned down during the previous term and Avis had not finished the First grade. Her mother had decided that she was small to have to go into Wells to finish the term so she, like Dale, had stayed at home half of the previous year.

****

38

"Now I lay me down to sleep,
I pray the Lord my soul to keep,
If I should die before I wake......"

Diphtheria! Anna had heard that dread word spoken in such hushed tones by Mama and Papa as they lay in their bed across the bedroom from her cot that she had to still her heart-beat in order to hear what they were saying.

Papa said, "Little Junior Overton is so sick with that damned diphtheria that they don't expect him to live through the night."

"It's an epidemic that's been all around us but now it's right in Wells," Mama whispered.

"I remember when my two little brothers died one after the other. Orville died first, then Oliver. They just gasped and wheezed and struggled to breathe. I'll never forget it. But I'm afraid of that toxin-anti-toxin they want to vaccinate the children with. They could get the diphtheria from it," Papa said.

"It's been around a long time and they've improved on it, Charlie, I think we'll have to sign the note the children brought home. What if all the other children were vaccinated and Dale and Anna weren't. Then they might catch the disease from all the children running a fever from the vaccination."

"We'll see in the morning," Papa said, as though he just had to put off thinking about it as long as possible.

When Dale and Anna went to school the next morning, Miss Comfort announced that little Junior Overton had passed away and that the County Health Officer would be out to administer the toxin-anti-toxin to the entire school. Those who had forgotten to bring their permission slip from home would not need to go home to get one. All children would be vaccinated. No one said that his parents had objected.

At five minutes until ten, the Big Room teacher knocked on the door. Miss Comfort went to the door and talked to her. Then she turned around to face the class room.

"The hearse is across the street at Overton's house right now," she announced. "Out of love and respect for our kind neighbors who have lost their little boy before he was old enough to go to school, we will all file out and form a line down the sidewalk and face the street. We will quietly stand at attention while the hearse is passing by. Turn. Rise. Pass."

The Big Room children were already filing through the door and would form the line first while the fourth graders from Anna's room would fall in behind. That meant that she would be the last one in the line and stand closest to the schoolhouse. On this solemn occasion no one spoke. Only sobbing was heard.

"There will be no funeral service for this little boy, owing to the very contagious disease in our community," Miss Comfort said, as the children filed back in the classroom.

Nothing further was said about the toxin-anti-toxin that the County Health Nurse administered to the whole school; in fact, Papa seemed to be relieved that Dale and Anna had been vaccinated without his having to make a decision about it.

"Papa, did a hearse come to get your little brothers when they died of diphtheria?" asked Anna that evening.

"No, honey, they died within a few hours of each other. So we made a pine casket to fit them both and Dad and I took them up to the Hall Cemetery and buried them by ourselves."

"Why didn't your whole family go?" asked Dale.

"Your Uncle Bert was also very sick at the time. We thought he might also be gone by the time we got back from the cemetery, but he was older. Diphtheria is a real killer. If they can last four or five days the membrane that grows in the throat and chokes them will begin to break up," Papa explained.

"Couldn't you give them any medicine?" asked Anna.

"In the cities when every home had someone dying of diphtheria, they set up hospitals and doctors could insert a tube down the throat and into the windpipe and save some of them but Orville was just past one and Oliver was not quite three and they weren't strong enough to fight for air. Bert was five. Mother would put a drop of coal-oil in a teaspoon of sugar. When Bert would try to swallow it, he would start to cough and cough up pieces of that membrane. Mother never left his bedside for a week," explained Papa. "He got so spoiled that someone had to sit by his bed all the time and entertain him or he'd get to crying and start coughing and Mother would be right back worrying over him."

"He was probably lonesome without his little brothers," said Anna sadly, "And maybe that's why Grandma still spoils Uncle Bert like Mama says."

"I'm sure that's it," agreed Papa, "Or maybe that explains the old saying, 'Only the good die young'."

"Why didn't all the rest of you get it?" Dale asked.

"Diphtheria is a very contagious disease and once you get it you don't get it again. Hank and I had already had it and so had Dad and Mother when we were younger. Epidemics came oftener in those days," Papa said.

"And that's because the County Health Nurse comes out to all the schools and vaccinates everybody nowadays, Miss Comfort said," Anna explained.

That night as Dale and Anna were going to bed, Dale on his cot in the living-room and Anna on her cot in the bedroom, they paused to say, in unison:

"Now I lay me down to sleep
I pray the Lord my soul to keep
And wake me with the morning light
To do what's right with all my might."

Mama and Papa both said, "Amen."

School resumed as usual next morning; no one got diphtheria from his vaccination and Anna and Dale, at least, appreciated school and life in general a bit more.

****

"We are not here to play, to dream, to drift-
We have hard work to do, and loads to lift."
by Maltby Davenport Babcock

Anna had been very proud of Dale's ability to read the whole Primer - but now he was ahead of her! He and Avis had a First reader which they finished after Christmas and were reading in a supplemental reader while she and Averill were starting the First Reader.

"Now, Anna, you'll be ready for the Second Grade next fall at the same time Dale is," Mama explained. "Just be sure you learn your numbers and how to print and write your alphabet. Then next year, Avis and Averill will be with you and Dale - all in one class again."

So that became her goal. Dale already knew all about numbers but writing was difficult for him. He printed everything. She studied very hard and neither she nor Dale missed a single day of school that year.

"School's out! School's out! The teacher wore her bloomers out." the Big Kids were singing at the end of the day.

Tomorrow would be the Last Day of School. They had the first year, all eight months of it, behind them. They had pieces to speak, the Big Room kids would be there, everyone would be in the program and the teachers would hand out the grade cards.

"Everyone must have passed," Mama had said last night.

"How do you know?" Dale asked.

"Oh, the teacher would probably have passed out the grade cards today without all the parents there if someone had failed," she had explained as she separated the whites from the yolks of eleven eggs. Mama had baked a big angel food cake for the Dinner. She and Papa would both be there. Aunts and uncles, grandpas and grandmas, baby brothers and sisters, no one missed the Last Day of School Dinner.

****

School Days. School days!
Dear old Golden Rule days.
Readin' and Writin' and 'Rithmetic.
Taught to the tune of a hickory stick........

"No, you cannot put your bare foot in the wet concrete of this sidewalk," Papa said. He was down on his hands and knees troweling the lovely sidewalk he was just finishing on the northeast corner of the big school yard in Wells. That sidewalk ran all the way across the south side and all the way along the east side of the big school yard - just outside the fence. Papa had made all that sidewalk. The section which was closest to where they lived just across the sandy road, would soon be hard and dry. "This is a public sidewalk and belongs to all the people in Kansas. When we build a porch on our own house we can put your footprint in it and the date you did it - but not in this sidewalk."

Anna thought of her father's words as she listened to the sound of the trowel in the soft gray mud. Soon it would be dry and she would run across the street, down the sidewalk and turn the corner - more lovely sidewalk.

Later, when she was going to school, in the little room yet, however, she recalled her father's words about how the school with its lovely yard, fence and sidewalks belonged to all the people in Kansas.

The Big Room Teacher was taking one of the big boys into the Big Room by his shirt collar, and a couple of the big boys were explaining what that was all about.

One said, "You know the rules the teacher wrote on the blackboard the first day of school. One of them was, 'No jumping over the fences.' Well, we told Charles that he was foolish to walk down the sidewalks when he could run and jump over the fence and be home in half the time at noon."

The boys laughed, "He'll probably get a lickin' with a rubber hose. They say she's got one."

"Has anybody ever seen it?" asked another.

"No, but my dad's on the school board and he said they got one for her and we'd better mind the rules or we'd get to feel it," said Gilbert. "He said, 'we don't own the school just because we're in the Big Room, and we'd better mind the rules and learn respect for public property.'"

"Maybe Charles can't read all those rules," Carroll said.

Philip spoke up, "Dad says ignorance of the law is no excuse. I'll bet she's teaching him to read right now."

They all laughed, the five minute bell rang, the boys went to their outhouse, the girls went to theirs', they came back, washed their hands in the big basin in the cloak room, got a drink each with his own tin cup from the fresh bucket of water the teacher had just pumped - and the noon hour was over.

Anna liked this time in the school day best of all, she thought as she took her place in the line of boys and girls to march in. The Big Room teacher started the Victrola playing a lively marching song, then both teachers came out of the center door and each took her place in front of her line of pupils.

"March" came the order and everyone was supposed to start on the same foot and march up the steps and into the center door, going left into the Big Room or right if one were still in the Little Room.

Sometimes the Victrola was wheeled into the Little Room and the small children listened to music for their "Opening Exercises" and at other times the teacher read a chapter or two in some exciting book the children had selected. Continued stories sometimes took two weeks or more to read and the children didn't want the teacher to stop reading. It seemed the chapters would end in the most exciting places and one would have to wait until tomorrow to find out what happened next.

* * * * * * * *

The teacher stood straight and tall in front of the room full of small children. She had in her hand several little pieces of crumpled paper. Until that moment this had been a lovely morning, - another school day beginning.

Then she spoke, "I've been finding all these notes on the floor when I sweep each night and I wonder if you people would like to claim them?" She straightened out one small scrap and read from it: "Did you see Mona color her shoes white with chalk?" Mona was mentally retarded. She was bigger and older than the rest of the Little Room children but little was expected from her and she did whatever she chose to do as long as she didn't disrupt classes.

Miss Krinkle looked around the room. "Agnes, did you write this note?"

Agnes sat near the back of the room in the last row to the left. Next year she would be in the Big Room. She nodded her head, "Yes," she had written the note.

Miss Krinkle walked down the aisle and said, "Stand up, Agnes." Agnes stood up in front of her and without more ado the teacher pocketed the rest of her notes and, taking Agnes by both shoulders, shook her until her head bobbed back and forth and her teeth rattled. "You may be seated, Agnes, and I hope you have learned that you are not to be passing notes in school after this." Agnes sat, crying, with her head on her desk.

The second note the teacher read from the front of the room said "Give me them creans." Miss Krinkle pocketed the note and looked directly at Anna sitting right in the front of the second row of seats.

"Anna, did you write this note?" she asked.

Agnes was still crying quietly but the rest of the children were very quiet and you could hear her all over the silent room.

"No!" said Anna, knowing very well that people go to Hell for lying. But Hell was not right here and now and the teacher was!

"Dale, did Anna pass this note to you?" the teacher asked. Dale sat directly behind Anna and was the keeper of the one box of crayons they always had to share. Mama was reared in a Quaker home and two boxes of crayons would have been wasteful and unnecessary for two children in the same grade in school. Crayons were for 'busy work' after all assignments were finished and you were told you could play quietly; or for after the last recess on Friday - when the whole school room was

43

allowed to have ciphering matches, spelling matches or geography matches - or do art work with teacher supervision.

"No!" said Dale with equal fear of damnation.

"Anna, you and Dale can both stay in at recess. I want to talk to you both some more about this," Miss Krinkle said. "Children, you can all take out your books. There will be no opening exercises this morning."

Recess finally came and the rest of the children filed out to play as Dale and Anna sat huddled in their seats.

"Anna, how do you spell crayons?" asked Miss Krinkle. Anna knew how she had been spelling 'crayons.' She thought it must be wrong so she spelled, "Cranns?"

"No!" came the answer.

"Crins?"

"No!"

That wasn't right either. If she had ever got to keep those crayons in her desk for any length of time at all Anna would know how to spell the word, but then she wouldn't have to be forever asking Dale to pass those crayons to her when the teacher wasn't looking in the first place. It seemed there was no way out of this terrible situation.

"Dale, do you pass the crayons to Anna when she writes notes to you?" the teacher asked.

"No!" said Dale, and this time he was telling the truth.

"Did you ever see this note, Dale?" Miss Krinkle asked.

"No!" he answered truthfully again. Of course he hadn't. It fell on the floor.

"You may be excused, Dale. Anna you can sit right there in your seat till you get ready to tell me the truth about this note," the teacher said. "And you can go home for dinner but when you come back to school you must come in and take your seat. You will not play outside with the children unless you tell me now that you wrote this note."

Mama was down to the creamery when they went home at noon so Dale and Anna ate crackers and peanut butter and apples but the peanut butter kept sticking in Anna's throat so she couldn't swallow. They both knew that there was no turning back now--they had both said "No!" and "No!" it would have to be if she had to spend the rest of her life inside while everyone else played outside.

Anna asked Dale how to spell 'crayons' - he told her - but, after all, why shouldn't he know? He got to keep the crayons in his desk all the time! Anyway she still didn't know when the teacher asked her at noon. She just shook her head and said she didn't know .

Anna spent recesses and noon hours inside for two days, and became less and less knowledgeable about anything. At last the teacher gave up the struggle, perhaps realizing that she had punished her quite enough.

So the crime of lying is still on the books for Judgement Day.

* * * * * * * * *

44

"Anna, have you finished studying your spelling words?" the teacher asked as Anna was fidgeting around and looking back to see what Dale was doing at his desk behind her.

"Yes, and I wrote them each ten times," Anna replied, drawing out her Big Chief tablet to show her completed assignment.

"That's fine," said the teacher. "Hand it in tomorrow. Would you like to get a library book - or look at the <u>Books of Knowledge</u>?"

Anna loved to look at the <u>Books of Knowledge</u>. There was a whole row of them and she could look and look at them and never run out of pages to turn and new pictures to look at and read about. She was in the fourth grade now and listening to the smaller children recite was not as interesting as it used to be. Next year she would be in the Big Room and all the other classes would be older than her class and she'd have lots of things she could listen to when the sixth, seventh and eighth graders recited.

There was the beautiful brass sun with the long arm out to the side with the smaller brass ball on the end of it that showed how the earth turned around the sun and the earth turned over once every day so the sun could come up and go down for you depending on where you lived on which side of the earth. Anna wished she could play with that on her desk but the teacher brought it in just once from the big room to explain about 'gravity', - and why one didn't fall off when the world turned over.

Suddenly her attention was called to the front of the Room. The second graders were reciting their spelling, standing in a straight row behind the recitation bench. Kathryn had been spelling every word correctly when the others missed them.

"Kathryn, why are you studying your hand as you spell each word?" the teacher asked.

Kathryn hung her head and didn't answer, so the teacher rose from her chair behind her desk and walked over to Kathryn. All eyes in the room were on the class standing at the front of the room by this time. Kathryn held her hands tightly behind her back.

"Hold up your hand for all to see," the teacher said.

But Kathryn stood silent with hands clenched behind her back so the teacher had to take her hands apart.

"Kathryn, you have written your words on your hand. That is cheating. It isn't fair to stand at the head of the line and spell the words that others can't spell if you are reading them off of your hand. Now you must tell your classmates that you are sorry to have cheated them that way," the teacher said sternly.

But Kathryn stood silently, her little mouth in a straight determined line, while the entire room awaited her answer. Her big sister, Mary, cried softly at her seat. Mary was in the third grade, was such a good student and would never do such a thing. One wouldn't have thought that Kathryn would do such a thing either. She was a good student also but apparently more headstrong and less obedient than her big sister.

At last the teacher walked over to the blackboard, picked up a piece of chalk, drew a ring on the floor in front of the classroom and told Kathryn to stand in that ring bent over with her hands touching her toes, while the rest of the spelling classes recited their spelling. The rest of her class filed back to their seats and the third and fourth grades were called to recite. Mary continued to cry the rest of the period. When the rest of the children were all dismissed for recess, the teacher told Kathryn she must remain inside as she wanted to talk to her.

Anna felt sorry for Mary but, like all the rest of the children, teased her as she sat there crying because her little sister was in trouble. Anna remembered how awful it was when she and Dale both had to stay in. She hoped that Kathryn wasn't as stubborn as she had been in never admitting to the not she had written. Dale never did tell Papa and Mama about how she had lied. "I'll just have to keep that a secret for the rest of my life," Anna thought, sighing.

Mary and Kathryn had to ride the bus home with all the children from the Fairview District and Avis told Anna the next day how they all teased them and said that if they didn't tell their folks about how Kathryn had to stay in, they would.

Mary was quiet and studious and never appeared to get angry about anything, but the next day the teasing kept up while the country children ate their lunches on the shady side of the schoolhouse. Mary always brought milk to drink in a milk of magnesia bottle. Anna lived so close to the schoolhouse that she and Dale went home to lunch. Mama was apt to be down to the Cream Station so they would eat bread and peanut butter and select an apple from the basket. That way they could be back in the school yard before the country children had finished eating. Mary always chewed each bite 100 times and drank her milk last.

Anna ran unsuspectingly around the corner of the schoolhouse and "POW" she caught that heavy blue milk of magnesia bottle on the side of her head. She saw stars and bright circles for a few seconds but decided Mary had reached the end of her rope with all that teasing and planned to waylay the first one who came around the corner. Anna decided not to take it personally and they were fast friends all through grade school.

****

Humpty Dumpty sat on a wall.
Humpty Dumpty had a great fall.
All the king's horses and...
All the king's men
Couldn't put Humpty together again.

"The bank broke and all our money is gone," Papa reported. That small red brick building had always been there - The Wells State Bank - a solid place for Dale and Anna's savings. Papa and Mama had always said they had a savings account in that bank! Thirty dollars each from Baby Bonds that were bought for them during World War I. It was 1923 and the economy was pretty good, everyone thought. Mama and Papa put checks people gave them and Mama's check from the Concordia Creamery Company that she got for buying cream to ship to them - in that bank.

Mama seemed very unhappy, "Charlie, how do you know? What does Leslie Clay say about it? Surely there is some mistake."

"He's gone. He roomed with Jessie Palmer and his clothes are gone. He left in that Model T. It's gone, too," said Charlie. "I hope it kicks him like it did just three months ago when he tried to crank it."

Anna remembered. She was just seven and not very tall but she could fill people's tanks with gasoline. Leslie Clay drove up to the gas pump in front of the cream station and wanted five gallons of gasoline put in his car. It was after dark but Mama was testing cream, her elbows deep in a ten-gallon can, stirring with that long, long stirring rod to get a good sample of some farmer's cream. He was waiting for her to test it, weigh it and figure the butterfat content and write him a check so he could go to the grocery store to buy groceries and get home before midnight. He had brought in chickens to sell also and Papa and Dale were weighing his chickens out at the tin shed and untying their legs to put them in the long batteries and feed them. Then, when Papa got a truck load of chickens, he'd haul them to Salina in crates.

He had the gasoline lantern out there, but Mama lighted the wall lantern and Anna hung it outside on the Creamery wall, away from the gas pump. Mr. Clay seemed in a hurry as Anna filled his tank with gasoline. He handed her a five-dollar bill and Mama didn't have change for it in the cash drawer so Anna ran down to Copeman's Store to get change. Just as she was getting back to hand Mr. Clay his change, he got out to crank his car. It had two levers on the steering column, one for 'gas' and the other for 'spark.' It was easier if the driver stayed under the wheel and someone else stood in front of the car and twisted the crank. But Papa wasn't there to do that, he and Dale were still busy out at the chicken batteries.

Mr. Clay twisted the crank and the engine fired just as he let loose of the crank and it 'kicked' him--the crank came back around and whacked his wrist - breaking it. As the poor man held it under the wall lantern to view the damage Anna could see a small bone about to break through the skin on his arm. He sank down on the seat in front of the Creamery and Mama pumped water and wrung out a cloth to mop his forehead. Anna ran to tell Papa to come quick.

Papa left Dale to finish feeding all the caged chickens, and came in a hurry. He helped Mr. Clay into the car, the farmer waiting for his cream check offered to crank the car so Papa got behind the wheel, the car started and Mr. Clay was on his way to the doctor in Minneapolis.

But Mr. Clay's arm was out of the sling and good as new the last time Anna saw him. And now he was gone and the bank was broke.

Anna slipped out of the house, ran across the sandy street, down the long sidewalk beside the schoolhouse, cut across Fred Payne's yard, up the alley and across the street from the Cream Station. She stood in front of the bank with its 'CLOSED' sign on the door. She intended to see if she could find where the bank broke. Maybe she could find a crack somewhere around it where her thirty dollars might have leaked out. She walked around the building several times. It seemed to be as solid as it always had been, no cracks in it anywhere. She climbed the fence to Mr. Dyar's yard beside it and climbed the big cherry tree. She could look on top of the bank from the top of that tree. It was just black tar paper. No holes or cracks in it, either.

It was still a mystery the following Sunday morning at Sunday School. George Miller, who ran the garage and filling station just north of Papa's tin shed was the Sunday School Superintendent. He had a way of discussing things and bits of news pertinent to the morals of the community and that morning his remarks were about Mr. Clay and the closing of the Wells State Bank.

"At the close of Friday's business, I took my accumulated cash across to the bank. Leslie counted it, - we filled out a deposit slip as we had done many Friday evenings at the close of business and he made no mention of anything being amiss at the bank. I believe I am the last person to have seen him in Wells. He filled his car with gas - said he was going to take a short trip. The bank had that 'CLOSED' sign on the door and I asked when it would open. He explained that the State Bank Examiners would have to decide that and they were not expected to arrive in town for another week."

"So I said, 'Leslie, why didn't you tell me when I deposited all my cash in the bank Friday night that I wouldn't be able to get it out for the start of another business day? I think that would have been the Christian thing to do.'"

"His answer was that if I were a real Christian I wouldn't expect him to treat me any different than any other businessman in Wells. The bank examiners have not arrived, Mr. Clay has not returned from his short trip and I fear he never will."

George Miller's fears were valid. Leslie Clay never returned. No bank examiners ever arrived and, it was reported, Mr. Clay took all the money in the bank, including Dale's and Anna's life savings and drove all the way to Mexico. He was never heard from again.

****

*"..Snips and snails and puppy-dog tails
.... and that's what little boys are made from..."*

Saturday morning Stella always had so much to do at home so she let the few farmers who had cream to sell just put the cream in the creamery while she took care of chores at home. It was two long blocks from the north end of Wells to the cream station down on Main Street. Anyway, Charlie was down there building new batteries in the long machine shed just north of the creamery. Before too long the farmers would start bringing in their young fryers and they would hold them in those batteries until they had a truck load to take to Salina. Buying chickens was getting to be as big a job as buying cream. Stella almost wished she hadn't set the incubators this spring.

It was the Saturday before the Children's Day program at the church and both Dale and Anna had a part in the program. Dale's bath should come first before he got busy somewhere out of her sight. The Saturday baths were always a big job. She brought in the wash tub, sent the children for pails of water and more kindling to build a warm fire. The reservoir and teakettle were full of water. She was ready to begin on Dale. She had to wash his ears and he always hollered as if she were cutting them off. His shock of golden hair had to be washed, too, and slicked back while it was wet. Such a hassle.

At last that was over and it was Anna's turn. The water was warm. Her braids were loosened, hair brushed and washed, elbows scrubbed, toenails cut and one last warm rinse all over. Anna loved having a bath and getting clean clothes to wear. Her dark hair was parted in the middle and combed out long and straight. It was shiny and squeaky-clean. Now she could sit in front of the big oval mirror while her mother braided it on each side and they talked about what color ribbons she should wear at the top of each braid when they went to Sunday School in the morning.

Mother had promised Dale he could help her candle the eggs that were in the incubator down in the cellar. That was a job that came in the middle of hatching chickens every spring.

So they went downstairs to candle eggs and Anna tagged along. Mother had a box with a lamp inside and two holes in its side the size of an egg. As Momma held each egg up to the hole, the light would shine through. If the egg was fertile, the shape of a baby chick could be seen inside. But if the egg was not fertile it would show up cloudy and Mother knew that egg was rotten, and it would have to be thrown away.

Well, Anna thought, there must have been four or five hens that the old rooster couldn't catch because there were that many rotten eggs in the incubator that Saturday morning. Dale was very happy because Mother told him he could take them out away from the house and throw them away.

Anna tagged along, having no desire to do any throwing. One had to have a good throwing arm which girls were not supposed to develop even if they could. She was there because Dale said he'd throw them hard and when they hit the ground they'd pop - just like a firecracker.

"Move back out of the way so I can throw," Dale said, as he picked up a rotten egg gingerly in his hand.

Anna stepped behind him as he drew back his arm for a mighty throw. The egg slipped from his hand backward, catching her on the forehead with a "POP" as the egg broke and the rotten contents splattered her clean hair, her face, her dress, her arms and legs and even her new brown canvas sandals she wanted to wear to Sunday School in the morning.

Anna was stunned and almost asphyxiated with the stench of the rotten egg, blinded by the liquid dripping off her eyebrows, chin, hands, even her hair which had been so squeaky-clean and freshly braided. She was too devastated to cry. Dale came leading her back to the house to their mother. Years later he might possibly tell the story of this episode as though it were funny. But that morning it was no joke.

Mama was horrified. The fire had to be rekindled, the tub brought back in, the reservoir refilled, buckets of water heated with the teakettle - the stinking hair unbraided and rinsed out of doors several times before Anna could believe she could ever live with herself again. Even her new canvas sandals had to be washed and set in the sun to dry. Dale helped carry the water and the kindling without a murmur. Her filthy clothes were set to soak and rinsed repeatedly before they were put in soapy water to be washed, dried and ironed so she could ever wear them again.

It wasn't until Papa heard the sad story that Dale began to think it was funny. Papa laughed in true Allison fashion and even Mother was forced to smile ruefully as the story was told and retold at every family gathering. However, it never was funny to Anna.

****

Oh, for boyhood's painless play,
Sleep that wakes in laughing day,
Health that mocks the doctor's rules'
Knowledge never learned of schools, --
excerpt from "The Barefoot Boy"
by John Greenleaf Whittier

Dale and Anna stood on the front stoop of their little two-room house in the north end of Wells. It was the noon hour and the boys and girls were already coming out into the schoolyard after eating from their dinner pails. Dale was in a hurry to get back over to the school yard to play ball. He didn't really have time to finish his wedge of watermelon at the table. Mama insisted that he eat it and brought it to the door for him as he was hurrying out with his baseball mitt. He tucked it under his arm as he reached for the wedge of melon.

As Dale spit out the seeds, the ball mitt slipped from under his arm and fell in the sandburs beside the porch. Anna jumped down off of the porch, picked up the ball mitt, handed it to him and took the melon rind he had finished. He slipped the mitt on to his hand but a big healthy sandbur was stuck to the leather thumb.

Dale stuck the thumb up to his mouth to pull the sandbur out of the leather, and sucked the sandbur right down his throat. He coughed and sputtered and Mama came to the door to see what was the matter.

"I swallowed a watermelon seed," Dale lied as he hopped off the porch and went running back to the schoolyard to play ball.

Anna followed after him worrying to herself about that sandbur in Dale's throat. Maybe he could spit it out and Mama wouldn't know he had lied about what made him cough. But he didn't spit it out.

In fact, Dale couldn't spit or swallow either so he drooled all afternoon. Anna handed him a handkerchief to wipe his chin and the teacher kept him in at the last recess.

"Dale, what is your problem?" she asked.

"I got a watermelon seed caught in my throat," Dale insisted.

"Would you like to go home?" she asked. "You could be excused after the last recess." She knew that Dale and Anna both didn't want to miss school. They had been neither absent nor tardy since the first grade and neither one wanted to be the first one to miss school.

Dale shook his head "No" and continued to drool. She tore a section off of a clean dust cloth she had brought from home and sent him out to finish recess.

When Mama got home from down at the Cream Station she was shocked to see her little boy, his shirt pocket soaked with saliva he had been spitting into handkerchiefs one after the other as they became soaked; and still he continued to drool.

"Dale, what is the matter with you?" she implored.

"I just got a watermelon seed caught in my throat," Dale insisted, trying to spit into an old coffee can beside his cot in the living room.

"Well, if you're not better in the morning, we'll have to take you to the doctor." Mama was frying potatoes and hamburgers while Anna set the table. "Maybe if you eat something the watermelon seed will go on down your throat. I've never heard of a watermelon seed causing that much trouble," Mama said.

Anna couldn't forget the sandbur that she had seen slip down her brother's throat but she could not tell on him either when he was obviously so miserable. She knew why he kept insisting it was just a watermelon seed that was caught in his throat. He didn't want to go to the doctor and miss school. She wouldn't want to either. And she knew Dale loved school just like she did.

Dale tried to eat supper but he couldn't swallow food if he couldn't swallow spit so he just kept on spitting and insisting that he'd be better in the morning.

But the next morning was no different. Still Dale kept insisting that he was fine as he searched for something more to spit in as he got ready for school.

"Anna, what does your mother think about Dale not being able to swallow?" Miss Comfort asked, as Anna was going out to play the first recess.

"Well, she says that Papa will have to take him to the doctor if he doesn't start trying to swallow," Anna said.

"Well I should think so," the teacher agreed as she watched the little boy wipe his chin and stuff that sopping wet cloth back in his shirt pocket as they went out to play ball.

Days went by, soon it would be a week since Dale had been able to swallow any food. Mama was at the end of her patience. She cooked rice that morning and handed Dale an ultimatum.

"You will either eat this bowl of rice and milk or Papa will take you to the doctor this morning!"

Dale burst into tears as she scooted him up to the table and pushed the bowl of rice in front of him. He opened his mouth and tried to swallow the rice. Dale coughed and choked and suddenly spit out the sandbur in his hand.

"There's your old sandbur!" he said. Mama burst into tears.

"Dale, you could have died," Papa said. "Why didn't you tell us it was a sandbur you swallowed instead of a watermelon seed?"

"Because he didn't want to miss school," Anna piped up as Dale was finishing his bowl of rice.

Mama was still looking at that sandbur; it appeared to have festered on each of its prongs where it had stuck and lodged in Dale's throat.

"Dale, the teacher would have excused you after the last recess and you could have gone to the doctor the day you did that. Don't you ever lie to us again about so serious a matter," Papa said.

Anna heard Mama saying to Papa, "God is certainly looking after those two," as they went skipping off to school that morning without a care in the world - for the first time in a week. 'Yes, indeed,' Anna thought, 'God did. That's what the song means that starts 'His eye is on the sparrow and I know he watches me!'

****

"Where did you come from, Baby dear?"
"Out of the blue sky into here."
"And where did you get your eyes so blue?"
"Out of the clouds as I came through!"

"Mama, this is the Fourth of July! Are we going down to Uncle Roy's for a picnic? Why can't they come up here? Philip and Chester Miller's papa has a lot of fire crackers and sky rockets to shoot off tonight and we want to watch them."

"Honey, your papa is going to bring you and Dale and Leta, Lela, and Lola back up here to play today. You can have a picnic right here in Wells and then you'll be here when Millers have their fireworks tonight."

"But why can't Uncle Roy and Aunt Blanche come up here today? And little Kenneth? He has just learned to walk and he's fun to play with. And why can't you come back with us?"

52

Anna was full of questions about this sudden change of plans for the Fourth of July. Last year they all went fishing and the little children played on the sand bar, waded in the shallow water and made sand pies.

"Now, Anna, you're going to have to help your papa with the picnic. He's going to have to watch all five of you children today since I'm going down to your Uncle Roy's house. Your Aunt Blanche is getting a new baby today," Mama explained.

"A new baby!" Anna's eyes opened wide. "Where's she getting it?"

"Honey, the doctor is going to bring it. Now run out and get in the car, we have to hurry and be there before he comes. And no more questions, Anna," Mama said sternly.

Anna crawled up into the box her papa had built on the back of the car for Dale and her to ride in, and to carry everything they didn't want up in the front seat with them. Mama shut the door behind them and hurried out to climb into the front seat beside Papa. Soon they were driving into the yard at Uncle Roy's house. Leta, Lela and Lola ran out and crawled up into the box with Dale and Anna. Papa turned from his seat under the steering wheel to say they were to stay in the car; he was going straight back to Wells.

Just then a car drove in the yard and a man got out and carried a small black bag into the house. Leta said it was the doctor. As Papa turned the car around to go back to Wells, Anna watched to see if the doctor would come back out to get a baby out of his car but he didn't. If that baby was shut up in that small black bag she hoped the doctor was opening it to take the baby out right now!

The four little girls played house in the grape arbor while Dale and Papa worked around the yard. They had bologna sandwiches for their picnic lunch and Papa made potato soup for supper.

That night they made a bed in the box in the back of the car and all five children laid out under the stars watching the sky. Dale saw the first fire cracker. Soon the whole sky was alight with fountains of bursting lights in all the colors of the rainbow. "Zooooom," they would go - away up into the sky and then burst into hundreds of beautiful colored lights arcing across the sky to rain down and then disappear before they hit the ground.

Papa sat in the front seat of the open car and watched, too. He said, "Every year since July 4, 1776, we celebrate the day the Continental Congress signed the Declaration of Independence from England and the thirteen original colonies became the United States of America."

"Did Great Britain celebrate too?" asked Dale.

"Not much," laughed Papa. "They sent their armies over from England and tried to win the Revolutionary War and tear up our Declaration of Independence."

"Did we drive them back down the hill like we did Kaiser Bill?" Anna asked.

"We surely did!" said Papa. "And we've kept adding states since the thirteen original states won that war till we now have forty-eight."

"Papa, can we get some firecrackers next year?" asked Dale.

"We'll have to see, Dale, but Leta, Lela, and Lola have something to celebrate this year. Your Uncle Roy just called before we came out to watch the skyrockets. They have a new baby sister," Papa said.

"Where did they get her?" Leta asked.

"Mama said the doctor would bring her," Anna said doubtfully.

"Well, he must have," said Papa. "Now, I'll cover you up with this army blanket and you can sleep out here under the stars and we'll go down to Uncle Roy's house in the morning and have breakfast and see the new baby."

"Aunt Blanche didn't need another baby. She already had Kenneth. Why couldn't we have her?" asked Anna.

"Because the doctor brought her to them," said Papa, shortly.

"Kenneth isn't a baby anymore," said Lela, "He walks. Anyway, it will be fun to have a new little baby to play with."

"That's right," said Papa, "She'll be growing, too, just like Kenneth did, before you know it. Babies don't stay babies very long at all. Now go to sleep, children."

"Mama is too busy at the cream station," Dale spoke up. "We can go down to Uncle Roy's and play with the babies. I like to build railroad tracks for Kenneth, anyway."

"Mama's sad sometimes because we didn't have any more babies but now she's just too busy, I guess, to order one," Anna said.

Papa agreed with satisfaction. It had been a good Fourth of July, after all.

****

Mother

Most of all the beautiful things in the world come by twos and threes, by dozens and hundreds! Plenty of roses, stars, sunsets and rainbows, brothers and sisters, aunts and cousins, but only one mother in all the wide world.

Kate D. Wiggin

Dale bounced into the creamery one evening in the spring and said to Mama, "Dad wants me to ask you what you want for Mother's Day, Mama?"

Mama's eyes lighted up and all the tired lines left her face. "There's a glass dish, it's the new Pyrex stuff that you can put right in the oven - it's oval shaped and it's got a lid. It's down at Copeman's over there with all the dishes and kitchen stuff. It costs fifty cents but for Mother's Day... Of course, I don't need it, I've got plenty of oven pans but, once you've baked something in that glass pan, you could put it right on the table," Mama finished, with some misgivings about the expense of such a gift, since, of course, it wasn't an absolute necessity.

"OK, I'll tell him," Dale bounded out, never sitting long anywhere, but Mama moved with more dispatch as she finished testing the cans of cream that had been brought in that Saturday evening.

Papa was down to Copeman's store, sitting on the loafer's bench, catching up on the week's happenings. He had been out with his truck all that week, hauling produce and implements for hire and Saturday night was a time for relaxing. The cans of cream were small four-gallon cans that evening so Anna could help Mama wash cans and finish up in the creamery. Mama hummed as she worked and soon was writing the checks for the farmers who kept dropping in to pick them up and go down to the store and pay for their groceries. Dale came in and sat down, it was almost time to go home. Mama closed up at ten o'clock if there was no more cream coming in and Papa wasn't home yet from hauling. But tonight Papa was still visiting down at the store.

"Dale, what did Charlie say about that dish?" Mama asked, as the little boy came in and sat down.

"He said that was a little high for a dish but he'd look around and see if he could find you something," Dale said casually.

Mama's face fell. "Doggoned all, I stay here and work and wait for customers and I'm right here every day, day in and day out. And the one day I might have to stay home and cook a meal - and if I want something new to cook with 'it's a little high'!" Dale and Anna seldom saw Mama really angry and never at Papa. And tomorrow was Mother's Day.

"Dale, do you know what Papa got for Mama?" Anna whispered. She knew Mama was near tears and she was feeling every bit as bad as Mama. It did seem most unfair! Dale just shook his head and looked sad.

Papa came bustling in. "Time to go home," he said. Mama took the change out of the cash drawer, stuffed it with the bills and checks into the leather pouch, turned out the gas lamp, turned the kerosene heater off under the can washer and they were ready to go home. Mama didn't say a word to Papa.

They all slid into the front seat of Papa's new truck. He bought a new truck every year since he could get a good trade-in price on the old one and soon the tires or the battery or the front-end or something would go bad on the old one and it was cheaper, he reasoned. Mama always agreed with him but Anna sat silent and so did Mama as they rode up to the north end of Wells and stopped in front of the door on the little two-room house they called home.

Anna was thinking, 'Papa can afford a new truck but he can't afford a new dish for Mama' - and she knew Mama was thinking that, too.

Papa went in first and lighted the kerosene lamp. There on the table sat the pyrex dish. Mama sat down at the table and burst into tears, of frustration or joy? She would have been hard put to tell which.

Papa patted her back and smiled. He had told Dale to tell her the dish was too expensive because he knew she'd be indignant. Papa loved to tease Mama, and so did Dale. Papa had bought the pyrex dish and handed it to Dale to sneak home with so that it would be there on the table when she got home. He didn't tell Dale to say he'd find something cheaper but that was Dale's story. Between the two of them they had created a Mother's Day gift that would never be forgotten.

* * * * * * * * * *

Anna recalled the 'ever-so-funny' story Papa loved to tell about when she and Dale were two and three years old:

"I came home from working on the road," he'd say. "And Stella would tell me all the things the kids had gotten into that day. They had played out by the wagon and I had left the open coffee can of axle grease down where they could reach it and they smeared that all over their clean rompers, so she had to change them and put the rompers to soak in kerosene, and then they had found the tar bucket, where I had left it when I got through patching the roof on the well house. So that took a second pair of clean rompers with two sets soaking in the kerosene, and then they had found the whitewash that I had left in the paint bucket when I got the chicken house ready for the young hens. I had to interrupt her before the kids ran completely out of rompers. 'Stella, I said, I just don't know what we're going to do with those kids now. I guess we just should have knocked them in the head when they were younger and fed the milk to the pigs.'"

Everyone would laugh and Mama would shudder. Anna didn't know if he had mended his ways about leaving grease cans and paint buckets around or if they had finally quit getting into such things. It was just Papa's way of teasing Mama.

Dale and Anna had ways of getting into messes of their own creation also. Anna remembered the little episode of the syrup pail:

Mama had bought a fresh pail of syrup, a full half-gallon which she had just opened to fill the syrup pitcher that morning. It was sitting on the corner of the kitchen cabinet when she got ready to go down to the Cream Station with Papa that morning.

"Stella, I'm ready to go," he called from the cab of the truck. Mama swallowed the last of her breakfast, picked up the cash sack and the latest <u>Woman's Home Companion</u>, and glanced in the mirror to see if her face was clean.

"Anna, you straighten the kitchen and sweep the floor. I know it's awfully dirty but the scrubbing will just have to wait till Sunday morning when I have time to do that. Dale, now you help Anna, do you hear?" Mama said on her way out the door.

Anna had hid Dale's ball mitt. She started washing the dishes in a big pan of soapy water, rinsing them in another pan and fishing them out for Dale to dry.

56

"Anna, do you know where I put my ball mitt?" asked Dale.

"Sure, I do," said Anna. "I'll find it for you when you get these dishes dry and put them up in the cupboard."

"You find it and then I'll dry the dishes," said Dale.

Anna picked up the dish towel and twisted it at the corners to take a swipe at Dale. Dale got the broom from behind the door to defend himself from the snap of the dish towel. So they snapped and parried and swiped and swung and danced around in the kitchen. They often did this when the folks were gone. After all, they had all day to get the dishes done, the floor swept and the kitchen straightened up. Mama would probably send them down to the store for peanut butter, bread and apples for lunch if they came down to the creamery about noon... Suddenly they looked around toward the kitchen cabinet - someone had knocked over the big bucket of syrup and most of it had poured out onto the floor!

It didn't really matter who had knocked it over. They both had to clean it up. Dale tried to sweep it but that was no use - it was too sticky. Anna set the pail upright. There was just a little syrup left in it. She hurriedly finished washing the dishes and poured the whole pan of dishwater in the floor. Dale continued to sweep. They swept it all out the back door. It still was sticky so they used the bucket of water from the wash stand. Dale handed the broom to Anna and went out to the well house for a fresh bucket of water. Anna kept sweeping up water from all four corners of the kitchen. A bucket or two more and the kitchen was clean. Anna wiped off the cabinet and put the very light pail of syrup back to the back of the cabinet where they always kept it. They had a pitcher of syrup and maybe Mama wouldn't wonder what happened to her new pail of syrup for a week or two at least.

Dale dried the dishes and put them away while Anna made the beds. That little two-room house never looked so good! Even the back step was clean and it looked as though someone had even watered the moss roses by the back step!

When Mama came home that evening she hugged each of those guilty little wretches and bragged on them to Papa when he came home, "Charlie, you should just look at this floor. The children mopped this morning - they had the dishes all done and put away and the beds made. I didn't even know they could mop."

"Well, it wasn't easy," Dale said.

"I hid his ball glove," said Anna. "And he had to help me mop after he dried the dishes, before I could find it for him."

"Well, whatever caused it, it was well worth it," said Mama, happily. They both resolved to do it again sometime without having to lose a pail of syrup to cause it. Te children never knew whether their mother ever wondered what happened to most of a gallon pail of syrup.

* * * * * * * * *

"Why can't I go with Papa and you stay home and do the dishes and sweep the floor, Dale?" asked Anna. She would be nine in the fall and it seemed that she was being left all the time to take care of the little two-room house all by herself.

"Because I'm a boy," said Dale as he finished his pancake and wiped his plate clean of syrup with the last bite. "And boys are supposed to work outdoors, Papa said so. Didn't you, Papa?"

"Yes, I did, Dale, but Anna can go with me sometimes when I'm hauling chickens and eggs to Salina and you can stay home and help your mother in the cream station. People are bringing in their young chickens every day now and she needs you out at the tin shed to weigh them and put them in the batteries," Papa said, trying to be fair with his two children.

"But who will do the dishes and make the beds and sweep the floor when you and Mama both have to leave early?" Anna argued.

"Anna, you don't want to grow up to be a tom-boy. Your mother was so glad when you were born. We had a little girl who could help her in the house. Come along, Dale, I promised Erv Baker I'd be there to load those calves at seven," Papa said as he bustled out with Dale right behind him.

But the very next Monday morning Papa said, "I have to haul the chickens to Salina - I've got a dozen crates of young broilers. Copemans and Overtons have at least a dozen 30-dozen cases of eggs to sell. Dale, come along down to the creamery with me and help me put those chickens in the crates. I'll pick up the grocery and hardware orders and see if the elevator and the lumberyard want anything from Salina. Stella, you and Anna can get the morning chores done here and come down to the creamery in about 30 minutes. Anna can go with me to Salina." Papa had been worrying about his little tom-boy after all, Anna thought.

Dale looked a little sober as Anna climbed into the seat beside Papa. Mama said, "Dale's going to buy chickens for me today and feed them when he gets them in the batteries. I'm glad I've got help today." And they were off to Salina.

When they were done with all the business for the two grocery stores, the elevator, and the hardware store they went shopping. Papa bought Anna two beautiful new dresses. One was blue and one was yellow. They had smocking and embroidery on them and would have been very nice for Sunday School but Papa explained that wasn't what they were for.

"Now, Anna, we'll get you some new knee socks too, and bright garters with ribbon bows on the side. And new brown canvas strap sandals - so that every morning after you have the morning work done, you can dress up and come down to the creamery and Mama will send you down to the store to buy the day's groceries. That way you can be the lady of the house." Papa had her summer outlined for her.

* * * * * * * * *

58

It worked quite well, also, except for a few catastrophes. Anna decided one day to enlarge on Mama's arrangement on the kitchen cabinet. Mama kept the sugar in a two-quart jar so it wouldn't draw moisture, she had explained to Anna.

Anna went down in the cellar and brought up three more two-quart jars. She emptied the flour into one, the coffee from its can into another and the salt into the third one. Now she had four two-quart jars lined up across the back of the cabinet - four canisters for coffee, flour, salt and sugar. When Mama came home that evening she seemed pleased to see what Anna had done, not enthusiastic, maybe, but pleased.

Mama seemed to be learning where those four items were and cooking breakfast and supper with her usual speed and efficiency till one evening just before supper Papa came in with his hat full of big, ripe strawberries.

"Stella, can we have strawberry shortcake for supper?" he asked, pouring them out into a colander. "Anna, you hurry and wash and clean these. I'll go chop some kindling for your mother and she can whip up a one-egg cake to go with them."

Mama stopped in the middle of peeling potatoes for fried potatoes and started whipping up the cake. She put in one-half cup of shortentng, one egg, one cup of milk, two cups of flour, two teaspoons of baking powder, and one cup of sugar, beat them altogether, poured the batter into the pan to bake, cleaned the spoon with her finger and licked her finger. BRINE!! She had grabbed the salt canister instead of the sugar!

Mamma grabbed the pan of cake batter, ran out behind the well house and scraped it out on the ground. The little chickens came running and began eating it up. Mama panicked, thinking the salt would kill them or the baking powder would make their craws swell. She scooped it all up in the pan and took it to the outhouse - to dump it down the toilet hole.

She came out looking a bit calmer and said, "Too many cooks in the kitchen, I guess. Anyway I can't have the salt and the sugar both in two-quart jars, Anna. We'll just have to give that up."

****

Seein' Things

I aint afeard uv snakes, or toads, or bugs, or worms, or mice, An' things 'at girls are skeered uv I think are awful nice!

Eugene Field

Anna stepped out on the little front stoop of the little two-room house that was home to her - her special world. It was a hot day - Mama had gone down to the cream station early. Papa and Dale had left in the truck. She had had the morning to herself to wash the dishes, sweep the floor and make the beds. All that behind her, she still had the day to check the bird nests in the trees in the yard - and then she glanced down.

A rattlesnake!!!! All curled up sleeping beside the porch in the sun. His rattles were plain to be seen. He must have crawled out of the cellar; Anna's beloved cellar where Mama had the incubator and all the jars of fruit. Anna ran up and down those cellar steps without a care in the world - up until now!! That little window with the ledge beneath where they stored the overshoes for winter when it was summer and one could always go barefoot. He must have crawled through that window. "Did he live on that ledge? Well, he must never crawl back in that cellar again," Anna thought, "But what to do??"

Should she run down town - two long blocks and tell Mama - and risk the snake crawling back into the cellar - and what would Mama do? She wished Papa wasn't always away at work ....

There was the parsonage across the street. Mr. Gunkle might be at home, but would a preacher kill a rattlesnake?

Anna ran across the street, climbed the fence and crossed the garden. The preacher wasn't home but Mrs. Gunkle was. She lay there on an old chaise lounge in the shade with a wet washcloth over her forehead. She often had a headache and folks said she was 'sickly.' Reverend Gunkle often had to go to church functions without her.

"What do you want, dearie?" she asked, in her kind, weak voice. Anna hated to say but maybe Mrs. Gunkle could tell her where to turn next for help.

"There's a rattlesnake all curled up right by the porch. He's asleep but I'm afraid he'll wake up and crawl back down in the cellar," Anna hesitated. Mrs. Gunkle sat up, her eyes wide. She did look sick with those big dark circles under her eyes. She spoke not a word. She just laid the wet washcloth aside, walked over to the garden gate and picked up the hoe. She swept through the gate and along the path, her long skirts dragging at the weeds beside the fence.

Crossing the street, she paused at the gate to Anna's yard. "You stay here, honey," she said, her voice stronger and her whole manner changed to suit the occasion.

"There he is, still curled up, asleep," Anna spoke softly, pointing toward the porch.

Mrs. Gunkle walked over toward the snake with her hoe poised and deliberately hoed the sleeping snake out to the middle of the yard. Anna watched with wide eyes as she chopped at the aroused creature. He leaped into the air, his entire length, following the hoe; Mrs Gunkle backed up and followed him down chopping furiously. He struck several times before her hoe landed squarely behind that head with its darting fangs. The head was severed but the body with its dreadful rattles continued to writhe.

"He'll die in a few moments," Mrs. Gunkle said, as though she were an authority on killing snakes. "Meanwhile, don't touch him. The poison in his fangs can kill even after he's dead. We'll put him in this box and your father can bury him when he gets home." She picked up the head with the hoe and tossed it into the box, scooped up the body the same way, being careful to keep it far away from her flowing skirts. She walked back across the street briskly. Anna thought she didn't look sick at all anymore.

It was almost noon, time for Anna to go down to the creamery and see what Mama had planned for their dinner, Papa and Dale probably wouldn't be home till evening but they'd eat something, cheese and crackers and maybe an apple from Copeman's Store. Anna couldn't wait to tell Mama about how Mrs. Gunkle had killed the snake for her.

"My goodness, Anna, whatever possessed you to ask that poor sick lady to kill that snake? It's a wonder she didn't die of a heart attack right there in the yard!" Mama exclaimed.

"Mama, he might have crawled back in the cellar and then I could never go down there again," Anna wailed.

"Nor me either," agreed Mama, saying no more till Papa and Dale got home that evening.

Papa cut the rattles off of the snake before he carefully buried the thing. He came bringing them in for Mama to see. "Mrs. Gunkle really chopped that snake up. Do you suppose she will want these rattles to show the preacher?" he asked.

"Charlie, I can't imagine what possessed Anna to go across there and ask that poor sick lady to kill a snake for her. It's a wonder she didn't faint just thinking about it!" Mama was embarrassed that Anna had to call on a neighbor. "I'll have to go over and see how she is this evening and tell her we are pleased that she was on hand when Anna needed her. But I won't carry those horrible rattles and I doubt if she will touch them either."

Papa laughed, "Stella, what would you do if you had a headache and a little neighbor girl came over and told you that there was a rattlesnake curled up by her door?"

"Why, I suppose I'd do just what she did. I'm sure I'd forget my headache for a minute or two anyway," said Mama as she changed her dress and combed her hair.

"And I'll bet Mrs. Gunkle is feeling better for getting the exercise. I'll give the preacher these rattles. I'm sure he'll be proud of her, when I tell him how much we appreciate what she did," Papa said as he opened the screen door for Mama.

****

The Red River Valley

The Big Room was a very real milestone during grade school years. Dale and Anna were in the fifth grade so they could listen to the 'Big

Kids' recite. The books were harder to read in the library and for many of their friends, that was the last four years of education they would ever get. Radio had been invented and small radio stations began to spring up. Several of the families had a radio and some of the boys could sing the old country songs like "Save My Mother's Picture From the Sale," "The Face on the Barroom Floor," "The Wreck of the Old Number Nine" and "The Red River Valley."

Anna yearned to sing songs like that from memory. "Avis," she said one noon hour when they were visiting, "Do you know the words to "The Red River Valley?""

"Oh, sure," said Avis. "Toy and Swede sing it all the time."

"I only know two verses," said Anna.

"What will you give me to write the words to the rest of it down for you?" asked Avis.

"Are you sure you know the rest of the verses? There's a lot of them - if you write them all down for me tonight, I'll give you a five-cent sucker tomorrow," Anna bargained, knowing that it would have to be a big sucker, five inches across to get Avis to work that much.

"I want a big red one, strawberry flavor." Avis drove a hard bargain.

"What if all they have at Copeman's store are the green lime ones? Marvin Overton doesn't keep them in stock. I could get you five licorice pipes at his store. If I can't get a big red sucker, would you rather have five licorice pipes?" Anna continued, knowing the green suckers were all they had left in the showcase at Copeman's the last time she looked.

"I don't want licorice pipes," Avis decided. "Mama wouldn't let me smoke them around her and I'd have to give them to the boys anyway."

"All right, I'll see if I can get you a big red sucker, and, if I can't, I'll get a green one and bring it at noon," Anna assured Avis. Mama held the purse strings - on a leather pouch with an Indian head printed on the side. She kept it in the cash drawer in the cream station where Mama was always to be found. There was a gasoline pump in front of the creamery, and Papa also kept spark plugs and light bulbs and other small parts to keep the Model-T's running. Anna often pumped gas for people, or sold them fuses, bulbs, plugs, etc. when she was around and Mama was busy washing cream cans or measuring acid into the testing bottles for the cream. So the little girl knew she could convince Mama that she needed a nickel without having to give too much explanation as to 'What for?'.

Anna brought the big green sucker back to school at noon. Avis handed her the sheet of paper on which she said she had written all the verses to "The Red River Valley" as she reached out her hand for the sucker.

"I don't like lime," she said as Anna opened the folded paper to see that she had written only the first verse and the chorus - which Anna already knew. Avis was licking the big sucker.

"Where are the rest of the verses?" asked Anna.

"Toy and Swede were both in a hurry to go somewhere last night and said they'd help me later with the rest of the verses," Avis answered between licks.

* * * * * * * *

Postscript: Approximately sixty years later Avis delivered the rest of the verses to "The Red River Valley." She said she had found them in an old folk song book. Anna was a little too proud to admit that probably she couldn't have sung them anyway.

****

"I dream of Jeanie with the light brown hair,
Borne, like a vapor on the summer air:
I see her tripping where the bright streams play
Happy as the daisies that dance on her way."
Old song by Stephen Foster

"Stella, if you hurry I'll give you a ride down to the creamery." Papa was always in a hurry to begin his day. He always had something to do with his truck. On his way by he could drop Mama off at the cream station. There she'd be for the whole day - ready for business. "But you'll have to hurry. I'm taking Dale with me, we're going over past the old Hugo Crumm place where Roy used to live --" Papa paused as he picked up his gloves from the corner of the kitchen cabinet.

Mama was standing by the sewing machine brushing her long brown hair. She was bent over to get all the long hair on the back of her neck to go the same way as the rest of her hair - up.

"Aren't you about ready?" demanded Charlie.

"Charlie, I've a notion to ask Bertha to cut my hair. Edith and Edna both have short hair and she cuts theirs all the time. I never have fifteen minutes to get ready to go to work and it takes that long to put up my hair. Anna, what did you do with the box of hairpins?" Mama sounded flustered as she always did if Papa was waiting on her.

Dale and Anna had been picking walnuts with a couple of hairpins and the box was over behind the door where they had been cracking black walnuts on the bottom of the flatiron. If they got enough that they didn't eat as they cracked them - maybe they'd have black walnut ice-cream on Sunday. Anna hurried to bring the box back to the sewing machine. The comb and hairbrush and hairpins and ribbons and buttonhooks and shoe horns and all the things like needles, pins, safety pins, thread, etc. all were to be kept on or in the drawers of the sewing machine that stood in front of the big mirror that hung by the bedroom door.

"Stella, if you cut all that lovely long hair," Papa said, "You'll never be able to wear picture hats again or have any use for hat pins any more.

I wonder what Vern Heald and Tom Yonally said when their wives came home from visiting their mother with their hair all bobbed off like a horse's tail?"

"I've never worn a picture hat, I don't own a picture hat or a long hatpin either and what would I do with one?" Mama rolled her hair up in a long rope and twisted it around hastily to make a tight bun up on top.

As Mama jabbed in a few wire pins, Anna thought, "Aunt Belva had blond tortoise shell pins and Mama had some pretty brown ones once but they were all lost somewhere."

"I have to run out to the toilet a minute, Charlie. Anna, you'll do up the dishes and straighten up the place before you come down town, won't you?" Mama asked.

"Sure, she will, - Stella, that's what I built that toilet out behind the tin shed down there by the creamery for. Can't that wait?" Papa was always hurrying Mama.

She just gave him a sideways glance on her way out the back door. It was the kind of a look that told anyone who knew Mama that they would be wise to say no more. Papa went on out to the truck.

"Mama, I'll bring down the comb and brush and my ribbons and you can braid my hair later," Anna said as Mama came in the back door and gathered up the mending.

"That will be fine, Honey, brush your hair good this morning. That will make it grow thicker. I see Charlie is still waiting on me." Mama hurried out the front door, stopping to take the scissors down from the nail. Papa had driven that nail high up on the door casing so they could all return the scissors there when they were done with them. "Will you see if you can find my little embroidery scissors for me and bring them down? I seem to have misplaced them somewhere and I don't like to take these," Mama explained as she disappeared through the door.

"Papa didn't like the idea of Mama getting her hair cut," Anna thought to herself as she brushed awhile longer, hopping up on a chair so she could see herself in the mirror. She bent over and brushed her hair up from the back of her neck. A lot of it wasn't long enough to reach the top of her head. She tried to twist it around and make a bun on the top of her head like Mama did. It was no use, it was too thin and short up there. She wondered how old Mama was when she could do her hair up on top of her head. She knew she'd be a lot older before she could ever make a bun on the top of her head. Mama was past forty years old. If it took that long to grow it, it would be a long, long time before she could ever look grown up. Anna hopped down off of the chair and made a bundle of the hairbrush, comb, bow clasp and ribbon and put it by the door so she wouldn't forget it.

Sometimes she liked playing house - doing the dishes, making the beds, sweeping the floor. She didn't like emptying the slop jar (Mama called it a chamber pot). She carried it out to the toilet and stopped on her way back to rinse it, catching water in it where the pipe emptied into

64

the tank for the horses and cows at the edge of the corral. It was just a job that had to be done every morning and Mama didn't have time to do it. She didn't even have time to brush her hair. Anna felt sorry for Mama. Papa and Dale didn't have to spend time brushing long hair - boys and men had always been able to cut their hair or leave it long if they wished - and they could jump in the truck and be off in the morning without a care in the world. There were barber shops for men and little boys got their first haircut almost when they learned to walk so they wouldn't look like sissies! "That's what I am - a sissy!" Anna thought. She didn't blame Mama for wanting her hair cut! Anna hurried back into the house, slid the 'thunder mug' as Papa called the chamber pot, back under the bed, gathered up the brush and the ribbons and hurried down town.

"Mama, I've decided I want my hair cut even if you don't," said Anna as she came into the creamery. "It will be a long, long time if it ever gets long enough to put up and you'll be having to take time to braid it every day and we have to take a whole day off when we wash our hair."

Anna paused for breath and Mama said, "All right, Anna but I'm going to order Dale a new pair of these little long pants. They are in the catalog this spring, see here," said Mother, pointing to a page in the Montgomery Ward catalog. "Then Charlie won't think that all we're thinking of is ourselves. After all, we all have to keep up with the times. And those knickers that little boys wear - they never keep them buttoned below the knee. Look at these cute little overalls."

Later that day the little town was quiet, there was no cream waiting on the scale to be weighed, a sample to be taken and tested, no cream can to be washed and no check to be written.

Mama said, "Anna, I think we'll just run up to Bertha's right now and get your hair cut; I'll just leave a note on the desk saying I'll be right back and if someone brings in any cream they can just leave it. Let's go."

Mrs. Brown had barber shears and such a nice house, almost as nice as Aunt Belva's in Concordia. Mama was so lucky to have such a good friend. Mrs. Brown was almost Mama's only escape from the world of business - her only job was being a homemaker. Anna settled herself on two catalogs on a chair on the back porch and in no time at all she had bangs, her hair was parted on the side and cut straight around - just below her ears. Anna flipped her head around this way and that but it wouldn't fall in her eyes. She liked it!

"Stella, you should let me cut your hair today, too," said Mrs. Brown.

"Oh, I'm not sure that I'll have time, I should be getting back to the creamery - someone might come in who is in a hurry for his check."

"Mama, I'll go back and sit in the creamery and tell them you'll be right back if you want me to," offered Anna, hoping Mama would decide to cut her hair. She knew Mama was thinking that Papa wouldn't like it. Anna thought he probably wouldn't like her haircut either but she did and, as Mama said, they had to keep up with the times.

"Well, run on back, honey, while I make up my mind."

Anna would have liked to have stayed but she knew better. No one showed up with a can of cream and by and by Mama came back to the creamery with her hair cut! It would take a bit of getting used to but Mama had short hair.

"What do you think Papa is going to say, Mama?" Anna asked hesitantly.

"Well, what can he say? It's done, isn't it? I guess he'll just have to live with it. At any rate, it's lots cooler and with summer coming on, I'm going to enjoy it - as soon as I get used to it - and as soon as it gets used to being combed down instead of up. Bertha says there's new bobby pins that will stay in it but my combs and hairpins just slide right out. What do you think, Anna?" Mama began to have some misgivings.

"Copeman's have some pretty brown barrettes, Bertha said. Anna, will you take this half-dollar and go down and buy a card of them, if you can find them?" Mama said as she shut the cash drawer.

"Mama, you look so pretty, and these will hold your hair back," Anna spoke admiringly as she watched her mother arrange her thick short hair. Mama was standing behind the door looking into a small cracked mirror that she kept hanging under the calendar. She fastened her hair back on each side and decided to face the new world without hairpins, but she was obviously apprehensive.

"Ed Luthi must have decided to sell that breechy cow in Salina or Charlie and Dale would have been home by now; they were just going to help him find her and haul her home. They seem to be taking an awfully long time," Mama said as the day wore on and the shadows from the trees across the street lengthened.

At last they drove up. Dale came hopping out of the truck with a big hatbox, almost as big as he was. He didn't even notice Mama as he set it on the seat by the cash register. "See what Papa bought you," he exclaimed.

"Well, shades of O'Henry," Mama said as she lifted the lid.

There was the most beautiful picture hat anyone had ever seen - complete with two hatpins and trimmed with pale green satin leaves and rolled satin vines around the brim, a rose bud and a big peach satin rose. Mama looked up at Papa standing in the door and Anna saw tears in her eyes.

Papa just said, "That millinery store was going out of business, Stella, and all their hats were on sale. The saleslady said that nobody was buying hats anymore - everyone has short hair."

****

66

"How dear to my heart are the scenes of my childhood
When fond recollection presents them to view..."
(The Old Oaken Bucket by Samuel Woodworth)

"Hurry home from Sunday School, children," said Papa. "Stella wants to come back from Concordia and visit her folks, so we'll have the cream cans loaded in the truck when Sunday School is over."

Papa shipped the cream that had been brought to town on Mondays, Tuesdays, and Wednesdays to Concordia on the train. But he couldn't hold over the cream that had been brought to town on Thursday, Friday and Saturday until Monday to ship it by train - it would become too sour in the summer heat and boil over. He had built a vat in the back of the creamery - like a six by eight foot bath tub - to set the ten-gallon cans in as they accumulated. It had a pipe running into it from the well and out of it to the garden behind the creamery. Dale and Anna kept that vat full of cold water from the well by pumping a half-hour or so morning and evening every day all summer long.

Even so, the farmers who brought the cream to town may have saved it a few days where it was not so cool so it was necessary to take it by truck to the Concordia Creamery Company on Sunday.

They were the buyers whom Mama worked for under contract. She had bought the cream from the farmers and paid them for first grade cream but if the cream was too sour they would dock her wages and pay her for Second grade cream. That would cut her commission so that she would have a very small check from the company for a whole month's work. So the Sundays all summer long had to be spent in the same way - a trip to Concordia with a load of cream was the center-piece of whatever else was done on Sundays. They took along picnic lunches and they always had an ice cream bar at the Creamery. Once they went through the plant and watched them make butter and dried buttermilk which they sold to the feed stores for food for baby chicks.

But this Sunday they were going to come back by way of Grandpa and Grandma Jordan's farm. It was ten miles east of Delphos so it wasn't really out of the way. It just had to be a nice day with dry roads. The farmstead sat right beside Pipe Creek and the roads would be so muddy that one couldn't drive over them. It was such black, sticky mud, not at all like the sandy soil around Wells, and the big truck tires would ball up until the wheels wouldn't turn.

Anna looked at the sky. It was a beautiful day for visiting Grandma and Grandpa Jordan. They hadn't had much rain lately and they hadn't been up to Grandma and Grandpa Jordan's lately, either.

"Grandma is sick," Mama explained. "Uncle Ney called this morning to tell us the doctor said she has had a stroke. She is in bed and wants to see us."

"Uncle Ney and Aunt Ethel will be there, won't they?" asked Anna.

"Oh, yes, honey, they live there now since Pa is not able to do the farming or milking," Mama looked worried. "And, now that Mother can't move, all the housework will fall to Ethel and she's certainly not much force where that's concerned."

"Well, maybe it is not as bad as it sounds," Papa urged Mama not to worry, "At any rate, we'll get to see them today."

They unloaded the cream on the dock in Concordia and bought an ice cream bar from the big cooler just off of the office as Papa was getting the forty cans of cream weighed, counted and receipted for. Then they were on their way back to Grandma's farm.

Mama had two brothers and three sisters. Uncle Frank, the oldest had gone to work for his grandfather when he was ten years old. Aunt Lula would have been nine, Uncle Ney, seven, Mama, five, Aunt Belva, three and Aunt Elsie, the youngest, hadn't yet been born.

"Mama, why would Grandpa let his oldest boy go to live with his grandparents? Wouldn't he have been lonely?" asked Dale as they were riding along. They could all ride in the cab if Anna sat on Mama's lap.

"That was a very bad time for Pa and Mother." Mama always said "Pa" with an 'AH' rather than an 'AW' sound as was the old English way of speaking. "Mother was very sick and all of us children went to stay with Pa's sisters or brothers. Pa was a carpenter and helped to build the State Capitol Building in Topeka while Mother was in the hospital there. Belva and I stayed with Aunt Annie, Pa's old maid sister. She had homesteaded one hundred and sixty acres herself when her brothers did, lived on it and proved up on it too," Mama spoke of her aunt with a great deal of pride.

"Was I named for your Aunt Annie?" asked Anna.

"No, dear you were named for Mother. You know, her name is Anna. She didn't want me to name you after her. She said, 'They'll just call that poor baby "Annie" just like they do me.' But, so far, they haven't, have they?" Mama said as she squeezed her little girl.

"Who is 'they,' Annie?" Dale piped up. "She could be Little Orphan Annie but I call her Calamity Jane."

Anna ignored him, "So when Grandma got well and you all got back together again , Uncle Frank just stayed with his grandparents? Why did he do that? Didn't Grandma want him to come home, too?"

"Yes, she did," Mama explained, "but Pa had two sons and only one farm and his folks wanted your Uncle Frank to stay with them. All their sons, four of them, each had a farm of his own that he had homesteaded when they came to Kansas just after the Civil War and so his father promised Pa that they would deed their homestead to your Uncle Frank if he would live with them and help them in their old age. Mother didn't like it but that was the English way of doing things."

"So, now Uncle Ney lives with them and he and Aunt Ethel can take care of them. Do you think Grandpa will deed the farm to Uncle Ney?" Dale asked, "I'm ten years old and I could use a farm."

"Oh, no, not so fast, little man, you're my little boy and I need you, too," said Papa. "Anyway, we're almost there. Now children, your grandma is sick so play outdoors or help your Aunt Ethel in the kitchen after you have spoken to her."

* * * * * * * *

Mama was very quiet on the way home after her visit with her mother. Anna knew Mama kept turning over in her mind her mother's weak voice. She had overheard her grandmother, so she knew what Mama was thinking. Anna understood why Grandma felt she must talk to Mama, "I wanted you to come to see me so I could explain what we have done before I got so weak I couldn't talk," her Grandma said. "It might not have been my wish that we deed our farm to Ney and Ethel but Pa would have it no other way," Her voice trailed away.

Mama patted her hand to assure her and Grandma began again, "Pa is really not able to farm anymore and Ney has been trying to catch up on things since he has come home to recover from that bad accident at that elevator."

"How does Ethel feel about earning a farm caring for you and Pa?" Mama had asked Grandma.

"Oh, she doesn't complain, she can't lift me to change the sheets or help me change my gown, and Pa can't either, but you know Ney has always been a good nurse. Ethel cooks meals and feeds me. I'm such a care," Grandma began to cry.

"Has Belva been down to see you?" Mama asked. Aunt Belva had married a State Senator's son after teaching for thirteen years, and, although she was two years younger than Mama, she was much more opinionated about what should be done in the family.

"Yes, she came right down; Ney called her to ask what doctor she would recommend. She wanted to take me to Concordia to a hospital but the doctor didn't think that was necessary. He said I may gradually get better right here," Grandma sighed. "And we don't have money for that - Pa hasn't been able to pay the taxes on this place yet this year."

Mama knew how proud Pa was. He thought maybe if Ney owned the farm he could get a good crop of corn and pay the taxes. Frank was living on Belva's river-bottom farm east of Concordia. He had the homestead leased out and was really doing well farming for Dave

Coughlin, too. Belva and Dave had moved to southern California in 1923 and Aunt Belva had driven back to Concordia for a visit.

"Did you tell Belva that Pa had deeded the farm to Ney?" Mama asked.

"Pa told her - that's why I wanted you to come and see me. She told him he should have talked to all of you children first, you know how Belva is," Grandma had started to cry. "Stella, if you say anything to Pa or Ney, tell them that you think deeding the place to Ney was the best thing we could do. You will, won't you?"

Stella had agreed, but she knew that Belva would be down to Wells. She was so strong and capable. She had driven that car across the desert, she and her nine-year old son, Kerry, all the way from California in July. Now she was up to Concordia visiting Frank and Erma. She was probably telling Frank how to run that big 640 acre farm. Stella wondered how Erma was putting up with living in the new house that Belva and Dave built on it just five years ago. She was probably having to keep her mouth shut and just listen. Frank's farm that he had earned by living with his grandparents was rocky and small by comparison. And it didn't sit on the Republican River. Belva and Dave must be doing awfully well out in California in the real estate business to leave their beautiful farm to a brother-in-law to live on and just come back to over-see things.

Charlie broke into her thoughts, "Ney was really glad we came. He seems to be getting the farming under control. Of course, he needs rain on that corn crop if it is to make much corn. And I suppose, if he keeps farming he'll need a tractor. He's not as crazy about that big team of Percherons as your Pa."

"That big team of Percherons won't be very crazy about a tractor either," said Mama, "I'll never forget the first time they saw a car."

"Tell us about it," begged Dale and Anna both at the same time. They really admired that big matched team of horses, they were so beautiful, their hide was the color of molasses candy and they had cream-colored stockings on all four legs, long blond manes and tails and their skin just rippled as they walked.

"Belva and I were hauling a load of corn to Delphos and we had gone a mile or two when the team began to snort and prance and toss their heads. Then we heard it before we saw it. They had smelled the gasoline. That car was a quarter of a mile away but that team wouldn't go another step toward it. The car pulled over as far as they dared without overturning in the ditch and stopped. The team just stood right up on their hind feet and snorted. They kept backing up with that wagon loaded with corn and we were afraid it would overturn on the other side of the road. Two men got out of the car and walked down the road to meet us. They took the horses by the bridles and pulled them down to

70

earth, patted their noses and talked to them and finally led them by that big car," Mama paused.

"What kind of a car was it?" Dale asked.

"It was a big Packard touring car. They said they had been two days coming from Kansas City to Concordia and had frightened teams and caused runaways all the way. They wanted to find a dealer to sell cars in Concordia," Mama sighed, shifting Anna's weight to the other knee. "That was about 1907. I think there's been a Packard dealership there ever since."

****

"Blessed are the peace-makers: for they shall be called the children of God."
The Beatitudes - Matthew 5:9

Anna had followed the path across Fred Payne's yard and came up around the long machine shed where Papa kept the chicken batteries. Sitting there beside the cream station was that big brown Franklin Air-Cool car with a California tag on it. Aunt Belva had come!

She should have put on a clean dress and those knee-socks and slippers before she came down town, It was too late now. She decided to come in the back door of the creamery. She opened the screen door and slipped inside. No one noticed Anna and she stopped to listen. Mama was saying in her very firm voice, usually reserved for preaching to Dale and Anna, "Belva, you know how our Ma and Pa are - they are devout Quakers and English - they oppose law-suits and believe all questions should be discussed and settled in meeting."

"But they didn't discuss deeding the farm to Ney with the rest of their children, now, did they?" Aunt Belva spoke up and Uncle Frank said, "That's right, Stella."

"Pa didn't feel there was any need to," Mama said. "Frank, you already have a farm Grandpa Jordan deeded to you and as far as we four girls are concerned, we are all married and have husbands to look after our needs. That left only Ney and he was there helping to care for Mother when she had her stroke. It seemed to Pa the only fair solution."

"Stella, that may be the way it's done in England but this is America and women have rights here. And we can take this to court and break that deed. That farm should be sold and the proceeds used to care for Pa and Ma. They have a right to be cared for with dignity." Aunt Belva spoke as though she were explaining things to children.

"Belva, I went up to see our mother and she asked me to protect Pa's right to deed the farm to Ney. I know that Mother will be a great care to Ethel and Ney but they have shouldered the burden and I feel we have no choice but to let them carry it. That's what Pa wants and so

71

Mother wants us to abide by his wishes." Mama seemed to want to close the discussion .

Anna came on into the creamery. Aunt Belva seemed to be pleased to see her. "My goodness Anna, how you've grown. We didn't bring Kerry with us this morning. He had gone into Concordia with his cousin, Nile, and we were coming this morning on business, anyway."

"Are you coming down again before you go back to California," asked Mama as Anna settled herself on Uncle Frank's knee.

"Oh, yes, Stella, I really didn't come back to disrupt the whole family. I had only just arrived last week when Ney called about Mother. If you won't cooperate with us, we can do nothing except go along with what Pa wants. We are going back by way of the farm to see how Mother is this morning," said Belva. "Kerry and I will be down to spend a few days with you the first of the week.

Mama seemed relieved when they left. Anna began to make plans about how they were going to entertain Kerry and Aunt Belva next week.

"I wish we had a little more room in our house when we have company," Mama said, more to herself than to Anna. "It's a good thing it's summertime, Dale and Kerry can sleep out in the box on the back of the car and Belva can have Dale's couch in the living room. It folds out on both sides..."

"There's room for me too, and I like to look up at the stars, Mama," Anna's eyes twinkled with excitement as she explained. "Papa showed us how to find the North Star and the Big Dipper. Dale and I haven't got to sleep outdoors for a long time...Please, Mama, can I?"

Cousin Kerry was younger than Dale and about six months older than Anna but he seemed to be a mere baby to both of them. Anna remembered when they went up to Aunt Belva's for Christmas when she was six and Dale was seven. Kerry wouldn't be seven till next June but he was a plump little boy and taller than either Dale or Anna.

"I'm building a shelter for the bunny rabbits so the hunters won't find them," Kerry had said as he sat on the floor, stacking a set of new blocks Santa Claus had brought him for Christmas.

Dale had said, "Who wants to build a shelter for the bunny rabbits? Papa shoots them and dresses them out and we eat them in a rabbit pie."

Kerry began to cry and went to tell Aunt Belva how awful Dale was, "Dale's father kills bunny rabbits and eats them!" wailed Kerry.

Papa and Mama sat in silence and so did Uncle Dave and Aunt Belva. At last Aunt Belva said, "Play with your train, dear."

Kerry had a magnificent train that he said Santa had brought him for Christmas. It had a train track that ran through tunnels in the baseboard from the parlor through Uncle Dave's den into Aunt Belva's sewing room back into the dining room and back to the parlor where the depot was. Kerry did need a lot of help to just watch that train run.

"I hope Kerry isn't quite such a baby now that he's nine years old, Mama, he might even be afraid to sleep outdoors," Anna worried.

"Well, Belva is by herself without your Uncle Dave to help spoil him and I can tell her that you children will be perfectly safe out under the stars and up off of the ground in the box on the back of the car," Mama said with some satisfaction.

"And I'll tell Kerry that if the coyotes howl and start to eat us, Dale will shoot them with Papa's twenty-two," laughed Anna.

"Now don't try to scare him, dear. You can talk to him about the stars. Belva shouldn't mind that."

The visit with Cousin Kerry and Aunt Belva was uneventful. Anna thought Kerry was a sweet nine year-old and Dale was a bit disgusted that he preferred playing with girls to playing ball with the boys.

"He's a real sissy," Dale said later, "And he's still talking about shelters for animals."

"Now, Dale, he was telling about how all the children in their school were selling postcards pictures of the animals that they are getting for the San Diego Zoo. It's going to be the biggest zoo in the world when they get all the animals from all over the world for it. and the children in the schools in San Diego intend to sell enough post cards to buy an elephant for the zoo," Anna defended Kerry.

"Yeah but he said the mean old hunters down in Africa were killing elephants just for their tusks and someday he intends to go down there and put a stop to that," Dale snickered as he told about Kerry's bragging. "He's moved up from protecting bunny rabbits to elephants in just two years."

"Dale, I've been reading about the slaughter of elephants in Africa just for the ivory in their tusks and I think Kerry is right about that. You remember that we killed the rabbits to eat. We didn't let them lay there on the ground to rot," Papa said.

"Yeah, but how's he going to put a stop to that? Is he going to shoot the mean old hunters?" Dale argued.

Papa laughed, "I guess we'll just have to wait and see."

****

Over the river and through the wood,
To Grandfather's house we go;
The horse knows the way to carry the sleigh
Through the white and drifted snow.
                    --Lydia Marie Child

"Are we going to stop back by Grandpa's again?" Anna asked. "We've been there nearly every Sunday since I can remember."

"Honey, your grandmother doesn't get any better. She just has to lie there and it must be awfully lonesome for her," Mama said. "I wish there was something I could do to help but I can't stay for a week. Sunday is the only day we're not buying cream, eggs and chickens. Don't you like to go see your Grandma?"

"Oh, sure," said Anna, "Uncle Ney plays games with Dale and me or he and Papa take turns trying to beat Grandpa at checkers. It was more fun last summer when we could play outdoors."

"Well, you can help Aunt Ethel get dinner. Maybe she gets tired of company every Sunday, too. Mother has been right there in that bed since last July and that's a long time for everybody," Mama explained patiently. Anna remembered Mama cooking and washing and caring for everybody when Grandma Allison was sick. "You help your Aunt Ethel now that it's too cold to play outdoors, will you, honey?"

"I'll carry in wood and help Uncle Ney with the chores if he's got any left to do," Dale said, "while Papa plays checkers with Grandpa."

They delivered their load of cream to the Concordia Creamery and got back to Grandpa's farm on Pipe Creek before noon. Grandpa, Grandma, Uncle Ney and Aunt Ethel all seemed so glad to see them.

"What did you do last night?" Uncle Ney asked at the dinner table.

"Oh, that's a big night in Wells, now that the dances have started again," Mama said.

"You managed to get some music, did you, Charlie?" Uncle Ney's eyes brightened. He loved dances - knew all the calls for square dances and would have been in Wells every Saturday night himself if Grandma weren't so sick.

"Sure did, and George McCain is helping me manage. He comes to town early with his cream and goes down to the Woodman Hall and builds a fire. It seems like everybody brings his cream to town on Saturday night and I have to stay and help Stella," Papa said.

"And what do you kids do?" Aunt Ethel asked.

"Myrtle Yonally, Norline Heald, their little sisters and a whole bunch of us girls go up behind the stage and dance to the music," Anna explained, "We have to be quiet, though."

"Are you learning to dance, Dale?" asked Aunt Ethel.

"No, we play Wolf and Dog," Dale explained with some finality, like that was the only thing for boys to do when all the country boys came to town.

"How do you play Wolf and Dog?" asked Uncle Ney.

"Oh they just run all over town in the dark barkin' and yippin'," Anna piped up.

"I keep telling Dale that he should come in the Hall and behave himself," Mama explained, "But there must be at least 20 boys, all between 10 and 15 or so, who run wild every Saturday night."

74

"Aw, there's more to it than that," Dale finally defended himself. "We decide who's goin' to be wolves an' who's goin' to be dogs and the dogs chase the wolves and when the last wolf is caught the game is over."

"How can you tell which is which out there in the dark?" Aunt Ethel asked.

"The dogs bark and the wolves yip," Dale said. "And, once you catch a wolf he has to start barking like a dog. The only thing is some of the wolves cheat - they keep yipping after they've already been caught. And that way we never get down to the last wolf."

"Dale, you're never going to learn to dance or learn square dance calls if you're out playing in the dark every Saturday night," Uncle Ney said. Uncle Ney could call for square dancing all evening long and never call the same call twice.

"Ney, they aren't dancing squares much anymore," Mama said. "It's all fox-trot, waltzes, two-step and now the Charleston."

"How do you dance the Charleston?" asked Aunt Ethel.

"Like this." Anna jumped off her chair and showed them with the snap of her fingers and the twist of her heels while she sang, "Yes, sir, That's my baby! No, sir, I don't mean maybe. Yes, sir ! That's my baby - now".

"My, goodness, Dale. See what you're missing - running around out in the dark," said Aunt Ethel. Grandma managed a smile. Uncle Ney had carried her out to the table and propped her up with pillows so she could eat Sunday Dinner with the family.

"Yeah, that's all girls have to do is learn that stuff," Dale wasn't envious.

"Well, I think before another fall, you're going to have some new long pants and dress up and stay inside the hall," Mama said. "Have you seen the new long pants for little boys in the catalog? They surely do look funny after seeing little boys in knickers all my life."

"Well, I suppose we'll get used to them," said Uncle Ney. "I had to learn to keep those knickers buttoned and Ma had to keep reminding me and sewing on a new button because somehow they'd get torn off and I'd be going around with the buttonhole tag flapping below my knees."

"Like Dale's are right now?" teased Anna.

"Well, there aren't any buttons on these either," Dale said. Anna thought to herself that she should have sewed some buttons on when she took Dale's knickers off the line after the last wash. Mama had so much to do and Anna thought, 'I could sew on buttons.'

Uncle Ney changed the subject, "Anna, how would you like to come up and stay with us for a week when your Christmas vacation starts?"

"Oh, that would be fun," agreed Anna, thinking of Christmas as a long way off.

"Stella, when does the kid's vacation start? Maybe you and Charlie could bring Anna up for a week. Does she have two weeks off from school?" Uncle Ney was busy planning for her visit.

"I need Dale, or he could come, too," Papa said. "I have three farmers that I've promised we'd come out with the chicken coups and cull their flocks and buy the culls. Dale climbs right up on the roosts after they go to roost and hands them down one at a time. I've been waiting till Dale's vacation starts - the kids don't stay up at night too much on school nights."

"It's all that practice Dale gets playing Wolf and Dog, I'll bet," Uncle Ney teased, "He can see in the dark and he's learned to steal in like a coyote."

"He's getting so he can tell a laying hen from one they just as well sell or eat and save the chicken feed."

Papa always bragged on Dale and Dale just lowered his white eyelashes over his big blue eyes and looked shy. Anna wished she could help catch chickens sometimes - but it was a dusty, smelly job - worse than helping Mama wash cream cans. Anna couldn't wash the ten-gallon cans - her arms were too short and she always got sour cream on her elbows washing the tall three-gallon cans.

"When is Christmas vacation?" she asked. "We're already practicing for our Christmas program. We're going to have it down at the Woodman Hall because we need a stage so we went down there to practice Friday."

"Your program is next Friday night, Anna, so we can bring you up next Sunday for a week and Christmas isn't till in the week after. Maybe you can help your Aunt Ethel get the Christmas Dinner and we'll come to get you Christmas Day." Mama didn't seem to need her at home for anything.

"You can sit by my bed and keep me company, Anna. The days get so long when you're just lying there," Grandma said, and Anna thought, 'Well, at least Grandma needs me for something.'

* * * * * * * * *

"Anna's going to tell us about the Christmas program this evening," said Uncle Ney as Mama and Papa and Dale were getting ready to go back to Wells that next Sunday afternoon.

"Yes, and I can speak my piece for you," Anna said cheerfully.

"Get Ney to speak 'The Night Before Christmas,' for you, Anna, he knows it all from beginning to end," Mama always spoke proudly of her big brother's ability to recite everything in the old <u>McGuffy Readers</u> from beginning to end. Anna looked forward to listening to Uncle Ney - he was so funny.

Grandpa Jordan sat in the parlor reading the <u>Capper's Weekly</u>; Grandma was back in her bed in the front bedroom; Uncle Ney had gone out to do chores and Aunt Ethel was embroidering a dresser scarf when Anna came in from the outhouse, 'toilet', Mama always called it though many people called it a 'backhouse' - by whatever name, its purpose was all the same.

"Do you know how to embroider, Anna?" asked Aunt Ethel.

"No, but I can sew on the sewing machine if you have any torn sheets you want me to sew." Anna walked over to the treadle machine by the front door. It was covered with another of those dresser scarves and was piled with Grandpa's papers and magazines.

"Well, maybe after we get the washing done tomorrow - there are plenty of sheets and pillow cases to patch but not on Sunday," Aunt Ethel was threading a needle with embroidery floss. She had a scrap of white muslin in her hand and an embroidery hoop. "It's easy to make daisy petals and outline stitches and cross stitch or feather stitching for borders. Sit here by me and I'll show you."

Anna was busy making daisies all around the edges of the scrap of muslin when Uncle Ney came in from the barn with a pail of milk. They had a separator and Aunt Ethel went out to the clothes line to get the old dishcloth that was used as a strainer. Uncle Ney put the separator together. "We don't have a separator," said Anna. "Mama says it's just something more to wash and keep up and she gets enough washing of milk and cream things down at the cream station."

"Your papa just has one cow for milk for the table and for clabber for the chickens but you have to put the milk somewhere, don't you?" Uncle Ney said as he poured the bucket of milk through the strainer rag into the big separator bowl.

"Oh, we have three big crocks out in the pumphouse on a bench that's low enough for me to reach, and I can skim the cream off of the milk the next morning with the skimmer. We have two syrup pails for the sweet cream and the sour cream on the second and third bowl. Then I empty the clabber into the slop pail and Dale stirs mash into it for the chickens. Then I wash the bowl that had the clabber in it and it's ready for Papa to bring in the pail of fresh milk from the barn and strain it into the empty bowl," Anna explained as she wondered to herself who was doing that tonight at home. 'I'll bet they are missing me after all' she thought with some satisfaction.

Uncle Ney was grinding away on the separator and a thin stream of cream was coming out of one spout into a small pail and a big stream of skim milk was coming out of the other spout into an empty pail. "Do you want to go with me out to slop the hogs?" he asked as he finished the separating. He poured some of the milk into the potato peelings and table scraps from their big Sunday dinner. He stopped on the back porch and scooped some bran into the slop, got a bucket of corn from another sack and they were on their way out to the pig pen.

"We had some cute little pigs just a few weeks ago but they are getting big - growing like weeds just the way we want them to," Uncle Ney spoke with pride as the young pigs came racing up to the trough by the fence to be fed.

"Papa is going to get Dale and me each a pig to feed next spring so we can buy our school clothes and books in the fall," Anna said as she watched the squealing pigs crowd each other away from the trough.

"Well, I'll keep that in mind and if I have a couple that are getting crowded away from the trough when they are little maybe I'll just give them to you and Dale."

Anna skipped all the way out to the henhouse with her basket in hand. She could gather the eggs. She had already done this a lot of times at Grandpa's farm. 'Now that the farm is Uncle Ney's, Grandpa seems perfectly content to just sit and read or play checkers if anyone has time to play with him,' she thought. 'Aw, well, that's the way it should be,' Mama would say.

Grandma seemed to be dozing when Anna looked in the bedroom after the evening chores were done.

"Do you want to play me a game of dominos?" asked Uncle Ney.

Dale was always much faster than she was at adding so he always beat her and she hadn't developed any great liking for that game. "Why don't you play checkers with Grandpa and I'll watch?" Anna said.

"No, you're company and I want you to play with me," said Uncle Ney. Aunt Ethel was back at her embroidering, sitting almost under the big Alladin lamp so she could see. Grandpa sat there smiling - waiting for her to pull up a chair and play dominos. There was nothing to do but show them how slow she was at dominos.

The game went better than Anna expected and after all she should be able to add combinations up to six - she told herself - she'd be in the fifth grade next year - she was already nine years old. It was just that Dale was so much faster than she was at Arithmetic. Uncle Ney didn't seem to be in any hurry. She beat him one game.

Uncle Ney and Grandpa had to go help Grandma up on the chamber pot and get ready for bed. Aunt Ethel made Anna a bed on the couch in the parlor. When she fell asleep the lamp was still on.

The days crept by. Uncle Ney was shucking corn. Aunt Ethel was washing and cleaning and cooking. Grandpa was reading or dozing in his chair. Anna sat by her grandmother's bed and listened to her talk.

"What do you do to help your mother when you are at home?" Grandma asked.

"On Monday mornings we wash," Anna said. "I bring in the kindling and wood and keep the woodbox full so we can have hot water in the boiler. I can carry in half-pails of water from the pump-house. Papa fills the boiler and the tub with rinse water and the reservoir is full when he leaves on the truck. Mama hangs all the big things on the line before she goes down to the creamery and when Dale and I come home from school at noon we hang the socks in the squares on the garden fence and the underpants and Dale's knickers and shirts."

"Don't they blow off?" Grandma asked.

"Oh, we use clothespins if Mama leaves us any and we take them off the fence when we get home from school. We roll the socks in pairs and if one is missing we go out and hunt for it where it's blown off the fence."

"I'm sure you children do all you can to help your mother, Anna," said Grandma in a weak voice, "But I want to tell you that Stella was never as strong as my other children and after she had scarlet fever when she was twelve years old she would tire so easily. Walking a mile and a half morning and night after that was almost more than she could do. She would come home from school so tired she couldn't eat. She could run like the wind before she was sick so long and ran such high fevers and after that she just never did regain her strength."

"Mama has never told us about that," Anna said.

"No, I'm sure she wouldn't and she probably hasn't told Charlie, either or he would never have thought she could run that cream station and take care of a house and family all at the same time. I don't know what he's thinking of, anyway," Grandma's voice trailed off as she started to cry.

"Mama says other women work in the fields, drive teams and do all sorts of outdoor work on the farms and no one thinks anything about it but, since she's right on the main street of Wells every day, people notice." Anna tried to take Papa's part, "And Papa helps her in the creamery whenever he's not busy with the truck - and Dale and I help her when we can. I try to wash my face and comb my hair and find a clean dress before I come down town. She says we look neglected if we come in the creamery with dirty feet and hands."

"Well, I just wish she didn't have to go down there every day - she just has to neglect something, that's for sure." Grandma seemed sleepy so Anna slipped out to see what Aunt Ethel was doing.

Aunt Ethel was hanging sheets on the line. Anna went out and found the corners of the ones left in the basket so her aunt could pick them up easier. Aunt Ethel said, "Ney will have to change his mother's bed again when he gets in from the field. Her bowels and kidneys are getting weaker by the day."

"Isn't she going to get any better?" Anna asked, istfully. She missed the grandma who made cookies and pies and knit socks and mittens. She was always working in the nice warm kitchen and when she and Dale would come in from playing in the snow, she would let them put their feet in the oven and their wet shoes on the oven door. Anna shivered.

"Honey, it's too cold for you to be out here without a coat," Aunt Ethel cleared her throat and spit. "My catarrh is always worse this time of year."

"Dale and I never catch cold," Anna bragged. "You know, neither one of us has ever been absent or tardy from school since we started in the first grade."

"Well, it's a good thing. Stella wouldn't have time to take care of you if you had to stay home," Aunt Ethel pinned the last sheet on the line. "Come on. let's hurry in out of the cold."

The kitchen was cold and smelled of wash day without the beans. Mama always put on a pot of beans to cook while she had a fire going to heat the boiler anyway. Aunt Ethel poked at the fire.

"You know, your mother never caught cold much either, Anna. She always seemed so frail but I remember when Minie Winsett was so awful sick with the flu and Claude had it and several of the kids had it all at the same time and your mother took you kids and went out there and took care of Minie - the doctor thought maybe she wouldn't pull through - she was awful sick. That was that bad flu when the soldiers at Fort Riley were all dyin' with it. I don't suppose you remember - no, no - you wouldn't - you were only three." Aunt Ethel talked as she peeled and sliced potatoes. The skillet was heating on the stove and Uncle Ney would be in soon for dinner.

Anna didn't remember the Winsetts all having the flu when she was three but she did remember how much fun she and Dale had when they went out to that farm just east of Wells to play with the Winsett kids. There was Dorothy and Vernie, and Babe and Josie, and Irene and Bob and Verl and they played hide and seek all over the place. "They moved away and we sure do miss them," Anna said.

"They live up here not too awfully far from us now. We sometimes see them when we go into Delphos," Aunt Ethel as she some pork strips in the skillet.

Uncle Ney came in from the field. "Who do we sometimes see when we go into Delphos?" he asked.

"The Winsetts - you know they used to live down by Wells," Aunt Ethel said, turning the fried pork. "Ney, as soon as you warm up a little you'll have to go in and change the sheets on your mother's bed."

"Couldn't that wait till after we've eaten?" Uncle Ney asked quietly, more to himself than to Aunt Ethel. He sat down tiredly at the table.

Anna hurried to set the table - a place for Grandpa, Grandma, Aunt Ethel, Uncle Ney and one for me, she thought. "Will you bring Grandma out to the table?" she asked.

"No, but leave her plate there," Uncle Ney said, "You can help me feed her after she has a bath and clean sheets."

"No wonder Uncle Ney wanted me to come up and visit," Anna thought. "This is an awful sad place - and I'm beginning to feel like I'm not so happy either."

"I'm not very hungry," she said. Anna never did like fat pork - not even at home - but the frying potatoes smelled good, kinda.

"Oh, you have to eat a little," Aunt Ethel said, "Food keeps you warm in the winter. Could you cut the bread and put the jelly on - it's there in the cupboard. We'll have to bake some fresh bread for supper - I think there's just a piece of a loaf left."

The potatoes stuck in her throat and the little strips of lean in the fat pork didn't slide much either. Anna wondered what Dale was doing right now??? - probably eating those beans with catsup on them, or maybe Mama opened a can of tomatoes to go with the beans. She wondered if they missed her. Anna almost cried, thinking how sad it was that she wasn't there to help Dale eat those beans and tomatoes.

"Honey, you're not eating anything," Aunt Ethel said. "You'll get sick if you don't eat."

Maybe I'm already sick, Anna thought. As Anna was picking up the dishes and scraping the scraps into the slop pail for the hogs, Uncle Ney came back into the kitchen. Aunt Ethel had made Cream of Wheat for Grandma.

"Anna, do you want to feed your grandmother her Cream of Wheat?" he asked.

"Oh, sure, - does she like it?" Anna thought it looked awfully tasteless as she watched Uncle Ney dishing it up. Maybe the sweet cream and the spoonful of sugar would make it taste better. Grandma couldn't move her hands and arms to feed herself and it seemed hard for her to swallow even the Cream of Wheat. Poor sick Grandma. Anna felt like crying. She took the half-finished bowl back to the kitchen, scraped it into the pail and put it in Aunt Ethel's dish water.

Uncle Ney was pumping a tub of water for the soiled sheets and night clothes from Grandma's bed. They had a cistern and a pitcher pump right in the end of that long kitchen. He stoked the fire and put on the boiler again. They'd be washing again on the back porch this afternoon. Anna picked up the dishtowel to wipe the dishes. At home she'd be arguing with Dale - it was his job to dry the dishes. Suddenly she felt like she was going to cry. She put down the dishtowel and disappeared out the back door without a word. The outhouse was the most private place there was when you felt like crying.

It was cold out there. Anna's nose was running and she had nothing to wipe it with but her dress tail. She didn't want Uncle Ney to know she was crying. If he asked her why she couldn't tell him. She didn't

know why she was crying. Maybe she was sick. But she couldn't be
sick - she never got sick. She just felt so sad. She shivered. The tears
were dry on her face and her nose had stopped running. She'd have to
go back in the kitchen - she couldn't stay out here forever.

Anna started back to the kitchen - no, she decided to slip in the front
door and into the front bedroom. She'd sit by Grandma's bed - if she
still looked like she had been crying she could say she was feeling sorry
for Grandma. She really was.

"Anna, could you look in that trunk?" asked Grandma. "There's a
book called The Life of Christ in the tray right on top. It's red leather
bound. Could you bring it and turn the pages so I can see the etchings?"

Anna found the book - it was a lovely book but some of the pages
looked as though they had been water soaked - they stuck together.

"Grandma, some of these pages are sticking together; what happened
to this book?" asked Anna, picking her way through the pages. It was
nice big print - she thought she could read it herself if the pages would
turn without tearing.

"It was in a trunk that went through a cyclone," said Grandma. The
cyclones in Kansas were killer tornadoes. Anna's eyes opened wide.

"A cyclone! Where were you, Grandma?"

"It was our first year here. Your Uncle Frank, our first baby was
just 5 months old. Your grandpa was digging a well a few feet from the
back door. It was three feet across and about 5 feet deep by that time.
He brought up a bucket of dirt and noticed the clouds and the storm
coming across the prairie this side of Delphos already. He opened the
door of our new little two-room house and told me to grab up the baby
and come. He helped us down in the well and turned to shut the door
when the twister hit. It scooped that little house up like it was kindling.
He crawled down in the well with us and we huddled there while it
roared over our heads." Grandma gathered energy as she spoke.

"And where was this book?" Anna asked in wonderment.

"Our new little house was nowhere to be found but the trunk was
lodged in a fence corner down by Lamar. It had burst open and
everything inside was water soaked. The neighbors put us up till Pa
could build another house and we just started over..." Grandma seemed
to be sleeping as she finished talking.

Suddenly she opened her eyes. "You know, Anna, I didn't want
Stella to name you after me. They always called me 'Annie' but now
I'm glad - I want you to have that book. I wanted to send it away and
get it restored but I was always afraid I'd never get it back. Maybe,
some day you can get that done."

Anna's eyes filled with tears as she thought of her grandmother's
years right here on this farm where she raised six children and still
couldn't get her Life of Christ book fixed so she could turn the pages.

82

Grandma wanted to say more, "You know, Anna, my folks were all such strict Quakers and didn't believe in spending on furniture or clothing or making any noise about what they believed. Even music was frivolity. But Pa bought me that organ and I want my cousin, Allie Woodward, to play it and sing at my funeral. Ney knows what I want." She seemed to drift off to sleep and Anna went out to the kitchen to watch Aunt Ethel make the bread out into loaves.

"Now, young lady, I'm going to teach you how to make gravy," said Uncle Ney when he came in from the chores. "I'll bet you've never made gravy."

Anna shook her head. She had been afraid her uncle would ask her why she had run out to the toilet to cry when he left after dinner. Now he was trying to cheer her up, she knew. Her eyes filled with tears again but he seemed not to notice.

"You put two tablespoons of meat-fryings in the skillet and stir it around till it gets hot. We'll need two tablespoons of flour, one teaspoon of salt and 1/4th teaspoon of pepper and three cups of milk. Can you remember all that?" Uncle Ney was getting a pencil and the back of an old envelope, "Here, write it down."

Anna wrote it down while he scooped in the meat-fryings and the flour and stirred, "Where's the salt and the pepper? Ethel, is the milk in the icebox still sweet?"

Aunt Ethel hurried to get the big pitcher of milk she'd saved from the morning's milking.

"Here Anna, you stir, you'll have to stand up on this chair." Uncle Ney measured the milk into a cup and began to pour it in. It was warm up over the stove - Aunt Ethel had been baking bread all afternoon - it was cooling on the breadboard. He poured in another cup. "Stir faster."

Anna was beginning to feel better, "Pour in the other cup," she said, "It's getting too thick."

"Oh, I thought we were making pudding here," said Uncle Ney with a straight face. Anna laughed.

The table was set and Grandpa was waiting at his place. Uncle Ney poured the gravy into the gravy bowl and they were ready to eat - boiled potatoes, breaded tomatoes and roast pork. Anna ate a good meal.

"What day is this?" she asked as she and Aunt Ethel were doing the supper dishes. Uncle Ney was helping Grandma into her night clothes. He had fed her breaded tomatoes and a little potatoes and gravy and brought the dishes back to the kitchen.

"It's Friday. I don't suppose they'll have a Saturday night dance this close to Christmas, since it's next Tuesday," said Aunt Ethel.

"Oh, yes they will," Anna assured her. "I heard them announce it last Saturday night." All that ache and pain in her chest came back with a rush. She was so far away. She had to go out back again.

"You'd better carry the lantern, Honey," said Uncle Ney. "It's awfully dark out there."

"I'm not afraid of the dark," boasted Anna, forgetting for a moment her need to escape to cry. "Sometimes I shut my eyes and imagine I'm blind and see if I can do things without seeing them. Some people have to, you know; and the longer you leave your eyes shut the easier it is to do things without seeing them."

"When I have to go out back before I go to bed, I make Ney carry the lantern. Suppose there was a spider on the toilet seat and you sat down on him in the dark?" Aunt Ethel shivered all over as she spoke.

Anna laughed, "Or a skunk - Mama keeps telling Dale that sometime all those boys chasing around in the dark are going to run onto one of those - playing Wolf and Dog."

Grandpa spoke up, "Well, hurry back and I'll tell you about getting lost in the dark once."

"Oh, I can wait till Uncle Ney carries the lantern for Aunt Ethel and I'll go along." Anna wanted to hear Grandpa's story - he so seldom spoke.

Grandpa had been making his way back to the parlor and stopped to listen to Anna telling how she wasn't afraid of the dark, "Well, let me sit down first, this is a long story," said Grandpa, sitting heavily in his easy chair.

Anna settled herself on the settee as Grandpa began, "I was born in Nova Scotia. Pa and Ma lived in a settlement of English people who had migrated to that British colony just before the Revolutionary War - they had left some of their families in Pennsylvania. They didn't want to fight against their Mother country and lots of the colonists were ready to fight for their rights. Of course, Quakers always look for a peaceful solution so they were being persecuted and called Tories.

"At any rate Pa and Ma were born there, grew up and married and our family was all born there. I was born in 1850. There were a number of children in the settlement and we had plenty of places to play as long as we stayed right in the settlement. Nova Scotia is heavily timbered and the men in the settlement had to keep hacking away at the forest to keep it back. One afternoon we were all running between the log houses playing hide and seek - I was five years old - big enough to play outdoors but I was strictly forbidden to play in the edge of the forest."

"'Thee must heed thy father's word if thou wouldst play outside in the settlement,' my mother said. 'Only the bigger boys go near the trees and that is with their elders to help with the timber.' So we knew to stay away from the logging road that led into the timber, for Pa might be coming home with the other men and big boys, dragging logs back to the settlement."

"But the big friendly trees just a few feet from the log houses made a good place to hide as well as behind the big wood piles, and, as you modern children say, 'all the other boys were doing it.' By four in the afternoon the sun would disappear from the sky - the trees were so tall and dense. All the little boys were hiding around close, darting between the trees when I realized that I hadn't heard anyone call, 'All Outs in Free' for quite a while. I looked around and could see no one hiding behind any of the trees close at hand. And I didn't know which way was back to the home base. I kept running first one way and the other - trying to break free of the dense forest."

"I would have been glad to find the logging road - I could have followed it back even if Pa might have been coming home with the logging crew and I'd have had a sound threshing for disobeying. I knew then why we were admonished never to play in the edge of the forest. I just wished I could find the edge."

"By now Ma would be out bringing me in by the ear - it was too late to be outside - it was growing dark. I sat down by a log. Maybe if I was very quiet I could hear someone calling. Surely someone would miss me and come looking."

It was hard for Anna to imagine in the middle of the wide open spaces all around Wells that you could get lost in dense timber where it got so dark you couldn't see the sun when it was still high in the sky. Uncle Ney put a stick of wood in the Round Oak heater with its chrome foot fenders where you could put your feet up by the heat if you were careful not to touch the black jacket and scorch your shoes. Anna shivered and moved a little closer to Grandpa's chair.

"Didn't anyone ever find you?" she asked. "Could you hear anyone calling?"

"Not a sound, it was as if the forest had swallowed me up. I must have cried myself to sleep - I woke up to deep darkness and dense quiet. There was not a sound but I could see eyes in the dark - big ones, wide apart and smaller ones close at hand - all looking at me."

Anna remembered how she felt in that straw stack - like she was smothering - Grandpa went on...

"The biggest set of eyes moved closer and I felt a cold nose brush my cheek but nothing bit me or growled and I didn't move a muscle for a long, long time."

"How could you see eyes when it was so dark?" Anna asked.

"They say it's because eyes draw whatever light there is and reflect it back," Uncle Ney said. "The animals saw your eyes too, Pa."

"Oh, I'm sure they did, and heard me breathing and smelled the cold sweat breaking out on my forehead, too," agreed Grandpa.

"How did anyone ever find you, Grandpa?" Anna wanted to hear the rest of the story because Grandpa was here - now - so it must have had a happy ending.

"Well, it must have been morning because I got so I could see the outline of the trees and I started walking. I remembered my big brother saying that when you're lost you walk in a circle and can't walk out of the trees - you come right back where you started from. I must have walked in a circle around the settlement. Anyway, I stumbled onto the logging road and there stood one of the men from the settlement. He began to holler, cupping his hands at the sides of his mouth. There's not much echo in the timber but the closest one hearing takes up the hollering and soon we could hear several calls coming from the timber."

"He picked me up and carried me down the road toward the settlement. Soon there were twenty men at least following us. Pa broke through the timber and took me on his shoulder and we arrived at the edge of the clearing in high style."

"Did you get that sound threshing?" asked Uncle Ney.

"Pa was reluctant to punish me at once because I was pretty bedraggled and Ma was there to take me inside. I hadn't had anything to eat or drink since noon the day before and it was time for dinner. I think Ma thought I had already been punished and told Pa so. I'm sure I learned my lesson and so did all the boys in the settlement. There were several sermons of thanksgiving at the next Quaker meeting. It wasn't as quiet as some."

"Ney, I'm going to have to go out back, will you come with me to carry the lantern?" asked Aunt Ethel. "Anna, you'd better come along so you won't get lost in the dark."

Grandma had been resting peacefully all the while Grandpa was talking and when they got back from the outhouse Grandpa said she was ready for Uncle Ney to help her up onto the chamber pot and get her ready for bed.

'Uncle Ney certainly had his work cut out for him, having to care for Grandma, carry lanterns for Aunt Ethel, do the farm work and even teach me how to make gravy!' Anna thought. She wondered if Dale was missing her - maybe Mama needed her or was lonesome for her??? She heaved a sigh as she fell asleep.

Saturday morning, Anna stood at the kitchen window looking south toward Wells. Uncle Ney was fixing oatmeal for breakfast. Maybe she could eat some of that, but her eyes kept filling with tears and she couldn't swallow.

"How far is it to Wells?" she asked casually so Uncle Ney wouldn't know that she just ached all over and wanted to be home so bad she couldn't swallow.

"Twenty miles," Uncle Ney answered, "The same distance General Sheridan had to ride to turn back his soldiers and save the day for the Union forces!"

Uncle Ney could recite poetry and prose chapters and verses. Anna heard him recite 'Sheridan's Ride' many times. In fact she could recite it herself but this morning was no time to have to worry about the Union forces and 'the steed that saved the day by carrying Sheridan into the fight from Winchester, twenty miles away!' - and Uncle Ney knew it.

"But we don't have to depend on Sheridan's fast horse," he said. "We'll just call Josie Winsett. She's going with a fellow who takes her to the dance in Wells every Saturday night. Maybe she'll swing by here and take you home in time for the dance tonight."

Anna's world was full of sunshine at once. And that evening when Josie and her beau dropped her off at the cream station she thought her mother and brother's world brightened up the same way.

Dale asked, "Can I go out and play Wolf and Dog with the boys, Mama? Anna's here to wash the three-gallon cans."

And Mama's face lighted up, too. "Oh, I guess so, you're about done anyway, Dale. We were going to come up tomorrow on our way to Concordia with the cream -" Mama smiled as she spoke, "But I'm glad you're here tonight."

The winter dragged on for Grandma as she became steadily more helpless. Uncle Ney hired a trained nurse to care for her the last three months of her life. Lottie Kitchener was a stiffly-starched lady with a blue chambray shirt-waist dress and matching cap who was there to do nothing but take care of Grandma.

"It's costing Ney five dollars per day, but, as Belva says, 'He's getting the farm so Mother should be worth it,'" Mama explained.

Grandma died July 14, 1925. She had lain abed one year to the day from the stroke that had started her illness.

They had her funeral at the farmstead. She was laid out in her casket in the living room and people sat in the long kitchen, the bedrooms, the back porch, and many sat on the running-boards of the cars. All her Quaker relatives were there from Glasco, and, in spite of Quakers frowning on organs and music, her cousin Allie Woodward played the organ and sang, just as Grandma wished.

****

Papa was a little boy too:

"Snips and snails and puppy-dog tails--
That's what little boys are made from---"

"Did you know that poor little Inscho woman is in the family way again? And they're still hauling water from Pipe Creek. They just can't find good water," Mabel's tongue moved as fast as her needle.

"Oh, my, I wonder if they've tried water-witching? We had real good luck with that," Esther said.

Eight ladies sat around the long quilting frame in the kitchen. They had come, each with her horse and buggy to Elizabeth's house to help her finish her quilt. The children who were too small to work with their men folk were all playing somewhere. The little girls were busy with their ragdolls and the boys had gone down to the creek. It was such a nice afternoon in the late summer of 1886.

This was one of Papa's stories of his childhood and he was one of the little boys who had gone down to the creek.

"Now, Charlie, you can't go with Port this morning, you and Henry will have to stay here at the house. All the neighbor ladies will be coming over today to help me finish this quilt and they will all bring their children. You boys can go down to the creek ..." his mother was bustling about their little frame house. "I want to scrub this kitchen floor and bake three pies. Will you bring up about a peck of apples. Choose the ones that have spots on them. We always use them first, you know."

Yes, Charlie knew. His dad had made a trip to eastern Kansas with two other farmers and brought back eight barrels of apples in each wagon. Every family in the settlement had at least one barrel of apples. They had two to eat by spring. His father had just got home and already they were being told to eat the spoiled ones first. Papa always told Dale and Anna to pick out the very best apples when he brought home a bushel because he said they were always eating the bad apples first when he was a little boy. Papa went on with his story:

"The kitchen was scrubbed. the pies were baked and the ladies began arriving. In those days all ladies wore long skirts to their ankles and at least two petticoats. They wore high topped shoes..."

Anna interrupted, "Even in the summer? Did they wear stockings too?" she asked. Hardly anyone wore high topped shoes anymore.

"Boys wouldn't know. You couldn't peek under those skirts and ladies didn't show their ankles. Anyway there were about a half-dozen of us boys who went down to the creek to fish, well, really we weren't doing much fishing - we were all barefoot and were throwing water and mud. John had a bucket and we began catching frogs and putting them in his bucket."

"Do you suppose they are about ready to cut those pies?" Hank wondered. Hank was always hungry.

John had almost a bucket full of frogs and, of course we couldn't just dump them out so he carried them along back up to the house.

"How old was Uncle Hank?" Dale asked. They had just heard that Uncle Hank was coming back from Montana and bringing his family with him - they were going to try to find something to do and live in

Wells. Dale and Anna didn't know too much about Papa's brother, Hank, because he had taken his family and moved to Montana and didn't even get back when Grandma Allison died.

"Oh, he was about six because I was eight years old - the oldest one of that bunch of little boys, as Mother pointed out later but how was I to know what was about to happen and I couldn't have stopped it if I had known...," Papa was a good story teller.

"Well, what did happen?" Mama asked. Papa had so many stories so maybe Mama hadn't heard that one before.

"Well, I was busy thinking how muddy we all were and how Mother had scrubbed that wood floor with lye water so it would be white and clean that morning. I didn't know how we were all going to get cleaned up so we could get any of that pie. By that time we were at the back door - all standing on the back step. John opened the back door. My cousin John was spoiled, both Mother and Dad said so, and we were always told that when we went to anybody's house for dinner if we ever behaved like John we'd get a thrashing when we got home.

John's mother was sitting around the long quilt frame with all the other mothers but she was nearest the back door. "My goodness, you are all so muddy!" she said sweetly, "Did you catch any fish?"

And John said, "No, but we sure caught a good mess of frogs. Want to see?" And he just deliberately lifted that bucket by its bail and the bottom and tossed that whole mess of frogs and dirty water out across the floor under the quilt frame. And all Hell broke loose! All those women were screaming and jumping up on the chairs and the frogs were jumping every which way under those skirts - some of them got caught between those petticoats - in all my life, so far, I've never seen such a mess."

"I'll bet you never did get any pie," Dale said.

"No, but it took those women so long to corral those frogs and clean up that mess and everybody's shoes and the bottoms of those long dresses were muddy and they were all so mad at their kids that nobody got any pie. Each put her own children in her own buggy and had to hurry home before it got dark," Papa paused as though that were the end of the story.

"And, did you get a thrashing, Papa?" asked Anna.

"No, but I got one of the most awful tongue-lashings Mother ever handed out. And we never got to go to the creek again when we had company. We were just told to play hide and seek out by the barn."

"Did she give Uncle Hank any pie? It wasn't his fault." Dale liked to hear about Uncle Hank. He and Anna could hardly wait for them to get back to Kansas from Montana.

"Oh, I guess we all got pie for supper - we had three pies to eat," Papa laughed. "Dad really thought that was one of the funniest things that John ever did. He was the worst one of my cousins when he was little."

****

"Oh, the Martins and the Coys
They were reckless mountain boys ..."

Old song.

"Your Uncle Bert was about four when Hank and I were six and eight years old - but I guess Bert was spoiled - you see the winter before an epidemic of Diphtheria had taken Oliver and Orville, our two little brothers, when they were about one and three years old and Bert was Mother's only baby left. When Hank or I were four we could get up in the night and go out to the barn with Dad and hold a lantern if a cow was having trouble with a new-born calf, or we could take a lantern to the chicken house and bring in the eggs or go to the well-house for the pail of lard if Bert had the croup - he got croup every time he caught cold..."

"What was the lard for, Papa?" Anna and Dale liked to hear Papa tell how things were when he was a little boy but sometimes it didn't seem as though Papa was ever little - he was always the big one who was responsible for everything.

"Mother mixed turpentine with it and Hank or I would run out to the woodpile and pick up chips to start a fire and heat the teakettle and we'd help Mother make a tent over Bert's crib - steam and the turpentine in the lard she rubbed on his chest would begin to help him breathe. Dad was gone a lot - helping the neighbor men put up wood - they'd stay a week at a time down along the river."

"We have to put up wood, too, Papa, but we don't stay overnight." Dale said.

"Dale, they had no cars or trucks in those days and it would take a day to bring home a wagon-load of wood if you had a good team. So they stayed long enough to put up wood for everybody, then loaded the wagons and hauled to everybody's farmstead," Papa tried to explain some of the hardships of those days before cars or telephones.

"But what if a cow was having a calf when Grandpa was gone for a week?" Anna asked.

"Mother and I sat up many a night out at the barn with a sick colt or a calf that didn't learn to suck right off or Mother would spot a roupy chicken when she gathered the eggs. We had to dope the roupy ones with turpentine and lard too or the whole flock would get sick and die," Papa said.

90

"Now they sell the roupy ones," Dale interrupted. He was the chicken buyer and he had to dock the farmers for their sick chickens and make them take them back home. He was always glad if Dad was there to tell them he couldn't buy sick chickens.

"But didn't you have to go to school the next day after you sat up all night with a sick colt?" asked Anna.

"Oh, yes but school was always the easiest thing. I liked to read and cipher," Papa's eyes always lit up when he talked about school. "But we always had to quit school in March to help with the spring work. But I stayed with it till I got through the <u>McGuffy Sixth Reader</u> and that's as far as school went in those days."

"Mama, you went to high school, didn't you and taught school?" Dale asked.

"Papa means it was compulsory for parents to send their children to school till they finished the Sixth Reader or got to the age of sixteen - whichever came first, and Charlie liked school and finished grade school in spite of having to quit to help with the farming before school was out. It was harder for boys to finish than girls because they did have to work outdoors more," Mama explained.

"Some parents sent their big boys to school till they were twenty-one in the dead of winter because they didn't have much else to do and hadn't really learned to read well and, as their folks said, 'A little more book larnin' won't hurt 'em,'" Papa laughed, "I remember a bunch of big fellows coming over to our school from Meredith. We were having Lyceum that night..."

"What's Lyceum?" Dale interrupted.

"Well, it's a school program or a lecture. Some school districts tried to have them once a month, especially if someone on the school board liked to lecture. They sometimes had a pie social to go with them. We were having a pie social that night, and this gang of big guys came and disrupted the whole proceedings. The young ladies in the district would bake a pie and bring it - well, all the ladies did - and they'd auction off the pies - only the auctioneer would know who baked the pie (the name was on the bottom). That was supposed to be a secret but some girls would have their brother leak to some neighbor boy - what kind of a pie she'd baked and he would bid till he got her pie - then they could sit together to eat it."

"Where would the boys get the money?" Dale asked.

"Oh, their dads might give them the money - but that time that bunch of guys pooled their money and one did the bidding. It was well known that one of our young guys was sweet on the prettiest young lady in our school."

"How old was she, Papa?" Anna had heard the expression "Sweet sixteen and never been kissed" and she wanted to know how old she must be before baking pies and eating with boys at pie socials should interest her.

"Well, I suppose she was fourteen or fifteen - she was through with her <u>McGuffy Reader</u> and could cipher down anybody in the school. She helped the teacher with the little kids - you see, there was no way she could go on to high school very handy and she'd probably be marrying some fellow in a year or so and have some children of her own..."

"Now, Charlie, sixteen is too young to be thinking of getting a family of your own," Mama interrupted. Anna had heard her say that Grandma was only fifteen when she and Grandpa Allison were married. Mama would tell Anna what a hard life Grandma Allison had had - she had fourteen babies and only eight of them lived to grow up to have children of their own.

"Long courtships aren't good either," Papa said. "Stella, you were lucky, you and Belva, to have Ney to take you to dances and take you home. Not all girls who want to go to dances have a brother to squire them around. Of course, that's how you both got to be old-maid school teachers, too," Papa liked to tease Mama about being so old when they were married.

"Papa, go on. I want to hear what happened at the pie social," Dale urged.

"Well, when this young fellow started bidding on the pretty girl's pie - these fellows run the bidding up till her beau had to drop out of the bidding and all six of those ruffians got her pie. They got to fighting amongst themselves, somebody threw a pie - and the fight was on. The ladies were screaming and pie was flying through the air. It broke up the social and everybody went home mad at the gang from the other school district."

"So we had to get even and the next month a gang of us boys from our district went over to Meredith when they were having a Box Supper. When we got there they were still having their program so we marched in by the side door, about eight of us and lined up between the stage and the audience. Two or three of us had mouth harps and we were playing 'Turkey in the Straw.' Some of us could sing."

"There was a big old gal with her black, straight hair parted in the middle and peeled back and the blackest eyes you ever saw - sitting right on the front row - right in front of me. We paused to catch our breath and she said, 'Boy, where was you raised?'"

"I bowed real low and answered, 'Heaven's my home, Madam. I'm just here on a furlough.'"

"What happened then?" Dale was anxious to know.

"Oh, everybody yelled and laughed. They seemed to like our music so we sang:

"Oh, the Martins and the Coys;
They were reckless mountain boys

There was fuedin' and a fightin'
And wrongs that needed rightin'..."

"Nobody interrupted us and we sang a few songs and marched out," Papa concluded.

"What's a Box Supper?" Anna queried, "Did you stay for that?"

"The ladies and all the young girls fix up a box and that's a secret too. They decorate them all up. Each lady hopes her box will be the prettiest and bring the most money for the school. And then they fill them with sandwiches that will impress the fellow who buys the box and cake or pie or cookies..." Papa paused and Anna interrupted.

"Did you ever take a pretty secret box to a Box Supper when you were sixteen, Mama?"

"Oh, yes, but no handsome young feller like Charlie was there and I always had to eat with some old geezer who had enough money to bid higher than anyone else - My experience was that one always went to Box Suppers with high hopes and went home disappointed ..." Mama smiled. "Oh, some matches were made at Pie Suppers and Box Socials but, somehow I escaped till Charlie came to my school when I was teaching and ciphered down everybody and then outspelled everybody at the Community Meeting."

"Did he beat you too, Mama?" Dale wanted to know.

"Oh, I was the teacher, I pronounced the words. But your Papa was still standing there when we pronounced the last hard word in the Speller and everyone else had missed a word and had to sit down."

"Papa, you said Uncle Bert didn't have to work like you and Uncle Hank when he was little - did he get to stay in school in the spring?"

"Bert didn't seem to like school like I did, and he was always getting into fights - I was done with school before he got very big so I don't remember much about his school except that Dad was always having to settle some scrape that Bert got into." Papa didn't like to talk much about Uncle Bert's fights.

"Papa, what did you do when you got out of school so young?" Anna asked.

"Oh, we used to have to herd cattle in the upper pasture. Farmers didn't have as many fences and didn't put up hay. Dad was paralyzed when he was only thirty-seven years old. I was only nine at that time and either Hank or I usually had to go along with him on any work he did. Sometimes we both worked with him. Herding cattle was a long boring job but we had to do it in the winter on any days we could be outdoors and we had to take turns because we couldn't work together and leave Dad to do chores alone. In the spring it was more fun to herd cattle but we had to help with the planting."

"I remember one time in the late spring when Bert kept getting into fights at school and getting sent home and Dad said he could just stay home. Dad said he had to take his turn herding cattle in the upper pasture. Well, he did for a couple of long days and then he began to bawl every morning it was his turn - he'd tell Mother he saw a big rattlesnake and was lucky he saw it first - it was just ready to strike, he said. And then Mother would worry about Bert and she had Floyd and Florence and Roy and Carrie - they were all little - she had enough to worry about without having to worry about Bert all alone in the upper pasture all day."

"What did he eat? Could he come home to lunch?" Anna wondered.

"No, he'd take biscuits and jelly - Mother would make cookies and fry chickens and save a drumstick for in our lunches. He had plenty to eat. Mother would say, 'Now, Bert, don't eat the sheep-sorrel - if it doesn't have a lavender flower on it - it might be snake-sorrel.'"

"What would happen if it was snake-sorrel?" Dale wanted to know.

"Oh, I don't know - the early settlers sometimes ate things that grew wild and were poisoned and your grandmother was always worried that one of us would eat something poisonous. At any rate, she worried and that gave Bert something to try to worry us all about. He didn't want to take his turn herding that day so he said, 'By God, I'll eat all the snake sorrel I can eat - what kind of a flower does it have on it?'"

"'Yellow,' Mother said, 'but, please, Bert, tell me you'll leave all those plants alone - too many of them will physic you. You have plenty of lunch if you just eat what I send.'"

"But when he came home that night he was feeling abused for having to spend all that day alone so he said, 'By God, I ate all the snake-sorrel I could eat.'"

"'Oh, Bert, you didn't!' Mother began crying and Hank and I started teasing him. I said, 'Maybe we better drench him like we do the horses when they eat too much green cane.'"

"Hank said, 'Maybe he needs an enema.'"

"'Bert, do you feel sick?' Mother worried."

"'No, I don't feel sick, I'm just hungry. In fact, I'm starved. I didn't have near enough dinner. That's why I had to fill up on snake sorrel.' Bert loved to hear Mother worry over him," Papa went on.

"Well, he ate a big supper and went to bed and along in the middle of the night - we heard Bert holler and, of course, we all showed up at his bedside. He hadn't just wet the bed - he had befouled it - he hadn't been lying, he had eaten an awful lot of sheep sorrel and it all came through him just like it went down. And Mother was right when she told him it might physic him. And he sure didn't need an enema or any other treatment except he had to get up and take a bath and Mother had to change his bed and he never did live that down. Every time it was his turn to herd cattle again, Hank or I would say, 'Bert, you better eat all the snake sorrel you can eat.'"

"Couldn't Uncle Floyd go along with him, or Aunt Florence?" asked Anna.

"No, they were six or eight years younger than he was. He was closer to Hank's age but he never did quit fighting. He used to want to go to dances with Hank and me and he always got into a fight - he'd start them someway and he'd carry a bolt in his pocket - 'Just in case I need an equalizer' - he'd say."

"What did he mean by that? What did he do with the bolt?" Dale queried.

"Oh, he'd reach in his pocket and come out with a clenched fist - and he'd be holding that bolt in the palm of his hand. If you hit someone with a bolt in your hand you could break a jaw. Hank and I never wanted to go with him. In fact we played a trick on him one time. We were all planning on going to the dance and he came home early - Dad had sent him over to help a neighbor put up wood. Mother fed him supper before we got home and he laid down across his bed and went sound asleep."

"We came home, ate supper and got dressed and ready to go to the dance and didn't wake him up. Mother wanted us to but we told her he'd be mad if we didn't let him get his rest. 'When he wakes up he can get ready and come along,' Hank said, 'He'll be in a better humor.'"

"When we got home from that dance after midnight, he roused up when we walked in and jumped up. 'What are you trying to do,' he shouted, 'Thought you were going to run off from me, didn't you. Well, I'm goin' ta beat you there - I've got a score to settle with one of those guys...'"

"Mother came out of her bedroom. 'Bert,' she said, 'now don't go picking fights at dances.' She didn't realize that the dance was over and she couldn't have stopped him if she had. He flung on his clothes and even stopped long enough to shave and put on a tie, 'I'm planning to take Tom's girl home tonight after I beat him up so I'm taking the buggy.'"

"So Hank and I tried to get to the wash basin and finally put our ties back on - hunted for our belts that we'd already taken off. We went out to the barn to get our saddle horses that we'd just put away and Bert came flying by with his mare hitched to the buggy. We waited till he pulled out of the yard before we started laughing."

"It was three o'clock in the morning before he dragged back in the house. 'I got up there to that barn dance and there wasn't even a light in the house. Where did they have that barn dance?' he fumed as he threw his clothes down and fell across his bed, as Hank and I rolled off our bunks, laughing."

"It is a wonder that he didn't hit you with a bolt in his hand," Anna said, "Wasn't he awful mad when he realized he'd slept through the whole evening?"

"Oh, yes, but what could he do? Hank and I both were ganged up on him. Mother would always get up to keep Bert from getting hurt and Dad would order us all outdoors if we were going to fight. He'd threaten to use his crutches on us." Papa was always patient with Grandpa Allison and Dale and Anna came to know why - and, when they thought about it they realized that Grandpa was pretty much the head of the household that Papa grew up in - even if he was crippled by paralysis when he was thirty-seven.

****

The Town Clown

Papa somehow never got too old to play a prank on someone and he loved to tell stories to make people laugh. Wells was a bustling little community of about one hundred people serving the farmers who surrounded it. The train came chugging through the town every day bringing supplies to the hardware store, the grocery stores, the elevator and hauling the cream to Concordia. Everyone who wanted to work could find something to do and Papa always wanted to work. So it was when he and Mama came to Wells in 1910 shortly after they were married. They had rented a farm across the road from the Clarence Brown family. Edith and Edna were young ladies at the time and became fast friends of Mama's. There were card parties and socials and church activities and they were soon acquainted with the entire community. Play was always mixed with work, and, when farming slacked off in the fall Papa worked on the railroad.

One evening he came home laughing about what a trick he had played on the Mexicans who lived down along the railroad track in the Mexican shacks as the old boxcars that set along the siding were called. They had come up the railroad tracks from Albuquerque to find work along the tracks. The train companies hired them for very little to keep up the track so the heavy trains would not derail.

"I was sitting down in front of the restaurant visiting with Charlie Comfort and Everett Payne and there were two or three Mexicans sitting over a little ways chattering amongst themselves in Mexican," Papa told Dale and Anna. "I reached down and picked up a couple of pop bottle caps out of the dirt, took out my jackknife (and a couple of pennies that the Mexicans didn't see). I just idly pried the corks out of those tin caps and said to Charlie, "You know, sometimes you can find pennies under these caps. There's one under this one!"

"I picked up a couple more caps and found another penny and by that time those Mexicans had started digging up bottle caps and by morning there won't be a bottle cap left in the dirt around the grocery stores or the restaurants either."

"Don't they throw the caps back down when they get the corks pried out of them?" Dale giggled. "I'd think they'd catch on after they'd pried out a few caps."

"No, they are filling their pockets with caps and fanning out all around town finding bottle caps to take back to the shacks. Everett Payne fixed a couple of corks with pennies and threw them back down before we got up and left to come home."

"Charlie, don't you feel sorry for those men? They are so far from home and they've left their families..." Mama worried about them freezing in the winter in those shacks.

"Oh, some of them are smart and they are picking up English and before long they will be bringing their wives and kids. I'm sure they are living better than the families they left behind," Papa laughed, "And they're getting smarter every day."

* * * * * * * * *

"Charlie Allison and Pat Watkins have a bet on - and whichever one loses will pay for the treats for everybody in town," Vern Heald reported to Marvin Overton. He studied the showcase in Overton's Grocery.

"What's the bet about?" Marvin asked.

"They didn't say. They just said for you to set up the treats - a nickel each for everybody who comes in and keep a record of it. One or the other of them will pick up the tab when the bet is settled. Have you got any good five-cent cigars, Marvin?" Vern said, as he proceeded to collect his share of the bet.

All afternoon various people came in to get their five-cent treats. Children got a sack of candy or an ice cream cone - women got a bottle of pop. Whip licorice was popular with the boys. The box of cigars was empty and the list on the tab got longer and longer. Marvin Overton was used to Charlie Allison and Pat Watkins and didn't worry about being paid. One or the other of them would come in and settle up. He was confident.

A couple of weeks went by and the tab laid there behind the counter. Papa was in the store on day and Marvin said, "By the way, Charlie, which one of you won the bet you and Pat had?"

"Oh, it hasn't been decided just yet," Papa said. "But just as soon as it is, one or the other of us will be in and settle up for the treats."

Overton's Grocery wasn't as big as the big general store on the east side of the street. And that had been a big afternoon when everyone who was in town came in that Saturday to collect his share of the treats. They had bought something else, some of them and so Marvin wasn't in a hurry to be paid. He just thought to remind them.

A month or so went by and Marvin jogged Charlie's memory again. He and Pat were loafing in front of the store with a half-dozen or so of the regular fellows, "Say, who finally won that bet?" Marvin asked once more.

"It still hasn't been decided yet," Pat answered.

"Well, what was the bet, anyway," Marvin finally asked.

"Pat and I were discussing the new elevator," Charlie explained, "And I bet that when it ever falls over - it will fall north - Pat bet it would fall south."

"Now, Marvin, whichever way it goes, you're bound to get paid for the treats," Pat concluded amid the hoots of laughter.

****

The Man in the Moon as he sails through the sky
Is a most remarkable skipper
But he made a mistake when he tried to take
A drink of milk from the dipper.
He dipped right out of the Milky Way
And, slowly, carefully filled it
But the Big Bear growled and the Little Bear howled
And frightened him so that he spilled it.

...recited by Ada Harder

The two men were stealing silently along in the darkness toward the old blacksmith shop on the west side of Wells. They followed a pair of parallel paths called Wells Street on the plats, paths made by countless wagons travelling to and from the blacksmith shop.

They made no sound - their plans already made and their night's adventure already set like a mouse trap - ready to spring when the moment arrived.

It was 4:00 a.m., May 18, the year 1910. The newspapers had been full of stories about the return of Halley's Comet. People's reactions had been varied. Even some righteous souls had deeded their homes to the church, sold their cows and chickens and totally dispensed with their livelihood, the papers said. The big general store with its hitching posts for the horses and long benches for the local farmers to sit out in front -

while the ladies bought the groceries inside - had been the scene for days of all sorts of discussion about what was going to happen when Halley's Comet hit the earth again.

Halley's Comet had been tracked by astronomers since before the birth of Christ and there was some evidence that it was the Star of Bethlehem. All these thoughts and apprehensions had been expressed for some days around Wells and each resident had his own private thoughts about the Second Coming of Christ??? or just some dire calamity such as the earth catching fire as the comet went by??? Would it be a giant explosion and the earth just disintegrate 'in the twinkling of an eye' as the Bible said???

Charlie Allison and Jim Whitley were young men at that time and full of devilment and this nocturnal prowl was their reaction to the yet unknown but upcoming event.

They had discussed what one could do to make the loudest possible noise when Halley's Comet was supposed to hit the earth. Accordingly, they had already put together black powder and blasting caps which they planned to set off at about 3:00 a.m.

In Papa's words, "There was total darkness in Wells. Everyone was supposedly sleeping the sleep of the just.. Several had expressed assurances that nothing was going to happen in Wells anyway but Jim thought that everybody was worried, even the ones who said nothing. Jim and I carried his anvil off of its stand and out west of the building. We turned it upside down and filled the hollow in the bottom with black powder. Then we put another anvil on top and lit the fuse. When the moment arrived 'BOOM' every house in town had a light on instantly. They must have all been lying there in their beds, wide awake, just waiting for that comet to hit."

Anna always loved to listen to Papa tell about his escapades. His eyes would twinkle and he'd be so happy. This Halley's Comet prank had happened five years before she was born. It wasn't that Papa never took life seriously. He was always worried and worked very hard to keep paying bills and keep food on the table. He just never missed an opportunity to make people laugh. Papa was a Wesleyan Methodist from the Hall neighborhood as a little boy and must have never been afraid of dying. Little was known about the heavens at that time - but like the nursery rhyme of the 'Man in the Moon' that starts this story, he seemed to never fear that all the stars were friendly - why not? God made them all.

****

Make me, dear Lord, polite and kind
To everyone, I pray.
And may I ask you how you find
Yourself, dear Lord, today?

by John Bannister Tabb

"Grandpa Allison can sleep with me, Mama, my cot folds out on both sides," Dale spoke with enthusiasm. Grandpa Allison was coming back from Montana and, of course, he'd stay with Charlie. Charlie was his oldest son. No matter that the little two-room house in the north end of Wells was already bulging with Mama, Papa, Dale and Anna. And Mama had no time to stay home and tidy it up each day.

"Grandpa can help me with the dishes, Mama," Anna volunteered. And she could sweep around him, she thought. Grandpa was on crutches. Anna had never known him any other way. He kept all his belongings in a battered old suitcase and traveled by train or bus from Montana to Kansas from time to time after Grandma died - living with his daughter Florence and family or his daughter Carrie's family or Uncle Hank and his family.

Kalispell, Montana, was where Papa's two sisters and beloved brother, Hank had gone to raise their families. Anna wished she could travel to Montana sometime. It sounded almost as far as China. "You could reach China if you started digging, and kept digging completely through the earth," Dale had told her - which sounded about as unlikely as getting on a train and traveling to Kalispell, Montana.

"Well, we'll just have to do the best we can," said Mama resignedly, as she hurried to clear the breakfast table. And Anna knew she was thinking of one more place around the little round table and three square meals a day with her down at the cream station all day. Mama hadn't yet figured out how to be two places at once.

"Dale, will you feed the chickens in the batteries in the barn?" Papa spoke hurriedly from the kitchen door, "I've got to go up by Lamar, I've got a load of hogs to haul to Salina today. Stella, do you want to ride down to the creamery today or walk down a little later?"

Mama glanced around the house - looked over toward the kitchen cabinet and said, "Oh, I might as well go with you now. My cupboard is pretty bare but when the kids come down town they can buy some groceries for me - I can think what I need down there as well as here. Anna, you'll finish up here, won't you, honey?"

"Your Grandpa will be here tomorrow morning to help you with the dishes, Anna," Papa said. "He's coming in on the bus to Salina and I'll

100

pick him up when I get the hogs delivered to Butzer Packing Company and gather the groceries and hardware goods for the stores - it'll work out about right if I don't waste any time." Papa was always in a hurry.

Grandpa Allison settled down into the routine of living with his oldest son with surprising ease. Anna was sure he always felt himself to be useful to Charlie and his family. He explained that to her as he wiped the dishes and stacked them on the kitchen cabinet for her to put away.

"Anna," he said to her one day soon after he arrived, "You're not scrubbing your mother's griddles and skillets till they're clean. Just wiping them off is not enough."

"That's what Mama said to do with them," Anna argued.

"Well, she's just too busy to notice how thick with stove soot and burned grease the bottoms of these pans are getting," Grandpa edged himself from the table to the stove without crutches, twisting his crossed legs so that his crossed feet balanced his tall body. He had long powerful arms and could move about the small room easily as long as he could reach a piece of furniture.

He examined the drawer full of bread pans and muffin tins, too, in Mama's big Peninsular Wood Range. It was a beautiful cook stove. Uncle Ney had brought it down to her when he moved Aunt Ethel's cook stove into Grandma's house. Papa didn't like it as well, Mama said, because the oven was up on a level with the cook-top and he couldn't dry his shoes and socks on the oven door. He had to stack them on a chair close by the fire box on the other side and they dried slower. But Mama liked it better - she didn't have to stoop to see if the pie was baking or run into the open oven door when she was in a hurry.

"Anna, where does your mother keep the lye she uses when she makes soap?" Grandpa asked. He was piling every pan on top of the stove that Anna had tucked away in the long drawer under the oven.

"Oh, Mama keeps that out in the pumphouse on that long shelf where Papa keeps things we are not supposed to bother. She said I was never to open the lye can for any reason. It will burn a hole in your hand if you touch it, you know," Anna explained as she watched Grandpa messing up her kitchen by dragging out every pan, griddle and skillet she had carefully tucked away.

Grandpa edged himself about till he could reach his crutches and proceeded out the back door, pausing to take down the wash tub that always hung by the back door except on wash day and Saturdays when it was time for a bath.

"Mama, Grandpa is going to clean your pans and skillets and the pancake griddle with lye water, I think, so I just left," Anna reported to Mama when she got down to the cream station. She was hoping to be vindicated for running off and not helping grandpa carry the pans and fill the tub with water etc. Even so, she was not quite prepared for the outburst her report provoked.

"Doggonnit all, he'll ruin every pan I've got," Mama walked the floor and stomped and cried and wrung her hands. "You know all your Grandma Allison ever had to cook with was enamel pans. I hate enamel - it comes in holes and he'd even mend them with rags and screws and washers. I'll just thank Port Allison to keep his hands off my pans."

Mama was right. When evening came and it was time to go back to the little two -room house to cook supper, the pans and skillets were still soaking in the tub of lye water out in the back yard. Mama carried bucket after bucket of water out to the tub and dumped the water and rinsed the pans and rinsed again. She wiped them dry finally with clean rags and brought them inside to dry out on the stove and in the warming ovens. But, with all that care, they all had rust spots on them and the skillets didn't look better - they looked worse.

Grandpa was out to the barn helping Papa and Dale feed the chickens in the batteries so Mama explained to Anna, "I'll get a hot fire and put some lard in the skillets and the griddle and see if I can season them again so pancakes won't stick and steak will brown but I'll just have to get some new pie tins and bread pans. You can't do much to help a rusted tin pan. Now, Anna we won't say anything in front of Grandpa about the lye water. It would just hurt Charlie and do no good, anyway."

Grandpa continued to be helpful in the kitchen every morning. Dale was happy that he was relieved of having to dry dishes but Anna was getting more possessive of her kitchen every day. She liked to straighten the kitchen and put everything away so the cabinet was bare. The sink where everyone washed his hands in the wash basin and looked in the looking glass to comb his hair was right beside the cabinet where food was prepared. The pail of water with its big dipper had a place to sit right beside the washbasin in the sink - in Anna's kitchen - but not in Grandpa's kitchen. His notion was that, since everyone drank water from the dipper - the pail should stand on the cabinet - away from the basin with the soap dish and comb and toothbrushes that were on a little shelf under the mirror.

One morning when Grandpa finished drying the dishes and putting them in the cupboard he sat down by the table to watch Anna wipe off the stove and the cabinet. Then she used the same dishcloth to wipe out the wash basin and sink. She threw out the dishwater and hung the dish pan with the dishrag spread across it to dry just outside the door. She came back in and looked over her kitchen - the bucket seemed out of place on the cabinet and in the interest of neatness she placed the bucket down in the sink beside the wash basin.

Grandpa spoke sternly, "Anna, bring me my crutches."

Uh oh! she knew she had displeased him somehow as she hastened to carry his crutches from beside the front door and hand them to him. He arose and stocked over to the sink. Standing on one crutch, he lifted the bucket out of the sink and placed it back on the cabinet. "Young lady, you'll die of germs before you are thirty," he said sternly.

Mama just laughed when Anna told her what Grandpa said.

"But, Mama, if I was going to turn the washbasin over and wash my face and hands I'd lift the bucket up onto the cabinet then. And I wouldn't comb my hair over the water bucket!" Anna was indignant.

"Honey, I think Charlie and your grandpa are going after a horse and buggy for your grandpa this evening. He needs to get out of the kitchen. He probably tore up girls' playhouses when he was a little boy, too "

"A horse!" Suddenly all the little problems of 'too many cooks in the kitchen' was forgotten. "What will Grandpa do with the horse and buggy? Will he take us for rides?" Anna asked.

Grandpa had the dealership for Diamond lamps and lanterns. In fact, he and Papa had ordered gasoline lanterns and lamps for the cream station, and out to the tin shed where they bought chickens. Mama even had a Diamond iron. Anna still had to use the old sad irons that sat on the back of the stove top if she wanted to press a doll dress. That Diamond iron had a shiny chrome ball in front of the handle that was filled with gasoline. Then it was pumped up with a cute little air pump that came with the iron. It had little windows along its sides where one reached in with a kitchen match to heat the generator. When the generator was hot, a knob on the front was turned to "ON" and a whole row of little gas flames came on and heated the iron. Grandpa had ordered Mama's gasoline iron and gave it to her for Christmas.

"He wants to drive around the county and sell Diamond irons to all the housewives. Your grandpa is quite a salesman, you know. We have seven lamps, and lanterns that have to be filled with gasoline and pumped up every evening at dusk so we can run this creamery, the gas pumps out in front and the scales out at the shed where we buy chickens. He convinced us they'd make a much better light than a coal oil lantern - and they do," Mama explained.

After that Grandpa was gone from the kitchen before Papa every morning. He brushed Madge, his new horse, till her coat was shiny and fed her her morning oats with a feed bag over her nose. She was gentle but her back was so wide that Anna's legs stuck straight out when Papa set her up on Madge's back. She wasn't for riding - she was a buggy horse. Grandpa painted his buggy wheels red and the rest of the buggy had a new coat of black paint. The leather was cleaned and shined. Grandpa was in business.

Thereafter there were always several irons sitting around the creamery with a tag on them. Some farmer's wife had brought it in to be fixed or for Grandpa to order a new generator and install it. Grandpa would go to visit Uncle Roy in Oakhill or Uncle Bert - down in the Finn District or Uncle Floyd out in Luray but in a few days he would be back with his battered suitcase to live with his oldest son, and fix the lamps and irons that he had sold. Or he would hitch up old Madge and drive out to some farmstead to return an iron and sell them a lantern.

Grandpa was a great pal to Dale but seemed to believe for sure that little girls should learn to cook and sew and clean early so they could be a good housewife and mother as soon as possible.

One Sunday after Grandma Jordan had passed away, Uncle Ney and Aunt Ethel brought Grandpa Jordan down to Wells to visit Stella and her family. It happened that Uncle Roy and his family had also come to visit from Oakhill. Grandpa Allison and Grandpa Jordan had each lost his wife and each was living with his son and family. So they had like experiences to visit about. They were sitting out in the shade of the big maple tree by the little house in the north end of Wells.

"Ed, what do you think of these women all getting their hair bobbed off? Do you know what it says in the Bible about that?" Grandpa Allison asked, shaking his head at the very thought of a whole generation of women risking their chance at eternity that way. "And the way they are dressing, hardly any clothes on at all - dresses clear up to their knees, almost."

"Well, Port, I haven't seem too much of the high fashions lately, I just hadn't thought about it," Grandpa Jordan answered.

"Well, just look around you," Grandpa Allison clucked his tongue, "If Gabriel blows his horn any time soon and I think he's going to - I'll bet a whole generation would be lost."

Grandpa Allison came from the Hall community Wesleyan Methodists. He often said he had never taken a drink of whiskey or danced a step or played cards. Anna, Leta and Lela were taking turns swinging in the swing not too far from this conversation. They stopped swinging - they had all had their hair bobbed off and their dresses were all above their knees. Mama had quit wearing two underskirts a long time ago and her hair was short - so was Aunt Blanche's. They wondered if Grandpa Allison was saying they would go to Hell?

Grandpa Jordan spoke slowly and didn't seem at all concerned about the world coming to an end any time soon, "Port," he said, "I'll tell you what I think. Now that we've raised our families and they are all out on their own and we're living in someone else's home, it's just best to be like those three monkeys that hear nothing, see nothing and speak nothing."

"Oh, I suppose," Grandpa Allison agreed without much conviction.

'My two grandpas are as different as night and day,' Anna thought. 'Grandpa Jordan had to have the daily newspaper and read the news and talked about the tariff, prices and politics and Grandpa Allison could tell you how many words there were in the Bible but he didn't care if the paper came that day or not. He might look at the advertisements to see how short the dresses were after Papa got through reading the paper but he didn't read the news, ever.'

Grandpa Allison had to be doing something to feel useful. Grandpa Jordan didn't worry about whether he was useful or not. He played Solitaire with a deck of cards and whiled away many hours with cards. Grandpa Allison considered cards sinful - but then he was a Methodist and Methodists didn't play cards or dance. Anna often wondered how Papa could play pitch and even run the dances down at the Woodman Hall. He didn't seem to be afraid of Hell or damnation and he'd heard it preached every Sunday when he was a boy.

Anna remembered reporting to Mama and Papa what George Miller, the Sunday School Superintendent at the Wells Methodist Church had said one Sunday morning after Papa started the dances last fall, "I wonder if all of you God-fearing brothers and sisters realize what is going on in our little town," he had asked from the pulpit. "I went down to the restaurant to tell a fellow parishioner that we had the new sparkplugs in and his car was ready and as I was passing by the Hall, the music was deafening and I glanced through the window and the men and women were dancing so close together you couldn't get a case knife between them!"

Papa just laughed. He thought it was so funny he told George McCain. George was a farmer from up by Lamar who liked to bring his family to dances so he helped Papa keep those dances going - he'd get the music, collect the money for tickets and pay the orchestra. Papa belonged to the Woodman Lodge, collected rent for the hall and kept up the dance floor. He'd buy a bolt of ribbon at the store and a package of pins when he got home from hauling produce every Saturday night. He'd cut the ribbon into two-inch pieces for tickets. They worked together.

"George Miller wants to close the Woodman Hall for dancing and card playing, too," Papa explained. They both laughed and joked and seemed not to fear the wrath of the Almighty, at all.

"Well, I guess it's jest as a feller sees it," George McCain said.

Anna came to realize that there was no real dyed in the wool or set in cement way of looking at anything. Old George McCain was right, "It was jest as a feller sees it."

****

Lake Coming

"The bands played, the crowd waited as the rains fell. Governor Ben S. Paulen arrived 5:30 P.M. Oct 13, 1925. - taken from the <u>Minneapolis Messenger</u>, Minneapolis, Kansas, October 15, 1925.

"Stella, they're finally going to get the Governor to take a look at our lake site," Papa was excited as he put down the paper and began to pace the floor. "They'll be here next Monday or Tuesday. They are going to blow the fire whistle in Minneapolis and delegations from Delphos, Lamar, Bennington, Lindsay, Vine, Niles, Culver, Verdi, Tescott, Solomon and Wells - every town in Ottawa County will get a line ring. And, since Wells is so close, Doc Goodwyn wants everybody in Wells to be the delegation from here to go down to Rehberg's pasture and be there when the Governor arrives. He wants a thousand people waiting; that lake is going to be the greatest thing to ever happen to Ottawa County."

"Well, they've been talking about it long enough, but, it says here, there are two excellent sites in Ottawa County and there are dozens of sites across the state that he's going to visit with his core of engineers." Mama didn't want Papa to get too excited about the prospect of a big lake, covering more than a hundred acres being only a couple of miles from Wells - and then be disappointed.

"They'll not find a better place for a lake in Ottawa County and the way it's been raining, - a lot of places will be hard to get to. Yeah, it will take a lot of doing - but we're going to get that lake!" Papa was enthusiastic. "We'll do what we can - the whole town of Wells will be down there next Tuesday, anyway. I'll take a truck load - and a truck load of chairs in case the Governor wants to make a speech." Papa talked of little else from that day on.

He brought a bathing suit home for Mama - Dale and Anna could wear some old clothes - Dale could cut off some old coveralls with worn-out knees and Anna could put a safety pin through the skirt of an old dress so it wouldn't ride up and show her underpants - Papa wanted to be sure all his family could swim long before the lake was finished.

"Why, Charlie, do you want me to put this thing on and get out of the car in front of people and go prancing down to the water. You know I can't swim," Mama's face was red as she looked at the suit.. "Can you take it back?"

"Well, I'm not going to. Girls and women drown more often than men and boys do because, of course, they can't swim - they have never tried. Next spring as soon as it warms up we're going down to the slab just below where the dam will be. That's a real good swimming hole,

106

and I'll teach you to swim in no time. We'll be ready when they open up that lake for swimming."

Mama smiled; she had a reprieve that would last till next spring and they didn't have that lake yet. She folded the suit and put it in a dresser drawer. Papa had to do something while he waited for next Monday or Tuesday to come.

"Don't you think we'll get a lake, Mama?" asked Anna. "I want to get a swimming suit, too."

"Of course you do, honey, and maybe you can wear this one when you grow up. I hope they get the lake - it seems to mean so much to Charlie. But I wanted them to get a high school here in Wells and whatever came of that?" Mama snorted.

"Papa is sure we'll get it, Mama, and he's sure you'll wear that suit, too," Anna said, "What are you going to do next spring?"

"Next spring is a whole winter away, Anna, and I just can't see me in that bathing suit," Mama's face turned red again at the thought. "Let's get by next Tuesday, first."

It rained for several days - roads in much of Ottawa County were almost impassible with mud but around Wells it was sandy so, though the rain made puddles in the street, it soaked in leaving dry sand. Papa talked to the school board - the teachers were told that Papa would haul the school children down there, and their folks should find rides, too. He said he'd make as many trips as necessary to make sure everyone got down there who wanted to go.

Tuesday dawned gray and cloudy but the news from Minneapolis was that Governor Paulen and his party were in Mankato for a noon meeting and that they'd had to cancel several of their visits to lake sites but the Game and Fish people in Minneapolis were still planning to have the dignitaries out to the lake site. It was eight miles east by way of the cemetery. The roads would be muddy but bands from Bennington and Delphos were planning to be there - rain or shine so Minneapolis would be there in force, also.

"I'll take the tarp for over the truck bed so the kids won't get wet if it starts to rain. Everybody will just have to think about that - the way this weather looks," said Papa, "But, if the people from Bennington can get up there with their band over that muddy road from Bennington, all of Wells can get there. It's all sand from here to the lake-site."

Dale and Anna went fishing every summer in Sand Creek in the pasture just west of Wells - they waded in the shallow places, and caught sunfish and mudcats. Oh, yes, they were old hands at playing in Sand Creek. One time they had caught a leather-back turtle who swallowed the hook. They dragged him home, dug a small hole in the yard, filled it with a pail of water and gave him a home. They cut the string long enough, drove a stake in the ground and tied him there.

107

"Papa, look what we brought home for your supper." Dale bragged, laughing as he showed-off his prize catch when Papa got home that evening.

"Well, I'll be danged! You don't eat leather-back turtles - or, at least I never have. Now, if you'd catch me a few frogs - are there any bullfrogs down there?" Papa was always interested in fishing.

"There are lots of frogs but how would you catch 'em?" Dale asked.

"Oh, we used to catch 'em by hooking a little piece of red ribbon on the fish hook and dangling it in front of their nose," Papa explained, "but you gotta have patience."

Patience was something neither Dale nor Anna had ever developed to any great degree. There was a railroad bridge across Sand Creek and a few holes for fishing but they were mostly whiling away their long summer afternoons where it was cooler than the hot sandy streets of Wells. They would run home on the railroad ties - keeping out of the Mexican sandburs with their bare feet. But this was going to add a dimension to the play they had never before imagined would happen to Sand Creek.

Springs fed many of the streams that flowed through Central Kansas and many of the early settlers had a spring on his back porch or a spring that filled a pond in his pasture. So it was that Sand Creek didn't ever go dry - even in long periods of dry weather.

Anna could see little that suggested a hundred acres of water when they arrived at the spot where the people from the county-seat were supposed to bring Governor Paulen. They had dragged a small wooden platform out in the middle of the pasture along side of parallel ruts that had been made by wagons or cattle on their way to the creek-bank. Sand Creek had cut a deep channel through the pasture in this section. It wasn't wide but it was too wide to jump across and too deep to wade in a lot of places.

"That lake will fill with water and stay full," Papa assured every one.

"But a hundred acres of water will cover a lot of good buffalo grass. There aren't any trees around for picnics," some would argue.

"Oh, the state will plant trees and build boat docks and concession stands and bathhouses. They'll hire lifeguards so everyone can learn to swim." That barren pasture became a gorgeous campground before one's very eyes as he listened to others.

Some were very skeptical - the afternoon wore on - the bands set up their instruments and played as evening approached. The crowd swelled as teams and wagons brought people from as far as ten miles. Some walked from the little country schools close at hand or their folks picked up their children and brought them - if there really was going to

108

be a lake or if the governor was really going to be dragged out to that pasture in the middle of nowhere - no one wanted to be the one who missed it.

At last the procession of cars arrived, mud spattered, but triumphant. Governor Paulen got out and began shaking hands. He seemed so happy that so many people had come and had waited so long, after all, it was five-thirty in the evening in the middle of October - many would be getting home long after dark. He came by Papa's truck as all the children reached out a hand.

"It was a long wait but Dale and Anna both got to shake hands with the Governor," Papa reported later.

Flags were set up on the platform - six chairs were placed about and Doc Goodwyn as president of the Ottawa County Game and Fish Committee introduced Governor Paulen - the bands played and everyone thanked everyone for coming. As the crowd dispersed everyone was in gay spirits and the lake seemed close at hand. Everyone went home expectant and hopeful.

"Now, when are they going to start building the lake?" Dale asked. He had been swimming with the boys in ponds for quite a while. Papa found him a little green swimming suit which he left at home with Mama's suit.

"Mama, Dale swims naked all the time with Wendall Todd and Philip and Chester Miller and Fred Payne's boys. Why didn't he buy me a swimming suit?" Anna complained to her mother.

"Honey, I asked him that and he said they didn't have any in the stores. Little girls just don't learn to swim, I guess. They said they had no call for them. I don't want you and Dale going swimming in Sand Creek by yourselves, anyway, Anna." Mama worried all the time that they would drown.

A two-inch column a week later mentioned that the Governor was very impressed with the large showing of Ottawa County citizens at such a late hour in such inclement weather but that no decision about the lake would be forth-coming until next spring.

"We'll get it, you just wait and see," Papa assured his family.

April 22, 1926, a front page column was headed, "Lake Decision Soon." The article went on to say that engineers, wildlife advocates, financial advisors and legislators were meeting in committee in Topeka. A trip by engineers was being made to lake-sites across the state that were missed in the fall. The time was right for making a decision. An aide from the Governor's office had said that the Governor had been most encouraged by the enthusiasm and interest shown in Ottawa County, it had been the high-light of the trip. So far, there was $40,000 set aside with which to start a program of water impounding and more would be forthcoming as needed.

Papa was more confident than ever, "Now, Stella, this is one we're not going to lose. You see, we just have to have patience." Papa folded the paper and flew out the door to talk to everyone he met on the street. People gathered in front of Copeman's Store and he'd find several to talk to about how lucky we were in Ottawa County to be getting a lake. And Papa was right.

The Minneapolis Messenger, June 3, 1926 carried the headline, "Lake Site is Formally Adopted" and underneath this caption, "$175,000 to begin a program of water impounding for recreation." Sportsmen across the state rejoiced. Congratulations were in order for Dr A. R. Goodwyn of Minneapolis, a dentist, who had worked tirelessly on the Fish and Wildlife Committee. He had been instrumental in bringing carloads of fish by rail to the county-seat and stocking the streams in Ottawa County for several years. And now, largely through his efforts, everyone, sportsmen, sightseers and happy people, young and old could take pride in their very own lake in Ottawa County.

Work on the dam began the next spring.

****

110

Moving!!!!!!!!

Anna lay on her little cot in the south end of the bedroom pretending sleep. Maybe Mama and Papa's low voices woke her.

"Stella, we have got to get closer to that cream station and the tin shed. That's where you work from dawn till midnight and you just sleep here. I've been thinking - we could rent part of the Dyer House and be just across the street from the creamery," Papa's voice was low and hesitant.

"Why, Charlie, all our beautiful fruit trees, the grape arbor - I thought you loved this place!" Mama sounded disbelieving, her voice still tired from her short night's sleep.

"I don't have time to plant a garden or water the trees, Stella, and we can't be two places at once; besides I've lost some interest in this place since I found out that Carl Comfort didn't take the money I handed to him to pay my delinquent taxes for me. Instead he used the money to buy a Tax title for himself, the damn crook," Papa swore under his breath and said no more.

But the seed had been planted in Anna's mind as well as her mother's in the spring of 1926 and by fall it had all been done.   Anna and Dale each had a bedroom as did Mama and Papa - in the upstairs of the Dyer House - so much room and so little furniture to fill it!

The north downstairs room that had once been the parlor in the Dyer House became the Allison family's living quarters downstairs. It had a washstand and a bucket, a hall tree for coats, a cot for Grandad when he came for extended visits, stove, kitchen cabinet, table and chairs. Its door to the rest of the downstairs was locked because John and Louise Stilwell and their two small children, Marjorie, three, and Junior, five, lived in the rest of the downstairs just beyond that door.

The Allisons shared a front porch and the entryway. The south door in the entryway opened into John Stilwell's barber shop so one could run into almost anyone when coming down the long staircase that led to the bedrooms upstairs.

The togetherness of shared living quarters was an experience that taught the families many things about the private lives of friends and neighbors that they wished they'd never learned.

There was no place for Mama's new washing machine except on the back porch which led from Louise's kitchen. Also, the well from which Anna and Dale carried the pails of water for the washstand in their kitchen-dining-living room was right beside the back porch. So Mama made an agreement with Louise that she could use the new washing machine on her back porch and heat her wash water in Mother's copper boiler on the little two-burner kerosene stove.

Louise had been using a washtub and a stomper with a washboard for badly soiled clothes so she was happy to have Mama's washer on her back porch. Louise had been heating water for her washing in a five-gallon lard can on the porch, so she was glad to use Mama's boiler too.

They agreed that Louise would wash on Monday and Mama would wash on Tuesday or Thursday - which one might assume would accommodate two families using the same facility with no friction whatever.

Papa had chosen that new washing machine because it operated like a cradle. One put the clothes in and the soap and water through a steel lid in the top. The tub was shaped like a crescent and had an upright wooden handle in the middle. Dale or Anna could swing it back and forth and wash the clothes because there were big springs on each side of the tub, which, when hooked to the framework, helped with the swinging of the wash load. Papa was always looking for ways to help Mama and keep Dale and Anna busy and out of mischief at the same time. So they took turns pushing the handle back and forth - ten minutes for each load.

"Now, the way to keep that washer helping you is to always unhook the springs on each side when you are done washing and have drained out the tub. That way you can flip the washer over so the inside will dry out and never rust," Papa explained to Louise and Mama as he moved the new washer with it's galvanized tub and water-tight lid onto the back porch of the Dyer house.

At last Mama was home - just across from the cream station. She could look out the window and see anyone driving up with a can of cream and bake a pie in her own kitchen at the same time - and hear John and Louise and their children's problems at the same time also - through the thin walls in the Dyer house.

But Mama still spent most of every day in the cream station, except for wash days and Sundays and early mornings.

"Charlie, didn't you tell Louise that she should unhook those big steel springs on that washer when she finishes her washing and flips it over to dry out?" Mama asked.

"Yes, I did," Papa explained, "But she works so fast she just forgets. Maybe you should remind her - we don't want those springs to get all stretched so the machine won't operate so easy."

"I did remind her," Mama said. "She said that's the first time she'd heard of it and she went back in her kitchen and slammed the door."

"Yes and I heard her telling somebody - right through that thin door," Anna piped up, "That if Stella would spend a more time mopping up after she washed and worried less over that damn washer, the back porch would look less like a pig sty when she was finished with it."

"Sshhh! Sound travels both ways, you know," Papa spoke softly, "We'll just have to check it ourselves after she's finished and unhook it each time." But Anna could see that Papa would liked to have said a lot and spoken a lot louder if that locked door had not been so thin.

* * * * * * * * * *

112

"Louise is a Kircher - and you remember her brother, Mike, Anna," Mama explained over in the cream station later that day, "You remember how quick he flew mad when Charlie asked him to bring back the tools he had borrowed out of the tin shed."

Anna did remember that night very well:

It was a clear moonlit night; Grandpa Jordan was spending a few days with his daughter in Wells. That was just last year after Grandma died. Mama and Papa had spent a long day in the creamery and on the produce truck. Grandpa had been sitting on the porch of the creamery all day visiting with people. Now they were all tired and ready to go up to their little house in the north end of town for the night. Dale, Anna and Mama sitting in the back seat of their Model T touring car. Grandpa was sitting in the front seat. Papa was settling himself behind the wheel when Mike Kircher walked over the creamery porch on his way home for the night. He was a friend of Uncle Hank's son, Melvin. They had been working on an old car in Papa's tin shed and when Papa needed pliers or wrenches or the hammer - they were nowhere to be found.

"Mike, I'd like to talk to you a minute," Papa stopped him beside the car. "I wish you and Melvin would bring back the pliers you borrowed out of the--"

"Why, you son-of-a-bitch , I never stole your pliers!"

Papa came uncorked. His doubled fist caught Mike's chin as Papa jumped over the steering wheel and landed on the ground where Mike had stood just a second before.

But Mike was running and screaming, "I'm a minor! I'm a minor! I'm only a kid!" Papa caught him in about ten steps.

"I'll bring 'em back, I'll bring 'em back!" he blubbered. Mike was more than six feet tall and raw-boned but he wasn't twenty-one years old yet. Papa let him go after a bitter tongue-lashing when he promised that he and Melvin would bring back the tools.

Grandpa Jordan talked all the next day about how Papa could hit a guy, jump over a steering wheel, land a-running and catch him in ten steps. "I guess you'd have to say," he concluded, "that nobody better call an Allison a son-of-a-bitch."

But the situation worsened with the washing machine. Anna was washing dishes the next day in the kitchen when she overheard little Junior telling his mother, "Guess what I did, Mama. I hid their old washing machine lid so nobody can use that washer." And Louise just laughed like she thought it was cute.

Of course, Anna reported the crime to Dale and Mama over in the cream station and Dale devised a plan for getting it back. Anna's clever big brother - he was already twelve and she wouldn't be eleven till November - could always solve a problem. The problem was that te washing machine couldn't be used without the water-tight lid because all the water would splash out when it was swung back and forth.

Anna went back across the street to sweep the floor and watch out the window. Soon she saw Dale playing in the soft sand under the big maple tree across the street. He had a wooden train engine and four cars and was busy making train tracks. It wasn't long before little Junior and two more boys were helping with the train project.

Anna was busy making a coverlet for her doll's bed when she heard five-year-old Junior's high-pitched voice, "Mama, I dug their old washing machine lid out of the ash pile and put it back on the porch. And I told Dale I had found it for him."

His mother's voice, "What did you do that for? Why didn't you let them look for it for awhile?"

"'Cause Dale said that his dad had gone to Minneapolis to get the sheriff to look for that ole' lid. That's why," Junior sniffled.

"Aw, he was just pullin' your leg. The sheriff wouldn't make a trip out here just to find a little ol' lid for a washing machine. You should never have let on -" his mother scolded.

"What's this?" John Stilwell's deeper voice, "Louise, what do you mean teachin' that boy to steal. Sonny, you did just right, and don't go carryin' off stuff that don't belong to you anymore, either."

"Well, you don't have to put up with that tribe splashing around on your back porch either. Those kids spill more water filling that boiler than they ever get in it. I don't know why that lazy woman don't just do her own work and get it over with," Louise fumed.

"What's that got to do with teachin' a little five-year-old boy to steal?" John persisted, "I suppose you want him to grow up to be just like all your brothers - they've all been in jail for stealin'."

"They have not all been in jail - only Mike - and Mike wouldn't have got caught if he hadn't gone back after that last batch of chickens...," Louise paused for breath.

"My God, Louise, how dumb can you get?" John went back in his barber shop where their voices rose and fell but Anna could no longer hear what they were saying.

That one episode was over but, at least, housework was never boring since they had moved to the Dyer house.

****

July 4, 1927

"Anna, that darn phone is ringing...," Dale was reaching over to help Anna put the box of picnic supplies in the back of the truck. "Listen. There it goes again," he said, resignedly.

They had hoped against hope all week long that Fred Windhorst would hold off starting to cut wheat till the 5th of July. Papa had promised to be on hand when the new combine started into the field of ripe wheat on Fred Windhorst's farm. In fact, wild horses couldn't keep him away from the job. Papa was going to haul the wheat to the elevator in Wells from the new combine - the very first one in the whole area. He's explained it was a big machine that moved through a field to cut the wheat and thresh it at the same time. It cut the wheat straw off - chopped it all up inside the machine and knocked the kernels of wheat out of the heads. The wheat ran into a big bin in the top of the machine. Then Papa would drive his truck under the spout and the wheat would pour into the truck box. He'd haul it to town and sell it for Fred Windhorst the very same day.

Remembering the long process of harvesting, Anna understood why Papa was so excited about hauling that wheat. A binder usually cut the wheat in June and bound it in bundles. A half-dozen men shocked that wheat and then they waited their turn to have a threshing machine come to their field in August. Teams of horses hauled bundles on hayracks from the field where they had been in shocks. Six hayracks would be along side a big threshing machine that was blowing straw up onto a high stack and pouring a thin stream of wheat into a wagon beside it. Anna shivered as she thought how she had learned that one couldn't play in a fresh straw stack. Papa had to lose his turn on the bundle wagon to come up on that stack and pull her out.

This new invention wouldn't make any straw stack - it would just chew up the straw and spit it out the back and string it all over the field. Then they'd plow it under and make the soil better for raising another crop. It was going to take twelve horses to pull it and Fred Windhorst would be up before dawn to get those horses into their harness and ready to start as soon as the sun had dried the dew off the ripe wheat.

The phone in the cream station across the street kept ringing. Dale and Anna were all dressed up to go to the big 4th of July Celebration in Markley's Grove in Minneapolis. There was to be a band and a speaker and fireworks. They had a tank full of watermelons they had hauled from Oklahoma, the paper said. There would be flags and hats and Dale had a pocketful of spit devils. Anna had on shoes and so did Dale. You couldn't grind spit devils on cement with your bare heels. But, best of all - Markley Grove had a big wavy slippery-slide and Anna loved to climb to the top of it and let go and feel the wind in her hair as she came swishing down with her skirts flying only to alight running - around to climb the steps again. They had been there one other time when the Modern Woodmen had their annual picnic - that was a long time ago.

The phone kept ringing. Mama and Papa were still inside the Dyer House getting ready to go. Mama had baked pies and fried chicken and packed the basket and now she was getting dressed up to go. Papa still had to shave.

"Shall I go tell Dad the phone's ringing?" Dale asked and Anna knew he was handing down a sentence of death on all their big plans for getting to go to a big celebration on the 4th of July.

"Yes, I guess you'd better," she said sadly. "If they'd have hurried a little bit more we'd have been gone - but Papa wouldn't miss hauling that wheat for anything."

Fred Windhorst had a windmill and a big tank with a watermelon floating in it that 4th of July. They had their picnic up there and Mama got to go along. They had fried chicken and home-made ice cream. Rovena and Anna went swimming in the tank. "It really wasn't a bad way to spend the 4th of July," Anna reflected as she drifted off to sleep that night; it was just that nothing compared with that big slippery-slide and she wondered if she would ever get another chance to slide on it.

****

Summer of '27

The summer of '27 was a good season for the farmers around Wells and Papa had lots of hauling to do. Fred's brother, Ernest, also cut wheat with that new combine. There were cattle and hogs to sell and people were milking as many as twenty head of cows on all the farms around. They'd be milking and separating the cream after dark many nights so they could work in the harvest fields all day.

The women and children raised the chickens, gathered the eggs, tended the gardens, cooked the meals, slopped the hogs, fed the calves, pumped the water, washed the clothes and ran all the errands. Even so, there were times that they had to have hired hands.

Mama was busy testing cream. The ten-gallon cream cans that were furnished by The Concordia Creamery Company would be full every two or three days - enough of them to make a truck load of cream to be hauled on Sunday to Concordia as well as a dozen cans to ship on the train in the middle of the week.

Dale and Anna bought chickens, candled eggs, pumped gas at the visible pump in front of the station, and sold fuses, light bulbs, spark plugs and quarts of oil. The oil came in barrels and had a pump on the top of each barrel. One just asked what weight they wanted and pumped the oil out of that barrel. They sold it by the quart. All the farmers could change their own spark plugs, pour in their own oil and change light bulbs, so, even though Dale and Anna both were small, about seventy pounds big, they could help their mother with all the mechanical sales when Papa wasn't there.

"A man's work is from sun to sun - but a woman's work is never done," Mama used to say, resignedly. Farm work was done with horses and men started to the fields by daylight and had to quit and bring in the teams to be unhitched, unharnessed, curried and fed, often by lantern light that night. Wives and children usually had the milking done and the cows were back out in the pasture. The milk had to be separated. That was done with a separator in the milk house or the end of the kitchen. The separator had a spout for the skim-milk to pour from as well as a spout for the cream to pour into the cream can. The skin milk was fed to the calves. Whoever was the strongest turned the crank on

116

the separator. The separating of cream from milk was done with centrifugal force so the crank had to be turned fast and consistently.

"I get to run the separator, it's my turn tonight," a big girl would say to her smaller brother.

"No, my arm is stronger," her brother argued. The other would have to take the first pail of skim milk and feed the calves and be back to take the second pail from under the spout and slide in the empty pail. Feeding those pushing, shoving unruly calves wasn't nearly as much fun as turning the crank on the separator.

Mash had to be mixed from the milk that had been left to sour from the morning before and fed to the pigs and chickens. Eggs had to be gathered and the baby chicks fed and shut in their pens. There was always dozens of small tasks in the evening as well as in the morning around the farm. Breakfast and supper came after the chores were done and the more hands to help, the sooner they all sat down to the table.

After supper the men had time to take the cream and eggs to town. In 1927 most of the farmers had a car and very few wives drove so they came to town to sell the cream and buy groceries at night. Mama and Papa would be buying cream and eggs, pumping gas and oil, and buying a few of their young roosters. Copeman's Store would be open as well as the hardware store, often till midnight. Much of the business in Wells was done by gas lamps and lanterns.

Dale played "Wolf and Dog" with the farm boys and Anna got to play with all the little girls who came to town. Social life and work were all tied together in the "Roaring Twenties."

****

"Let me live in a house by the side of the road
And be a friend to man.
excerpt from "The House By The Side Of The
Road," by Sam Walter Foss.

Charlie Allison woke Stella up before the sun hit the east upstairs window in the Dyer House that morning the last week in July of 1927, "Stella, I'm going to build us a house across the street just north of the cream station. There's plenty of room there for a house 24 by 28 and still leave room for a driveway beside the tin shed. I'm goin' over and stake it out while you're gettin' breakfast."

Stella was used to Charlie's rapid decisions - to buy a new truck - to do today - what most people would think about for tomorrow or put off indefinitely. But - build a house! That was something she'd like to think about for enough time to have it just the way she wanted it. That was quite an undertaking! Stella sat up in bed - in time to see Charlie disappearing down the stairs.

When Charlie came back across the street for breakfast, he had already called Charley Comfort and Everett Payne and asked them to bring their teams and slips to dig the basement.

Anna and Dale were up and downstairs for breakfast. "Papa, will I have a bedroom of my own in our new house?" queried Anna, getting a word in edgewise between the rapid plans that Papa was outlining between bites. He could lay up the sidewalls of the basement in a couple of evenings - and he wouldn't turn down any hauling jobs, couldn't afford to - he said.

"Oh, sure. A house that's 24 by 28 has room for a front room and a kitchen and three bedrooms - plenty big enough for anybody. And with a big basement under it - the same size, we'll have more room than we know what to do with," Papa assured them. "Oh, yes, I almost forgot to tell you, Stella, there's a three-gallon can of cream on the scales somebody must have dropped off - they'll probably be by for their check before too long." Papa was on his way - he had a load of chickens to sell in Salina and hardware and groceries to bring back to Copemans and Overtons. "Just tell Charley and Everett to start digging between those stakes and I'll be back to help put in the finishing touches this afternoon."

"Doggonet all! That's just the way Charlie always does me," Mama fumed, more to herself than to her children. "'Oh, yes, Stella, there's a three-gallon can of cream waiting for you' - and - 'Oh, yes, Stella, I'm going to build a house' - and, 'Oh, sure, it'll be plenty big enough for anybody.'"

"Mama, aren't you glad Dad's building us a house?" Dale asked as he finished his pancakes and paused as he hurried out to help Papa load the crates of chickens.

"Well, I guess so," Mama said. "I'd just like to be asked something, some time instead of being told all the time," she paused, and as the voices and noise from the Stilwell side of the house drowned out her words, her face changed. "I'm sure I will be, Dale, when I've had time to think about it," Mama said. "It's just that Charlie goes at everything too fast for me. Of course I'm pleased."

Dale hurried out and Anna took up the discussion, "I'll be glad when it's done and we can move out of this one room downstairs and the three big rooms upstairs. And we won't have to keep our voices down and strain our ears to hear what the Stilwells are saying just through that door."

"Anna, eavesdropping is wrong but I quite agree: living so close to another family is no way to live for long if one can do otherwise. Charlie hasn't liked living here at all but I worry about the cost of a new five-room house, things like that. But, if Charlie thinks we can afford it and he can do it, I'm sure he can. We'll just have to help him all we can. I'd better get across the street and test that cream before that customer comes back and wants his check," Mama finished as she hurried out.

118

Charley Comfort and Everett Payne arrived across the street before Anna had the breakfast dishes done and put away. She ran across the street to watch them as they broke the ground for the new house. The ground scraped away easily - almost like brown sugar, she thought. Anna loved the ground in Wells anyway - it was never muddy because it was so sandy. Of course, when the wind blew, it whipped up the sand and stung one's face. About four feet down the scraper turned up a sardine can! Sand had drifted in there between Papa's big machine shed and the cream station - four feet of it since people had been eating sardines in Wells. Well, it wouldn't happen much longer! Papa would have a house there before long.

Charlie Allison took no time for food or water, much less sleep. He hauled in the bricks for the basement walls and foundation, laid the bricks himself, hauled cattle, pigs, chickens, cream, groceries, feed, hardware and anything anyone wanted hauled for hire and brought back lumber, shingles, nails, all the things it took to build a house. His hammer and saw could be heard far into the night.

"I want to get this house ready for us to move into before school starts, and that's just a month away," Papa explained - and he did it too!

Papa hired a finish carpenter to make the window and door frames. There were nine window frames and two door frames. The carpenter charged him $22. "I made twice that much with my truck hauling while he was making those frames so I just couldn't afford to take the time," Papa apologized to Mama. He also hired several men to help him shingle the house. It took a lot of shingles because the sidewalls were shingled as well as the roof.

"Let's put our name on this inside sheeting before they put on the shingles," Dale suggested.

Armed with a hammer and nail, each, they stood side by side on the south side of their new house and hammered dents in the new wood, their names and the date: August, 1927.

Their house was ready for the house-warming so they had a dance and everyone came from far and near before Papa put in the partitions.

"There's still a lot to do on it," Papa said, "but we're going to move in before school starts. I made $274 hauling things for hire and still finished building it in one month. Stella just couldn't slow me down."

"We'll paint these drywalls for a few years - we can paper them later - and Stella is going to get to pick out the paint," he added with a grin.

Mama heaved a sigh as she smiled and said, "Why, Charlie, you've done so well making all the decisions, why stop now?"

****

The Death Of Floyd Collins

"Oh come, all you young people,
And listen while I tell
The fate of Floyd Collins,
A lad we all know well;
His face was fair and handsome,
His heart was true and brave,
His body now lies sleeping
In a lonely sand stone cave."

The radio brought the news of Floyd Collins into every home across the land in the twenties. Newspapers that came daily in the cities and weekly or biweekly on the mail routes had kept people abreast of what was going on in the world if they were inclined toward reading. But the radio brought tragedies home through daily updates on progress and people gathered around the radio in the lumberyard to see if they were going to get that poor boy's foot free from the big boulder that had rolled on it down in that cave in Kentucky.

"Papa, if you were there you could break that boulder and get his foot loose, couldn't you?" Dale asked.

"Well, I'd sure try, but the paper says people are coming from far and near to see if they can help. - Everybody has an idea but nothing seems to work. He must be wedged in a crevice that the boulder made when it rolled onto his foot. They can't get to him or they could amputate his foot and pull him out with ropes," Papa worried aloud.

Anna shivered, "I'm never going down in one of those places. The paper said his mother begged him not to go. Why would he want to go down in a place like that anyway? I didn't go to sleep for a long time thinking about him fastened down there so he can't get out."

"Oh, there are a lot of caves in Kentucky that have never been explored," Papa said. "And curiosity kills more than cats when it comes to wanting to probe into the unknown. I was never very crazy about wanting to go down in caves either."

"Charlie, I worry when you go down in wells to clean them out for people. You shouldn't do that either," Mama said.

"Stella, I always put a fruit jar with a lighted candle in it - down on a rope and if the candle goes out I don't go down. Too many people have died going down in wells without checking to see if the air is bad in the bottom of a well," Papa explained. "I'm going over to the lumberyard and see if they've got any more news on that boy."

Graham & Fury Lumber Co. had put new Atwater Kent radios in all their lumber yards in all the towns around to increase the communication to their operators. When they were going to have a sale they'd put an advertisement on the radio at the station in Abilene. Frank Sommers ran the lumberyard and he knew to listen at a certain time of day to pick up the items that would be on sale that week.

Anna wished she could go along with Papa when he went across from the creamery to hear any news - he and Dale left as she said to Mama, "Dale said that they put on earphones to hear and he heard, 'This is KDKA, Pittsburgh, Pennsylvania.'"

"Oh, well, now, Honey, - girls don't want to go over there - there's just a bunch of men and boys hanging around the lumber yard. Charlie will be back soon enough if there's any news. The paper said that the Ladies Aid from a church had brought in pies and coffee and soda pop and set up a stand nearby and a local grocer was setting up a stand to sell hot dogs. So I guess they are going to stay right there till they get that poor young man out," Mama explained to Anna.

"I just wish I could put on those earphones and hear something sometime. Where is the paper?" Anna said.

Mama arose from the padded seat by the cash register, lifted the lid and handed her the newspaper that had come that morning.

"Oh, how the news did travel,
Oh how the news did go,
It traveled through the papers
And over the radio:
A rescue party gathered,
His life they tried to save,
But his body now lies sleeping
In a lonely sandstone cave.

But on that fatal morning
The sun rose in the sky,
The workers still were busy,
We'll save him by and by;
But oh, how sad the ending,
His life could not be saved,
His body then was sleeping
In a lonely sand stone cave.

Young people, oh, take warning
From Floyd Collins' fate
And give your heart to Jesus
Before it is too late;
It may not be a sand cave
In which we find our tomb,
But at the Bar of Judgment
We, too must meet our doom."

(Excerpts from a long song written by Rev. Andrew Jenkins in 1925.)

Anna didn't hear 'The Death of Floyd Collins' sung, all its ten verses, till some time later. The very first year after they moved into their new house, Papa built a stand with doors on it so he could hide the battery and the Allisons had a new Kolster radio in their living room. It had a loud speaker on top and one could get stations as far away as New York or Los Angeles. But the sad plight of the young adventurer who went down in that cave in Kentucky would remain in her memory always. She heard it first in the back of Copeman's store. Their radio also had a loud speaker. An additional verse was added:

> *"The mining experts gathered.*
> *They sought to find a plan*
> *To lift poor Floyd's body;*
> *From far beneath the sand;*
> *And oh, how they did struggle,*
> *With hearts so brave and stout,*
> *But the cave that swallowed Collins*
> *Would never let him out."*

****

Play Ball!

It looked extremely rocky for the Mudville nine that day:
The score stood two to four, with but one inning left to play,
So, when Cooney died at second, and Burrows did the same,
A pallor wreathed the features of the patrons of the game.

A straggling few got up to go, leaving there the rest,
With that hope that springs eternal within the human breast.
For they thought: "If only Casey could get a whack at that,
They'd put even money now, with Casey at the bat."

"Casey at the Bat"
by Ernest Lawrence Thayer

Uncle Ney could recite all thirteen verses of "Casey at the Bat" as well as many other poems and Mother said he liked to play ball too. Mama must had played some ball too when she was a girl going to Meridith school up in Cloud County. She told how Grandpa Jordan was able to walk up to the school on Sunday afternoons to watch the local ball players when he felt it was too hot to get out in the sun for any other activity.

Papa and Dale went to ball games and Anna even helped Dale save up money to buy a ball glove - a must if you were going to play ball.

Wells had always had a baseball team - in fact, a silver Loving Cup, hung on the north wall of the Woodman Hall - a trophy from 1910 when Wells won all but one game in the whole season.

The entire community had a hand in the Woodman team. Papa said the uniforms were made by the womenfolks and the Woodman Lodge bought the material. The cup was presented to the team at the end of their victorious season by the A.J. Reach Company of Philadelphia because, during the season the team had bought a gross (twelve dozen) of baseballs.

"There were two requirements for players," Papa said. "You had to be a Woodman and you had to have a fighting spirit."

Players on the Wells team at that time were:
> Charles Goodfellow, center field.
> Frank Goodfellow, catcher.
> Bert Goodfellow, shortstop.
> John Goodfellow, manager and 2nd base.
> Irvin Baker, pitcher and 3rd base.
> Bert Baker, pitcher and 3rd base
> Herb Kay, 1st base.
> Ollie Clanton, left field.
> Carl Comfort, right field.
> Fred Payne, coach at third base.
> Hallie Payne, score keeper.
> Clarence Brown, umpire.

In those days there were few cars. People traveled by team and wagon, horse and buggy or a posse with fast horses.

"One time we borrowed a car in Minneapolis to go to Culver to play," Charley Goodfellow recalled. "It was a racing car and I think we maybe travelled 25 miles an hour. Folks thought we were travelling too fast. They were afraid we would kill ourselves."

Claude Baker, Irv Baker's son had been a mascot for that famous team. They lived north of Wells and it was two or three miles to any school so Claude stayed with Papa and Mama a week at a time before Dale or Anna were born and had been a regular visitor all their lives. So they heard the stories about that Woodman League team of 1910 whenever the subject of baseball came up.

However, Anna was not prepared for the scene in the living room when she came home from school in the fall of 1927. At least half a dozen men and women were sitting around the radio listening to the World Series - several of them may have been players on that team in 1910 - all grown up and sitting around listening to some other champion team play ball.

Mama had a big poster on the kitchen table, had a box score for each team set up on it with their names in batting order, RBI's (runs batted in), PO - put-outs, SB - stolen bases, etc. She really enjoyed the World Series as did everyone else in Wells who could gather around the radio and hear those games instead of reading about them in the newspapers the next day. Radio brought the world right into the front room! Anna found that each one had picked the winner and there were baseball pools all over town. For a quarter one could pick a number up to ten and maybe if one had drawn a seven and the score ended three to four, one could win two dollars and fifty cents.

"Mama, that's gambling, isn't it?" asked Anna.

"Oh, well, honey, if it's all in fun it's not so bad, especially if it's right in your own house and you can stand to lose a quarter every day for a week - there's seven games, you know," Mama explained.

But Anna knew it was just for the grown-ups. Children did well to have a nickel for candy at any one time.

To have a house right next to the cream station was certainly a luxury for Mama. And the radio furnished entertainment right at home for the whole family - especially when they had company. Mama could run out to the cream station and test the cream in about thirty minutes and be back in the house to take the cake out of the oven and the radio would have entertained the company while she was gone.

There were three cans of cream around the scales out in the cream station that afternoon when Anna came home from school - they belonged to three of the men sitting in the house listening to that World Series game. They were in no hurry - Mama could test their cream later.

****

*"There was a little girl
And she had a little curl
Right in the middle of her forehead;*

*When she was good
She was very, very good
And when she was bad she was horrid!"*
old Nursery Rhyme

"Well, I wish I had a little curl," Anna thought as she looked in the mirror at the plain little face with the shiny brown straight bangs across the forehead.

"Pretty is as pretty does," Mama had said as Anna went out to the kitchen sink to wash her face and comb her hair.

"Myrtle and Norline had made spit curls at each side of their foreheads and combed their hair back when they came in to doll themselves up for the dance last Saturday night," Anna mused as she set the glass down.

Anna made spit curls with soap and a little water...from a soap dish and a glass of water on her dresser.

Anna had been in the Big Room for three years now. She remembered last fall when she and Mary wrote poetry about Avis and

124

stood around in the Big Room at the Noon Hour while the teacher was gone for lunch - reading the verses aloud:

> *"Look at her,*
> *She thinks she's pretty*
> *With her painted face.*
>
> *The cupid's bow lips are drawn from a stick*
> *And the curls are made of soap...ick!*
>
> *She may think she's pretty but..*
> *I think she's dippy."*

Avis had cried and gone down to the basement and wouldn't come up when the afternoon classes were called. Miss Boettcher had gone down and brought her up to class.

When it was time for recess she announced, "Anna, you and Mary will stay in this recess. The rest of the class is dismissed."

Anna's face burned as she remembered Miss Boettcher's words: "I think a word to the wise will be sufficient," she said. "Teasing others about their appearance will not be permitted in this school. Is that understood?"

Mary and Anna nodded dumbly.

"You are dismissed," she said. Mary and Anna were forced to go out in the yard where the rest of the school children gathered round to tease them.

"You had to stay in, Ya, Ya!" and, "What did you do?"

"I would have liked to have danced around Avis and sang, 'Teacher's Pet, Teacher's Pet! Bawlin' to the teacher an' what do you get?' but I knew what we'd get if we teased Avis any more," Anna was thinking. She could almost feel sorry for Avis if she hadn't been so pretty. Avis was fourteen when Anna was eleven.

"I don't dare use any of these samples in the daytime. Papa and Mama both would have a fit. Crystal gave them to me just to wear on Saturday nights." She put the lipsticks and little tins of powder back in the drawer. "I'm just too short," Anna thought. She tipped the swinging mirror forward so she could see all of her as she stood in front of the big three-drawer dresser Papa had brought home from a farm sale right after they had moved into their own house.

Papa was always buying things for Anna - like the awful high-topped shoes that were her size last year. She hated to wear them to school but she wouldn't hurt his feelings so she wore them a few days and it was one of those days when they took a school picture for the whole year. And there she was with those corny high-top shoes on and all the rest of the girls had on slippers. And her flannel underskirt was showing too! Dale even had his hair slicked back. He had gone down to Mrs. Copeman and borrowed one of her old silk hose. She told him he could cut off the top and use it for a sock-cap to sleep in. That way his hair would be slicked back for half a day at least.

"Well, at least I won't go to school with my underskirt hanging - I can see the bottom of my skirt. And my beautiful new slippers. I get to wear them to school. They even have one-inch heels. Papa took me into a real shoe store in Salina and paid $5.00 for them....."

"Anna, come and set the table for breakfast, the pancakes are ready," Mama broke into Anna's 'primping' as she called it. Anna knew that Mama felt Papa had paid too much for her shoes but she only felt a little guilty as she tripped around the table placing the knives and forks at each place, making sure the spoon-holder and butter dish were on. Mama was making hot syrup so she got the pitcher from the cupboard.

"Don't you look nice!" Papa said as he came through the back door and Dale even turned as he was washing his face and observed, "Yeah, and she's wearing spit curls too!"

And Mama only said, "Now if she behaves as well as she looks she will have a fine day. Dale, did you remember to wash your ears?" So Anna knew that Mama liked her shoes too.

****

Election-1928

"Republicans are always doing things for the big companies. Mama says we should quit protecting the big companies with high tariffs and have free trade so prices of the things we have to buy wouldn't be so high. Mama and Papa are going to vote for Al Smith," Anna said at school one day in the fall of 1928.

"But he's a Catholic and he wants to bring back liquor," Mary Kinsey said. "My Papa says the Democrats have made a poor choice of a candidate."

"He's for states' rights to choose if they want to prohibit the sale of liquor. He just wants to repeal Prohibition in every state because it isn't working," Anna's brown eyes flashed as she spoke. All the Jordans could argue politics and she'd been listening to Mama discussing the issues with Grandpa Jordan as far back as she could remember and, now, the radio was bringing speeches into everyone's living room.

"Who says it isn't working?" Miss Edith asked.

"Papa says that anyone who has a habit of drinking can get liquor from a bootlegger but he has to pay twice what it used to cost," Anna explained.

"Has your papa bought any?" Avis asked.

"No. But he says that the dances down at the Woodman Hall are harder to run than they used to be. Drunks stayed in the saloon and didn't bother neighborhood dances. And now he or George McKain have to order someone out who has a bottle in his car nearly every Saturday night," Anna explained.

126

"The dances should be closed down, too," Helen Miller said.

"What good would that do but spoil the good times for everybody else?" Dale asked.

"Dancing and drinking are both sinful, my Dad says," said Chester Miller.

"Chester, you can sin anywhere, even in church," Anna retorted.

"I'm not sure we should be discussing sin or politics either," Miss Edith spoke up. "It's time for the five-minute bell."

All fall the discussions kept up and became more heated, particularly about Catholics. Robbie Comfort came to school telling that a group of Ku Klux Klan were seen out on a hillside over by Ada - burning a cross.

"Why were they doing that?" Mary asked.

"They are against Catholics - they think that if Al Smith were elected they'd drive out all other religions - we'd have Catholic Wars like they did in the old days," Robbie explained.

"That's what the Pilgrims came to this country for in the first place, Robbie. They couldn't do that," Anna argued.

"That's right, Robbie. Freedom of religion is a Constitutional right," Miss Edith said.

When Anna came home from school telling what Robbie had said, Papa added to the gossip that was going round: "Yes, I heard today in Salina when I was visiting in the Salina Mercantile while they put up Copeman's order, that when they were building the chapel out at Marymount the dray wagons kept hauling great big solid wooden boxes from the depot that it took two or three men to lift and finally they dropped one of them on purpose. It burst open and it was filled with gun parts. They were storing those boxes under the pulpit."

"Charlie, did you ask that man if he had been going to the Ku Klux Klan meetings?" Mama asked.

"No, but I know a lot of people are," Papa said.

"Who, Papa,?" Dale wanted to know.

"Well, nobody will come right out and say they've been there but I've been told where they are meeting by men who have seen them around their bonfires in their white sheets and white masks. And some have seen crosses burning out on the hillsides," Papa explained. "I thought I might get in my truck tonight and drive over by Ada and see if I could see any burning crosses."

"Charlie, I wish you wouldn't," Mama spoke quietly. "Paying any attention at all to that kind of scare tactics only adds fuel to their fires of hatred they are trying to stir up against Catholics. It only looks like an awful waste of good white sheets. And they are so high priced to buy. The price of cotton to the cotton farmers keeps going down while workers get less for picking cotton. And, of course the high tariff on anything shipped in protects those big mill owners so that they can get richer and richer, selling high-priced sheeting."

"I know you're right, Stella, but no one is discussing the real issues this year, just booze and Catholics, and Tammany Hall, whatever that amounts to." Papa went back to his paper and Anna skipped down to Copeman's store. She hadn't seen Crystal for several days.

Business was slow between four o'clock and time for the farmers to be done milking and chores and ready to come to town in the evening. No one was in the front of the store so Anna went on back. She paused in the Dry Goods and Notions section. The new bolts of rayon goods were beautiful.

"Mama didn't think rayon would wear well or wash well either but Anna wished she could cut out a dress for herself out of some of it. Mama ordered remnants out of the catalog and Anna made plain cotton print dresses for herself and her mother, too....But when she bought yard goods for nice dresses, she had Angie Comfort sew for her," Anna was thinking to herself as she wandered between the bolts.

"Come back and listen to this speaker," Mrs. Copeman invited her. She had two big oranges in her hands. "You and Crystal can peel these and we'll have an afternoon snack."

Of course Anna was always hungry, she forgot her interest in the new rayon yard goods as she settled her self on a couch by a counter in Copeman's make-shift living room. Mrs. Copeman and her daughter always made her feel welcome.

"What's been going on at school lately?" asked Crystal.

"Have you heard about the Ku Klux Klan?" Anna volunteered and was quite unprepared for the startled reaction of both Mrs. Copeman and her daughter. Since neither Gene nor Ocea were anywhere around she almost wondered if they had gone to organize another meeting of that dreadful organization.

They neither one spoke for a moment, then Mrs. Copeman spoke crisply, "I think they do a good work for people in times like these - somebody needs to do something to keep that Catholic from getting in the White House."

Anna ventured a question, "How will that harm the people?" Mrs. Copeman was a big woman - many people were a little in awe of her - they saw her as a bossy woman who snapped the paper-clip on her pencil as she ordered her husband, Ocea as well as her brother-in-law, Gene, around. Even her daughter, Crystal, who would be twenty-one in time to vote that fall, always jumped when she spoke.

"Harm the people? Harm the people? Why, we'd be in a civil war in thirty days! The Catholics would take over this country."

Anna looked at Crystal and saw actual fear in her eyes. Still Anna said, "I think Mama and Papa are going to vote for him."

"Well, they'd better arm themselves," Mrs. Copeman snapped. "There will be blood in the streets!"

Crystal started to cry and Anna told her, "He probably won't get elected, anyway; Mama says a Catholic never has."

"Well, that should tell you something about the people's good judgment," Viola Copeman said. Anna remembered that she had to get back home for supper.

The word, 'Democrat' got to be more dirty as the month wore on - still Mother never wavered in her belief that the economy of the country was the real issue and that the laboring classes should organize, particularly the farmers, to have more power in Congress instead of allowing big companies to control legislation so that the poor farmer, unorganized and without a power bloc in Congress would be the last man thought of. Her words fell on deaf ears - even Papa's, it seemed. At least, he said less and less, probably realizing that words were useless against the scare tactics put forth by the Republicans.

At last Election Day came and every eligible voter came to Wells. Both Ladies Aids were selling pie and coffee. No one was discussing who they were voting for but everyone was there to vote and wait for the votes to be counted. The radios were turned on and people gathered to hear what little news was offered. Little came in till midnight. It was as if the nation was holding its breath to see what was going to happen.

Anna was in the back room of Copeman's Store with a number of people when the election news came in that Al Smith had carried New York City.

Crystal was sitting behind the counter running the radio. She dropped her head in her arms, the tears starting, she exclaimed, "The Pope will be in the White House in the morning!!"

Papa came home from the Woodman Hall as Anna was leaving the store. They had finished counting votes for Grant Township. He said Al Smith got sixteen votes in the whole township.

Anna ran ahead of him up to the cream station where her mother and Dale were waiting, "Mama, Al Smith only got sixteen votes in this township - but he's carried New York City."

The next morning it was announced that Herbert Hoover had won by a landslide, carrying all but five states.

"Stella, don't you wonder who the other fourteen votes were in Grant Township?" Papa asked.

"Well, at least we'll be able to say, 'I told you so' to nearly everybody in the whole country one of these days," Mama assured him.

And she was proved right, when, just eight months after Hoover took office the stock market crashed in October of 1929.

****

"The breaking waves dashed high
On a stern and rock-bound coast;
And the woods against a stormy sky,
Their giant branches tossed
And the heavy night hung dark
The hills and waters o'er-
When a band of exiles moored their bark
On a wild New England shore----"
(from 'Landing of the Pilgrim Fathers)

Anna's mind jumped to:

> *"Tell me not in mournful numbers*
> *Life is but an empty dream!-*
> *For the soul is dead that slumbers*
> *And things are not what they seem.*
>
> *Life is real! Life is earnest!*
> *And the grave is not the goal;*
> *Dust thou art, to dust returnest,*
> *Was not spoken of the soul."*
>
> *(from a* Psalm of Life)

"No, that won't do," Anna thought. She wished Mr. Stauffer, her sixth grade teacher, hadn't assigned just two verses of two different poems to be learned for recitation all in one day - her mind always mixed them up when she was reaching for something to calm her thoughts.

> *Be strong!*
> *We are not here to play, to dream, to drift;*
> *We have hard work to do, and loads to lift;*
> *Shun not the struggle-face it; 'tis God's gift.*
> *Be strong!*
>
> *(by Maltbi Davenport Babcock)*

"That's it," Anna told herself. She had a decision to make. "Shun not the struggle, face it." - that's what she'd do!

Anna was never sick. She had never been absent or tardy since she had started to school in Wells in the first grade. Now she was in the eighth grade and she had complained of the sore throat till Mama decided to look in her throat: "My. Goodness, Charlie, look at this child's tonsils!" Papa always worried about Dale and Anna's health; he dropped his paper and arose to take a look.

"We'll just take you down to Dr. Hinshaw, right now," he said, "while I've got time and you are home from school. Stella, maybe he can give Anna something to gargle with that will heal up her throat. The vinegar and salt we've been prescribing hasn't done much to help."

But Dr. Hinshaw looked in Anna's throat and said, "These tonsils have kept her from catching all sorts of diseases but now they've had it. They are pitted and badly inflamed. They should come out - the sooner the better."

"Well, Doc, when can you do it and what will it cost?" asked Papa. He was never one to quibble when something had to be done.

130

"Any time you are ready," Dr. Hinshaw said to Anna. "How old are you, little lady?

"I'll be thirteen in November," Anna said as she drew up to her full height.

"Let's see what you weigh, honey. Sixty-two pounds - that's a little light for her age, Charlie. But she'll probably gain and start to grow pretty fast when she gets those diseased tonsils out," Dr. Hinshaw talked to Papa while Anna looked at his equipment. She had heard Avis describe her experience with getting her tonsils out. It all sounded pretty gruesome.

"Let's see, you've got a brother, Dale, haven't you, Anna?" Dr. Hinshaw interrupted her worried thoughts, "How old is he?"

"He was already fourteen in June," Anna replied. "And he doesn't weigh much more than I do - and he's not much taller either. But we never get sick. We have neither one ever missed a day of school in all eight years."

"Boys don't take a spurt of growing as fast as girls do but when they do they run off and leave little sisters," Dr. Hinshaw explained. "That's quite a record - never being absent or tardy for eight years - both of you."

"Maybe we could take your tonsils out on Friday afternoon and you'd be ready to go back to school the next Monday," Dr. Hinshaw suggested. "Oh, your throat would be a little sore but you must have gone to school today with a sore throat, didn't you?"

Anna had to admit that she did, and her head ached, too, but she wouldn't mention that.

"Doc, how big an operation is this?" Papa was getting concerned about Anna not wanting to miss a day of school - when she should be thinking of getting well so she could start growing as she should.

"Well, I do it two ways. I use chloroform and put children to sleep - it takes a little longer and costs a little more - $40, for that. Bigger people just sit in this chair and I take their tonsils out with a local anesthetic. I just charge $25 for that," Dr. Hinshaw explained. "The chloroform makes children a little sicker at the time - but it works better for them. You can decide - no hurry till we get ready to do it."

"Maybe, Anna can get excused at the last recess next Friday," the doctor suggested. "That way she'd have two days and three nights to heal. She could be eating fried potatoes by the next Monday," Dr. Hinshaw laughed.

"All right, Doc, we'll be in at about 3:00 next Friday and we'll decide how she wants it done by then," Papa agreed.

Neither Papa nor Anna had much to say on the way home. He did say, "Now, Anna, don't worry about the difference between $25 and $40. I"m going to spend $40 either way. If you decide to sit up in that chair and watch the doctor take your tonsils out, I'll spend the other $15 on a new winter coat for you. But you have to have a new winter coat, either way - so don't let your decision rest on that."

Anna was remembering what Avis had to say about getting her tonsils out. Robbie Comfort, who was also in their class in grade school had his tonsils out at the same time. Robbie's father talked to Mrs. Hanes about Dr. Cheney, in Minneapolis doing tonsils in a sort of assembly line process and Avis's mother gave Bob Comfort the money to pay for Avis's operation. Robbie and Avis had it done at the same time. Avis said that Robbie fought the chloroform and hit the nurse who tried to make him count to ten.

Robbie said, "I didn't mean to hit her. I just didn't want that mask put over my face."

He was supposed to be asleep before he got to ten but he kept counting and fighting the mask they tried to put over his face.

Anna smiled as she thought about Robbie's experience - but it really wasn't funny at all.

Avis said she cried, but then, Avis cried when Anna and Mary wrote poetry about her. She cried when she wasn't really hurt at all. She said it kept her from being hurt a lot of times.

"'Shun not the struggle, face it; 'tis God's gift.' That's what she'd do," Anna thought, "Be Strong!"

"'Faint not-fight on! Tomorrow comes the song.' That's the way that poem ends," she thought. Thank goodness, she had learned it all. Of course, it was only three verses.

"The 'song' will be if I can eat fried potatoes the next Monday - or popcorn, like Robbie did before the week was out...," Anna decided to herself.

By the time Dr. Hinshaw cut out one tonsil with all the sound of tissue being gnawed off - and laid it there on the little round white table beside the chair, Anna felt she'd made the WRONG decision - and that if she even lived through the ordeal of the other one being sawed on - she would so advise anyone would might ask her. "DON'T SIT UP AND WATCH!"

Uncle Phin and Aunt Blanche Comfort had taken Mama and her to the doctor's office in their touring car. They weren't really Anna's aunt and uncle - Papa and Mama weren't blood relatives of anyone in Wells - but everyone in Wells seemed like brothers and sisters if one really needed help. Papa had stayed home to mind the creamery.

As Anna looked back she couldn't recall the extraction of the last tonsil or of getting out of the chair. Her memory started as she was lying with her head on Mama's lap riding home. She was spitting up blood in a coffee can they had brought along on the trip.

"Be Strong! Tomorrow comes the song." That promise of being able to eat popcorn was two weeks away. Anna had no appetite for anything but strawberry pop and lost twelve pounds. However, she was on the mend and growing again by her thirteenth birthday in November.

Dale and Anna would both be graduating next spring - after eight years in Wells Union II. In order to graduate students had to pass the County Examinations with a 75 percent grade average. Otherwise, they would have to continue going to grade school till they passed or reached sixteen years of age. Only then were they allowed to just quit.

During the seventh grade, all the children prepared for the 'county exams' as well as the eighth graders. They went to another school on a designated Saturday in the spring and took an exam in Geography and Spelling. If they didn't pass, then they'd have the eighth grade year to study harder and pass Geography and Spelling as well as all the eighth grade subjects in the exam: Reading, Writing, Arithmetic, American History, Language or Grammar, Physiology, Civil Government and Agriculture.

Dale and Anna always liked school - never missed a day or were tardy all eight years and never wanted to. When they heard anyone talking about 'playing hooky' they could never understand why they'd want to - school was where things were happening that neither one wanted to miss.

Of course, they all looked forward to the 'Last Day of School.' It always came in April after eight months of school. They had a program, got all their awards for perfect attendance and perfect spelling and were handed their grade cards - which told if they had passed or failed and would have to repeat that grade.

Neither Dale nor Anna ever got failing grades, in fact they always competed with one another for the highest grades in their class. Dale usually excelled in Arithmetic and Anna would come out on top in Grammar and maybe, Reading. Perhaps the fact that they were competing with one another is why their grades were always good and neither one ever wanted to miss school - the other would get ahead! Maybe that's what Mama had in mind when she insisted on her 'two little children - just a brother and a sister' always being in the same class.

"Competition is a good word," Mama would say. "It means: to strive together."

"Is that what it means?" Dale asked her one day. "When another buyer comes to Wells to open another cream station, you don't act like it's 'striving together,' do you Mom?" Dale always liked to tease Mother.

Mama explained: "Now, Dale, that's different - there's only so much cream around here to be bought - and I was here first."

"Mom, they say competition is the life of business," Dale continued.

"Not my business," Mama declared.

****

The Little Brown Schoolhouse

The teacher, oh well I remember;
My heart has long kept her a place;
Perhaps by the world she's forgotten,
Her memory no time can efface.
She met us with smiles on the threshold,
And in that rude temple of art,
She left with the skill of a workman
Her touch on the mind and the heart.

Anonymous

Anna gazed down upon the little town of Wells from the hillside pasture a mile north. They had gone on a field trip just to pick daisies that April morning in 1929.

Miss Edith (Yonally) seemed to know when they needed to study and when they needed to relax. School would soon be over in Wells - the Last Day of School was no more than a week away. Tomorrow was Saturday - the day they would be taking the County Exams. There were five eighth graders, who, if they passed those exams would not be going to school in Wells any more.

They sat on the rocks at the top of the hill and ate the sack lunch that each had brought. Someone started naming teachers they had had in the long eight years of grade school. Dale, Anna and Avis had the same eight teachers, but Robbie Comfort had come to the Wells' school just a couple of years ago.

"Let's see now," Avis asked. "Which came first: Gladys or Mildred Comfort?"

"Oh, I can name them all in order," Anna spoke up. "It was Mildred I told that Dale could read the whole primer so you and he got to go on to the First Grade Reader and left Averill Yonally and me in the Primer till Christmas. Then, it was her sister, Gladys Comfort who always let me look at the pictures in the Books of Knowledge when I got my work done in the second grade. Zelma Krenkle kept me in for passing notes to Dale in the third grade"

"Wasn't she the one who tied Charley Sanderson in his seat that year?" Avis asked.

"No," Dale spoke up, "It was the Big Room Teacher, Miss Plunkett, who did that."

"Why did she have to do that?" Robbie wanted to know.

"Some of the big boys locked him in the coal bin downstairs and then he wouldn't come out when the teacher made them unlock it - they kicked the door open and he had the axe. He wouldn't come out when Miss Krenkle told him to, so Miss Plunkett grabbed the axe away from him and carried him upstairs and set him in his seat in the little room. He wouldn't stay in his seat so they tied him. He squirmed loose and ran home," Dale remembered very well.

A Pipe Creek feat & S/Pineapplis 1869-69

The Wells post office opened in 1887. For many years Fred and Cora Comfort were the postmasters. Their living quarters adjoined the post office.

Wells Union 2—The elementary school where Dale and Anna attended without being absent nor tardy for all eight years—from 1921 through 1929.

Charles F. Allison, father to Dale and Anna, was a man of many talents. This photo was taken on his 60th birthday March 28, 1941, in front of the Allison home in Wells.

Stella Jordan Allison, Anna's mother, holds her first granddaughter, Judy Constable. Easter Sunday, 1945.

Dale and Anna Allison. This photo was taken in 1927. Dale was 13 and Anna was 12 years old.

Dale Allison (left) and Jim Constable (right) by Jim's 1936 Plymouth. They were home for the weekend. Both sold magazines for Curtis Publishing Co. the winter of 1937.

Friends from Wells who visited the Constable and Allison families after they moved away in 1945. This was taken in the Sky Room of the ElCortez Hotel, San Diego, Ca. 1947. Left to right: Forrest and Myrtle Hanes, Dale and Evelyn Allison, Jim and Anna Constable, Ruth and Philip Miller.

Friends gathered at the Woodman Hall for the Farewell Dinner for Stella Allison, Anna, Judy and Terry as they were leaving Kansas in November 1945.

Five of the next generation at the Farewell: Judy and Terry Constable, (17 months and 3 months): Jean and Joan Lyne, twin daughters of Edith Yonally Lyne, and Douglas Geist, 11 month old son of Beth and Ernest Geist.

"They sent a member of the school board, Fred Payne, to talk to his mother before they let him back in school," Anna said.

"My goodness, what did you learn that year?" Miss Edith asked.

"Well, one thing I learned was not to fight the teacher and tear her blouse when she said 'Take your seat!'" Avis said.

"Miss Krenkle had strange ways to punish us," Avis went on. "She shook Agnes Payne till her head rattled for writing a note about her sister, Mona, and then she read a note about crayons and accused Anna of writing it to Dale. Anna said, 'No' she didn't write it so she kept her in every recess for two days." Anna was silent so Avis went on: "And wasn't she the teacher who made Kathryn stand in a ring drawn with chalk on the floor - bent over with her fingers touching her toes till she would say she was sorry for writing her spelling words in the palm of her hand and looking at it during Spelling class?" Mary and Kathryn Kinsey were both good pupils; and they both looked uncomfortable so Anna interrupted:

"The next year when I was in the fourth grade we had Miss Glenna Windhorst. I liked her and I read all the books in the little room library - some of them I read twice," Anna said.

Dale got a chance to speak, "Our very first year in the Big Room we had a man-teacher - Earl Goodfellow - I liked him but Swede didn't - he was in the seventh grade. He was fifteen then and bigger than our teacher. Earl was Swede's brother-in-law's little brother, too."

"Now, Swede liked Earl well enough," Avis said, in defense of her big brother, "He just liked to tease."

"And Mr. Goodfellow let him get away with it too - as long as he could," Anna said. "Remember how Swede kept pretending to toss Sumner Payne's cat 'Puddin' to Sumner and saying 'Cattcchhitt, Sumner, Cattcchhitt, Sumner,' till Mr. Goodfellow had to say, 'That will do, Wendell' and how Swede kept tossing his knife - playing mumblety-peg when he went up to sit on the recitation bench for class till the teacher took his knife."

"I'm afraid I would have, too," said Miss Edith.

"But what he expelled him for was having a fit of coughing," his sister, Avis defended him again. "And Mama wouldn't make him go back to school because she felt he was tired of school and was big enough to do something else. He wasn't learning much from Earl anyway."

"Didn't he ever get out of the seventh grade?" Robbie asked.

"No, he was already sixteen before school started in the fall so he went to work," Avis said.

"Gee, maybe I should do that," Robbie teased Miss Edith, "if I don't pass the exams tomorrow."

"You'll pass," Miss Edith assured him. "That's why we've stayed in reviewing evenings. Don't worry."

"Too bad Swede didn't get to go to school to Mr. Stauffer," Anna said. "He made me write the poem, "Trees" twenty-five times because

I forgot to memorize it for the next day's assignment. It's a nice poem, too, but I haven't liked it since. I'll bet Swede would have cleaned up on him."

"Do you suppose that's why I don't like the Preamble to the Constitution?" Avis wondered. "I had to write it twenty-five times that year, too. I'm sure Swede would have done something violent if he'd have been made to write whole poems twenty-five times every time he forgot an assignment."

"Well, you may have to remember the Preamble tomorrow for the test on Civil Government," Miss Edith said.

"Is that the one that begins, 'Four score and seven years ago...'?" Robbie asked with a sly smile for Miss Edith.

Anna was still remembering her dislike for Mr. Stauffer, "You know, I'll never forget the formula for finding the area of a trapezoid but I don't remember it fondly."

"Oh, was that the time Mr. Stauffer jumped up and pranced back to your desk and slapped you when you snapped, 'What rule?' at him?" Avis remembered that all too well.

"Listen, all he would have had to do is tell me that you do the process that is inside the brackets first and then multiply by the altitude and divide by two instead of making me stand up there at the blackboard all the second period making the same mistake over and over and then snapping: 'Take your seat and write that rule twenty-five times!' Who snapped first, anyway?" Anna's eyes flashed in anger, still, as she recalled that indignity. That's one time she bawled in school - and the only time, she thought.

Miss Edith said, "Anna, we'll have you demonstrate that formula when we get back to the schoolhouse - it's one we haven't reviewed and I need to be brushed up on it too." Anna really liked Miss Edith.

"Miss Boettcher was really a nice change after old Stauffer," Jim Wallace said, "And pretty, too."

"Mr Stauffer ran for County Superintendent that fall," Paul Comfort spoke up. "I remember he gave me ten cards with his name on them to pass out to each pupil in the Big Room to take home to his folks."

"Oh, yeah, and you always got to dust the erasers, too," Mary Kinsey said, "Not that I envied you that job!"

"I guess you know what we did with those cards with old Stauffer's picture on them, Don't you, Paul?" Avis asked.

"I do, I knew my folks wouldn't care if we tore them up and dumped them down the toilet hole," Anna said and everybody laughed.

"What was really funny about that was when the next day he was sitting in that swivel chair by his desk at the noon-hour, admiring his picture in the Messenger. He looked around at us and said, 'My name and my face is in many a place,'" Avis said. "I hoped he didn't have any idea what we were all laughing about."

"I must remember not to give my picture to all you children if I run for County Superintendent," Miss Edith laughed. "We've got to be getting back to the schoolhouse so Anna can explain that formula for solving the area of a trapezoid."

When Anna showed up in the cream station that afternoon she was feeling very sad and forlorn - not only were her school days in Wells almost over but she had discovered the start of menstruation for her - her childhood days were over, too!

"What's the matter, honey?" Mama asked when she saw Anna's unhappy face.

Anna started to cry - it wasn't that she had never been told about menstruation. Mama discussed that forthcoming event with her once but she dismissed it from her mind - it had to be a long way off, something for grown-ups to worry about. Now suddenly the Last Day of School was going to be the last day of going barefoot - looking forward to school in Wells - going fishing down at Sand Creek - chasing fireflies at night, running down to the store with three pennies to buy three sticks of whip-licorice - grown-ups didn't do things like that! Anna sobbed.

"Oh, my goodness, whatever it is, it can't be all that bad. Can't you tell me, Anna?" Mama entreated.

At last Anna managed to convey the message and Mama laughed with relief.

"Come on, honey, we'll go in the house and find something to protect your panties on those days - but it's nothing to cry about. I'll admit I felt the same way the first time - but your life isn't over just on that account," Mama said.

"I can't step my feet in cold water or play 'Pump, Pump Pull-Away' or climb ropes or anything anymore." Anna was still sure life was pretty well over.

"Honey, it's not all that bad. You might not feel like climbing a rope but some little girls never want to climb ropes anyway. Just keep still and be patient and you'll feel better in a day or so," Mama explained and then she thought of something. "Look here in the new Ladies Home Journal what they are advertising: Sanitary Napkins! We'll just have to get some of those for when you start to high school this fall. I wish something like that had been available when I was growing up and had to be away from home, going to school. Washing out muslin rags on the sly so nobody saw them was the worst nuisance and still is."

"Mama, you don't still have to do that every month, do you?" Anna was shocked!

"Oh, yes, honey, you'll get used to it," Mama said. "You'll get used to putting your "granny rags" as some old women call them, to soak in a coffee can in the closet and rinsing them out at the pump after so they'll be ready for the wash the next Monday," Mama continued.

"How does it happen that I have never noticed them around?" Anna still couldn't believe her mother had been so secretive.

"Now, Anna, you'll learn," Mama said patiently as she tore an old muslin tea towel in foot-square sections and produced from her dresser drawer a new white muslin belt with two tabs on it.

Mama handed two safety pins to Anna and the nine squares of old muslin, soft from much washing, "Now, here's your belt and pins and all you'll need till fall. By then you'll be used to the idea and we'll see when the new fall catalogs come if we can order you something you can just put in a paper sack and burn. What a wonderful new idea!"

"Well," Anna thought, "It might be a new idea for Mama, but it really wasn't all that wonderful - just another way of coping with the problems of growing up. It's just something I'm going to have to put up with," she said to herself.

Dale, Anna, Avis and Robbie as well as fifteen or twenty other seventh and eighth graders were on hand at 9:00 a.m. the next morning to take the County Exams. It was a very formal occasion. There was to be no visiting and very little asking the teacher's assistance. It was held on successive Saturdays at the end of April. Their papers would be graded by the staff of the County Superintendent and they would receive their grades in the mail. Then, on a designated day out in May they would have Eighth Grade Graduation which would be held in the auditorium of the Minneapolis High School. When that day came, Dale and Anna received scholastic honors as well as a big certificate from the State of Kansas for being neither absent nor tardy for all eight years of school.

"School days, school days, dear old golden-rule days" were over. It was both a sad and happy occasion for everybody.

Papa and Mama were both pleased with Dale and Anna's first eight years of school.

"They made good use of every day and had a very good school as Ottawa County Schools go. I think they have a very good foundation for high school. That's the next hurdle," Mama said.

There seemed to be no limit to the ambition Mama had for her children.

****

Growing Pains
and
Oil Fever

"Hey, Mom, guess what? They are going to drill for oil right here north of town!" Dale barged into the cream station all out of breath with his news.

And that began a long summer in 1929 for everyone in Wells. All activity had previously been directed to planting gardens, wheat, oats, corn or sorghum or raising chickens, pigs, cattle or sheep with little time off from any of the activities surrounding all the farmers' routines. Suddenly life in Wells took on a new dimension. Baby chicks to raise, gardens to plant, calves to feed, pigs to slop, fences to mend, machinery to fix, trips to make for parts, chicken feed, groceries, and to take the

138

cream, eggs, and young fryers to town had always kept everyone working a twelve-hour day on the farms and in the town. At harvest time people hardly slept at all. So only the news of an oil-well could have expanded time already stretched to beyond it's capacity.

This was destined to be a summer to remember. Everyone geared up to accommodate the increased activity: Mrs. Overton, who had divorced Marvin, the man who ran the grocery store on the west side of the street, had gone into business for herself. She had opened a restaurant in the next building south of the Woodman Hall. It had a couple of extra rooms upstairs that could be rented out to work crews from the railroad or single men who came to town looking for summer work. The Dyer House had rooms upstairs too, and there were others who rented rooms to the people who came to drill for oil.

Louise Stilwell had divorced John by that time. She had a Cook Shack to live in behind the cream station and barber shop that she ran just south of Stella Allison's creamery.

Miller's Garage had extra customers with all the roughnecks and roustabouts, tool pushers, ramrods, and supervisors, who all drove cars. Copeman's Store had work clothes, gloves, baloney sandwiches, canned baked beans, bananas, and ice to sell for little ice boxes and water jugs - yes, there was an exciting new activity going on in Wells that summer.

Gene and Ocea, Viola and Crystal Copeman had farm ground and pasture land just northwest of the oil-well site as well as the biggest general store in town.

"Mama, you'll just keep on buying cream and Papa will keep hauling produce just the same -- even if they strike oil, won't you?" Anna asked one day when she came back from visiting with Crystal in the back room at Copeman's Store.

"Well, of course, Anna, as long as people keep raising chickens, gathering eggs and milking cows, we'll be buying chickens, eggs and cream. And Charlie will keep buying another new truck every year to be paid for." Mama did a lot of worrying about being in debt. Their house wasn't paid for, yet, either.

"Mama, how much do we owe on our house?" Anna worried also.

"Well, Charlie borrowed a thousand dollars at the Ottawa County State Bank when we built our house and we make payments on that with interest every six months. You don't need to worry about it, Anna," Mama fretted.

"Mama, Crystal has been going to the seances that the Spiritualists have and she says Copemans have an Indian guide who has shown them where there is oil on their land north west of the place where they are drilling for oil," Anna reported.

"Oh, my goodness! The Copemans never took any interest in Spiritualism before. And I doubt if there are any Indian Spirits around who care if they strike oil on Copeman's farm or not," Mama scoffed.

Anna's mother had joined the Spiritualist Ladies Aid when she first moved down to Ottawa County and lived across the road from Mrs.

Brown. She would hurry home and bake a pie or some cookies whenever the Ladies Aid was serving lunch at a sale or they were having a pie social to raise money for something, but she didn't depend on spirits to help with her own fund-raising projects.

"And Crystal says she can see an Indian guide behind me, too," Anna bragged. "She said my guide led her all over this town and there's oil right under Wells. We could all be rich."

"Honey, I think your Indian guide is right behind you right now telling you to go over to the house and cook some macaroni and tomatoes. There's bacon drippings in the skillet to season it with. Charlie and Dale will be here for dinner before we know it. When I come in I'll fry a few slices of that pound of bologna that's in the icebox," Mama was talking to Anna, writing a cream check for somebody and planning dinner for her family all at the same time.

"Mama, when you fry the bologna, fry my slice last and when it turns up all the way around, can I break an egg in it and put the lid on till the egg cooks through? That's the only way I like an egg," Anna had forgotten the Indian guide. She was hungry.

"Maybe I'll do all the eggs that way," Mama said. "But run out and pull some radishes and onions, we must keep eating them while they're small. Charlie likes them so well."

The supervisor of operations on the oil-well was a man named Jess Cling. He drove a long, low roadster. He had no family with him so everyone supposed he wasn't married. The Allisons could study him first-hand from inside the cream station. He came into Louise's barbershop for a haircut at least once a week - or a shave, maybe. Mama's cream station had a big four-foot window on the south side and Louise's barbershop had a four-foot wide window on the north so the two women could keep tab on each other without meaning to. Oft-times Mama could look up from what she was doing and catch Louise looking right at her. The two buildings were just six feet apart since the barbershop had been built on there when Louise decided to run the creamery next to Mama's. It was sometimes more than Mama could bear in silence to see married men whose wives were her best friends laughing and talking to 'that woman.' Sometimes Mama even imagined they were talking about her. She was sensitive about the acid holes in her dress if she didn't wear that oilcloth apron to protect her clothes. Poor Mama, Anna was sorry for her.

Anna was thirteen years old that summer but she was wise beyond her years and size. One could say she secretly admired a big, burly young man who roomed and boarded down at Mrs. Overton's restaurant. He was a roustabout named Vic Paget who worked at the oil well. Vic had black patent leather-looking hair, and was among the men who frequented Louise's barbershop.

Overton's Restaurant was a hangout for kids of all ages who liked ice cream cones and ice-cold soda pop. So, when she had any spare time, Anna found the restaurant an interesting place to be that summer.

140

"Anna, could you come down afternoons and entertain Norma Jean, maybe take her up to the schoolyard to swing?" asked Mrs. Overton one day when she was in the restaurant for an ice cream cone.

Anna's time was not too well taken up at home that she couldn't entertain a four-year old. Mama thought that would be a fine activity for Anna.

"I imagine a little four-year-old does get pretty bored with life in that restaurant. Maybe you could play paper-dolls with her, Anna, when it's too hot to be out in the sun," Mama suggested.

And so it was that Anna was bringing Norma Jean home from an afternoon of activity as the oil drillers were getting off from work. Mrs. Overton (she insisted that all her customers call her 'Blanche' now that she was a woman alone and the sole proprietor of her restaurant) was standing in the doorway of her kitchen. She had had time to do her hair up on top with long thin curls in front of each ear. She was built as Papa said, 'a good bit like a lead-bottomed salt shaker - smaller at the top with a very wide base,' but Anna thought she was pretty cute.

Vic Paget was just coming in, smelling of hair tonic, freshly shaven and ready for supper as the whole crew was gathering.

Mrs. Overton greeted him with, "Big Boy! Does your mother know you're out?"

Paget retorted, "She'd ought to. I weighed nine pounds!"

Anna didn't have to report on that for the whole town to hear it. Vic Paget's birth weight was the talk of the countryside.

Every night after Papa and Dale were home from hauling and Mama was done testing cream, they'd drive up to the oil well. It had a night crew and the tall wooden tower was all lit up. Papa said they were drilling with cable tools and would strike oil any day now. A long line of tubing running from down in the hole out to a distance of thirty feet or so had a flame of gas shooting out from it. There was always a crowd of people there at night, cars parked out on the prairie grass. Some were interested in watching the process of drilling for oil while others were just sight-seeing. It was somewhere to go that was close at hand and a respite from the unceasing work that was everyone's lot in life if he intended to survive and advance according to his potential.

"Anna, did you slop the pigs after supper?" Papa had asked on the way up there.

"Yes, I took out the potato peelings but they won't eat the grapefruit rinds - Dale, we're about out of bran in that gunny sack in the tin shed," Anna reminded them. The pigs were Dale's project, too. They would both be starting to high school that fall and those pigs would be up to two-hundred and fifty pounds - ready to be hauled to Salina. Papa had bought them as weaners for Dale and Anna to care for all summer. When September came they would be ready to sell and they would have money enough to buy their books for high school.

"Why would they eat grapefruit rinds?" Dale asked, "I can't stand the grapefruit, either, it's so bitter." I'll get some more bran tomorrow."

Dale was already fifteen - just last week. Anna wouldn't be fourteen till almost Christmas. He had milked the cow they kept for milk and butter every evening for several years.

"Dale, when are you going to teach me to drive the Hudson? I could go over to the elevator and get the bran myself, if I could drive," Anna asked.

"When you learn to milk the cow," Dale smirked.

"Children, you are both growing up too fast," Mama said with some pride. "Why do you want to learn to drive that big old contraption with a sixty-bushel box on the back, Anna? You could take your little wagon and walk over there and buy a sack of bran."

"Well, here we are!" Papa said as they pulled up beside a touring car where several ladies were visiting. Their husbands and children of all ages were standing a little closer to the noisy rig, which was clanging and battering away at the ground beneath.

"Papa, when they strike the oil will it shoot up into the sky like I've seen in pictures?" Anna wanted to know what to expect.

"I'm sure everyone hopes so," Papa laughed.

"I heard Levi Comfort say that they'd probably strike it in the daytime when there is nobody here but the crew and they'd cap it and keep it a secret till they could buy all the land around here cheaper," Dale said.

"We'll have to wait and see, won't we?" Papa laughed as he got out and went around the new truck to help Mama out.

"Stella, why don't you sit here with us?" asked Nora Comfort, sitting in the touring car next to them.

The oil-well was also a place for the 'young bucks' as Papa called them, to bring girl friends. Mothers would allow their daughters to ride with a boy-friend to a public place like that - seeing no great harm in the numbers of people around them.

Mrs. Baker, who lived in the two-story house just west of the lumberyard - had two granddaughters who were just a year or two older than Anna. Norline Manuel lived in Delphos and Mildred Kirkby lived in Minneapolis. They came every summer to visit their grandmother. Norline had black hair and eyes and Mildred was a blonde.

That night Johnnie Baker from Minneapolis had brought Mildred Kirkby out to the oil well and they were sitting in his roadster 'necking' as it was called in Crystal's <u>True Confessions</u> magazine. Anna was several years from being up to that sort of grown-up activity so she joined several 'nasty little brats' in dancing around and around their car singing a dirty little rhyme about:

"Johnny Baker, Johnny Baker, the candle-stick maker,
Wiped his --- on a piece of brown paper!
The paper was thin and his finger slipped in!
And, OH, WHAT A MESS Johnny Baker was in."

Papa and Mama were busy visiting with friends so Anna got away with her part in that teasing episode and she was left to reflect on her own behavior - she hoped Mildred hadn't noticed her - she didn't feel as grown-up as she sometimes wished she were. "I must be having growing pains, Anna thought as she tossed and turned in bed that night.

The next evening as Dale was milking Pogius Maiden, Anna walked over to take a lesson in milking the cow. Anna had to learn to drive a car. She had seen Avis driving Lou Heald's car and Ward Comfort was riding with her - out at the oil-well last night. 'If Avis can, I can,' thought Anna, 'but, first, Dale said I have to learn to milk that cow.'

"I've come to learn to milk," Anna said.

Dale smiled an evil smile. "Look how I can feed the cat," he said as he turned the cow's teat sideways and a stream of milk hit the cat squarely in the face. Old Puss was sitting there waiting and lapped furiously, then backed away to clean her whiskers.

"Now, come a little closer, Anna, and I'll show you how I can hit that button on the front of your dress." She could still hear Dale chuckling as she beat a hasty retreat.

"Mama, Dale threatens to spray milk all over me every time I go over there to learn to milk and he won't teach me to drive the car till I take turns with him on milking the cow. He's so mean," Anna wailed to her mother when she got back across the street to the cream station.

"Now, Anna, don't you see that's Dale's way of staying ahead of you - and after all, he is older than you. He's proud of being able to milk and drive and you can't. It bothers him that you are taller than he is and weigh a few pounds more, too," Mama always excused Dale for his meanness, and Dad would only laugh if she told him.

"I don't care, I'm going to tell Papa on him!" Anna pouted.

"He'll just laugh. He thinks its fine Dale can drive you to high school and dances or anywhere you want to go. That way you'll get to go and won't have to hunt for a beau to squire you around. Your Papa always said how glad he was that your Uncle Ney always took me to dances so I wasn't married when he came along. You know, I was twenty-five when I first met your dad," Mama seemed happy when she talked about being an old-maid school teacher when Papa came along.

The summer dragged on - the gas from the oil well caused it to catch on fire and the wooden tower burned to the ground. They put up another tower made of steel and many thought they would strike oil any minute. Meanwhile Louise got better and better acquainted with the tool-pushers and supervisors who came to her barbershop.

One night about ten o'clock as business was winding down at the cream stations, barbershop, garage and grocery store, Anna was sitting in front of the cream station and overheard Louise say, "Peanuts, will you take the kids back to the trailer and put them to bed. I have to clean up this creamery and I'll be over."

"Mama, I have to go out back," she heard little Marjorie say. They used the church outhouse sometimes.

"Sonny, you go with her, and hurry along. Peanuts is waiting to put you to bed," Louise directed.

Louise was busy in the creamery when Jess Cling walked by from the garage and stopped to talk to her a minute before going on.

Dale appeared from somewhere and sat down beside Anna on the porch. "Come and go with me in a little bit and I'll show you something. Shhh! Don't say anything to the folks. OK. Come on," he said. They went in the house, out the back door, and through the alley over to the church.

"Hurry up," Dale whispered crawling under the wooden porch in front of the church. Anna crawled under behind him, unmindful of spiders or mice, she was so curious about what Dale had to show her. "Quiet!" he whispered.

Just then they heard someone approaching - and through the cracks they could see - illuminated in the moonlight - Louise! She sat down on the porch steps just above them.

They didn't have long to hold their breath till the long, low roadster slid up in front of the church with its lights off. Louise got up, got in the car and it drove away. Louise had a date with the oil well boss!

The two little snoops crawled out from under the porch and sauntered back toward their back door. "Dale, how did you know that was going to happen?" Anna asked.

"Oh, I've been watching her go out on dates that way for quite a while. You'd think Peanuts would catch on after awhile."

"Maybe he does know," Anna reasoned, "She's not married to him. She just told him to put her kids to bed."

"He thinks she's gone to the church outhouse if he saw her go by the trailer," Dale decided. "I'll bet he'll think she's sure constipated before she gets back." They both giggled.

September came and it was time for the big adventure of going to high school. The excitement over the oil well slowly died down. Some said they had struck oil and capped the hole till oil prices were better. No one knew. Only the Copemans were still planning to hire someone to drill for oil where the Indian Spirit had told them they'd find it.

"Hope springs eternal in the human breast" as Mr. Acuff would say.

Anna had been taught to listen with respect to Mr. Acuff's sayings. After his wife died, Mr. Acuff became the janitor at the school house. He had grown fond of Louise and hung around the barbershop a good deal. Mama heard him say one day while he was sitting on her porch, "Such is life in the far west," like it was something profound.

Mama suspected that barbershop had been built onto the north side of that old creamery with Mr. Acuff's money.

"I'd have to say where Mr. Acuff is concerned: There's no fool like an old fool," Mama intoned.

****

> *"Mica Mica, parva stella,*
> *Iris quantum sistum belia...."*

Dale was on top of the world! Dad had bought a 1927 Model T roadster for he and Anna to drive to high school. He sang as he drove with high self-satisfaction:

> *"Mica, Mica, parva stella,*
> *Iris quantum sistum belia...."*

At least that is what Anna thought he was singing. It was Latin for "Twinkle, twinkle, little star, How I wonder what you are!" Anna did not take Latin because it fell in the subjects recommended for the College Preparatory Course and she had told the Registration Officer that she wished to take Normal Training, the course recommended for teachers. Anna always knew that she wanted to be a teacher when she finished high school.

> *"No one dreamed that Hobo Bill*
> *Was taking his last ride......"*

Dale seemed to know just two lines of several songs and Anna didn't know any more. All she knew was that they had finally finished grade school in Wells and were now embarked on the road to higher education.

The road was dry and good in September and their fancy Ford Roadster skimmed along doing thirty-five miles an hour. They could get to school in twenty minutes. Anna didn't see any more of Dale till time to go home at four o'clock, except in Study Hall. Their classes took them to separate rooms with different teachers. All girls took Home-Economics - sewing and cooking so they could learn to be good homemakers - there were no boys in those classes.

They started that fall with students all about their ages from rural districts as well as young people who had finished the eighth grade in Minneapolis. There were forty-two enrolled in that Freshman class. Several were from Wells and vicinity - Avis was there as well as Robbie Comfort. Both had graduated with Dale and Anna last spring - from Wells Union 2 and Charlotte Comfort from the Schur School and, of course, Philip and Chester Miller, Wendell Todd, Albert Kay and Edna Comfort, all upperclassmen. Mother always lamented that there were plenty of young people from right around Wells to have had a good high school if the people around Wells had been able to get a high school right there. But they didn't so it was a real test of perseverance to get a high school education.

The ten miles from Wells to Minneapolis was a county road but it was sandy only until one crossed Sand Creek about a mile west of Wells.

Then it became slick and sticky mud when it rained - which it did a lot of - the fall of '29.

"Charlie, do you think those children can drive over those muddy roads this morning?" Mother worried.

"Now, Stella, Dale's fifteen and he's been driving over muddy roads since he was twelve or so - he can do as well as the rest of these boys who are driving from Wells," Dad assured her.

Dale was small and had to look through the steering wheel in order to keep his feet on the foot-feed and operate the clutch, brake and low peddles when they were needed, as well as the hand lever that put the car in high gear. That little roadster was not heavy enough to get down and pull when the going got tough - it often slid sideways and plowed four tracks instead of two going down the muddy hills. The ruts would get so deep and the mud so sticky that going up any little grade would take forever. And, of course one didn't want to be tardy. There was a rule that one had to call at the principal's office and carry a written excuse to get into class.

"That's a county road and it will be graded as soon as Tex Tiemy gets to it," Dad assured Dale and Anna. "But it has to dry out a little first and it's raining again this morning."

"He shapes the road up so high with those deep ditches and when its raining it's slick on top," Anna fretted. "I just keep my fingers crossed and my feet planted firmly on the floorboards for fear we'll slip in the ditch if we get up any speed."

"Dale, you must be a really good driver - no one has had to pull you out yet," Dad said. "Those ditches drain away the water that would stand in the road and keep it muddy for a week. Guy Peck was down to the corner west of his house with his team the other day when I went to Salina. Boy, that's a mud hole - it's low in there and so the ditches don't drain off much water, it just stands there. Tex had the county cat and grader down there, too, trying to dig some drainage ditches and the mud was a foot deep."

"Dad, that little Ford roadster just hasn't got power enough when the mud gets deep," Dale said. "I thought that Stromberg carburetor we put on that engine was supposed to do something for it."

Anna always took quiet pride in the fact that she went out when they were installing that fancy carburetor and looked at the blue print while they were trying to figure out how to install it. "Papa," she said, "That little wire with the hook on the end should go there instead of over here."

Papa looked at the blueprint and said, "Well, I'll be danged, that's right." He reached over and hooked it up right and said, "Now, hop in, Dale, and give it a whirl and see if she'll go."

It started with no more fuss. They had been working with it all afternoon so Anna didn't dare crow. It was just an accident anyway that she happened out to the tin shed and looked at that blueprint. She didn't know anything about why a car needed a carburetor, even. She was just

146

a girl! "Well, it does go faster when the roads are good," was all she said.

"Well, we'll have to look around for a heavier car for these winter months," Papa said.

Their next car was a 1926 high-wheel Dodge coupe with a three-speed transmission: high, intermediate and low and had all kinds of power. Dale had to look through the steering wheel to drive it because, if he sat up too high on a cushion his feet wouldn't reach the clutch, brake or foot-feed.

"But, Boy, does it have power!" he said, explaining to Dad that he liked it for those winter driving conditions.

There came a day when Anna and Dale put it to the test. They arose one Friday morning and looked out the window at a raging snowstorm. There seemed to be no question that they would go to school. They had never missed school yet so this should not be the day to start.

John Schur's family lived three miles west at the top of a long hill. The snow was drifting but they managed to break the drifts and keep rolling - till they topped that hill. They looked down toward the Bennington corner at drifts that obscured the road the entire way to the corner and the blowing snow was piling more into drifts that no one would drive through till the road grader pushed them out.

Seven miles to go - the two students surveyed the scene in wonderment. Nature was so much more powerful than any human or man-made device at that moment. There had to be a way around it. The snow had blown off of the field north of the road - the wind had swept it clean and the grader ditches were not as deep right there either - that was a rocky knob the Schurs had built their house on.

Dale turned the faithful Dodge to drive through the shallow rocky grader ditch to the north and out into that field where they could travel all the way to the corner, back up onto the road and a few yards beyond. Another set of drifts in front of the Atwells might have stopped them but there was a place there where one could get out in the field to the south.

"Anna, can you open that gate? I'll drive all the way over to the fence on the west side of the field. I think we can get all the way over to Doerings through the field." Dale laid out the course of action with no thought of turning back, and, in truth, they probably could not have by that time - had the thought crossed either of their minds.

Anna opened the gate in the barbed wire fence and the Dodge kept going through snow a foot deep all the way over to the fence that ran along the west side of that forty-acre field. She thought as she fastened the gate back up and turned to catch up with the big, black, lumbering vehicle - how frail and small it looked through the blowing snow.

Dale was out unhooking the wire from a couple posts and she stood on the wire while he drove through. By solving each insurmountable problem as it presented itself and traveling - first in the road and, next, in the pastures or fields they finally arrived at the high school.

Anna and Dale were surprised to find that only three other cars were parked by the school. They belonged to students who lived at the edge of town no more than a mile from school. Usually there were twenty-five cars lined up along the sidewalk - students drove in from the country from every direction.

The principal was surprised, also, to see two pupils from Wells in the office seeking tardy excuses so they could report for class. "There was no way to let anyone know that we had canceled classes by the time we realized how bad this storm was so we just went ahead with school anyway," he explained.

The storm subsided - the wind died down and the temperature dropped to ten below zero by four o'clock that Friday afternoon. Dale and Anna had company on the way home. Edna Comfort and Avis Hanes had been staying in town that week and asked to ride home. No other cars were travelling and no one had come from Wells to bring them home for the weekend.

Neither Dale nor Anna had gloves and no one had coats heavy enough to be out in below zero weather. Kansas was so unpredictable that no one could be expected to have proper equipment for every eventuality. Drifts were deeper even in the fields that evening and the snow was frozen. That faithful Dodge that had waded through foot-deep snow that morning got stuck in the drifts four times on the way home.

"Here, take my gloves, Dale," Edna insisted, as she was stuffing feed bundles under the wheels. Dale had robbed a shock of feed to find something to help make traction. He would jump in the car and throw it in low gear and then reverse - to rock it back and forth till the wheels took hold and climbed out to frozen ground.

Avis and Anna sat in the car and hoped he would shut the door when he got out or in but the heater would have made little difference anyway. Anna finally crawled out and went behind the car to push along side of Edna. She seemed as stoical as an Indian. "If she can put her bare hands on the back fender and her shoulder against the cold body of the car I can too - she's only three years older than I," thought Anna. "I was just as cold inside the car. Papa always said one could easily freeze just sitting still. It's better to move around and keep the blood moving." Anna whacked her hands together and pushed on the back tire cover. Dale rocked the car back and forth.

Those half-frozen youngsters got home at seven that evening, three hours after they started from school. Dale and Ann sat with their feet and hands in cold water and bragged about their experience. If Mama or Papa felt they should have done any different, they wisely kept it to themselves.

****

148

"O wad some power the giftie gie us
To see ousel's as ithers see us!......."
Excerpt from "To a Louse" by Robert Burns

Miss Lorenz was a young lady still at home at the time of World War I so in 1929, the fall of that freshman year in Minneapolis, she was a striking looking maiden-lady, possibly nearing forty. She was the English teacher for the Minneapolis High School so she had classes all day for freshman, as well as sophomores. Sophomores were much more unruly, Anna observed as she was passing through the hall one day. Miss Lorenz had one big boy (bigger than she was) by the ear and was leading him to Mr. Engstrom's office.

"What do you suppose he did?" Anna asked Dale on the way home that evening.

"Those big guys had freshman English last year and they know more what they can get away with," Dale explained. "When we came in for Freshman English there were chewed-up spit wads everywhere. Some were even stuck to the blackboard."

"Oh, Yuk! What did she say?" Anna was horrified.

"She had Issie Giffin and Russell Comfort cleaning up the mess before they could leave the classroom. Russell was saying that he hadn't blown any spit-wads at the blackboard and she said, 'Then you won't mind cleaning them off, will you?' Ole' Russell just sputtered." Dale laughed.

One day not long after that Anna's Freshman English class was assembled, each in his own seat earnestly trying to follow Miss Lorenz's pointer as she parsed the verb: 'go'. She was standing beside her desk with her back to the class, pointing at the blackboard, "I go, You go, He goes. We go, You go, They go ..." She reached the top line of sentences when the strangest thing happened.

A half-slip with a rubber back panel came sliding down beneath her skirt like a great, gray curtain and settled about her high-heeled slippers.

Not a soul moved, - even Robbie Comfort, who had never failed any opportunity to tease Miss Edith last year in the eighth grade in Wells - batted an eyelash. That entire class of twenty-two students sat dumb-founded as that lovely lady stepped with one dainty foot at a time, out of that encircling pile of gray rubber. She bent over, --- picked it up, folded it neatly and slid it into the top drawer of her desk.

That evening as Anna sat at home, searching the Montgomery Ward catalog for such a garment, Dale said, "Boy! If that had been that sophomore class - Al Powell, Butch Trow and Issie Giffin would all three have been up there, helping her out of that rubber trap - they'd have thrown it from one to the other or something and she'd never have seen it again! What's it for anyway?"

Mama intervened. "Ladies wear rubber-backed half slips to keep their dresses smooth in back so they don't cling, Dale." She gave Anna a look that suggested that big, blundering boys didn't need to be prying

149

into why ladies needed extra garments in back when they had to be standing on display every day in front of people.

After that, when Miss Lorenz went down the aisle, her smooth skirt making little "swish - swish" sounds as she walked - keeping track of misbehavior in Study Hall, Anna felt an extra kinship and sympathy with old-maid school teachers.

Study Hall was a test of control for teachers. When a teacher had a spare hour she was expected to be in charge of Study Hall. Students were expected to be there too when they didn't have a class. Freshmen had the left two rows, sophomores the next two, then juniors and seniors to the far right. They came to study and prepare for the next class. Some teachers could control a study hall with little commotion while others were constantly moving up and down the aisles keeping order.

The Home-Ec teacher, Miss Peters, was fair game for the big boys. In her classes she always dealt with girls so she could do nothing about the grades that boys got - she had no boys in classes. In afternoon study halls Miss Peters was there with her rolled-up paper - standing at the back of the room. From somewhere in the middle of the big hall came a whistle, "Here, Shep! Here Shep!" She carried her paper and travelled the length of the hall to hit the suspected culprit with the rolled-up paper. Someone else whimpered, "Oh! Me wittle cwavicle!" and the entire study hall snickered

Row after row began to tromp - like soldiers marching. She could do nothing to stop such organized rebellion. Suddenly Mr. Engstrum, the new Principal, with the football shoulders and the ice-blue eyes, appeared at the front of the room and the tromping ceased.

Anna came down with measles that winter and missed two weeks of school. She was too sick to protest being quarantined and missing school for the first time in her life. Dale brought home letters from Clea Johnson, Donys Dobson, and even a couple of boy-friends he didn't know she had. Anna was pleased and surprised.

In spite of these frequent intervals of interruption and diversion, Anna and Dale got good grades in their various classes and enjoyed a successful year in the Minneapolis High School.

****

There once was a girl from St.Paul
Wore a newspaper gown to a ball
The dress caught on fire
And burned her entire
Front page, sports section and all.
(from "Gem of the Day" - Ann Landers)

"Stella, what's the matter with you, tonight?" Papa asked. "You burned the potatoes and left the hamburgers you'd fried in the oven. Don't you feel good?"

150

Mama put her head in her hands and burst into tears, but only for a second. Dashing away her tears, she exclaimed, "Doggonnet all, I'm just mad. Marie Adee was in to visit me today while I tested her cream and wrote out her check. She's such a cute little lady. She said she had something funny to tell me. She said Ben was over to the elevator and some man told him he'd go into Louise's to get his hair cut but Stella Allison would see him and tell his wife. And she said another guy spoke up and said that Louise told everyone that she'd have a lot more cream customers as well as a lot more customers in her barbershop if Stella Allison wasn't always right there to report to their wives - all about just who sits in her barber chair." Mama jumped up and hurried to the stove - the coffee was boiling over.

She poured a cup of cold water in it to settle the grounds and went on before Papa could think of anything to say, "Charlie, I didn't plant my cream station right next to her so I could spy on her. She's the one who did that!"

"Of course, that right, Stella," was all Papa had time to say, before Mama broke in again.

"I know she's talking about me every time I look up in that cream station - I even hate to go out there anymore," Mama sniffed.

Anna had known that for some time but both Papa and Dale looked shocked. Mama had seemed to like to buy cream for as long as Anna could remember, almost. And even when the big rack of cream cans came down on her head and broke her front teeth and cut her head - she was right back out there as soon as she healed up. But this was different.

"Stella, you always get more customers than anyone in town - I don't know what we'd do without the cream business. We just can't let that kind of gossip get you down." Papa was trying to make Mama feel better. He was proud of her.

"Charlie, you get out and go places but I am just stuck there every day and I can't look up without looking at her bending over those men. Marie said Louise was making a good barber out of all the wives around - they all say, 'If you go and let that woman cut your hair - you don't need to come home,' - so they are all learning to cut their husband's hair - some do a better job than others."

"Anyway, you had a nice visit with Marie," Papa said.

"Yes and I've been sick ever since - I won't need any of the cold hamburgers and burned potatoes. I have a headache. Anna, if you'll pick up the dishes and clean off the table - I just have to go lie down." Mama's voice was weak and tearful.

"Dale, you can help Anna with the dishes," Papa said. "I've a little chore to do outside."

Dale and Anna cleared the table, got out the dish pan, dipped water from the reservoir on the side of the stove and Dale wiped as Anna washed - when Mama was sick nothing was right - they didn't even have enough spirit to argue.

151

Dale took the bucket and went out to the pump in front of the house to bring back a pail of water. He filled the reservoir every night. When he came back with the water he said, "Papa is building something out in the tin shed - I'm going out to see what he's making."

There was always about a one-hour lull at sunset - farmers were milking cows, slopping hogs, gathering eggs, sometimes there was no one in town till after dark and then the grocery stores, garage, cream stations and, yes, the barbershop would be busy till ten or eleven at night.

Dale came in to take the gas lamp out to the station, "Mama, there's a can of cream on the scales. Papa wants to know if you feel like testing it tonight?" Dale stood at the bedroom door.

"Oh, I suppose I'd just as well get up - my head pounds just as much lying here. My feet feel better anyway. I've been off of 'em for an hour." Mama arose, combed her hair and got out to the door of the creamery just as Papa was driving the last nail in the board fence he had built - right on the line between the creamery and Louise's barbershop. That fence was six feet high and six feet long and completely covered the view for either lady as she went about her business in either shop. It was just three feet out from each window.

"Stella, Do you know what day this is?" Charlie asked with a grin.

"Yes, September the tenth - and that is just about the nicest anniversary present you have ever made for me, Charlie," Mama said as she stepped inside the cream station and looked at the new board fence just outside her window. "You know, my headache's gone."

Fall passed, winter came with it's Saturday night dances, coyote hunts, ice-skating on the ponds and Spring was threatening - school would soon be out in Wells.

That particular Spring morning Louise sent Junior out to light the coal-oil stove under the can washer in her cream station. Sonny was about eight years old - he got busy with his little wooden cars under the big maple tree just south of their station.

Kerosene stoves had a way of 'running up' if one didn't stay to watch them after they were lighted. The chimney would fill with soot - the soot would catch on fire and if the stove were close to a wall the whole place would catch on fire.

"FIRE!" someone yelled from across the street. Louise's cream station and barbershop was on fire!

"FIRE! FIRE! FIRE! FIRE !" People could hear: "FIRE!" being shouted inside and outside of every home. Someone gave the line ring on the party-line telephone. Magically, there were people out everywhere. Someone helped Louise get her barber chair out but that was all they could save from that burning building.

Buckets of water were being brought from every pump in town. Even the school children and the teachers from the schoolhouse were hauling water in five-gallon buckets with Dale and Anna's little red wagon they had found in the tin shed.

152

Papa climbed up on the roof of Mama's precious cream station from a ladder on the north side of it and men kept a bucket-brigade of water going up that ladder to him. He kept splashing water down the side of the building and putting out the burning embers that kept landing on the roof all around him.

Soon the well at the north corner of the creamery was pumped dry. Water was brought from across the street and down the street. Someone brought a load of wet gunny sacks from the elevator. From the outset, no one tried to save Louise's building - it was a raging inferno almost as it was discovered to be on fire. If the Allison cream station caught on fire - so would the Allison house just eight feet north of it. The wind from the south was beginning to pick up. Papa had to come down from on top of the creamery - his face looked burnt and smoky. An old tank wagon pulled up with a load of water. Clarence Brown had a threshing machine - the separator was powered by a steam engine. So he had taken his tank wagon down to Sand Creek and pumped a tank of water. It had an eight-foot hose and he stood up on the tank wagon and directed the hose up on the burning roof and pumped water on the places where it was catching fire. Mama's privacy fence was burning but the side of her creamery hadn't caught fire. just the roof - so far.

Frank Sommers rushed up to Anna, "Get all your valuables out of your house," he said. "That wind is getting stronger and the whole block is apt to go up in flames. Your house is apt to catch fire any minute!"

Anna rushed inside the house. "What was valuable?" she asked herself. She stood on a chair and reached a blue-willow sugar bowl down from the top shelf of the cupboard. "Keepsakes" somebody said. That sugar bowl had an 1850 2-cent piece in it and a quarter that someone had polished smooth on one side and carved C. F. Allison on and drilled a hole in - so Papa could use it on a watch fob. Mama's little gold watch was there, too, and two of her opal rings. Now, that was valuable - but what else. Anna ran in her bedroom and took down a change of clothes, a blouse and a skirt and pulled out that top drawer which had her little tubes of lipstick and the little tins of powder. She grabbed a scarf and tied these things up like a hobo's bundle and rushed out the back door to the tin shed. She set them down carefully in a hen's nest and rushed back to see what was going on with the fire. More and more people were arriving with all sorts of ideas to keep the whole block from going up in smoke - as Frank Sommers said.

At last the fire died down - Louise's creamery and barber shop was just a pile of burning embers. Someone had thought to call the Minneapolis Fire Department. Perhaps it was George Miller. He always had a Minneapolis phone and his garage was just north of the Allison's tin machine shed. If the big house started burning on the roof and the wind caught the embers his garage was next in line.

The big red fire engine from Minneapolis pulled up in front of the smoldering building and played its hoses over the dying embers. The tar-paper was smoking on Mama's creamery and they soaked that roof some more. If the valiant efforts of all the neighbors had been unsuccessful that Minneapolis Fire Department would have come in mighty handy and maybe been able to save Allison's new house - after all, it was only three years old at that time. They were all so thankful.

Dale and Anna went in the house to get ready to go to high school. They'd be late but were sure they could get an excuse. There was not a stick of furniture inside. All the kind neighbors had moved it to the backyard. If the house had gone up in flames - they would have had furniture at least, with which to start again.

As they were driving off to school, Anna saw Papa walk up to the board fence - still standing three feet from Mama's south window. It was charred to a crisp - he kicked it and it crumbled and fell in a heap. "Aw, well," Anna said, "It won't be needed any more. Louise's barber chair will have to find a new home."

"I heard someone say that if it hadn't been for that board fence, there would have been no way to save Mama's cream station," Dale said. "It would have all gone up in flames."

"And so, as Mr. Acuff would say, 'Its a mighty ill wind that blows nobody good.' And Mama won't need that board fence anymore. Louise can put her barber chair somewhere else," Anna said with some satisfaction.

****

> *Have ye Poverty's pinching to cope with?*
> *Does Suffering weigh down your might?*
> *Only call up a spirit to cope with,*
> *And dawn may come out of the night.*
> *Oh! much may be done by defying*
> *The ghosts of Despair and Dismay;*
> *And much may by gained by relying*
> *On "Where there's a will there's a way."*
> *excerpt from a poem by Eliza Cook*

Dale and Anna didn't feel the pinch of poverty in their freshman year in high school though the Minneapolis National Bank where Dad and Mother had borrowed money when they built the house in 1927 had closed its doors February 9th, 1929. Dad had lost money in that bank but the note had been lost also.

"Charlie, what do you think will happen with that money we owe at the Minneapolis National Bank?" asked Mother one morning, "Will they pay on it with the money we had in our account?"

"I have no idea, Stella, but when they get done with the president and the bank examiner, Old Gafford and Harvey are both going to go over the road for embezzlement," Papa explained. "And I expect some of those crooks have spent what we had in our account and some of the stockholders are holding that note and will spring it on us someday when the smoke all clears away."

"Eleanor Harvey is in my class in high school. I wonder if it's her dad that's being sent to prison?" Anna asked.

"If he's a bank examiner he's mixed up in it; there are other Harveys in Minneapolis, though," Papa said.

"Well, I hope it isn't her dad, she's nice." Anna sighed, "She has such a pretty face but she's six feet tall."

"The big boys are all jealous of her," Dale said, "Did you hear ol' Griest holler at her as we were going in the school house at noon? He said, 'Hey! Altitude, is it snowing up there?' She just smiled and ducked her head."

"Well, a few flakes were falling even down where I was while I was walking back from Belknaps Restaurant," Anna retorted.

"What did you eat for lunch?" Papa asked.

"I had a hot beef sandwich and a cup of cocoa for twenty cents and spent the other nickel on a Hershey Bar," Anna said. "I ate it on the way back to school. I had to go all alone - where did you go, Dale?"

"Oh, I rode with some of the guys and spent my quarter for candy bars," Dale said.

"Anna, your meal sounds pretty good. Dale, why don't you take your sister down to the restaurant in the car and eat a hot lunch with your quarter?" Mama suggested.

"Maybe I will," Dale brightened at the thought of driving the car down town.

"Stella, can't we fix sack lunches for these kids cheaper than fifty cents a day?" Papa said. "That's two and a half dollars each week just for getting through the day. That's more than it costs for the gasoline to run their car."

Mama began making peanut butter sandwiches and graham cracker cookies with frosting centers. Dad bought a bushel of apples for two dollars and Dale and Anna ate with friends in their cars or on the sunny side of the building. Some ate in the Home Ec room - girls, only, of course.

Such were the small economies for the winter of '29-'30. The Stock Market crashed just seven months after President Herbert Hoover had assured the nation that the country was "in a healthy and prosperous condition." The 'crash' came back in New York City in October in 1929 and didn't affect the economy immediately for Dale and Anna that first year of high school in Minneapolis.

Mother could have said, "I told you so," about electing a Republican President but she was far too worried for that. She listened to the radio every day and assured Charlie and the children that "Governor Franklin D. Roosevelt of New York had said the situation was sound."

"That may be," Papa agreed. "But you should see the men out of work standing on street corners and walking the roads trying to find a job. People are starving in the cities."

Mother kept buying cream and listening to the farmers complain when butterfat went from thirty-eight cents a pound down to nineteen cents and eggs were dropping from twenty-five cents a dozen down to ten cents. Farmers began eating their chickens and selling their cows since they couldn't afford to feed them.

Dad was busy hauling livestock to auctions in Beloit, Salina, Concordia, Clay Center and even up into Nebraska where there was lots of corn to feed them and corn, like wheat was not bringing enough to pay the hauling bill.

"I heard on the radio today that President Hoover has mobilized public leaders to form a Committee on Social Trends, and he's pressing Congress to establish Bank Reform laws. He's establishing a Federal Farm Board for financing market cooperatives and Home Loan Discount Banks to prevent foreclosure on mortgages on hundreds of thousands of homes and farms--" Mama was giving the best news while Dale, Anna and Charlie were eating supper.

"That's like shutting the barn door after the horse has been stolen. Just so they don't find the mortgage on this house any time soon..." Papa worried, between bites. "Stella, your sisters and brother, Frank, have said 'I told you so' about Ney losing your Pa's homestead but it was mortgaged when he took it over and he had all that expense when your mother died..."

"I know, Charlie, we are all victims of the times. We'll just have to do the best we can," Mama said. "Ney did, and he still had Pa to care for - even after they lost the farm and had to move into Miltonvale."

"He's pretty worried right now," Dad shook his head.

But he has a job working for the light company, doesn't he?" Dale asked.

"Yes, but he doesn't know for how long," Dad explained. "I stopped in to see them on my way home from Concordia yesterday. He said the most of his work right now was shutting off the electricity because people couldn't pay their light bills."

"Oh, dear," Mother lamented. "I guess it's a good thing we've never had electricity in Wells. We've still got our kerosene lamps and gas lanterns."

"Who was it who said, 'It's a short way from corn pone to puddin' but it's a long way back?'" Dale asked, not waiting for an answer. "Dad, I think I can pull three wheat wagons behind the Dodge Coupe and that way we can take on more jobs of hauling in harvest."

"We'll keep that in mind, Dale, some of these farmers have a couple of wagons around and we have one -- " Papa spoke and Mama interrupted:

"Dale, that is dangerous. What if one of those trailers came loose going down a hill?"

"Oh, now, Stella, we'd fix them so they couldn't come loose," Papa explained. "You could bring them in at noon and unhook them and take them through the elevator one at a time." Dale was still small - didn't weigh a hundred pounds yet but everybody in town thought he could do anything his dad thought he could do.

But the farmers couldn't pay the hauling bill when they called Dad and Dale and had their wheat and pigs and chickens hauled to market.

The situation worsened daily the summer of 1930. Dad couldn't make enough to buy new tires for his truck or trade for a new truck before tires become worn - like he had every year for the last seven years.

Dale and Claude Noel, the section foreman's son hauled the cream from Mother's cream station to Concordia in that wagon hooked to the '26 Dodge Coupe - no more lazy Sunday mornings when Mama, Papa, Dale and Anna packed a lunch and took twenty-four to thirty-six cans of cream to the creamery and came back by Uncle Ney's to visit. Papa was busy hauling cattle to market.

They had a big garden behind the house and the cream station. Anna pumped water at the well by the station and it ran down ditches beside the beans and carrots, peas and corn, potatoes and squash, radishes, onions, turnips and yams. Mama and Anna canned at least three hundred cans of vegetables and fruit.

Papa brought home bushels of peaches to be canned - and blue plums. "The truckers from Colorado are selling them for fifty cents a bushel - I had to think about next winter - we probably won't be able to buy tin cans of peaches next winter and we'll have to have something to eat."

"We can take canned peaches in our lunches to high school this fall," Anna suggested, eyeing the beautiful peaches.

"I don't think you can plan on going to high school this fall, Anna. We're just not making any money from buying cream, eggs, and chickens, - and the hauling isn't paying enough to pay for new tires on the car and the truck....," Papa paused as he looked at the stricken face of his daughter.

"Not go on to high school!!!" That is when the crash came for Anna. "How could she teach school when she got to be eighteen - if she couldn't finish high school?" Her ears pounded as she thought of the long winter ahead. Her stomach churned. She put down the peach and went to her bedroom.

"I'm sorry, Stella, but I just had to tell her," she heard Papa say before she shut the door.

"Not go on to high school ......!" Anna's head reeled. "What happened to 'Where there's a will, there's a way.' and 'We are not here to play, to dream, to drift. We have hard work to do and loads to lift!' Anna thought as she lay on her bed pondering her fate. "If Dale were ever around to talk to maybe they could work something out but he was swimming with the boys or hauling fifteen cans of cream to Concordia. Papa told him they weren't getting paid enough for the hauling from the creamery to pay for the trip!"

Anna worried for several days. She tried praying, "Our Father which art in heaven, hallowed be thy name -- thy kingdom come, thy will be done --" but it did little to solve the awful problem of what to do with one's life in Wells with no school to go to - she just had to finish high school. Of course Myrtle Yonally wasn't going - none of her brothers or sister had gone - she didn't seem to worry. Myrtle and Norline were Anna's best girl friends, but they both lived out in the country - she hadn't gone to grade school with them - none of her friends seemed to be in the same predicament Dale and Anna were faced with.

Suddenly it came to her! Uncle Ney lived in Miltonvale where there was a high school! Maybe she and Dale could go up and stay with Uncle Ney and Aunt Ethel and go to high school in Miltonvale. Grandpa Jordan had passed away last spring and even though his daughter, Pearl, was there with their little grand daughter, Peggy, there would still be room for Dale and Anna. Anna went out to the creamery where her mother was testing a batch of cream.

"Mama, I have an idea. Do you think Dale and I could stay with Uncle Ney and go to high school in Miltonvale?" Anna's voice sounded doubtful as well as hopeful.

"Now, Honey, that is an idea," Stella's voice sounded hopeful as well.

"We could have Dale drive us up to see Uncle Ney and Aunt Ethel before we mention it to Papa," Anna said, tentatively.

"That's right," Mother agreed, "Charlie wouldn't want to ask Ney, himself. We'll just go up there for a visit and see if it's possible before we tell Charlie."

And so it was that Dale and Anna changed schools and started their sophomore year in the Miltonvale Rural High School the fall of 1930.

Miltonvale had two schools: the rural high school - which was a public school and a parochial high school where Wesleyan Methodists from all over the United States sent their children to keep them away from 'worldly sins'. Those young people were different already - they still wore long hair - the girls had to wear dresses with long sleeves and skirts no more than fourteen inches from the floor - no rouge nor lipstick was permitted on the premises. Students in the rural high school called them 'Hillbillies.' Their campus was in the southwest end of town on a hill. The rural high school was north of U.S. Highway 24 in the west side of town.

Uncle Ney and Aunt Ethel lived just south of Main Street at the Phelps Furniture Store corner. It was ten long blocks - a mile - to the high school. Aunt Ethel's, Ruthie Watson, came in from the country and started her freshman year that fall so Anna walked with Ruthie, morning, noon and night - four miles a day to school. Boys who drove in from the country every day cruised the streets and picked up girls and gave them rides back to school at noon. Anna was the only girl from any town in the sophomore class that year - all the others were country girls and batched with a partner or sister at someone's house in town.

Anna was instantly popular - a new girl in school - and she and Ruthie seldom walked back to school at noon. Some boy would pick them up - maybe two boys who had eaten a sack lunch in the car. Dale had other friends that he rode with. The noon hour was the social life of teenagers in Miltonvale. Everyone was in off of the streets at nightfall.

The City Dads, as the Town Council in Miltonvale was called, was controlled by a majority of Wesleyan Methodists so there were no dance halls - no modern Woodman Hall where entertainment of a worldly nature was held. Dale and Anna went home to Wells over the weekend in the big Dodge and Dad and George McCain were still having Saturday-night dances. Wells was home - the best place in the world to spend their weekends.

*****×*********××

Opportunity

Master of human destinies am I.
Fame, love, and fortune on my footsteps wait.
Cities and fields I walk; I penetrate
Deserts and seas remote, and, passing by
Hovel, and mart, and palace, soon or late
I knock unbidden, once at every gate!
If sleeping, wake-if feasting, rise before
I turn away. It is the hour of fate,
And they who follow me reach every state
Mortals desire, and conquer every foe
Save death; but those who doubt or hesitate,
Condemned to failure, penury and woe,
Seek me in vain and uselessly implore-
I answer not, and I return no more.
                    by John James Ingalls

Dale and Anna had both felt the drive to avail themselves of the extra opportunities that were offered in high school when they started their freshman year in Minneapolis. Philip Miller was a student from the Wells school who went out for Debate. He was a Senior and on the first team. These bright people travelled to other towns to tournaments. It gave students a chance to spread their wings.

This extra-curricular activity that was offered was an opportunity they could both grasp. Dale and Anna were not born in a home with musical parents - they had no skill at the piano or extra ability to sing. Some students went out for Chorus or Band or Orchestra or Football. Physical Education was part of their regular curriculum. Dale was small but he could play baseball - a summertime sport. Anna had no particular athletic abilities except an interest in swimming - at the lake and bike riding in Wells. But Debate - now here was a skill they could both work at - an opportunity being offered now.

Debate became Dale and Anna's extra-curricular activity the winter of their first year in high school. The question to be debated that year was: 'Resolved, that installment buying of personal property, as now practiced in the United States is both socially and economically desirable.' Four debaters became a team. Dale and Anna were negative. Two other debaters were the affirmative side of their team.

Mother said, "Arguing is not a new skill for you children. You've been doing that ever since you learned to talk."

"But keeping still until it's their turn will be a trick for them to learn, Stella," Papa spoke up. "I think it will be good training."

"And we'll both be on the same side of the argument," Dale said. "I don't know that Anna can stand that!"

"Well, it won't be easy," Anna agreed.

When they moved to Miltonvale, Dale went out for tennis but Anna stuck with the debating. Ray Hauck became her partner. That year teams across Kansas were debating the Question: "Resolved, that the chain store is detrimental to the best interests of the American public." Ray and Anna were on the negative side of that question also, attempting to prove that the chain store system was economically sound, that it benefitted the public by its high efficiency of operation, and that chain store methods made for greater efficiency of the general working public.

Not all high schools had debate teams, but Miltonvale always had enough students for a first and second string. Anna and Ray were a team for the rest of her high school years and it always was the very best time of the school day - they laughed and 'cut up' and Mr. Evans seemed to enjoy it also. He would challenge their minds to prove their statements with research, statistics and understanding. It became the most fun to travel with the team to Concordia, Washington or Ellsworth.

Miltonvale seemed to be the only school around close that had enough students interested to make up teams. Of course they didn't have a pep squad to follow their success but when they won at a tournament they were introduced to the student body at the next pep assembly. Nothing like excelling at football or basketball but as good as a girl could do! Girl's Athletic Association (GAA), took the place of inter-collegiate sports for a few years and it was only the boys who matched games with neighboring towns.

All girls belonged to Girl Reserves: "Girl Reserves are high-minded; they work hard and don't mind it - all day long!" was their theme song. Their slogan: "I will try To Face Life Squarely," and their pledge: "I will try to do my best to honor God, my country and my community to help other girls and to be in all ways a loyal true member of the Girl Reserves."

One of the teachers was the sponsor of Girl Reserves. Her material and ideas came from the Girl Reserve Department through the National Board of the Young Women's Christian Association.

160

Other opportunities to do something extra came in Dramatics. Anna went out for Dramatics every year. She had always 'spoke pieces' at community meetings. Grandparents would teach their four-year olds to speak at "Lyceum" as they called community gatherings:

> "As I stepped upon the stage
> My heart went pitty-pat
> I thought I heard somebody say:
> 'Whose little dunce is that?'

But Dramatics in high school was different. Besides speaking clearly so that even people who were a little deaf could hear, there was much to learn. One chose a story in prose and delivered it with eloquence. Competing in one's own school with sufficient ability to get to go to the county competition in Concordia was a very real goal. Anna had good coaches and won in several competitions.

Miltonvale had school plays and students with B averages could try out in their Junior and Senior years. The plays were the highlight of the year and Anna had lots of fun at play-practice every evening for weeks.

In her Senior year the school adopted a system of grading where, as well as good grades in the regular classes, extra-curricular points were given for all these fun-filled activities that Anna had enjoyed every year. This system resulted in her graduation with Summa Cum Laude honors - the top grade in the system.

Many discussions were held in regular classes in Civil Government and Internal Affairs as well as International Relations about "Prohibition." Anna was a Democrat and a champion of the "New Deal," introduced by Roosevelt when he was elected in 1932. Nothing aroused her ire like calling her a "Wet" Democrat.

Sometimes Anna felt ostracized in Girl Reserves. One time she said that prohibition of the sale of liquor in open markets resulted in bootlegging and drunkenness at dances intended for healthful exercise and enjoyment for decent people. Anna discovered that most girls were more strictly raised than she and had never gone to a dance, had no idea about 'bootlegging,' except that it was a dirty word not spoken by young ladies. However, Anna's speech teacher came to her rescue with a suggestion that she enter a competition sponsored by the Women's Christian Temperance Union. They offered cash prizes for the best orations on the subject of 'Prohibition.' Anna won Third Prize and received $1.00. Her delivery was excellent, the judges said but the First Prize of $3.00 went to a young lady who sounded like she was quoting from some of Carrie Nation's speeches.

Anna also went out for Chorus and sang in the Second Soprano section with sufficient success to attract no particular notice. Music had never been a skill she excelled at but she really enjoyed trying.

Curiosity, an attitude that some young ladies considered prying or nosey, opened many doors for Anna and she encountered many friends along the way. Her attitude of caring and kindness provided many opportunities for lasting friendships and always proved to her that prying paid off.

"Grasp time by the forelock" became her motto and she came to feel that if it were true that 'Opportunity Knocks But Once' then she should always be alert to listen.

****

"Tis heaven alone that is given away,
Tis only God may be had for the asking:
There is no price set on the lavish summer;
And June may be had by the poorest comer."
From "The Vision of Sir Launfal" by
James Russell Lowell

"Now, what is the matter with her?" Anna heard Papa say as he came in from the tin shed at 12:00 noon, as usual, for his dinner. Anna was lying across her bed sniffling. She had been studying the Sears Roebuck catalog that morning. She wanted a swimming suit.

"Mama," she had said, "Look at this pretty swimming suit for girls. Could we order it? I have to wear an old dress and tuck it in my bloomers. And I want to learn to swim so bad. When Dale and I and Leta and Lela went down to the lake we had to sneak away over on the east side. I just know I could learn to swim if the water didn't get under my dress and drag me down..."

"My goodness, Anna!" Mama had said. "Do you girls have to go straddling way off down there to the lake with Dale every time you are out of my sight? Some day one of you will get in over your head and drown. Dale might not be able to pull all three of you out."

Leta and Lela, Uncle Roy's two oldest daughters had come down from Oakhill to stay a week and Mother said when they went home, "Now, maybe you'll be content to sew or help me around the house, Anna. I guess the old saying, 'Two girls is half a girl and three girls is no girl at all' is right when it comes to getting any help from a daughter."

"Mama, Dale can swim! Now how did he learn how? And when Papa found out he'd been swimming naked with Wendall Todd and Philip and Chester Miller and Buck and Gilbert Payne and could dive and everything, he bought him a swimming suit..."

"Hurry and set the table, honey, it's five minutes till twelve and Charlie will be in in a minute for his dinner. I wonder where Dale is?" Mama had brushed off Anna's plea for a bathing suit without so much as looking at the page in the catalog. Anna laid the catalog down in her chair, hastily spotted the forks and knives around the table, dealt out the plates, put on the spoon-holder and beat a hasty retreat to her bedroom before her eyes spilled over with tears so she couldn't see.

162

"Oh, she wants a swimming suit," Mama said.

And Papa interrupted. Dale was coming in the front door from playing ball in the street. "Dale, you can take Anna into Minneapolis and get her a swimming suit. Penney's ought to have something a girl could learn to swim in..."

Dale was more than glad, he was down right happy to get to take Anna into Minneapolis to get a swimming suit. Papa couldn't stand to have Anna unhappy about a thing like that. Everybody should learn to swim, girls as well as boys, he always had insisted.

But he was pretty much alone in that opinion. J.C. Penney didn't have any swimming suits for girls. "There just wasn't any call for them," they said. However, Anna found a boy's suit that had a white top and black pants and a webbing belt around the waist. Dale paid for it with the five-dollar bill Dad had handed him and took the change home. Anna could have done that but Dale was taking her so he could take her down to the lake too, and they could appear over on the west side of the lake. She could swim between the 'SWIM HERE' signs. People might think she was a boy but at least she wouldn't be wearing an old dress tucked into her bloomers!

Anna was dog-paddling along just north of those 'SWIM HERE' signs not long after that when she dropped into a hole that was over her head. Dale was no where about to help her. He was down closer to the concession stand where they were building the new bath house. She came up to the top and tried to holler for help but her throat was full of water and she couldn't make a sound. She thought how her mother had warned her about drowning. She kept trying to stand up but she could not touch bottom. She tried not to breathe. Her lungs were going to burst. How awful Papa would feel when they found her lifeless body floating on the water, like Tom Sawyer - she remembered the chapter where they thought he had drowned and mourned for him. Mama wouldn't say 'I told you so' - she'd be so sad to lose her little daughter....

Anna's head came up above the water, she gasped and kept clawing at the water, floundering and sputtering. Suddenly her flailing arm touched the submerged bank of the old channel of the creek. She clawed at the bank and pulled herself to shallower water. The dam was just built the year before and had backed up the water of Sand Creek to make this wonderful body of water. Anna crawled out on the bank and looked across it. "Grandad was paralyzed and couldn't walk without crutches but he could swim across that lake," she thought. "You won't drown. You'll float," Grandad had said. "As long as you keep your lungs full of air."

"Well, I won't tell Mama nor Papa I almost drowned. I'll just keep trying," she thought to herself, "But no more today."

Play was mixed with work for Dale and Anna as well as all their friends. Summer was for baseball and bike riding as well as being on hand to run errands and help with all the tasks around gardening, cooking, sewing, canning, cleaning, buying cream, chickens and eggs, and hauling groceries, feed and hardware to the stores in Wells, as well as hauling produce to the bigger markets. Charlie Allison had a Produce Business. It was going down hill every day due to the depression, but there was still plenty of work to do and a lot of time to play also that summer.

"I'm either going to have to buy a new truck or a new set of back tires - and they are about $250 apiece. Dale, we have to load up the chicken crates and go help Sanders catch his chickens off the roosts. I'm hauling them to Salina for him tomorrow. He says it doesn't pay to buy feed and sell eggs any more." Papa said.

"Dad, I want to go down to the corner of the lake - Roy Gawith and Ray Allison are putting up a roller-skating rink," Dale said. "What relation is Ray Allison of yours?"

"He's a first cousin - let's finish eating and run down there right now - Stella, you and Anna can do the dishes when we get back." Papa was always just as ready to play as to work. "Sanders' chickens won't settle down till it gets real dark anyway. Come and go along, Stella," he urged, studying his wife's tired face.

That trip down to the Skating Rink was a turning point in Dale's life, Anna often thought afterward, but no one realized it at the time. Ray and Roy were just opening up a new business. They had acquired a big tent and the framework over a big hardwood floor - a skating rink and several hundred pairs of roller skates to rent. They were setting it up at the southwest corner of the Ottawa County State Lake. It was an ideal location to attract people from everywhere that summer of 1931. Charlie was full of ideas to help them and he and Dale were full of enthusiasm as they buzzed around the new place to play. Ray and Roy had smaller children but Dale was seventeen, just the person they needed to help them run that rink. He got a job that evening. They hired him at fifty cents a day and his meals across the road. Orpha and Nina Kaiser were running a restaurant on the south side of that corner. So Dale took care of the tent and was there for any emergency and he also learned to roller skate like some people learn to dance -- on his toes - on his heels - in circles and to music. Many people who could skate equally well came from everywhere. Skates could be rented for twenty-five cents a pair. Dale was a skate boy. Ray and Roy were there in the evenings.

Crowds came and sometimes they were a rowdy crowd. Roy Gawith and his wife were beautiful skaters and they skated as a couple. When she wasn't there he slowed the crowd down by waltzing alone. They told Anna she could always skate free. They wanted small girls and big ladies and anyone who wanted to skate to get on the floor and learn.

"Mama, what is Dale going to eat down there at the Skating Rink? It sounds like he's going to guard the place, too, when they go back to Minneapolis," Anna worried to her mother that first evening when Dad and Dale had brought them home, loaded up the chicken crates, and left to get the load of chickens to take to Salina.

"He'll eat most of his meals at Orpha's across the road, Ray told Charlie that they have a place to heat coffee and make soup in that little office - I imagine it will be just one long picnic for Dale the rest of the summer," Mama said.

"Maybe I can ride down there on my bicycle sometimes," Anna suggested.

"Oh, Goodness, no, Anna, that's three miles. And, besides, I need you at home to help me at the cream station, and to candle the eggs when someone brings in a case. You can ride Dale's bicycle around town and run errands for me but I don't want you straddling off across the country. What if you should fall off and break your elbow somewhere out by yourself, like Dale did right here in front of the cream station?" Mama was adamant about that.

"Anna, Mabel needs cherry pickers. We have a big cherry orchard and the cherries are ripe right now," Lou Sheffler said, when he brought in the cream and eggs that June. "I'll pay you $2.00 a week!"

"Can I go out to Shefflers and pick cherries, Mama?" Anna asked, thinking that sounded better than standing in the dark basement sliding thirty-dozen cases of eggs over onto the table with its kerosene lantern behind the mask with the two holes. Picking up thirty dozen eggs - one at a time and keeping a record of the ones that showed blood spots when they were held up to the holes in the mask, wasn't very exciting work.

"Stella, I'll only need her for this week, probably. Ellen Heck works for Mabel all the time but harvest is coming on and we have six men to feed this week - those dang cherries always get ripe right at harvest. What do you say?" Lou was a good customer and Mabel did need help.

"Well, I guess you can go. Anna. Charlie has lost his help this week, too, Lou, Dale's working down to the Skating Rink," Mama explained.

Anna ran in the house and gathered up a change of clothes in a sack. Two dollars a week was just a little less than Dale was making and it was a paying job, Anna thought as she rode back out to the Sheffler farm with Lou Sheffler.

To be called out of bed at 5:00 AM was a new experience for Anna. She set the table and carried in the biscuits, fried potatoes and huge platters of fried eggs, bowls of sausage gravy and a big fruit bowl with two quarts of canned peaches in it - to be dished up in sauce dishes. There were twelve places around the table. Lou was still cutting his wheat with a binder and the men were shocking the bundles. They'd have a threshing machine in to finish the job of harvesting.

Mabel was angry at Ellen Heck. Ellen had arisen at about 3:30 AM, saddled Mabel's horse and rode out to the pasture to bring in the cows for the morning milking. Mabel had arisen at 4:00 AM to find Ellen gone to the pasture on her saddle horse. "Horse-back riding is the only real pleasure I get these days and the early morning is the very most pleasant time of the day to do it. Ellen has just spoiled my whole day. I'm sure she thought she was helping me, but she could have picked an extra bushel of cherries this morning and be in here slicing these potatoes by this time......"

Anna soon learned that there was so much work to do and so little time to do it in that there was no way to please Mabel Sheffler. She was frustrated with too little help and too much to do. Dishes to wash, pies to bake, potato salad to make, eggs to boil for deviled eggs, bologna sandwiches to make for lunches to take to the field, chickens to kill, scald, pick and cut up for frying, as well as those cherries Lou had hired her to pick. Lou had said she'd only be needed for a week. Anna resolved to be sure she could help out only a week. She KNEW her mother needed her and she could help out at the Sheffler farm no more than a week! Candling eggs in the cool basement became more and more attractive by the moment.

At last the week was over and she rode back into town with Lou when he took in the cream and eggs. He paid her the two dollars. The cherries had been picked, pitted and canned but there was no end to the work she could have done for Mabel if her mother hadn't needed her so bad. She left with a wholesome respect for farmers' wives and daughters, and she knew what was meant by the old saying: A man's work is from sun to sun but a woman's work is never done!

Town life was definitely more fun than country life, Anna decided. They did have a big garden and Anna did a lot of sewing when she had anything to sew. When they had chickens in the batteries out in the tin shed she had to keep water in the troughs beside their cages so they wouldn't get too hot and die while they waited till Dad got a big enough load to haul to Salina. She had to pick beans when they were ready to can, clean radishes and onions for meals, but they never had twelve places at the table. Anna always loved summertime but she knew she wouldn't if they had to work as hard all the time as they did out to Shefflers!

One morning the mail brought a big box from Aunt Belva. She had had a young woman stay at her house who had moved away and left a closet-full of dresses and drawers of under garments. So Aunt Belva had boxed them up and mailed them to Stella. Aunt Belva explained in the letter that accompanied all these wonderful possibilities that maybe Anna could make them over for school that fall.

What a windfall! There was even a white rubber bathing suit - just a little big yet for Anna but definitely for a girl. And that summer Anna became a dress-designer. She loved studying the catalog and making one dress over like the one on page twelve and deciding that the design on page twenty-two would work out better for the striped one. She dyed pink material purple because Miltonvale's school colors were purple and white. She learned to rip out seams and press out the old stitch marks, making all sorts of changes and a different use of each scrap of material.

The summer was filled with canning, gardening, riding her bike, enjoying making new clothes out of old and swimming and roller-skating at the lake. It was a very good summer.

****

"Long 'bout June, when everthing's
Nice an' green, an' somehow brings
Joy into a feller's soul,
Till he wants to shout an' roll;
When ther bees are buzzin' roun',
Makin' jes' a heap o' soun'
Doin' nothin'- like a hen
Jes 'afore a snowstorm, then
I go fishin. "

An excerpt from 'I Go Fishin' by
Richard Stillman Powell

Charlie Allison was goin' fishin'. There was not much else to do. It had been a hot summer already.

"Stella, I need an old pair of Overalls. A bunch of us fellows are going over to the Solomon River. There's a place over there where the channel has changed and trapped a bunch of big channel cats. Get the skillet ready for some big fish!" Papa was talking as he took the wash tub down off the peg on the back porch and the big butcher knife out of the drawer. Viv Heald, Everett Payne, George and Frank Comfort, Otho Kay, Tom and Jim Yonally and several others were assembling in front of the house and climbing into the back of the truck. Grandad Allison was sitting in front of the cream station with his crutches handy. Dale and Claude and Ernie Noel came running up from somewhere. As they all piled into the back of the truck, Grandad slid himself into the passenger seat in the cab.

Papa leaned out of the window as they were pulling out to depart, "Anna, will you pump some water and irrigate those beans. It's just time they're setting on and they need rain. We'll need a nice mess of string beans to go with the fish we're going to bring home," he shouted back at his wife and daughter.

They would all strip down to old pants or overalls and wade barefoot into a pocket in the river where fish had been trapped when the river returned to its banks after a big rain. Charlie knew how to tickle the big channel cats down under the water with his fingers along their bellies, then he'd slip his hands into their gills and bring them out of the water.

"Charlie will come home with his arms and legs all scratched up with the fins on those big fish. He doesn't have the patience for bank fishing with a hook, line and sinker. Ney went along with him one time and came home telling me it was like watching a rodeo to see Charlie riding those big fish out of the water. And they are not all that good to eat, either," Mama worried aloud as she went about her work in the creamery.

"I wish I could go along sometime and watch Papa tickle those big fish out of the water," Anna thought as she went about making dikes in the little ditches beside the rows of beans. The peas, spring onions and radishes were about gone but there was still a big garden out in the back yard to be watered if they were to have tomatoes, potatoes, green beans and corn canned this fall and carrots, potatoes, big onions and sweet potatoes in the bins in the basement.

Anna like to irrigate, she had always liked to play in the mud and it was so sandy in Wells that it wasn't that old black mud that stuck to everything and stained dresses. She went barefoot to water the garden, too. But it was the monotony of pumping water for a half hour or so till the water had run down every ditch that wasn't much fun. "Girls never get to go along or have any fun," she complained to her mother.

Mama had brought the churn with its two quarts of sour cream they'd saved from milking the jersey cow for five days. It was resting in the trough where the cold water was running out to the garden. "Oh, my goodness, Anna, you wouldn't want to be along with that bunch of half-naked men and boys dabbling around in that old dirty river, now would you?" she asked. Mama picked up the churn and sat down on the porch to turn that crank till the paddles inside the glass had turned the cream to butter - another monotonous chore for girls and women.

When the men came home that evening in muddy clothes with their tubs of fish, they were still in high spirits. "Darrel Comfort got a big fish, too," Dale said. "He managed to ride him all the way to the bank."

The smaller ones were more tasty for eating and all the men had fish to take home. Grandad had watched the rodeo and helped gut the fish. "These fish would have all died in another few days if it doesn't rain," Papa said. "They'd have run out of oxygen - trapped in that lagoon."

Charlie Allison was a provider, he brought home sand plums and choke cherries from the river banks and kept the whole family busy storing up food for the winter. He planted a big garden and had watermelons and cantaloupe planted down by Sand Creek south of Wells and big patches of sweet potatoes in the sandy stretches along the railroad right-of-way. Bushel baskets of produce sat on the porch of the creamery to sell or give away to those less industrious but no less hungry. As long as Papa was busy he seemed happy.

The winters were not the best time of year for Charlie, however. He was sitting in his big leather-backed chair with the wooden arm rests reading the Capper's Weekly one bitter-cold winter day when Jim Yonally came bursting through the door. "Get all your warm clothes on and find your skates, Anna," Jim said, "We're all going down to the lake and play some shinney on the ice. Myrtle is coming with the boys and she wants you to be sure to come along."

"My Golly, Jim," Papa exclaimed, "Do you know it's damn near zero out there? It's too cold for these kids to be out on the ice for any length of time. They'll freeze to death!"

"You can't skate in the summertime, Charlie," Jim exclaimed, "We'll build a fire and if anybody gets cold he can toss on a stick of wood and warm up."

"Jim, those tin cans you fellows use for hockey pucks are dangerous. Someone will get his head cut wide-open one of these days. I've saved some little three-inch chunks of hard rubber tires off of an old Nash I stripped down," Papa was talking as he pulled on his felt-lined boots, "Let me give you a few of those and some wood. I've been cutting timber down at Herman Hohnsee's and I saw up a load to bring home every day."

"Man, those chunks of hard rubber would put somebody away for good!" Anna heard Jim Yonally say as she was out to the tin shed to get her skates down off of a nail. He and Dad had come out to the shed to load some wood into Jim's stripped-down Ford with the box on the back.

"No! they'll stay down on the ice better and scoot along when you hit 'em with a buggy-stay," Papa explained, as he reached up along the roof of the machine shed to find a few more. "Take two or three. They won't fly around like a tin can."

"Papa, do you know where my skate key is for these clamps?" Anna asked. That was the worst part of ice-skating - her ankles were so weak and she had to find some shoes with heavy enough soles to hold those old clamps. Papa had ordered her some ankle-braces out of Marion Boster's hardware catalog. They bolted on the sides of the heel and had a steel rod that strapped onto the leg above the ankle to hold her ankles straight.

"Such a contraption," she thought, "I wish there was money enough in the world to buy a pair of shoe-skates like I've seen in the catalog but I can't let these old clamp skates stop me. That's what most everybody has to wear."

Anna and Myrtle were the only girls at the lake that day and there were dozens of men and boys. "Orville Dick, the new depot agent. is a real skater. So was Huck Strewve, Papa," Anna explained to her dad when she got home that evening. "They had four or five barrels lying on their sides and those men would skate real fast and take a flying leap and jump over all of them, land on their skates and come right back around and do it again."

"How did your ankle-braces work?" Papa asked as she shrugged out of her coat and peeled off an old pair of Dale's pants she had worn to keep her legs warm.

"This one hurt a lot," Anna said, pulling off her knee socks.

"Well, I should think it would, Anna!" Mother exclaimed, looking at the red, angry hole she had worn through the skin over her shin bone.

"Anna, you can't go skating again till you get that healed up," Papa worried.

The ice at the lake didn't freeze hard enough to skate on very often and Anna had no opportunity to skate again that year anyway. The rubbed spot just above her ankle took a long time to heal. Zinc Oxide ointment was used but Charlie Allison suggested that sunshine and nice spring weather would be the best cure. "Leave all that salve off of that sore and let it dry up. Take off your sock and that patch over it and sit out on the porch in the sunshine. That's the best treatment." The scab at last came off the first of June and ice skating was forgotten for another year.

Everybody, young and old got into the act when they had a big snowstorm. Kansas had a few - some winters were open, as they said, and what snow fell just drifted and piled up in the roads but one winter after the lake was there they had a sixteen-inch snowstorm. By coming all the way over to Sample's corner before turning south they could find a place near the south end of the section north of the lake where there was a long slope down toward Sand Creek.

Everybody brought something to slide on - big old sleds came down off of pegs in the barns. Big innertubes out of worn-out truck tires, sections of binder canvas nailed to flat boards for runners, little sleds, home-made in Santa's workshop, and the most fun-thing to slide on of all - Papa's big scoop-shovel. Anna could sit on it with the handle sticking up in front of her to hang onto and slide a quarter of a mile down that slope. It was almost as much fun wallowing in the deep snow coming back up the hill to slide again. Mothers were in on that kind of play - they had to help get the sled back up the hill for the small children.

****

"An idle mind is the Devil's Workshop"

Over a hundred people lived in Wells, - some were railroaders, some had worked in factories in the bigger cities and lost a job. Families came back to the farms and small town houses. They had no electricity or running water - no bathrooms - but then, no one else did either. But they all had time for fun. The drought, depression and dust storms of the "Dirty Thirties" as they came to be called, were years when there was plenty of time for play.

There were no crops to be harvested, they had burned up in the hot summers of the early thirties and would blow away in the dust storms each spring of the 'dirty thirties' but through it all there was time to play.

Summer, winter, fall or spring there was always something going on in Wells. The wonderful people who lived there saw to that. Nearly everyone had his own specialty or contributed to the other person's effort - and if he had no specialty he came and clapped to show his appreciation. Two churches were busy, too. Births, deaths, marriages, baby showers, wedding showers made activities all week long as well as the ringing of the church bell on Sunday morning. Certainly, the

170

churches saw to it that there were no 'Idle Minds' for the Devil to use for his workshop!

****

Kansas Boys

Come, all young girls, pay attention to my noise,
Don't fall in love with the Kansas Boys.
For if you do your portion it will be,
Johnnie cake and antelope is all you'll see.......

- From the American Songbag

Dale Allison was seventeen years old and had a paying job the summer of '31. Anybody could work for his folks but there wasn't much money around for anyone. But Dale had a job. He was more than the skate-boy at the Lakeside Skating Rink - he was in charge when Ray Allison and Roy Gawith were gone. By the fall the depression had tightened its noose around everyone's activities.

Dale decided not to go back to school. "Not this fall," he said, "Maybe next year, I will have saved up enough to go back to Minneapolis. Maybe I can even buy a car," he argued with Anna.

"Mama, Dale says he's not going back to school this fall. The skating rink will be open till Thanksgiving, he says, and he can't afford to quit the end of August and go back to school," Anna was worrying to her mother when she came home from an evening of skating.

"I know, Honey, I don't know what you're going to do about school either, now that Ney has moved away from Miltonvale. Charlie has about given up. With eggs at nine cents a dozen and butterfat at nineteen cents a pound and wheat at twenty-eight cents a bushel I can't blame him."

"Where's Papa now?" Anna asked.

"Oh, he's down stairs making home brew!" Mama said very little about things she couldn't do something about and she would never, never criticize Charlie to Dale or Anna but they knew that sugar and malt that went into that home brew beer of Papa's cost money. And it was also illegal to make beer, especially if one sold it. Of course he wouldn't be selling it and it wouldn't be on the table to drink either.

"I guess I'll go down and watch him a little bit." Anna said.

"Now, Honey, don't say anything to him about Dale not going back to school. It will just worry him." Mama said.

"I won't. I just want to see," Anna said as she went out the back door.

Papa's beer brewing was just like all the rest of his contraptions: he had found a big (twenty gallon, at least) distilled water bottle. It was in a wooden framework and had a kerosene lantern under it and it was full of a brown, bubbly liquid. With a cork in the top and a tube running

171

from the big bottle of beer over to a five-gallon pail of water, it was simple but effective. The water was bubbling as the gas from the beer escaped from the tube into the water. That way it kept down the smell, he explained to Anna.

"I'm just washing up a bunch of catsup bottles that Charlie Comfort gave me," Papa explained to Anna. "This beer is about ready to cap."

"How can you tell?" asked Anna, watching the bubbles of gas coming up from the bottom of the water in the pail, "It smells terrible."

"Does your mother know you're down here?" Papa asked, ignoring Anna's interest in the process of beer-making. Papa was always concerned about what Mother thought of his activities.

"Sure, I told her I was going to see what you were doing. Do you want me to wash those bottles?" Anna asked. Dad had a little bottle brush out of the cream station that was working to scrub the bottles pretty well.

"Oh, no. this is my project. If you want to help somebody, find something to do for your mother. I'll be done here in a minute anyway. It's about dinner time. Go set the table," Papa dismissed her. "And we won't be talking about this home brew upstairs, either."

"OK, Papa," Anna grinned at him as she disappeared up the cellar steps.

Anna had to figure out what to do about school since Uncle Ney had decided to move away from Miltonvale after he lost his job with the light company. For a man to have nothing to do out-of-doors was a very depressing thing. Uncle Ney did a lot of reading in the daytime when Dale and Anna had stayed with the family in Miltonvale. Though he wired around the meter and stole electricity from the light company to run the little fifteen watt bulbs, no one could read with them after dark. He gardened some but didn't have water to water a big garden or seeds to plant so he and Aunt Ethel had moved to eastern Kansas where his daughter, Pearl, and little grand daughter, Peggy, had moved.

Anna had a friend, Maurine Savage, who was in her class in school. She wrote to Maurine, worrying about where she could stay to go to school that fall. She would have no money for board and room and no one to batch with.

Maurine wrote back that her step-mother, Ferrill, was planning to move into Miltonvale and send Maurine and Abe Savage and her son, Orville Wilson, to high school that fall. She said that if Anna could furnish potatoes, onions, and at least twelve quarts of fruit and vegetables a week, she could stay with them. They had a little neighbor girl, Martha Belle Weaver, who would stay with them, also. Though it was crowded and still a mile from the school, Anna's Junior year was going to be fun.

Although Anna missed having her brother in school with her for the first time in her life, she went back to high school that fall by herself. Dale worked in the timber with his dad after the skating rink closed just before Christmas. They grubbed timber, cleaning the roots out of the

172

fields for August Hohnsee down along the river. Papa invented a portable saw rig with a fancy iron table that would feed logs into the blade. They sold wood for two dollars a 'rank', as Papa called it (it was half a cord).

"Mama, do you think I could have a quarter to buy notebook paper? I keep borrowing off of everybody, but now everybody I know is out of paper," Anna explained to her mother on one of her weekends at home.

"Anna, Charlie and Dale give away more wood than they sell. Nobody has a quarter. If it wasn't for our faithful Jersey cow producing an extra half-gallon of cream a week that I sell to the Concordia Creamery Company, we wouldn't have sugar syrup for on the pancakes, even," Mother looked so worried as she spoke that Anna said no more.

Dad and Dale were always up to Miltonvale to pick Anna up for the weekend. She was grateful for that. She knew it took gasoline to run cars and everyone was just living from hand-to-mouth, so to speak. The men gathered in mother's living room to play cards when it was too stormy to cut timber and Dale learned to make 'good German 'beer from Herman Hohnsee. It was his special recipe that his dad brought over from the old country.

The next spring Dale went back to work at the skating rink. He had time on his hands and several friends who hung around the skating rink to help him spend it. Huck Strewve, a bachelor who worked for Roger Blanchard, was a good skater and had a reputation for drinking hard liquor a lot. He furnished the malt and the sugar, bottles and other necessities and Dale made home brew for him down along Sand Creek below the dam at the State Lake. This was a nice business deal f r Dale but like all nefarious schemes it was bound to backfire. Mama found out about it.

"Charlie, your son is going to be caught making that stuff and wind up in the penitentiary for bootlegging. I knew he shouldn't be getting so knowledgeable about how to make that darned home-brew!" Mama walked the floor and wrung her hands. "You should have made him go back to school - even if he didn't have any money to go on - he can't keep working down there to that skating rink another fall. He'll be in jail."

Anna had never seen her mother so unhappy. Papa tried to calm Mama's fears while she continued to rail about the sin of intemperance, and Papa continued to assure her that he'd see that Dale quit making home-brew down below the lake - and that, somehow, he'd see that Dale went back to school in September.

Herbert Hoover was President of the United States but it was an election year. Franklin D. Roosevelt, governor of New York was running on the Democrat ticket. Most folks felt that nothing could help the farm economy so they scraped together enough to eat each day and played a lot.

Mama was dismayed by the situation. "Hoover just has another conference and then goes fishing!" she exclaimed. "Roosevelt is running for president now, but I don't know what good that will do any time soon if he does get in......"

The Inventinest Man

"The inventin'est man that I ever did see
Is the feller who lives next door to me

He's always ferever a-figgerin' out
Sumpin' to make; 'n he'll stand 'n shout

At the fence fer me to take a look
At some new thing he's undertook......."

an excerpt from I Hear America Singing,
an Anthology of Folk Poetry by J.B.H.

Papa was busy out in the tin shed, (a long machine shed that housed all of his activities that he couldn't bring in the house). He had batteries for chickens in crates waiting to be hauled to Salina, the nice Jersey cow - in the winter when she had to be fed - storage, etc. in the back half. There was room for his truck, a complete blacksmith shop and a long shop bench with a vise and grinder, a wall cabinet with pigeon holes where bolts, screws, nuts and small tools were poked at random. All sorts of angle and scrap iron was stored under that bench, too.

Dad was building an end-gate for his new truck. The one that came with the new truck was an awkward contraption that took forever to undo when one was in the elevator ready to dump a load of wheat. He had just put up with that clumsy piece of junk long enough.

"You'd think," he told Mama, "that Ford Motor Company could come up with a handier way of emptying loads or getting into the back end of a truck than that, as many trucks as they sell across this country...."

Dad had more time now than he had before the 'crash of '29' to do things out in the tin shed. He had bought a new Ford truck, a 1930 Model, but the recession had slowed down all farming activity and the farmers who had produce to be hauled didn't get enough to pay for the hauling. He had not anticipated such a terrible economic slump.

"Charlie has to keep busy to keep from worrying and he's more excited about making that end-gate than I've seen him in a long while," Mother explained to Anna. "He has Dale out there turning that forge hour after hour, every spare minute he's home. Mr. Peatling told him he wanted to see that invention he had in mind that was going to be such an improvement over the one that came with the truck. Anna, why don't

174

you go out to the shed and turn that blower awhile and give Dale a little rest. Charlie will never rest till he gets it done and on that truck."

The blacksmith shop was warm in winter and a hot smoky place in summer. Anna avoided the job of turning that blower more than a few minutes just to see the sparks fly out of the forge.

"Dad won't like it for me to try to take Dale's place, Mama. He expects Dale to be just as excited as he is about those pieces of scrap-iron that he's heating red hot. He thinks Dale knows when to turn and when to idle the blower better than I do," Anna complained as she went out the back door.

Papa scarcely noticed as she slid in beside Dale and took the crank out of his hands. The blower was hooked to a hole in the bottom of the forge. After the fire was started, Papa burned coal-slack or chunks of coke in the little nest of white-hot coals - and one had to know just how much to turn the crank to keep those coals burning white hot when Papa laid a piece of iron in the fire and when to idle the fire but keep it ready while he hammered the white-hot iron on the anvil to shape it. He wore long leather gloves with gauntlets to protect his wrists from the flying bits of steel as he held the iron with a pair of tongs. It was hot, dirty work and breathing the coal smoke wasn't very healthful either.

Dale ran to the outhouse and then into the kitchen to get a drink of water. "Dad won't miss me till Anna lets those coals die down too much and he has to add some coke and wait for it to come up to the proper heat. He don't like to wait a second," Dale explained as he snacked on a piece of spice cake Mama had just taken out of the oven.

"I know, Dale, Charlie gets so wound up in his work and so impatient. And he's not well. I wish he would go have an operation on those hemorrhoids when Fred Windhorst and Everett Payne go up to Nebraska this fall to have theirs worked on. These men never take care of their health - never take time out for a drink or to go to the outhouse. Your dad will be fifty years old next spring and he just keeps swinging that sledge like he's thirty," Mama worried out loud.

"I'll see if I can get him to stop a minute and come in for a piece of that cake but he won't even hear me if Anna has kept his forge red-hot like he wants it all the time," Dale said as he finished the last crumb in his saucer and headed for the back door.

It was a clever contraption Papa was making, even Anna had to concede, when it began to take shape. It had a series of levers operated by a handle that hooked up on the left-hand side and operated a pair of hooks that slid into iron brackets on the bed of the truck. When one pulled down on the handle the hooks slid out of the brackets and allowed the end-gate to swing loose from the bottom and be held at the top at each side of the truck box by a pair of cradles for iron rods that were shaped and fastened at each top corner of the end-gate.

"Charlie, that's the slickest end-gate I have ever seen," Mr. Peatling told Dad when he went in to Peatling Motor Company in Salina where he had bought the truck. "You ought to get a patent on it."

Papa was really excited when he came home from making a payment on his truck. "Stella," he said, "Mr. Peatling is sending away for forms so we can apply for a patent on the new end-gate. He says, once we get the patent he'll take it to The Ford Motor Company in Detroit and sell it to them to put on all the Ford trucks that come off of the assembly line."

Mama became excited with that idea. People weren't milking as many cows so the cream business had slowed down. Mama was getting smaller and smaller payments for the cream she bought for the Concordia Creamery Company. Any new idea that would help the faltering produce business that kept food on the table and clothes on the backs of her family excited Mama.

"Charlie, you have to draw a scale drawing of your end-gate and write fifty words or more explaining the difference between your invention and these three end-gates that have already been patented. Have you looked at this letter that came from the Patent Office?" Mama was studying the contents of the thick envelope that had come in the mail that day.

"That's why I married a school teacher, Stella," Papa's eyes twinkled as he explained to her, "I made the end-gate and I'm trusting you to write the explanations of why it's better and how it's different. Yes, I looked at those drawings. I can draw a scale drawing of my end-gate, but any fool could see that those three end-gates don't compare with mine....."

"But are you sure that 'Any Fool' can write fifty words or more on how they're different?" Mama was laughing as she cleared the table and found her tablet.

They worked every evening for a week on those three fifty-word essays and the drawing that they mailed with it. Mama was confident that they had done their best but it was several weeks before they had another opportunity to clear up a few points of similarity.

Papa scoffed, "I'd like to know how those fellows got their job. Any fool could see that there's no comparison to be made there!"

"Now, Charlie, we'll just sit down and I'll write what you say - leaving out the 'Any Fool,' of course. At least they haven't turned you down." Mama was happy to get an answer back.

After a long process of clarifying points and waiting for letters Papa got a Patent on his end-gate. It was to keep anyone from stealing his idea for twenty years.

Twenty years seemed to be a long time to all of them. Papa said, "Well, in twenty years, I'll be seventy years old, and I won't be around to care."

Papa took the cute little scale model of his end-gate over to Harrison B. Peatling, complete with the Patent. Mr. Peatling assured him that he thought they had a sure deal with Ford Motor Company. He would just make a special trip to Detroit and show them what an inventor and user of Ford Trucks had made to improve their fine trucks.

176

Mother and Dad had dreams of getting - maybe as much as fifty cents on each truck-body that Ford Motor Company sold - and each year they might get thousands of dollars. It seemed too good to be true and, as it turned out, it was. These were hard times for Ford Motor Company, also.

Mr. Peatling was very disappointed. He said, "Charlie, they told me that it would cost one dollar more on each truck to build and install those sets of iron on each truck They sell a million trucks a year and they would be able to sell them without that improvement anyway. And they just couldn't afford to spend that extra one million dollars. They said that truckers were still buying their trucks but that their dealers were having to repossess a good share of them. The Great Depression was taking it's toll, and the wheels of commerce were rolling slower and with little or no profit for anybody."

It was a clever new invention but, due to the depressed condition of the trucking industry, there was no market for it. Papa continued to struggle to make payments on his truck but in the end, Peatling Motor Company repossessed it also.

Dad didn't go up to Nebraska with Fred Windhorst and Everett Payne for treatment on his hemorrhoids that fall either. "It would have cost a couple hundred dollars," he explained to Mother, "And I'm not riding in that damn truck anymore; so they aren't bothering like they were last year."

****

"What a Blessing To Have an Education!"

(An extemporaneous Reading about 'The Crooked Mouth Family' that Anna gave so often at any gathering around Wells that it became her trademark.)

Dale and Anna enrolled in the Miltonvale Rural High School in the fall of '32. Dale was a junior and Anna was a senior. They batched or stayed with friends who had little more means of support than they had. Those were hard times! Farmers paid taxes which were used to keep school doors open and teachers at the front of the schoolrooms each morning. Some teachers accepted script, (an I.O.U. which said that when funds were available the receipt was good for so much money). Anna had a Home Economics Course in her senior year and took Quantity Cooking at 11:00 a.m.

Students with fifteen cents could come in the Lunch Room and buy a salmon salad sandwich and a glass of milk at noon. Some days the sandwich was ground bologna with relish stirred in to make it stick together and spread on the white bread. Anna didn't have fifteen cents a day to spend for lunch so she went home for lunch.

Home was across the street where she batched with Fannie and Esther Lilliman. Eight girls batched there - two in each of four rooms. She and Ferne Trickle paid seven dollars a month, three and one-half each for their room. It was furnished with a double bed, a little trashburner stove for warmth and a washstand with a bucket and wash pan. The pump for water was down the outside staircase and out in the back yard - as was the outhouse a bit beyond. Anna tried to wait and use the facilities over at the school whenever possible.

A small two-burner kerosene stove that Mother had used in the cream station provided a quick fire to fry the left-over potatoes from the evening before - in a skillet with a piece of home-cured bacon. What Anna and Ferne ate each week depended on what they had brought from home on Sunday night. Ferne usually brought cakes and pies. Farmers raised wheat and it sold for as low as twenty-eight cents a bushel so they hauled a load over to Shady Bend, Kansas and had it ground into flour for the winter. Ferne's cakes and pies got so gluey by Wednesday that they resorted to cooking the potatoes and pork that Anna had brought. She brought quarts of tomatoes, string beans and blue plums they had canned in the summer, too. There was no need to starve but Anna often thought longingly of the salmon salad sandwiches - she didn't like milk but she'd have drunk it with relish if she had had fifteen cents and could have stayed in the schoolhouse and ate lunch there at noon.

The room was cold, too. Anna was small - about five foot-two and so was Mama. So Anna was wearing Mama's good winter coat with the fur collar that winter. Mama said she didn't go anywhere during the week, anyway. But Anna couldn't cook with a coat on - so last night's cold side pork and a dish of tomatoes eaten in ten minutes would keep her alive till evening when they would build a fire in the trash burner with the kindling wood provided outside under the staircase. Then they would cook potatoes, carrots, sweet potatoes and pork, enough to sometimes have something left over for the next day.

Dale batched with Raymond Stein or stayed at Savages. Savages had an old victrola and Dale had a box of floppy records from the supply he kept down at the skating rink where they played music while they skated. "Managua, Nicaragua," "Love Letters in the Sand" and "Five Foot Two, Eyes of Blue" were great to dance to and the school kids learned to dance that winter in Mrs. Savage's living room.

Boys were not allowed in Lilliman's house but Dale wouldn't have come in anyway. He was still a little scared of girls. Anna had a boy-friend, Lynn Chartier, who had a car. He had lived in Miltonvale all his life and had odd jobs with people of means around the town. So he had money to buy gasoline at seventeen cents a gallon and he sometimes took Dale and Anna home to Wells and stayed all weekend so he could take them back on Sunday afternoon.

When Dale and Anna came home for the weekend they both stayed in the Woodman Hall and danced to Tip and Bessie Parrish's fiddle and piano on Saturday nights. Mama was happier. She and Papa weren't any busier in the cream station, so they could both come down to the dances. Papa didn't dance much except the square dances but Mama could watch her children - Dale was in school along with Anna now and he was staying inside the hall dancing - not running out in the dark playing "Wolf and Dog" - or in jail for making and selling home-brew.

"Wells is having another Town Play again this year," Mother said to Anna one weekend, "And they want you to come up with a Reading for one of the Intermissions."

"When are they having the play?" Anna asked, as she sat at the breakfast table relaxing that Saturday morning. It was good to be home from school in Miltonvale after being away for a whole week. As she was cooking for herself, it was nice also to have Mama put pancakes on her plate and offer hot syrup at home on Saturday mornings.

"Oh, not for six weeks or so. Edna Goodfellow just got the play books and is having try-outs for the parts. They may not have a high school here but people try to keep busy and have something going on to occupy their time," Stella explained. "Oh, yes, Myrtle has a new piece of yard-goods and wants you to help her cut a pattern and make a dress for the dance tonight. She'll be along in a little while."

Mother already had the boiler on heating water to wash Dale and Anna's clothes so they could go back to Miltonvale with clean clothes Sunday night. Mrs. Savage had Orville Wilson, Abe and Jimmy Savage and Dale to cook for so Mama would be filling a box with canned goods and potatoes for him as well as baked goods for Anna. So they couldn't relax for long - Saturday would be a busy day.

"Next Friday night is the Community Meeting. Edna Windhorst is getting up the program and asked me to tell you she has you down for a piece, too. 'Something you already know,' she said. Charlie told her he'd go up to get you kids early Friday evening so you'd surely be home in time for the program," Mama continued to fill Anna in on all she'd missed at home in one week's time.

Ferne got the flu about Christmas time and her parents made arrangements for her to board with someone the last semester - they didn't feel she was cooking well enough to keep up her health. So Anna boarded with the Home Economics teacher, Miss Greep, who had just married Roudy Courser. He was in Kansas City learning to be a mortician so she said she needed a roommate for awhile. When he came home Anna went to board with Pauline Palmer's folks.

George Palmer was the banker in Miltonvale and Fannie Palmer was a wonderful mother and homemaker. They lived in one of the nicest houses in town. Anna continued to bring potatoes, sweet potatoes and home-canned string beans, tomatoes and peaches or plums but no money. Dad and Mother just didn't have any.

The Presidential Election of 1932 had brought a Democrat to the White House for the first time in Anna's memory. Mama was vindicated - she had preached that the Democrat Party was the party of the people and that the Republican Party was the party of money and power.

Well, no one had any money to speak of, in the State of Kansas, at least, and Herbert Hoover didn't even carry Kansas in his bid for reelection in '32. Anna was sure that the Palmers were Republicans, though, being a guest at their table, she didn't bring up the subject and was quietly there when March 4, 1933 arrived. Economic conditions across the nation were desperate. Most of the country's banks had been ordered closed and general economic collapse threatened the nation. As a preliminary move the President declared a Bank Holiday.

The Miltonvale Bank closed its doors on March 4th and bank examiners were on hand for several weeks but it was never declared solvent so that it could open its doors again. George Palmer was a quiet, patient man who said very little. In the weeks that followed, Fannie worried aloud as she dished up the portions of cornmeal mush for breakfast that would sustain her family for another day.

"Well, if we have nothing to fear but fear itself, as Roosevelt said when he took office, I'd like to know what he's doing about it? Can anyone get his money out of the bank yet? Or any part of it?" Fannie said one morning to anyone who might be listening. George remained buried behind his morning paper.

"Mama," Pauline spoke up, "You know, they said at school that Mr. Kerr, the Ag teacher had just thirteen cents in his pocket the morning the bank closed. I wonder what he's been doing for money since?"

"I wonder how much money anybody thinks the Palmers have had to live on, Pauline? I get the feeling that everybody thinks George had an advance warning and lined his pockets with it!" Mrs. Palmer said.

At last Mr. Palmer put down his paper, "Fannie, do you know what they do with bankers in China when a bank fails?"

"No, I have no idea!" she retorted.

"Well, they just come in and tie their hands behind their backs, take them out to the curb, ask them politely to kneel down and then they shoot them in the back of their heads at the base of the skull and their bodies fall into the gutter." Mr. Palmer finished speaking and resumed reading his paper in the quiet nook. No one ventured to say more.

Anna would graduate in May. The Class of '33, whose motto was "Don't Dodge Difficulties" was certainly having to meet them head-on. They had given class plays and charged admission in both their junior and senior years and had sufficient money in the Miltonvale State Bank to have hired Commencement speakers and special entertainment but when the bank closed in March their money was lost. Since the bank was insolvent and never able to pay its depositors, they had to do their own Commencement Exercises. There was no money to rent caps and gowns so graduates wore their best suit or dress, sang their own songs and delivered their own Commencement Address. Eleven of the twenty-five graduates had solo activities from the Invocation to the Benediction. Anna delivered the final address which she had written out in long-hand and committed to memory. It was titled, 'Thanks to the Community' and took up five minutes of the time. It was eloquent though wordy but, since it was her specialty - dramatics - Mrs. Courser, their class sponsor, allowed her to deliver it in its entirety. She thanked the Board of Education, the taxpayers, the members of the faculty, the business men of the community, and the ladies who had helped with banquets. It was sincere and ended with: "Let us pay our debt to the community by years of noble living."

Mother and Dad came to Miltonvale to Anna's Commencement Exercises along with Uncle Fred and Aunt Cora Comfort from Wells. They had a neat Ford Sedan. They were not really Anna's aunt and uncle but Aunt Cora always said that all the children in Wells belonged to her. They had no children of their own but they ran the post office and had taught children how to behave in the post office since they were toddlers. Aunt Cora gave Anna a box of handkerchiefs and told her that she was one of the real achievers in Wells. There had been no high school graduates for several years because the depression that had started in '29 had caused children to give up or drop out if they lived in Wells - Anna had to agree with her - it had been a real achievement.

Lynn had given Anna a big album for graduation. It had pages for pictures of classmates, sports, and activities. Lynn was a year ahead of Anna in school and had been the Captain of the football team and lettered in all four sports; football, basketball, baseball and track so it had places for pictures of all of his achievements too.

There were pages where friends could write their memories of the good times of the high school years and since Anna had the album at school all of Commencement week it was filled with the writings of the many friends she had made in Miltonvale.

Notable among them is a poem written by her dear friend, Pauline Palmer:

Dear Anna -
    (I write this with all due apology to James Whitcomb Riley):

Little Orphant Annie came to our house to stay;
To wash the cups and saucers up (??huh!)
    and brush the crumbs away.
To swing the kittens by the neck, torment and tease
    us all
To warm my feet in bed, by heck,
To laugh but never bawl

Little Orphant Annie came to our house to stay.
To bring a ray (Yes, a small r!) of sunshine
    and brighten up the day.
To fill the house with laughter and very often Lynn
To never stay up after -
Oh well, she always did get in!

And all us other children, when the supper things
  were done,
We'd sit around the dining room table -
And have the mostest fun
A-listenin' to the wise-cracks 'at Anna tells about;
We'd laugh and sing and talk and play
And sometimes even shout.

Little Orphant Annie came to our house to stay;
But now the school term's almost up -
  she'll have to go away!

She'll take a spot from in my heart,
She'll take a friendship true;
She'll leave a score of memories that will
  always be like new.

She'll go to better work, I know;
She'll go to more success;
She'll make some man so happy if ever she says "Yes"!

Always a friend,
Pauline

P.S. I'll count on seeing you every time you're in town forever.

****

"Now is the winter of our discontent....."

from "The Tragedy of Richard III"
by William Shakespeare

Anna was lost - she had graduated! She was at home in Wells - with the rest of her life in front of her!

Pauline Palmer's sister, Helen, had gone to the College of Emporia with a tuition-paid scholarship. She had worked for and boarded with a doctor and his wife there. It didn't cost her any money because she ironed seventeen shirts each week for him and baby-sat their children on the evenings they went out. Helen had finished her two years necessary to get a Two-Year State Certificate that spring and planned to teach in the fall.

"Helen can give you a recommendation so you can work for that doctor's family, Anna, and you can get a transcript of your grades from the high school to prove you're entitled to a valedictorian scholarship. Your only cost will be about $75 for books and other fees," Mrs. Palmer explained.

Anna was too proud to tell her that there wasn't $75 anywhere in the world as far as she was concerned.

Lynn Chartier, her steady boy-friend, had graduated a year before she did from the Miltonvale Rural High School and had an athletic scholarship but could not go on to college - he was an assistant coach at the high school. She thought Coach M. L. Sallee had hired him, himself, for a few dollars a week the year she was a senior. But after the banks all closed Lynn didn't seem to have money enough to buy gasoline to come down to see her in Wells very often. When he did, he might stay several days. Bartering with one's friends and neighbors became a way of life.

Charlie and Stella Allison had no phone. "What was the use worrying about a phone? No one else has one either, so we couldn't call anybody anyway," Mama explained.

Anna had taken Normal Training Agriculture and Biology in high school as well as Sociology and World Economics in her senior year in preparation for acquiring a Second Grade County Certificate to teach in the rural schools in Ottawa County. They were still giving the examinations in the Courthouse in Minneapolis and there were at least half a dozen schools operating in every township.

"At least, I can pass that examination and apply for a school to teach this fall," she told her mother.

"Anna, do you remember how Frank McCormick used to tell you every time he brought in the cream that if you needed money to go to college in Emporia, he'd be glad to 'grubstake you' as he called it?"

"Yes. Esther McCormick went to Emporia and holds a Three-Year State Certificate. She teaches Sand Creek - but he doesn't mention grubstaking anybody these days," Anna said, sadly.

"Well, he had three daughters to give a college education and no sons to help him with his farming. But farms aren't making any money these days. He's lucky he got his girls grown up and working on their own before the crash came. He was telling me that you should look into taking that County Exam and teach this fall - maybe save enough to go to college in a year or two," Mother explained. "He went on to say that Esther was saying that Aldine Crawford is going to teach this fall. She applied for a school to teach and got it so she's going to take the County Exam this summer. Aldine was one of Esther's pupils down at Sand Creek."

The great gray blanket that hung from the heavens to the ground obscuring Anna's future lifted an inch or so as she was riding to Minneapolis with her dad the next morning. "I've known Frank La Plant ever since he was a little boy," Papa related.

Frank La Plant had been the County Superintendent since Anna was in the Big Room in Grade School. He had been a real inspiration to all the school children to learn to write with arm movement. He had no hands - just hooks - and the teacher would put a long piece of chalk in the clip at his wrist where he held a pencil or a fork, knife or spoon to eat. Then he'd go up to the backboard and draw the most beautiful birds with long tail-feathers, sitting in a lovely nest of leaves and curling blades of grass - all with arm movement. Then he'd teach her class in Writing. When he left everyone's handwriting had improved a little.

"I went to see him just after he had those hands cut off," Papa went on, "He was only thirteen and he said, 'Charlie, I put down my hands to save my head. Maybe I should have let my head go.'"

Anna had heard the story many times - how he was driving a team of horses and riding on a mowing machine with a long sickle that reached out about six feet to the side and cut weeds. When one wanted to turn he pulled a lever to lift the sickle up in the air, which disengaged the sharp tines that made up one set of blades working parallel to cut off the weeds. They were powered by a set of gears that moved as the wheels turned when the machine was moving.

"There was an old bird's nest caught in tines of the sickle when I lifted it to turn," Frank had explained to Dad, "And I stood up in the seat to knock it off and the team moved. I fell in front of the sickle as it came down."

"Who found him?" Anna asked.

"You know, he got up and laid those two hands hanging by the skin - across one another and walked to the house. He kicked on the door and when his mother came to open it, she took one look at him and fainted!" Papa explained with tears in his eyes.

Anna was sorry she asked. "The La Plants were Canadian French," Mama had explained, "So they were part Indian and very tough people."

184

At least, she had her hands, Anna thought as she rode along. Frank La Plant got well and had gone on to get an education so he could teach and even get elected County Superintendent! He went around to all the rural schools in the county and checked on teachers to see how well they were teaching and keeping records. Those records had to be accurate - the children's names and their ages - their attendance and their grades. Frank La Plant's name was on the big certificate Anna had received from the state for perfect attendance all eight years in grade school. She knew he would remember her.

"So you've made it through high school and you want to teach school this fall, Anna," Mr. La Plant said, as he appraised her from behind his big desk in the County Superintendent's office. "You are not very big...you know they still hire teachers to make the big boys behave so they can get any teaching done. How old are you?"

"I'll be eighteen years old in November," Anna said, trying to look as grown-up as possible.

"Well, you are not eligible to take that examination this summer. Kansas law requires that you be eighteen when you take it," he said.

"Aldine Crawford is taking the exam - she has a school to teach already and she's six months younger than I am. Maybe she applied for the school first? Would that make a difference?" Anna was grasping at straws.

"Honey, you'd have to lie about your age, or I would," he said sadly. "It's as simple as that."

Anna swallowed hard, squared her shoulders and said, "It's not worth that to either of us."

It was a long way down the Courthouse steps back to where Papa was waiting in the car.

Summer passed quickly. Everyone went to the local rodeos. 'Drugstore Cowboys,' Dad called them, would ride into town with a fancy saddle on their horse, a bandanna around their neck and a lariat hanging on the saddle horn. They would practice roping anything that moved. The local ball teams flourished. And, of course, there was the Ottawa County State Lake!

Anna had learned to swim quite well and, for a quarter, one could rent a basket and towel and go through the concession stand, change to a swimming suit, put one's clothes in the basket, pin the number on a swim strap and take a shower at the end of a great afternoon.

Anna had grown into the white rubber bathing suit that had been in the box of hand-me-downs that Aunt Belva had sent summer before last. The Lake now had a sandy beach and if one was just learning to swim there was a chained area. Beyond the chain the water was deeper and there was a diving tower with several diving boards. Anna liked to climb up to the very top and jump off the diving board. She would hold her nose and go down, down, down...at least thirty feet without touching bottom. People came from Minneapolis, Bennington, Ada, Niles, Verdi, Vine Creek, Longford, Lamar. Delphos and all the farms in between so there always was a big crowd, especially on Sunday. There was always someone to water-fight with and throw sand and the wonderful, hot Kansas summer was free.

One Sunday, Robbie Comfort, who had graduated from Grade School with Anna and Dale, was swimming with all the other friends at the Lake. Anna went up on the diving tower and jumped off into the thirty-foot water. Holding her nose with one hand and extending the other over her head, she felt the snap at the front of her waist come undone as she hit the water. The white rubber top to her suit skinned off over her head. She was naked from the waist up!!!!

She swam over to one of the poles that held up the tower and surfaced.... there was Robbie with the white rubber top to her suit!

"Let me put it on you," he said, as she made a grab for it.

She hung on to the pole and kept kicking him to keep him away, while he dangled the white scrap of rubber just out of her reach.

He giggled and hollered until everybody was watching to see how this situation would be resolved. Anna might still be there if Robbie's father hadn't come to the water's edge and told him it was time to go home, so Robbie had to toss her top to her. It was intact - she snapped it in front and tied the rubber strings behind her neck and across her back so she could emerge from the water. But Anna never again jumped off the top of the tower with that suit on - she no longer had faith in that one little snap.

Summer passed all too quickly and Dale went back up to Miltonvale to finish high school. Lynn Chartier, had worked all summer for a farmer north of Miltonvale but he still had no money to go on to college. He was going to help Coach Sallee again. Lynn did odd jobs for all the business men in Miltonvale and kept his old car running.

Dale came home one weekend telling Anna about a bunch of Miltonvale high-school-age boys going up to Aurora to a dance. Anna didn't think she was jealous but, somehow, she wan not happy that Lynn chose to go north to Aurora with a carload of boys rather than come down to see her. However, not long after, Lynn came down one Sunday and asked Anna to go up to Miltonvale with him. He explained to Anna's mother that he had asked his mother and Anna could stay at his house and bunk with his sisters.

"The Junior Play is this week and the Basketball Tournament in Minneapolis will give me a chance to bring her home," he explained.

"I want to teach you to drive my car. Get behind the wheel," Lynn said as they prepared to leave for Miltonvale. Dale was batching with Raymond Stein so he had groceries to take and all his clean clothes and fresh ironed shirts. He wasn't yet ready to go so Dad decided to take him, and Anna and Lynn drove off.

Anna had slid in behind the wheel a few times when they were hooking on trailers or were stuck in the mud - so she knew how to change gears. She just had to become familiar with the open road and not over-steer the car.

She drove all the way to Miltonvale and when they drove up to Chartier's house she stopped in the road. The driveway was down hill and short. Lynn always parked his car with the bumper in front almost touching the side of the house.

"Drive it on in and park it," Lynn said with authority.

"I don't want to. I've driven far enough - you park it," Anna said.

"I insist!" Lynn said. "You'll never learn by stopping every time you think you've driven far enough! Finish the job. Park it - now!"

Anna opened the car door on her side, stepped out, opened the back door, removed her little overnight case, and went across the street. She turned north at the corner and walked up the street to the new little honeymoon cottage of one of her best friends in high school.

Maurine Savage had never gone with boys much in high school, but had met Gwynn Lassey that very next summer and married him after a whirlwind courtship - just what proper, wholesome young girls should do. Gwynn was older and worked with his father in the hardware and plumbing business.

Maurine couldn't believe it when Anna told her she had walked off from Lynn and wouldn't be going back. "Can I spend the night with you, Maurine? I can sleep on this couch."

"Oh, sure, but Lynn will be at the door in a minute," Maurine said, laughing. "What do you want me to tell him?"

"Don't tell him anything. - I'm done with him," Anna said, her eyes flashing.

"Just like that? Without an explanation?" Maurine couldn't believe a three-year relationship could come to an end so abruptly.

Anna couldn't explain it either, but she felt strangely footloose and fancy-free. The great gray blanket that had obscured her future was still there, but somehow it had taken on a rosier hue.

****

These Are The Times That Try Men's Souls

These are the times that try men's souls. The summer soldier and the sunshine patriot will, in this crisis, shrink from the service of their country; but he that stands it now, deserves the thanks of man and woman.......
from *The American Crisis* by *Thomas Paine*

The winter of 1933-1934 was a time between times. The Great Depression had rendered the country paralyzed. Men had lost jobs on the railroad, in the factories, in the schools and in construction. Bread lines fed the hungry in the cities and people just existed from day to day in the little towns and on the poor farms in the country. Wells was no exception.

"Papa, what is this brown liquid in this vanilla bottle?" Anna asked.

Mama was out in the cream station testing a small can of cream that Charley Goodfellow had brought in that morning. He wasn't in any hurry, of course. He was one of the men sitting around a card table in the living room. There were five men gathered there. They were playing Schafskopf, (pronounced: 'shoscup'). It was a German card game played with a pitch deck. One or two sat out - only three could play at a time so there was lots of visiting every day in Charlie Allison's living room while the men played Schafskopf (German for Sheep's Head).

"That's Pain Relief. Old August Hohensee let me take some out of his bottle a while back. Why?" Anna's dad looked up from his card game.

"Why? Well, I just put a teaspoon of it in some white fudge I was making. It just fizzed and boiled and fumed up in my face. I knew it wasn't vanilla!" Anna laughed, ruefully. "I guess I'll have to throw it out. I used two cups of sugar and a half a cup of butter,too."

"Oh, no, don't throw it out!" Everett Payne said. "Pain Relief won't hurt candy - might even make it better - cure anything that ailed you!"

"He loaned it to me to try on my shoulder," Charlie said. "I don't know that it should be taken internally."

"Why, they even give turpentine with a teaspoon of sugar for croup. A teaspoon of Pain Relief with two cups of sugar and a half a cup of butter is bound to ward off any germ for the rest of the winter," drawled Alvin Underhill. "You were going to let us try your candy, anyway, weren't you, Anna?"

When Stella came back in the house there were only a few pieces of candy left, "My Goodness, Anna! I don't have any vanilla. Where did you get the ingredients for white fudge?" she queried.

The men all laughed. "She made up a new recipe," Papa said, "If it don't make us all sick pretty soon, you should try a piece."

The days dragged slowly by. Edna Goodfellow coached a play at the Woodman Hall that winter and Anna had a part. They made their own posters to advertise it - "Fifteen Cents - Adult Admission - Children Free." The Spiritualist Ladies Aid had big family-sized bags of popcorn to sell at a nickel a sack. The proceeds went into a fund to buy play books next year.

Anna went up to Miltonvale to visit high school a few days. She stayed with Maurine and walked home with her friend, Geneva Shay. They had sat in the same seat in Miss Jones' English Class. Geneva had heard a new song on the radio: "But Annie Doesn't Live Here Anymore":

> *You'll know her new silk hat*
> *And her polka-dot tie.*
> *If you see her, tell her I'm around*
> *But Annie doesn't live here anymore.......*

Geneve and Pauline Palmer had gone all through school together. They were Juniors - played violin duets together and were practicing for a trio with Lola Barber that they would sing at the Music Festival coming up. Anna and Geneva had been cheer-leaders for the Pep Club and both sang second soprano in the chorus last year. They had lots to talk about. As they parted there on the sidewalk, Geneva said, "Well, if I never see you again, you'll know what happened!"

But Anna didn't know. The whole town was stunned. No one could believe what happened. Geneva Shay died the next afternoon of spinal meningitis, December 7, 1933. Beautiful and healthy, full of life and exuberance one evening and gone the next day! She had been stricken upon arising in the morning - lapsed into a coma and died by four that afternoon. Spinal meningitis was very contagious and throat cultures were taken of the friends she had been near the day before. Anna's throat tested negative but Lola Barber had to take a serum shot to ward off the disease. Those shots made people very sick and several people whose throats tested positive had to take them.

The coffin was placed in the Shay's living room behind a window and Pauline Palmer stood on the porch and sang "When I Take My Vacation in Heaven". A whole town of mourners stood silently in the yard holding flowers that the dread disease would not permit them to place on the casket. It was a cold winter day as they filed up on the porch and looked through the window at their young friend who:

"With a cheery smile and a wave of the hand
Had wandered into an unknown land.
And left them dreaming how very fair
It needs must be since she was there."
(paraphrased from the poem in Geneva's obituary)

Anna went back to Wells feeling a dozen years older than her eighteen years. Yes, she had finally reached eighteen on November the eighth, 1933, and could take that Teacher's Exam next June. But winter was still ahead.

Dale had danced with Geneva at a Pep Rally the night before her death, but he had no germs in his throat when they took the culture in the school the next day. He was healthy and busy in Miltonvale Rural High School. He was a senior that year - his grades were good and he had time to rent (borrow) a clarinet from the Music Department. He would bring it home on weekends to practice. "Mary Had A Little Lamb" was the only tune Anna could recognize one weekend at the end of January.

"My throat is so damn sore I can't swallow, Mama," Dale said, "It's no wonder I can't play this horn!"

"Well, put it down and let me look in your throat," Mama directed. She set the flat iron back on the stove to keep heating. She was busy ironing his next week's supply of shirts.

"My Goodness, child, it's all full of spots!" she exclaimed, "I hope it's not contagious."

"Some of the kids have the measles, but you said I'd already had the measles. I can't get them again, can I?" Dale worried aloud.

"Honey, you've got something. Charlie will have to take you down to Dr. Hinshaw in Bennington and let him look in your throat," Mama decided.

Dad and Dale came home from the doctor's office in a high state of agitation. Dr. Hinshaw had taken one look in Dale's throat and pronounced, "Son, you have scarlet fever."

"He wouldn't even let him go back through the waiting room - he ushered him out the back door and gave me all the instructions: There's a thirty-day quarantine on scarlet fever. Here's the sign to tack on the door. He dated it in ink and signed it so the County Health Officer can lift it in thirty days from today. Everything in this house will have to be burned when we get ready to disinfect - that is, papers - even books if he reads them or anyone else opens them in this house for the next thirty days! Germs of scarlet fever lurk in the scales of the skin he'll shed off when his fever goes down..." Papa paused for breath as Dale stood shivering by his bedroom door.

"Goodness, he's got a fever, too!" Mama said, hurrying to wrap him in an Indian blanket off the couch. "I'll move the books we have on a shelf in his room - put them in our bedroom, Charlie...."

Dale interrupted her, shaking his head and gesturing at his throat and scribbling in the air with his hand.

"He wants to write something, Mama," Anna said with her usual sensitivity to Dale's wishes, strengthened by her sympathy for his sickness. "His throat is so sore he can't talk."

They both hurried to produce pencil and paper for Dale: "How soft is that bed of Anna's?" he wrote and another sentence: "I'll get bed sores if I have to lay in that bed of mine for thirty days."

No need to move the books from Dale's room - he didn't want to use that for a sick room. Anna's room was closer to the stove in the living room anyway and if the door was opened it would be warmer.

"My bed doesn't have a good mattress either, but I'll move my clothes and stuff into your room off the kitchen and you can have my bedroom - if you think the bed will be more comfortable," Anna agreed as she and Mama hurried to get Dale to bed with that fever.

SCARLET FEVER! The dreaded disease that could leave one with rheumatic fever and a weak heart for the rest of his life had befallen Stella's fair-haired son and Anna's precious brother. They couldn't do enough to help - if anything could.

"Dr. Hinshaw said I could go down on Hohensee's to cut timber so long as I worked alone for the next month. I doubt anyone will want to buy any wood - but I'll stay out of the house as much as possible and then I can go down to the grocery store and tell anyone going in - what we need - and they'll put it in a box on the store porch for us." Papa had been dealing with contagious diseases for a long time. "And I'll test whatever cream comes in or turn it away, Stella. You can't take care of Dale and buy cream," Papa went on.

"A month without any income at all!" Stella thought. "It's a good thing there's still some fruit and vegetables in the basement. We'll just have to make do, Charlie. There is not much cream coming in, anyway this time of year," she said, aloud.

Dale was very sick for three or four days. His fair skin broke out with a rash that itched. Mama bathed him with soda water and make chicken soup out of every hen that was not laying that month. His sore throat subsided and he really had trouble staying in bed six days.

Neighbors brought magazines - <u>Argosy</u>, <u>Whiz Bang</u>, <u>True West</u>, <u>Redbook</u>, <u>The American</u> - no one ever threw a magazine away but these would have to be burned at the end of the quarantine period. They were old but Mama, Dale and Anna hadn't read them so they were very useful. They all read so many magazine stories - especially the westerns - that they found themselves reading on the second page before they realized they had read that one before.

The clarinet that Dale had brought home from the school that weekend remained at the Allison house for a month and was disinfected before he could take it back to school. He couldn't blow it, however, which was merciful. A whole month of "Mary Had A Little Lamb" would have been too much for even Dale's ears. It remained in the case.

Pup, Dad's little terrier dog went down to the timber with him each day. Some of the more fearful neighbors didn't want him running out about town. "They thought that he might be carrying some of those dreaded scales that would be peeling off Dale's body," Papa explained.

Anna had a few dates with boys she had gone to Minneapolis High School with her freshman year and local boys who had never gone to high school. Since they were quarantined for the whole month of February - two boxes of chocolates were delivered to the door for her.

"Look, Sister!" Dale interrupted her reading of one more short story.

There he stood, peeking around the doorway between the living room and kitchen. He was holding out the smaller of the two boxes of candy, "You thought you had this hid so I couldn't find it, didn't you?"

He whirled around and around on his roller skates in the middle of the floor, holding the chocolates high above his head, laughing at her frantic attempt to reach them.

"Oh children!" Mama wailed, "Someone is going to get hurt. Anna, you don't care if he has that little box of chocolates, do you? Give it to him."

"It isn't good for him! He's sick! And I have to stay cooped up in here with him. I can't go anywhere or even talk to anybody. They just left the candy for me - not him!" Anna said, angrily.

"Oh, Sister! You can't eat six pounds of chocolates all at once. We can play "I Spy" with those boxes. You know you can't hide them where I can't find them!" Dale taunted her, rolling behind Mama and out to the kitchen, laughing.

"Children! Children! Just two little children - just a brother and a sister - and you can't get along!" Mama was repeating for the thousandth time, at least, the same remembered lament. They both dissolved into gales of laughter as Dale used the box of candy as a violin and with an imaginary bow, set her words to music.

"Just two little children, just a brother and a sister and you can't get along," they sang. Mama sat at the table, resignedly.

If Anna was going to get the scarlet fever, she could come down with it anytime after fifteen days and they'd be quarantined for another month. Dale could go back to school, though, but wouldn't be able to come home.

Mama was turning the pages of an <u>American</u> magazine for the tenth time. All the magazines were getting worn out - they had all read the stories many times. That magazine had a story about a mountain lion, - a big, black shadow stretched across two pages.

"What Would You Do If a Puma Jumped On Your Back?" Dale sneaked up behind her and pounced as he read the title over her shoulder.

Mama finally had all she could take - she began to cry. They were all exhausted and bored to death with each other. One more week and they could start burning all the magazines and any other piece of paper that would burn.

"Mama, I'm going to save this piece of paper where Dale wrote us that he'd get bed sores if he had to stay in his bed for a month. I'm going to thread it on a wire along with every important paper for the County Health Officer to fumigate when he comes out."

"Well, you must not be going to get the scarlet fever, anyway," Mama began to laugh through her tears. "You're still able to tease!"

Dale went back to school with his disinfected and fumigated clarinet in the case the first of March. He picked up his school work easily and planned to graduate in May. Business resumed as usual at the Allison household. Mama started buying cream and the card players could gather in the living room again. The period of contagion was over and Anna had escaped the scarlet fever.

* * * * * * * * *

The winter was not yet over. Kansas had been hot and dry for several summers, but people always looked forward to spring. Papa had saved seeds from every plant in the garden and was making plans to plant potatoes, beans, yams, peas, onions and even popcorn when a blast from the north sent the temperature down to ten below zero. Before the cold snap, as he called it, subsided a light skiff of snow fell and enough

192

of it clung to weeds and bunch grass in the pastures to make a home for the poor cottontail rabbits.

Rabbits had multiplied during the dry years and provided one more kind of meat for people. Dad set aside his spring garden plans and organized a posse of rabbit hunters. "I'm going down to the store and get a bunch of guys to go out with me. We can walk right up to those rabbits by following their tracks in the snow. We won't even need a gun - I don't have any shells anyway."

Dad had twenty-two rabbits skinned, cleaned and frozen hanging out in the tin shed when Dale came home from school the next Friday evening. The diet had changed from chicken to rabbit. Cottontail rabbits were one of nature's provisions that were 'pretty good eatin' as the local folks said. Anna's favorite way to eat them was to braise them - cut them up in pieces and fry them and then keep adding water to the skillet over a low fire for about an hour.

Some people made rabbit pie. Cooked for an hour or so and then covered with gravy made from the pan-fryings and covered with biscuits, wild cottontail rabbits made a great feast in those Depression days.

President Roosevelt was making a difference, too. Dale had been hearing about the Civilian Conservation Corps, the CCC, as it was called, that was providing jobs for America's unemployed youth.

"They are recruiting right now," Dale said at the table that weekend. "I'm thinking about signing up."

"When would you have to report in?" Papa asked.

"April 4th," Dale spoke softly.

But Mama heard. "Dale you can't do that - school won't be out till the last of May and you're going to graduate!"

"Now, Mom, I've already talked to the principal. He said I could take my assignments with me for Bookkeeping and take tests for the rest of the subjects and I can graduate anyway. I wouldn't have to be there...," Dale talked rapidly.

"It sounds like you have it all cut and dried already," Mama said.

"I think it's a great thing, I wish the government would recruit fifty-year olds," Dad said.

"Dale, couldn't you go June 1 and not miss graduation?" Anna asked.

"No. They'll be shipping out April 4th for Minnesota," Dale couldn't keep the excitement out of his voice any longer. "Dad, I'll be getting $30 a month. They'll send $25 of it home to you and I get to keep $5 of it for spending money. They'll furnish my food and clothes and I'll sleep in the barracks -"

"Minnesota! Dale, you will be gone for years! Have you thought of that?" Mother had read about all the things Roosevelt was doing to get the country moving again and she thought they were fine - for others. But - her son - it was going to take a bit of doing to get used to.

"It will be quite an experience for Dale," Mama talked to Anna while they washed and ironed Dale's clothes and baked cookies for him to take back up to school. "And young men have to do something. The boys on the farms have something to do - chores night and morning for one thing and it's time to start planting oats and spring crops. But Dale isn't a farmer's son. Charlie and Ney would have been among the first to join if such a program had been available when they were nineteen."

"Oh, I know, Mother. Dale said Lynn was considering going and a lot of the boys from high school who graduated and haven't done anything since," Anna agreed. "And Dale says we will be able to keep the car running and sugar and flour in the kitchen and a lot of things on $25 a month. Are we going to spend his money?"

"The Works Progress Administration is being organized and Charlie is going to Minneapolis to see about that, too. Twenty-five dollars is more than I made last month buying cream. We'll try to save all we can for Dale. When he comes home he'll need it to get started at something else." Mother was looking ahead and making plans. Things were looking up. Winter was over.

****

Pippa's Song

The year's at the spring
The day's at the morn;
Morning's at seven;
The hillside's dew pearled;
The lark's on the wing;
The snail's on the thorn;
God's in his heaven-
All's right with the world!
Robert Browning, from 'Pippa Passes'

Anna had arrived! She was eighteen! She could take that Second Grade County Teacher's Exam and apply for a rural school to teach. The Summer of '34 was at hand. Dad had planted a big garden and was hoping for rain - a typical day in Kansas.

"Dad, I have to be in Minneapolis next Monday morning at 8:00 to take my Teacher's Exam in the Courthouse," Anna said. "Esther McCormick has taught three years at Sand Creek and she's planning to teach in Wells in the big room next year. She told me she'd speak a good word for me with the school board at Sand Creek."

"Well, we have a lot to do before fall if you're going to teach in the country. You'll have to have a car to drive these muddy roads. Sand Creek is less than five miles as the crow flies but there's some muddy roads between here and there any way you'd drive."

194

"Papa, I have to get the job first!" Anna interrupted. She'd think about the car and the muddy roads and going to apply for a school to teach - after she had that Teacher's Certificate in hand.

Papa laughed, "I'll see that you are at the Courthouse door at 8:00 next Monday morning. You'll get that Teacher's Certificate all right. Your mother was a school teacher, too, you know."

"And your Aunt Belva, too," Mother said, "For thirteen years!"

"Now, Stella, we're not counting on Anna being an old-maid school teacher like your sister, Belva." Papa always thought that the best thing for a girl to do was to teach long enough to find a good husband and settle down.

"But she might not find a dashing young man like you were - just waiting in the very first district where she teaches," Mother teased.

"There aren't any of them around like Dad was," Anna assured them. "I'll probably be teaching forever - if I can get started."

The test was in fifteen subjects: Reading, Writing and Arithmetic, of course, enriched by English Grammar and Composition, Physiology and Hygiene, American History, Civil Government and Geography, Elements of Agriculture. English Classics, Elementary General Science, Kansas History and Music. With Principles and Methods of Teaching - these subjects had to show a degree of mastery to produce an average grade of 80% with no grade below 65%. When Anna had started to high school four years earlier they were offering a Normal Training course to prepare high school graduates for teaching in rural schools. In the Miltonvale Rural High School she had taken a course in Normal Training Agriculture and learned to cull chickens, judge livestock, splice and graft branches and twigs and be able to recognize common species of plants and animals. This was to be able to teach young people so that they could become farmers right out of grade school. Many young men never went on to high school.

Had Anna been able to go on to college she could have avoided this tough test. Two years at Emporia State Teacher's College would be a requirement before too many years but, since every small community had a little school supported by property taxes in that district, young teachers were still needed who could teach for forty or fifty dollars a month and board with some family in the district. She learned that if she could pass the Second Grade County Teachers Exam and teach for two years, she would then be able to take The First Grade County Exam. It had stiffer requirements: a per cent grade average of 90% and the addition of two more subjects: English History and College Algebra. Her career was ahead of her!

She passed that exam with a grade average of 85% and, armed with a Second Grade County Teacher's Certificate, she was ready to send out applications. Since a 'good word' had already been spoken for her at Sand Creek she started there.

Three school board members were elected in each district to supervise - along with the County Superintendent of Education and the

Kansas State Board of Education - the schooling of the children living in their district.

Herb Essig, Guy Peck and Betsy Constable were on the school board at Sand Creek.

"Dorothy, will you drive me around to the houses down at Sand Creek to deliver my application?" Anna asked her good friend, Dorothy Noel. Dorothy had graduated in Minneapolis a year ahead of Anna and could drive her dad's car. Ed Noel was the section foreman on the railroad out of Wells so his family lived in the nice house provided for the section foreman down by the railroad track at the southwest corner of Wells.

Dorothy was always ready for a new adventure so the next morning they drove down to Herb Essig's farm since he was the clerk on the school board. Esther had explained that Herb was the clerk, Guy Peck was the director and Mrs. John Constable, (everybody called her 'Betsy') was the treasurer. The application should be delivered to the clerk who would present applications he had received since school was out - at the next school board meeting.

Two women were sitting on the edge of the front porch of the Essig house when they drove in the yard. Anna had dressed carefully and had even put on silk hose and her best summer dress. She hoped she looked scholarly.

Grace Essig and her neighbor, Betsy Constable, were snapping beans on the west porch in the shade. Both ladies were barefoot. Betsy's battered old straw hat was lying beside her; her white hair rolled up on top of her head with a few damp tendrils about her face.

Those kind ladies put Anna at ease instantly but she didn't feel that she was overdressed. She knew that, had they been out applying for a school to teach, they would have given the job the same respect but she wished her silk hose were not so hot!

Betsy was to say later that Anna was no bigger than a pint of soap but she felt that she'd be able to handle the job since there would be just five little girls ranging in age from six to twelve that next winter.

"Herb isn't here this morning," Grace Essig explained as Anna handed her the carefully written application, "But I'll see that he takes your application to the board meeting. Esther McCormick taught here for three years. We sure hate to lose her. My daughter, Margaret, and Avis Constable will both be in the eighth grade and will be taking the county exam to graduate. Darlene will be in the fifth grade and the Lipes have two little girls, Betty May and Emma Jean. Betty May will be a third grader but Emma Jean will just be starting."

"We have quite a stack of applications to consider, haven't we, Grace?" Betsy spoke with a twinkle in her blue eyes.

"Oh, three or four - all just starting out since we've let it be known that we won't be paying any more than $50 a month for a new teacher. Esther was making $70 last year and we couldn't go any higher to keep her. Margie was so disappointed."

196

Anna resolved that her two eighth graders would be among the top ten in the county to graduate next spring if she got the job teaching them - she and Dale had been and she knew what they should know in order to graduate with pride.

"Esther told me there would be an opening here and that I should apply," Anna hesitated, wishing she could say she had a State Certificate from the Emporia State Teacher's College. "I just got my County Teacher's Certificate yesterday."

"We'll let you know in just a day or so," Betsy said. "Harvest is about ready to start so we'll have to meet right away and get it over with. If you get the job, we'll call you to come down to Guy Peck's and sign the contract."

"My folks don't have a phone but my brother, Dale has gone into the CCC and, if I can get a job teaching, maybe we will have one before long," Anna explained hopefully.

"Well, Herb can call Esther and she will let you know."

And they did - the next day Mr. McCormick brought in a little can of cream and told Mother Herb Essig had called Esther to tell her that they'd appreciate it if someone would tell Anna Allison to come down to Guy Peck's and sign a contract. Now, that was easy! The next steps were clothes to wear and a car to drive and she had all summer to do that in - she could take a little time out for play.

"I wish it would rain," Dad said, every morning. "The bedroom was so hot last night I couldn't sleep. If we don't get some rain I won't be raising a bit of garden. This year is shaping up just like last year. People are going to be starving around here next winter if it doesn't rain."

"Charlie, sprinkling your bed only makes you hotter when the steam rises off of the sheets," Mother said.

"Now, Stella, if you'd let me sprinkle your half of the bed - we might be able to get to sleep before the whole bed dried out and turned into an inferno," Dad retorted.

"It was cooler down by the lake last night," Anna entered the argument. She and Dorothy Noel, Jo Noonan, the depot agent's daughter, Dorothy's brothers: Claude and Ernie and Jo's brother, Charles had all driven down to the lake - just for something to do the evening before.

"How late does that concession stand stay open down there?" Dad asked. "Maybe I could have got to sleep if I hadn't thought you'd be getting home long before you did."

"Oh, we were driving around hunting pelicans. Someone told Claude that when they introduced pheasants down around the lake they brought in a pair of pelicans, too."

"Somebody was just pulling his leg, or he was just wanting to drive around. You didn't see any, did you?" Dad asked.

"No, but until we do we can keep looking. What else is there to do in the evenings? We had a lot of fun. Ernie had his guitar and there were others down there with guitars - Robbie and Paul Comfort and Howard and Oliver Constable have been singing for KFBI in Abilene," Anna said.

"Well, if Ed Noel was a farmer, he'd have something for those boys to do besides drive up and down the roads and burn gasoline. Man, I wish it would rain - I pumped the well dry this morning, watering the garden, but it doesn't do much good - it's all drying up in this 100 degree heat," Dad worried aloud.

Anna went down the street to get the mail and stopped on Marvin Overton's grocery store porch to wait for Fred Comfort, the postmaster, to bring it up from the train in his two-wheeled cart.

"Boy, I wish it would rain," Darrel Comfort said. "It was just too hot in the house for sleeping."

Charley Comfort agreed with him, "I told Nora we'd move our bed out in the yard if it got any hotter. I don't think it cooled off at all last night - the thermometer was above ninety when I got up this morning."

The Allisons got a letter from Dale that morning telling all about the big mosquitoes and the ninety degree heat in Minnesota. He had a special job being an orderly for the officers in the main barracks. It was a Civilian Conservation Corps but it was managed by military people as a peacetime pursuit.

"Dale is learning how other people live in other states and how to be a forester, too. All those lakes in Minnesota causes those mosquitoes," Dad said, "- and the humidity makes ninety degrees suffocating."

"That's what I've been telling you when you sprinkle the bed!" Mother said.

"Charley Comfort said he and Nora were going to move their bed out in the yard if it gets any hotter," Anna told them.

"By Golly, that's what we ought to do," Dad said. "What would you think of that, Stella?"

"Right down here on Main Street! Not much!" Mother retorted. "Nora lives up there where we used to - with plenty of trees and no close neighbors - it might be nice up there but not in our back yard! It gets daylight before we wake up sometimes."

But Dad had an idea and before the day was over he had a plan all worked out. When the darkness came he took the quilts and blankets off the shelf in each bedroom and hung them out on the clothesline in the back yard. "Just airing the winter bedding," he told Mother.

Mother was busy out in the cream station that night and when customers had collected their cream checks and gone down to the grocery store she came in the house to discover her bed had been moved to the back yard.

"The house shields it on the west, the tin shed shields it on the north, the garden on the east and the clothesline hung with the winter bedding makes a south wall. And we have the moon and stars for a ceiling, Stella," Dad explained with enthusiasm.

Stella couldn't believe her eyes. Charlie had always been so modest - would never wear his shirt unbuttoned, even and here he was planning to undress down to his BVD's and sleep right out in the yard. "Well, Charlie, you must be badly in need of a night's rest to have gone to all this bother. I can't wear my skimpy nightgown and ever go to sleep out there. I guess I'll have to find an old house dress to wear - I'm too tired to argue," she said with resignation. "Where's Anna?"

"She and Dorothy and that Noonan girl were here awhile ago - said they were going to drive down to the lake. I didn't start moving the bed out till they were gone. Maybe we can get to bed before she gets home." Charlie was bent on getting a good night's sleep out there in the yard. So they went to bed out under the stars.

At a little after midnight Anna, Jo and Dorothy stole silently into the backyard and quietly gathered the bedding off the clothesline, folding each quilt and blanket neatly and placing them at the foot of the bed.

The next morning at breakfast Dad was in good spirits. He winked at Anna and said: "Stella thinks I won't want to sleep out in the yard anymore. She got up early and took all those blankets down off the line - but she didn't fool me."

"Ah Ha! I knew if I just kept still you'd have to say something. You did it yourself, Charlie Allison!" Mother laughed. "You should know I'd be too tired to pull some antic like that!"

So each believed the other did it and Anna didn't dare tell them otherwise. Charlie Allison's daughter was a 'chip off of the old block' but this was one 'antic' they must never know she pulled!

They continued to sleep out in the yard - Kansas was continuing to set a record for the century - "Fifty-one consecutive days with the temperature over one hundred and not a cloud in the sky!" Rainfall for the year of 1934 was 15.81 inches - far below the average of 25 to 30 inches geography books credited to the high plains states.

Anna cut a piece out of the paper to mail to Dale - up there in 'cool' Minnesota - and wrote him a letter:

"We went down to the cement sidewalk in front of the Woodman Hall with an egg this afternoon, broke it and fried it right there on the sidewalk! It's really not a good summer for going barefoot, Dale, one's feet blister right through the calluses."

****

These are the things I'll write him - our boy that's in the West;
And I'll tell him how we miss him - his mother and the
    rest;
Why, we never have an apple pie that Mother doesn't
    say:
"He liked it so - I wish that he could have a piece
    today."

I'll tell him we are prospering and hope he is the same -
That I hope he'll have no trouble getting on to wealth
   and fame;
And just before I write "Goodby from Father and the rest"
I'll say that "Mother sends her love" and that will
   please him best.

                              excerpt from "Father's Letters"
                              by Eugene Field

The Civilian Conservation Corps, composed of America's unemployed youth, rendered services of public value in checking soil erosion, and in reforestation, flood control, road construction and similar work. The United States Employment Service helped to bring men and jobs together.

So Dale Allison and Lawrence Underhill from around Wells joined in April of 1934 and were sent to Minnesota. Young men from Minnesota were sent to Missouri, etc. This served to broaden the horizon of the nation's youth as well as that of their families left at home.

Letters came every week from Minnesota. If Dale was homesick it didn't show:

Dear Dad, Mother and Anna,

The Army runs these camps - our clothes are Army issue - I even got scabies from the army blankets that were issued for bedding in the bunks on the train on the way up here. Scabies are little tiny mites that cause your skin to itch. Those blankets had been in storage for twenty years - ever since World War I.

There are 200 men in our camp - 4 barracks with 50 men to a barrack. We are called enrollees. The Army runs the camp. Army officers are in charge but forest rangers are our bosses 5 days a week 8:00 to 5:00. The Mess Hall, Officers Mess, the barracks and Officers Quarters are all run by the Army. We are issued weekend passes but we go into the towns in army trucks and we can't leave camp without a pass. So, I guess you'd say we're in the Army now......

The company officer who is helping me finish my work so I can graduate in Miltonvale with the Class of '34 wasn't there when I turned in my last test in Bookkeeping but the Officer's Orderly said he'd see that it got mailed back to Miltonvale in time for graduation. Are you going up to hear my name read off at the Graduation Exercises? Write and tell me all about it..........

Did you get my wages? I'm glad I got the $5 and bought a few toilet articles from the mess canteen before the poker games started. Spec Cooper (Minneapolis) is really cleaning up. Most of these guys have never played poker before - they don't know they're dealing with a professional till it's too late......

We're planting trees. We get them from a CCC nursery. There must be 200 CCC camps up here. And there's work for that many. We're clearing stumps and dead timber from burned-over forest land and then a crew comes along and plants the little trees we got from a nursery up by Ackley, that's run by CCC boys - they are also from Kansas...

We have LEM's - Locally Employed Men and Forest Rangers for our bosses but nights and weekends the army is in charge. Forest fires between here and St. Paul (Minneapolis) are turning the sun into a copper penny up in the sky. We need lots of rain up here, too. This whole country must be dry as a tinder box. Smoke in the air burns my eyes...

Payday ... The Eagle shits again. A truck-load of us are going to Bemidji to a dance. It's about 30 below zero but we'll wear five pairs of long-barrels and have a tarp over the truck.........

We rented one room in a hotel and took off three or four layers of underwear before we went to the dance. Then we went back to the room and put them back on before we came back to camp. One drunk buddy kept saying, "Ma, I can't dance in these draggy drawers." At least he wasn't freezing with all that alcohol in his veins. The Minnesota girls are called 'Rabbit Chokers.' There's an awful lot of Swedes and Norwegians up here who really like to dance........

I'm living in the officers barracks now. I'm called an Officers Orderly. My buddies call me a Dog Robber - since I'm eating in the officers' mess hall - that means I'm eating what the officers leave - so I'm robbing the dogs of some good food. I even shine the officers' boots and run errands for them. I drove an army car into Minneapolis - it was a hot trip - 90 degrees in that city with its hot pavement. I was glad to get back .....

The forest fires are starting up again. I've been going out on the pole trucks - we've been setting telephone lines out into the fire zones........

****

"Old Zeke Perkins went to town one day
He went riding on a load of hay
He went riding in settin' on a board
Came ridin' home in a brand new Ford---"

Folk Song Belle Comfort sang to her
grand children.

"Anna, I've just talked to Claude Baker; he's going to bring you out a car to drive to Sand Creek this fall," Dad announced as he came through the door.

"I won't have any money to pay for one with till I've taught two or three months, Papa." Anna seldom called her dad 'Papa' anymore but this was one place where she was going to have to rely on providence and, somehow, Papa had always provided. She knew he'd do it again.

"Well, when Claude needed to go to school and Irv and Betty Baker lived away off up there where he'd have to walk three miles to any school, we kept him. Don't worry, Anna, he'll find you something that you can drive and you can pay for it by the month. What are friends for anyway?"

"I suppose I could find somewhere to stay during the week and you could come and get me on Friday nights, Papa," Anna said, tentatively....

"Claude is going to bring out something for you to drive," Papa dismissed that suggestion with no more attention than it deserved. Charlie had lost his son to the CCC's and he had no intention of losing his daughter for a week at a time to some neighbor just five miles away.

Claude Baker was a used-car dealer in Minneapolis. He had grown up, married Freda Trow - and they were a young family in 1934. He drove out from Minneapolis with several cars - one over-heated making the ten-mile trip, "Charlie, this one won't do," he said as he arrived. "I believe it must have a cracked block. You know, these slick operators put water-glass in these engines and you can't tell that the block has a crack in it till you drive them awhile."

"Well, come in and eat dinner with us. Stella is just ready to put the meal on the table," Dad said.

"People will do anything to make a buck, anymore," Claude said, telling them some of the tricks of the used-car business. "I'd probably sell this car I'm driving and let the buyer find out what's wrong with it, but we'd better not saddle Anna with it," he laughed as he spoke.

"I guess I'm no salesman," Charlie said. "All I know is hard work and nobody has any money to pay for hard work. This drought is killing off the farmers. The Agriculture Adjustment Act that Roosevelt got passed last year might help bring the price of wheat up from twenty-five cents a bushel but there won't be any wheat this year, the government can't make it rain. I get thirty-five cents an hour working on the WPA.

202

I'll tell you Claude, I really don't expect to ever have $50 in my pocket that I don't know what to do with - again as long as I live."

"Oh, Charlie, don't be so discouraged!" Mother said, "Things are going to improve.."

Claude laughed, "Why, Charlie, you can find $50 accidently almost any day!"

"Not after you're fifty-three, you can't," Dad spoke as though he had reached a ripe old age.

"Well, Anna's got a job teaching school, Charlie," Claude spoke optimistically.

"Yes, we have got to educate these kids," Dad agreed. "Some counties west of here are so dry and so poor that no taxes have come in and schools are starting this fall without any money. The teachers will teach for script and teach till it gets too cold in the schoolhouses - and start up again in the spring."

"What could you do with script?" Anna asked

"Nothing but save it until times got better and the farmers could pay their taxes. Then you could turn them over to the school board and they'd write you a check for cash," Dad explained. "Sand Creek is better off than that. They have enough to pay Anna fifty dollars a month for eight months and coal enough in the bin so she can build a fire in the furnace and teach all winter."

"That is a new school house down there, isn't it? Lottie and Dana were so proud of it." Claude was talking about his half-sister and her husband who lived just a quarter of a mile west of the schoolhouse. "Aldine started to high school that fall - so it was built in '29."

"Yes, it has a coal furnace in the basement and registers upstairs," Anna said.

"Charlie always builds the fires," Mother said, "I don't know how you're going to get along on the cold winter mornings when you have to start from scratch and get a schoolhouse warm for children by 8:30 ..."

"Maybe you'd better learn to bank the fire," Dad said, "With coal to use you can do that you know."

Anna didn't know, but she thought she'd cross that bridge when she came to it.

Claude brought out several cars before her dad finally decided one would do that cost $105 - $35 a month for three months. "Dad, that will leave me just $15 for gasoline, lunches, school supplies, clothes and everything for three months," Anna exclaimed.

"I could maybe let you have it for $30 for three months and $15 the last month," Claude bargained.

"I'll give you $15 right now," Dad said, "and Anna will give you $30 at the end of each month. We'll have it paid for by the end of November. Is that fair enough?"

"She's yours," Claude said, "Wouldn't you like to drive it?"

Anna looked around at her father but she could see no sign of apprehension on his face - no doubt but that she could just get in and drive a car - she had been riding in cars since she was three. Why couldn't she drive one? She got in, turned the key in the switch and stepped on the starter. She managed to drive her car to the corner north, make a U-turn and drive it back down the street in front of the house and get it stopped. Dad and Claude were talking about something else.

"My Goodness! Anna! Did you just get in that car and drive it without anybody along? You haven't driven a car since Lynn made you drive his with him along - and you quit him because you didn't feel capable of parking it!" Mama worried aloud as Anna came in the house.

"I don't know, Mother, Dad just acted like anybody could drive a car, he wasn't worried so I just got in it and drove it. It was mine, not Lynn Chartier's and if I wrecked it we'd just be out Dad's fifteen dollars. But I'm going to have to drive it a lot more before I'm very sure of myself," Anna said.

An opportunity arose a few days later when the 'fifty-one days without a cloud in the sky' was broken by thunderstorms and a 'regular gully-washer' in areas across Kansas, especially in the Republican River drainage. The river, unlike the Solomon, had shallow banks. It ran east of Concordia and on down across rich farming country in Cloud and Clay Counties.

"Mama, Dorothy and Jo and I are going to go on a trip to see the high water. They say the Republican River is three miles wide in some places," Anna announced, coming in from visiting down the street.

"Oh. Who's going to take you?" Mama asked. "The radio says there's lot's of roads washed out between here and Clay Center!"

"We're going to take ourselves. I'm practicing driving," Anna said.

"Oh, no you're not! Just three girls going gallivanting off like that! Charlie isn't here to tell you that you can't but I can tell you - what if you came to a place where the bridge was out?" Mother was emphatically against such an adventure.

"Mama. I'm a big girl, now. Remember, I own a car and I have to learn to drive it!" Anna laughed at her mother's fears.

"Well, driving into high water is no way to practice," Mama said. "Surely the Noonans and the Noels will know better than to let their daughters go with you!"

"Mother, if I come to a place where the bridge is out - I'll just back up and turn around and go back to the next corner and drive north. That's what I need to practice - backing up and turning around," Anna made it sound so simple.

Dorothy, Jo and Anna set out to see where the high water was. They drove north to the Oakhill road and turned east. Passing Oakhill and following road signs to Clay Center took them to a hill overlooking the Republican Valley. They got no further. The entire valley floor was covered with water and here the Republican River was, indeed, three miles across with debris floating in rushing water where once the road had wound through the valley and rich fields of corn had weathered the heat. Mother and Dad had often mentioned Uncle Frank Jordan's good luck to be farming Uncle Dave Coughlin's whole section of Republican River bottom land up east of Concordia. If the drought didn't wipe out the farmers, the flood would, it seemed.

"Well, we can't go any farther in this direction. Shall we just go back?" Dorothy asked.

"Well, I told Mother we'd just back up and turn around and try to go north till we hit the Republican up closer to Concordia. I'm wondering what the water is doing to Aunt Belva's nice farm home just three miles east of Concordia. I need to practice driving, you know," Anna explained.

"Yes, we don't want to just go back home," Jo agreed, "I had to talk like a Dutch uncle to get to come."

"Did anybody doubt that I could drive well enough to be hauling passengers on such an outing as this?" Anna asked.

"Something like that was mentioned," Dorothy agreed, "But I told Mama that I knew how to drive if you didn't. She said it sounded more like the blind leading the blind - to her."

They backed around into a turn-out into a field and went back the way they had come till they came to the next corner and turned north. Traveling three or four miles brought them to another place where the river had washed out a bridge, trees were caught on the stone abutment where the bridge had been anchored. A cow was swimming in the middle of the river, her eyes wild with fright. A little dog was clinging to a limb of the tree caught on the rocks. The three girls stood in what was left of the road bed and watched helplessly as the tree broke loose and carried the little dog swiftly around a bend and out of sight.

"I believe we can go home now, Anna," Jo said, "I packed us a lunch but, somehow, I've lost my appetite."

Backing a car would always be something Anna would rather not do if she could avoid it. However, they got that green '26 Dodge Coupe backed up and turned around and headed back home.

"Let's stop and eat that lunch," Dorothy said when they were almost home, "It won't do to let our folks know we lost our appetite on this excursion."

"Aunt Belva left her nice home up there on the river, anyway, and it's Aunt Erma and Uncle Frank who will be losing their cornfields and pens of hogs. It's just as well we didn't know whose little dog was floating down the river," Anna said, sadly.

"Here, eat my sandwich, Dorothy," Jo said. "I'm getting sick to my stomach again."

Their mothers were all surprised and relieved when they got home about two o'clock.

"Well, did you enjoy showing off you new car to the girls?" Dad asked that evening after they had discussed the awful devastation of the rampaging Republican River.

"No, I didn't even think about it," Anna replied, "And I don't think Dorothy or Jo envied me, either. We were all relieved to get home."

It would take trial and error and recovery and trial again for Anna to drive in mud and snow and dust and wind, up Beaver Dam hill and backing down it onto the bridge that was built at an angle to the road - when her car didn't have power enough to get over the rocks to the top. Or deciding to go around - either east or west depending on which road had been worked by the road graders. She would just have to learn to do by doing. The car was but a way to get there. And teaching would be the real job - what she had been dreaming of and waiting for in this whole time between times.

****

206

Still sits the school-house by the road
A ragged beggar sunning:
Around it still the sumacs grow,
And blackberry-vines are running.
The first verse of "In School-Days"
by John Greenleaf Whittier

"Anna, can you find me a copy of a poem that keeps running through my mind - I'm out there plowing and it keeps going round and round in my mind - It's driving me crazy," Toy Hanes was standing in the doorway of the Allison house by the creamery. He continued, in desperation, "It goes: Still sits the schoolhouse by the road, a ragged beggar sunning...around it still the sumacs grow...and blackberry vines are running."

"Sure, I can - it's in the little blue book I got one year for perfect attendance, just a minute," Anna said, getting up from her sewing machine by the front door.

"By golly, I knew this was the place to come! A little more 'perfect attendance' in school and maybe I wouldn't have to be out there in this heat trying to break up the ground," Toy said, pushing his battered hat back from his dusty forehead - to show a white line where the sweaty headband had rested (and a 'perfect V' shape to the black hairline that framed his handsome face).

"Pretty tough plowin', I imagine," Dad said, as Anna came out of her bedroom carrying the little blue book

"Here it is," she said, "The name of it is 'In School-Days' by John Greenleaf Whittier. You had the first verse just right - but there's ten more."

"Just what I need. I'll bet I'll have them all learned before I get that field done," Toy said, "I might have known that an old maid school teacher would have it right at her finger-tips."

"Now, look! I haven't even started yet," Anna said, laughing, "And you're been keeping Myrtle so busy helping you, we haven't been fishing or stirring up trouble. I've got to do something with my time."

"Well, don't marry a farmer if you don't want to be kept busy cooking for hired hands, raising a garden, milking the cows, and washing clothes. I tell Myrtle she's not going to have time for all that if she marries me. I need her to run errands...She's been up helpin' Avis out since she's got two babies now. I'd better be gettin' back on that tractor."

"You can have that little book. Dale and I got two or three of them in grade school for not being absent nor tardy," Anna explained as he hurried away.

Forrest Hanes, 'Toy' was his nickname, was nine years older than Anna and seven years older than Myrtle. He was less than ten years old when his dad had died - young, leaving his wife and six children. Stella, their mother, was left with a section or so of grass and farm land and a farming operation to manage. As a family they pulled together and were one of the success stories of the Wells community. His baby sister was Anna's grade school classmate, Avis. Avis had already married Ward Comfort and had a baby daughter and now a baby son! Yes, Anna was rapidly becoming an old-maid and very soon she'd be a school teacher.

Anna had finally arrived as she rang the Half-hour Bell on the first Monday morning in September, 1934. Sand Creek had twelve pupils when Esther McCormick started teaching there four years earlier but they had graduated or moved away and now the number was going to be five. There were two eighth graders: Avis Constable and Margaret Essig: one fifth grader, Darlene Essig; one little girl in the third grade: Betty Mae Lipe; and her little sister, Emma Jean, six years old and just starting to school in the fall of '34.

The Kansas State Board of Education issued a Course of Study each year in August at Institute - a week-long school held each year in the county-seat of each county. It was just in time to shine up the wits of the teachers and issue the new Courses of Study. That was the very first year Kansas had grouped History, Geography, Agriculture, Physiology, and all the social sciences into one subject and called it Social Studies.

Anna was in luck because this concept of teaching was new to all the teachers - and new to the State Board of Education, also. Experienced teachers as well as beginners all were starting even that year in learning this new way of imparting knowledge and understanding to young minds.

One couldn't follow the Course of Study, however; they had not had time to print a course outline to follow. Bulletins were issued from the State Office from time to time with guidelines to be followed for each new topic. There were lists of words and questions whose answers could not be found in the school books still in use for that year. To Anna this was a real challenge.

One of the first topics was Transportation. What a broad subject for six weeks of study.

"Dad, what do you suppose the word 'macadam' means?" Anna asked as she was studying the latest bulletin that had come in the mail from the state that day. "I don't believe it's even in the spelling book."

"I don't suppose it is," her dad answered, laying aside his paper. "It's a way of hard surfacing a road by rolling on layers of small rocks. A Scotsman by the name of McAdam developed it about a hundred years ago. They call it macadamizing."

"Well, how about that? If you can't find it anywhere, just ask Dad!" Anna applauded.

There were no encyclopedias in many of the little rural schools. Sand Creek was no exception. Anna finally bought a set from a travelling salesman for $65 - to be paid at $7 per month. She taught at

Sand Creek three years so she had the books paid for and left them as her contribution to future students.

Anna felt her first year as a rural school teacher was a success when Margaret and Avis both passed their County Examinations to graduate with scores in the top ten for eighth-graders in the entire county.

No one learned more than Anna that year, however. She mastered learning to drive a car in mud, wind and blowing dust; how to build a fire in a furnace with kindling and coal; to build a path to the outhouse (just one path that year - the path to the boys' outhouse grew up to weeds) - a path made from clinkers from the ashpan when she shook out the ashes from the firebox each morning; how to clean the schoolroom and sweep the floor each evening with compound: a mixture of sawdust and oil to keep down the dust; how to play games out-of-doors at recess and noon so that no one was bored and everyone stayed healthy and growing, or when to stay inside and play in the basement; how to keep time - she carried her own alarm clock, there was no clock in the school. And, above all, she saw that each child learned to his own potential and kept busy. She planned a program and had community meetings each month and if 'An idle mind is the Devil's workshop' is true then they should all have been angels.

The school day was divided into four segments starting at 9:00 a.m. and ending at 4:00 p.m. with a morning recess of fifteen minutes, a noon hour and an afternoon recess. That added up to one and one-half hours for eating, playing and attending to daily functions. Drinking water was provided from a pump in the school yard and each child had a tin cup on her own hook in the cloak room.

Opening exercises took up thirty minutes each morning. On Mondays the children recited Bible verses. Darlene had learned a new one each Monday. "God is Love" or "Jesus wept" was used most often by those who had neglected to commit a fresh one to memory. Singing songs from Songs That Children Love To Sing was a favorite way to start the morning. There was no piano the first year so this was done a capella with varying degrees of success.

Each child provided her own school books for her year in school and a ten minute recitation was provided for each subject with assignments for preparation of the next day's work. Since first, third, fifth and eighth grades recited in the same room, powers of concentration were tested as well as learning from others - their mistakes or successes.

The dry summers and open winters of the past several years conspired to shrink the new wooden window frames of the seven windows on the west side of Sand Creek School. The continual wind brought fine dust that filtered in around the window frames. Anna and her mother had been noticing a film of dust each morning - both at home and at school.

"It's coming from western Kansas," Dad said, as Mother was tearing a couple of old dishtowels (originally made from flower sacks) into dust cloths for Anna. "Nothing stops the wind out there and we haven't really had a decent rainy spell since this house was built and that Sand Creek schoolhouse was built since."

One Friday night in early March, Doll and Darrel Comfort had asked Anna and Claude Noel if they'd like to go along with them up to Minneapolis to a picture show. When they came out of the theater about midnight the wind was blowing and the air was full of fine dust.

Doll was pregnant with her first baby, "Now, hon, you wait right here and I'll go get the car," Darrel said, "if I can find it - I can't see anything in this dust."

And, indeed, not even the street lights could penetrate the dirt in the darkness. Claude and Darrel finally located their own car in the dirt and drove up at the curb. All the cars were the same color - just the color of the blowing, swirling dust.

"Darrel, do you think we can find our way home?" Doll asked.

"Well, the headlights surely don't penetrate it - anyway we've got to get you in out of this dust. Maybe when we get out away from town and these street lights we can see better," Darrel worried.

Claude and Anna got out and walked beside the car at every turn. Darrel didn't dare drive over five miles an hour. The ditches were deep on that ten-mile trek from Minneapolis to Wells. Once in awhile a big tumbleweed would blow across the road close enough to be seen.

"If a cow or a horse should be out on this road we'd never see it," Claude said. "We need a cowcatcher like they have on a train engine to shove the animals out of the way. Dad says they're having a lot of trouble in western Kansas running over animals on the tracks. The animals are blind from the continual dust storms."

"Did you hear about that old blind steer that got lost in a dust storm and wandered into Kansas City?" Anna asked.

"No, what happened to him?" Doll asked.

"Well, they said he was wandering around running into buildings and somebody threw a bucket of water in his face," Anna explained. "Dad was reading about him in the paper."

"And, did that help?" Darrel wanted to know.

"No. He fainted dead away. They said it took a whole bucket of sand to bring him to!" Anna laughed.

"I guess we asked for that," Dolly crowed. "Didn't we, Darrel?"

"Yeah, that sounds about like something your dad would read in the paper!" Darrel agreed, laughing.

Kerosene lamps inside the houses gave off a faint glow for only a few feet so it was hard to tell when they reached Wells. Old Jimmy Comfort described it later by saying, "Lamps gave off about as much light as an orange peeling."

The next day, being Saturday, there would be no school at Sand Creek so Anna and her mother went down to the school house and cleaned and swept the walls and floors for several hours. That fine dust had made streaks on the plastered walls out from those west windows eighteen inches, at least.

"It's a good thing we brought along this wash tub to dump these dust pans as we fill them," Stella said, "We'll have to dump this tub in the grader ditch on the way home. It's half full and we don't want the children tracking it back in."

"Or the wind picking it up again," Anna added. "I'm glad you came down to help, Mother, I couldn't have done it alone."

They both had covered their faces with red bandannas but their hair had turned the color of dust, "I don't know how men stand plowing and harrowing in the dirt all the time - just cleaning house is bad enough," Anna complained as they swept the floor with compound one last time. She'd be ready to ring the half-hour bell on Monday morning.

Monday morning came with the sun obscured by dust in the air - dust had become a way of life - the seer-sucker bedspread, the top cover on Anna's bed had had crinkles and stripes of pale blue and white when Anna went to bed the night before. Now, as she opened her eyes it appeared to be smooth and dull gray. She coughed as she slowly rolled the spread back, and remembered the testimony made by Sybil Hardesty in church the morning before.

Mrs. Hardesty had arisen to say, "I arose yesterday morning to a house full of dust. There was a blanket of dust shrouding everything in the room. I lifted a crocheted doily from the library table in the living room and there was the most beautiful dust pattern on the wood I dropped to my knees and exclaimed 'Thank you, God, for the beautiful, beautiful dust'!"

Beautiful dust, indeed! Anna didn't believe even Sybil Hardesty could thank God for it. Anna wondered what God would do to Mrs. Hardesty for lying in church as she gathered the ends of the bedspread and headed for the back door to shake out the dust. Looking out at the dusty world she hoped God had nothing to do with it. But the worst was yet to come.

Tuesday morning after a hasty clean-up of every desk at Sand Creek School, classes were in progress when it became so dark the children couldn't see to study. Anna lighted the gas lamp. It was used for the community meeting at night so was kept in good repair, gasoline in the base, a pump to fill it with air for pressure, a good generator and gossamer white mantles to give off the best light anyone could have without electricity. But it only made it clear that it was dark outside! At ten in the morning!

"Look, Miss Allison," exclaimed Betty May as she looked out a window, "I can see another schoolroom out there. And the lamp! And all of us!

Anna looked around the school room. The children's eyes were as big as saucers. They seemed to be waiting for her to signal panic! Or calm - or something!

It was so calm outside - the wind was not blowing as it had last Friday night. It was just as if a great gray blanket had settled down on Ottawa County - thick enough to obscure the sun - the trees, the roads -

the outbuildings! Anna hoped no one wanted to go out to the toilet. She was sure they couldn't find it in the darkness.

Avis Constable lived a mile and a half east and a quarter south; Darlene and Margaret Essig lived a half-mile east and a quarter north, Betty Mae and Emma Jean lived a half mile west and almost a mile south. They couldn't walk home - the way they had arrived if they couldn't even find the outhouse in the dark!! The school had no phone so they were captive of this unnatural darkness...........

Anna suddenly thought of a piece of poetry she had read in the old pictured Books of Knowledge there in the bookcase just behind her. Those books had no way to find anything in them -she selected the first in the row and opened it miraculously to the page.

She began to read about a strange occurrence in colonial times that had happened in one of the original thirteen colonies when a House of Burgesses was meeting in one of the isolated communities. It was a group of twelve men had been elected, each to represent his own settlement, which met to consider matters important to their government. The sun had come up that morning as it was supposed to do and they had all arrived to convene at 10:00 a.m. As the men pondered they noticed that darkness was falling. Lamps were lit as the twilight descended. They looked out and noticed that the cows were coming home from the pastures and chickens were going to roost.

One man rose to exclaim, "I move we adjourn this meeting. Methinks the world is coming to an end."

But another dignitary disagreed, "If, indeed the world is coming to an end, were it not better that we stay at our elected duties?" he asked.

So they deliberated through the day and by evening the sun had reappeared in its usual place. A footnote explained that they had had one of the unusual occurrences of that century when the moon had totally eclipsed the sun for a short time bringing total darkness for about ten minutes and twilight over about 150 square miles for several hours.

The little girls were sitting, listening, each at her own desk when the door opened.

"I'm taking these girls home with me," Grace Essig said, from the doorway. "Herb says there's a cyclone behind this."

She had tied a big square dishtowel over her hair - carefully -so the embroidered red plate hung down her back, Anna noticed, as she disappeared into the cloakroom to pick up the dinner buckets.

"Mrs. Essig, the Lipe children had best stay right here - I'm sure their parents will come for them when they can see," Anna spoke reassuringly, as she looked at Betty Mae and Emma Jean's faces. "And what about Avis? Won't her folks come to the schoolhouse looking for her?"

"They don't have a phone and their car isn't there," Grace said. "If this lightens on up I'll take her home after dinner. Come on, girls, the car is right by the door. I almost ran into the porch - you can't see your hand in front of your face," Grace shut the door behind them.

212

"Miss Allison," Betty Mae said, "My grandma said when there's a cyclone coming you should lie down in the grader ditch and it will pass right over you."

"The wind isn't blowing," Anna said. "It's so still outside and Dad said you can hear a tornado before it ever strikes if one is coming. If we hear any noise we'll cross the road - there's a deep ditch right over there."

The little girls seemed relieved. Anna moved closer to the gas lamp with her Book of Knowledge - looking for something to read to small children.

"Mammy's been through a cyclone," Emma Jean said. "She told us how the wind tore out big trees and took them up in the sky - it made an awful noise."

They huddled around the lamp sitting on the front desk and looked for something to read. It was almost time to go to the cloakroom for their dinner buckets when the door opened the second time. Jack Lipe stood in the doorway.

"We were afraid you'd try to walk home across Wayne Peck's and get lost," he explained. "I'm glad you stayed right here. Dad drove the old truck and I rode on the running board. We couldn't see the edges of the road."

Anna was glad she had stayed at the school - close to a ditch (if a tornado was coming) and waited patiently till she could turn the children over to their big brother and father.

She ate her lunch, graded a few papers by the gas lamp, and noticed that it was getting a bit lighter out of doors. By mid-afternoon it had lightened up so she could turn out the gas lamp and drive home. However, the dust hung in the air for most of that spring.

Spring was always an exciting time for Anna. The daisies showed their white heads in the pastures, teachers planned field trips - and there were the scholastic and track meets in all the schools. That year the rules came out from the County Superintendent's office - the county was divided into districts, with sixty-five to a hundred pupils in each district. There were five other schools in the same district as Sand Creek: Lindsay, Caledonia, Burnham, Sleepy Hollow and Schur.

Each pupil competed with children in his own grade in both scholastics and track. On a designated Saturday Anna's five girls went to Caledonia and took tests in Reading, Arithmetic, Grammar, Social Studies and Spelling. Teachers from each school were there to conduct the tests and grade the scores. Ribbons were awarded for First, Second and Third place scores. Points were tallied: Blue ribbons: 5 points; red ribbons: 3 points; and yellow ribbons: 1 point. Anna's five pupils scored in every test.

The following Friday the track meet was held at Lindsay - they had the biggest school yard and the largest school with eighteen pupils. Boys competed with boys and girls competed with girls and each competition was with one's own age group. Each pupil could enter in four competitions. Margaret Essig had got all blue ribbons in the Scholastic Meet and Avis Constable got a red or yellow.

In the track meet the scores were reversed, Avis got a blue ribbon in her four competitions - she was the fastest girl in the district, Margaret got a red or yellow ribbon. Darlene Essig had all blue ribbons in scholastics in the fifth grade and Betty Mae Lipe won all blue ribbons in the third grade in scholastics and they both did well in the track meet. Even little Emma Jean Lipe won a blue ribbon in the basketball toss!

When the scores were tallied and all the fives, all the threes and all the ones were added together for each school and the number divided by the number of pupils in that school - Sand Creek School took home the CHAMPIONS pennant. Anna sensed that some of the teachers with a greater number of pupils -eighteen, for instance to divide into the total points for their school, felt it wasn't fair. But the CHAMPIONS Pennant, orange with dark green letters, proudly hung in Sand Creek School till the district was dissolved ten years later.

So what if the other teachers were upset - her students were in the top five percent of that one hundred or so pupils - that was all! Nothing unfair about it.

****

A Psalm of Life

Tell me not in mournful numbers,
Life is but an empty dream!-
For the soul is dead that slumbers,
And things are not what they seem.

Life is real! Life is earnest!
And the grave is not the goal;
Dust thou art, to dust returnest,
Was no spoken of the soul.....

by Henry Wadsworth Longfellow

Myrtle Yonally and Anna Allison were the 'tomboys' of the Wells community. Jim Yonally, Myrtle's dad, had always included Anna in every wild escapade Myrtle wanted to go along on - ice skating, sledding, and the local rodeos.

Charlie and Stella Allison both felt that Anna should be more 'ladylike.' But, after she turned eighteen, got a job teaching school, and bought her own car, there was little they could do except shake their heads.

214

"I'd like to know why you want to go straddling off down to Manchester, of all places, to a rodeo! I'll bet there's not even a place to sit down!" Mama fumed.

"Now, Mama, who wants to sit down?" Anna consoled her mother. "Myrtle and I are just going along with her dad and her brother, Art, and Lou Heald, and I don't know who else, to watch them ride the bulls..."

"Anna! No lady says 'bulls'!" Mama stammered over the word herself as she preached to her laughing daughter.

"Well, maybe they're steers! Anyway, Myrtle says they're some of the wildest rodeo stock in the country."

"Well, I hope they have stout fences to hold them in - and a safe place for you to watch from," Mama worried aloud.

Anna thought of her mother's words again later that day as she watched from behind a fence as Jim Yonally was riding a steer who reared up on his front feet and tipped over straight forward on his head with Jim still astride his back. The crowd of onlookers gasped as the man was under the maddened animal and all that could be seen was flashing hoofs and horns.

"Who is that?" someone shouted. "He'll surely be killed!"

Myrtle and Anna knew who it was before a voice was heard to answer, "That's Jim Yonally from Wells - you can't kill him."

Jim did emerge from under the steer, picked up his hat and beat a hasty retreat to the nearest guard rail, seemingly, none the worse for the wear. Jim's reputation for dare-devil pursuits was well known. He had coyote hounds and soldiers on leave from Fort Riley would bring up their jeeps and land rovers and chase coyotes through ditches and gullies, up hills and down, where four-wheeled vehicles had never before ventured. Major General George S. Patton, brilliant tank leader, who distinguished himself during the conquest of North Africa in World War II was one of those weekend coyote hunters with Jim Yonally.

So it was that the whole community was shocked and saddened when the next summer during the time of the Sunset Spiritualist Church camp meeting that Jim Yonally died suddenly at home in his bed. Alice had heard him make a small sound in his sleep, she thought, and when she reached out to touch him she realized that she had heard the last breath he drew - his departure had been so sudden. Anna had seen Jim Yonally with his family at one of the meetings in the big tabernacle tent just a few evenings before he died - looking fit and as enthusiastic as ever.

The Spiritualists were building on their church for several years after they moved their 'Chautauqua grounds' from Delphos to Wells in the early twenties. The summer Spiritualist Camp drew crowds from all over the United States. They raised a huge tent to accommodate the worshipers, mediums, (those with the divine gift of being able to talk with friends and loved ones from the spirit world) and those who came to seek healing and messages from their loved ones from beyond the grave.

Jim Yonally's wife, Alice, was a Heald and closely related to the Comforts. The Comforts had brought the Spiritualist teachings to the Wells community in the early days and so Spiritualism was as firmly entrenched as the Methodist religion in the daily lives of the people around Wells..

The Methodist Episcopal Church had an equally impressive following and it's building had been there since 1901. Sunday School was well attended by all the children and Children's Day, held usually in early June during Sunday morning services drew parents who were Spiritualists also. Only a few people were positive that their religion was the only path to heaven.

Jim Yonally had a nephew who had been the minister of the Methodist Episcopal Church in Wells a few years earlier. Anna had taken piano lessons from his young wife. As Anna had no piano of her own, she had practiced in the church and sat on the piano bench in Reverend Mac Yonally's parlor. They lived in the parsonage just across the street from Anna's house when the Allisons lived in the north end of town.

As Jim was gone Alice couldn't ask him about funeral arrangements, so she did what she thought would suit him best. His family decided to hold the funeral in the tabernacle Tent on the Spiritualist Camp Ground. The Reverend Von Strode, a medium from back east who came every year to the summer meeting, gave the opening remarks. Reverend Mac Yonally, Jim's nephew, out of deference to the Mike Yonally family, Jim's brother, and a staunch Methodist, was asked also, to return for the occasion and to say a few words for his uncle at the funeral service.

Reverend Von Strode was tall and dark, with a Lincolnesque sadness about his gaunt face. "I can see Jim now," he said, "moving among his loved ones. He has his arms about you, comforting you in your time of deep grief. He wants you to know that his spirit will be with you always. He has more freedom now to be with you. He is not bound by the shackles of a body that needs food and drink. Jesus said, 'In my Father's house are many mansions' and I'm confident that Jim's mansion is right here since here is where he is today seeking to bring comfort to all of you mourners. His spirit isn't dead. He's reaching out to all who care."

When it was Rev. Mac Yonally's turn to speak, he made it clear that talk of anyone's ability to come back in body or in spirit was utter nonsense.

"The man is dead," he thundered. "He's in that coffin," he glared down at the coffin sitting in front of the podium and lifted his fist as if to drive in a few more nails. "And there he will remain until the resurrection morn."

Anna stumbled out of the back of the big tent into the bright, hot sunshine, blinking back her tears. She was making her way between the cars and mourners when she overheard Chester Miller, one of the real believers from the Methodist Church, congratulating the Reverend Mac

216

Yonally, "You really set them straight about what the Bible says about your Uncle Jim joining the ghosts and goblins around here. This was the best opportunity we've had, too. God sent you to bring that message, I'm sure."

But Anna wasn't sure. She didn't think that Mac Yonally knew his Uncle Jim as well as she did or he'd never think a few boards and nails could hold the soaring spirit of Myrtle's father for long. Von Strode was nearer right - Anna could never see those spirits as many of her friends had done but she was sure that Jim Yonally was already organizing the wildest angels in heaven on another coyote hunt.

****

Time You Old Gypsy Man

Time, you old gypsy man,
Will you not stay,
Put up your caravan
Just for one day?

All things I'll give you
Will you be my guest,
Bells for your jennet
Of silver the best,
Goldsmiths shall beat you
A great golden ring.
Peacocks shall bow to you,
Little boys sing,
Oh, and sweet girls will
Festoon you with may,
Time, you old gypsy,
Why hasten away?

by Ralph Hodgson

"Mother, I got a letter from Jo Noonan!" Anna said, with some excitement, "She's homesick down there in Wichita; she wants me to come down on the train and visit her for a week."

Anna had been down to the postoffice. Her friend Dorothy Noel was helping Everett Payne with his daughter, Vivian, and the house and farm work after his wife died. And since Jo's folks moved away and Jo had gone down to Wichita to Beauty School, Anna had some free time on Main Street in Wells.

"Anna, that would be quite a trip, getting south just a hundred miles to Wichita - by train, would take you all day. You'd have to change trains at Strong City and again at Newton. Trains all try to run east and west across Kansas," Mother said.

"But what else have I got to do with my time? I think it might be fun. Since her dad is a depot agent, Jo thinks that's the only way to go anywhere. You know she was always trying to get me to go with her to Albuquerque. She didn't know anybody in Albuquerque. She'd just ride down there on the train because that's where the Santa Fe was going. She'd get off and walk around the old Indian town that was right by the depot and return to catch the next train back," Anna explained.

"But she had a pass, Anna. It would cost you train fare, and what would you two eat for a week?" Mother was thinking of everything as she worried aloud.

"Oh, I'll borrow twenty dollars out of Dale's CCC money we have stored in my dresser drawer for him when he comes home - and I'll pay it back a little at a time when I start teaching this fall. Everybody's working somewhere, Mother!"

"It's too hot and the garden isn't producing and there's no cream coming in. I guess you could take a week off to visit your friend. We won't be canning anything next week," Anna's mother finally agreed. No doubt she thought of her own girlhood and how few avenues were open to girls as childhood gave way to womanhood and responsibilities rapidly replaced the carefree moments.

The round trip ticket cost $8.00. Jo met her at the depot in Wichita and they walked back to her room along the city streets. A big city where one didn't know everyone she met was new and unknown to Anna and to be walking the streets in it at dusk was an awesome experience.

"I'm so glad you came," Jo said, There's so many things we can do - the two of us - that one couldn't or wouldn't do alone."

Jo's room was in a rooming house up two flights of stairs but, once inside it was very much like the rooms girls batched in a week at a time in Miltonvale when Anna was in high school - except it was hot! It had a small window in the kitchen end and a larger window beside the double bed. This provided cross-ventilation. A small table, two chairs and a sink, a wash basin and a dish pan beside it with a two-burner gas stove provided for cooking, cleaning, eating, and washing. The loo, as Jo called it, was down the hall and was shared by the occupants of four other rooms.

A corner cupboard with a small counter beside the stove had dishes, cooking pots and an electric toaster. Jo also had an electric fan that would pull in air from the outside when the windows were opened. Five feet from the window by the bed was another rooming house just like her own, except no window directly across - just a blank wall. The small window in the kitchen end of the room was a transom window over a small door opening onto a fire-escape.

After a trip to the loo, they took assessment of their options. Jo was out of money - Anna had spent most of $2.00 on that eight-hour train trip buying peanuts and an apple and something to drink at each lay-over, so they were down to $10.00 for the week.

Jo's father was an alcoholic. He had been sent by the Santa Fe Railroad to Wells because it was a small depot and he could handle the agent's job easily. Jo's mother, Ellen, was an abused wife who had coped with her husband's addiction for as long as Jo could remember. Jo had a brother, Charles, a year older than Jo and a brother, Jimmy, about twelve at that time. They lived in the depot. It was a strong Catholic family - the first Catholic family Anna had ever known. They were in Wells for one stormy year - the beauty school was to be the way out for Jo.

"I thought Mother might be able to send me a few dollars but somehow Dad managed to find her grocery money. He won't get paid again till next week. When I asked you to come, I guess I was hoping to have a little something to finish the month on. I'm so sorry," Jo's dark eyes filled with tears.

"Well, we have $10. That will be plenty for this week," Anna answered cheerfully. "What do you have in the cupboard?"

"Nothing but some flour and salt; I ate the last crust of bread this morning! You see, you just came in time to keep me from starving to death," Jo said, "but we could spend all of that $10 before we could get one meal."

"But we won't," Anna assured her. "Let's go to that little grocery store on the corner we just walked by - I noticed they've got canned peas on sale for ten cents a can. We can buy a quart of milk, a loaf of bread, and a stick of butter for less than a dollar. We'll have creamed peas on toast every day - with money to spare!" She had fed herself on less than ten dollars a week many times getting through high school.

"I had no idea creamed peas could be so good," Jo said later, "Dad always made lots of money when I was little and we had a nice house provided by the railroad. Mother always fixed roast beef and baked a pie every day. I guess I'm just spoiled."

They went to church the next morning. Wichita had a big Catholic church within walking distance

Jo said, "We have to cover our heads." She dressed her best and tied a black lace scarf over her hair, "You'll have to wear that little white hat you wore on the train, Anna."

"But it's dirty. I wore it to protect my hair from the coal dust," Anna demurred, "Maybe I'd better stay right here." Anna was a bit reluctant to go to a Catholic church anyway, remembering the dread fear of Catholics that so many people around Wells had in 1928 when Al Smith was running for President.

"Oh, no, it will do just fine. The church is dark. No one will notice you - but they would if you went with your head bare. Put it on, we must hurry - we will be noticed if we come in late," Jo said.

A huge red brick building with foyers and small niches where candles were lighted and worshipers were kneeling for special private prayers did nothing to make Anna feel at home as Jo hurried her along to the big chapel; hundreds of people had already arrived and more were coming as they slipped into a pew and became a part of the congregation.

This kind of worship was a far cry from the little white Methodist Church in Wells where everyone knew everyone and a stranger was greeted and made welcome and coal dust on a little white hat would be noticed for sure. Anna would forever remain in awe of Jo's religion.

She began to understand a little better how the whole Noonan family could have patience to cope with their father's alcoholism. They had been brought up with the faith to accept what they could not change, not even with all their mother's prayers.

Anna got her hair washed and waved at Jo's beauty school for a quarter and waited each day while Jo and her friends practiced on the ladies who came to get their hair fixed. She was glad that she had decided on school teaching, however. Pleasing ladies sitting in front of mirrors while standing on your feet all day, every day did not seem to have a long-term goal like helping children learn to read. That, to her, was far more exciting.

Jo had made friends with a girl at the beauty school who had a boy-friend who was a bell-hop at the Allis Hotel. So she knew several young men who worked there.

They rented a boat and three of them invited Anna, Jo and her friend, Martha on a two-hour boat trip down the Arkansas River. It was cool on the river, the boys took turns at the oars and they all laughed and told stories while gliding down the river, around the bends and turns as it meandered through the city.

"Did you hear about the two snakes who were traveling across country looking for a cooler climate where it rained once in awhile?" one of the boys asked.

"Yeah, but you go ahead and tell it and be careful your tongue don't slip!" Martha's boy-friend said.

"Well, these snakes were coming from different directions and they met on the Kansas-Colorado border. The wind was blowing and the dust was flying and they stopped to talk. 'Where are you going?' the Colorado bound snake asked. The Colorado snake said, 'I'm hunting someplace where the dirt don't blow all the time. I'm headed for Kansas.' The Kansas snake shook its head, 'You might as well turn around and go back. The dirt is blowing there, too. It's hot and dry.....'"

"Just a minute," Martha's friend said, lifting the oar up over the speaker's head as he laughed and continued, "Here's where your tongue always slips!"

The story-teller went on,"'It's hot and dry and dusty. It hasn't rained this summer,' the Kansas snake said, 'Honestly, you won't even find a Pit to Hiss in!'"

He made a grab for the oar over his head and in the ensuing struggle and general laughter, somehow, the oar slipped into the river.

No one noticed the oar was missing as they all laughed and talked all at once until someone noticed that the two hours was almost gone and they'd have to be back or pay another $3.00. They had each chipped in a dollar as it was and there was no more money in the crowd. One of the boys was skillful with the only oar that was left and, dipping it in the water, first on one side and then the other, maneuvered the boat around the bends and back to the dock, shipping the oar as they rounded the final bend.

The caretaker was out on the dock, yelling, and pointing to the watch on his wrist. All the girls disembarked and hurried to the car with one of the boys who slid under the wheel while the other two boys argued with the burly timekeeper and entertained him with their watches, diverting his attention from the missing oar.

"Boy, that was a close call," one said as they jumped in the car and made their getaway.

"If he had thought to have us check in our oars, instead of worrying about ten minutes we'd all be - being held for ransom," Martha's boy friend said.

The next day Anna made the train trip back to Wells with more appreciation about how kids, the world over, work and play in whatever circumstances they happen to be born. Jo took a job in a beauty shop in Wichita, leaving Anna with only memories of her and her courageous family.

****

Happiness

Happy the woman, and happy she alone,
Who can call today her own;
She who, secure within, can say,
Tomorrow, do thy worst,
For I have lived today.
(Paraphrased to change gender from
Dryden's "Imitation of Horace")

"You have a letter," Mother said. "It's there on the radio."

"Who's it from?" Anna asked, as she dumped her armload of books, alarm clock and dinner pail on the kitchen table.

Mother smiled, "Look at the fancy square on the back," she said.

"Oh, it's from my good friend, Ray Hauck," Anna said, as she tore it open carefully at the end, "He told me he'd write me when he had an address in Manhattan."

She sat at the kitchen table and her mother poured her a cup of tea, "He wants me to come to Manhattan now that I have a car - to the Royal Purple Beauty Ball December 15th," Anna read.

"My goodness, Anna, I thought he knew you! A girl! Driving an old car clear to Manhattan and hunting him up on a college campus!" Mama sputtered.

"He has four or five roommates and they're all getting dates. He says they'll get me a room at the Hotel Wareham where the ball is being held," Anna read on...

"The ball will be formal for women. He's sent a clipping, 'Pee Wee Brewster's music makers will provide the melodies. Thirty-four aspirants for the title of 1935 Royal Purple Beauty Queen will parade their charms before Taylor Biggs Lewis, Kansas City artist and manager of the Muehlebach Grill......The queens will be chosen on personality and pulchritude alone. They might all happen to belong to one sorority...'" Anna finished, reading silently a bit more.

"Well, how did school go today?" her mother asked, thinking to divert her daughter from even considering such a proposal. Surely such a trek would be impossible.

Anna read her letter again that night before she blew out the light and fell asleep. She and Ray Hauck had lots of fun in high school when they were a debate team. They travelled to distant towns with Mr. Evans, their sponsor, and several other teams for debate tournaments. Anna knew she'd have a lot of fun in Manhattan but, as Mother said, it was all so impossible...

Friday, four o'clock - the end of the school day - the end of the week - the end of November. Anna went by Guy Peck's house to get a voucher, took it by Mrs. Constable's place for her signature and picked up her check from Herb Essig on her way home.

A plan was taking shape in her mind. Tomorrow she'd go into Minneapolis and see what Penney's had to make a formal gown from - something sophisticated enough to wear to a formal ball.

Anna wrote to Ray Hauck that night, telling him how she felt about her car - she could drive it to Minneapolis or Salina but to strike out on her own and drive to Manhattan! No one would believe she could do that alone - least of all, herself!

The next day when she brought home a length of black silk crepe and a remnant of silver metallic for trim, her mother said, "What in the world are you thinking of? You are not planning on going to Manhattan to a formal dance, are you?"

"Not really, Mother," Anna smiled, "I need a good dress, made with new yard goods. Do you realize I haven't made anything from new yard goods since I made that green skirt to go with my dark green sweater Dad bought me in Wichita two years ago?"

"Yes, and Charlie realizes it, too. And he's been so discouraged - it would worry him to death if he thought you were planning to take that old car clear to Manhattan. And by yourself, too!" Mother worried aloud.

"Never mind, Mamma, that would worry me too. I'm not going to do that - I don't know how I'm going to make this up anyway but two yards - the width it is, would make it floor length if I wanted...," Anna's voice trailed off as she looked at her mother's face. "Don't you think the silver metallic for the trim looks Christmassy?"

"It might if the dress was green," her mother retorted.

Ray's reply came the next Wednesday: his buddies had talked it over - she could come on the train from Salina. He'd send her a ticket and they'd get her a room at the Hotel Wareham, where the ball was being held. One of the guys had a car and they'd bring all their dates there. You weren't supposed to have anything to eat in the rooms, but they could smuggle in some pop and cookies or popcorn and they could party there afterward. All she'd have to do is go to Salina - leave her car there and take the train. He'd meet her at the depot in Manhattan. He sent her a clipping from the paper, 'TAYLOR B. LEWIS WILL PICK BEAUTY QUEENS FOR 1935' and under that in smaller letters: 'He Is Manager Of Plantation Grill of Hotel Muehlebach, Kansas City.' and in the smaller print: 'He will make the final choices for the yearbook staff at the Royal Purple Beauty Ball December 15 at the Wareham Ballroom.'

That night Anna cut out the formal and made the silver metallic cummerbund - just to see if there would be enough left to line the boat neckline so the silver lining would show.

The train ticket came on the 12th and, though Mother and finally Dad, when she told him, seemed resigned that she'd lost her mind and they'd just have to keep still about it around Wells, Anna went ahead with her plans and dreams about Manhattan.

"Anna, do you wish your folks had been able to send you to college instead of having to go down there to Sand Creek to teach school every day?" her mother asked one morning as she handed Anna the sack lunch she had put together for her.

"No, Mother, I bypassed college when I took that exam last summer. I look forward to each day, teaching. I love teaching," Anna said sincerely, and then added thoughtfully, "That Second Grade County Certificate will only last for another year and then I'll have to get more schooling probably. Thank you for packing my lunch - I really like those graham crackers with frosting between them to finish up with. No, Mother, if I were in Emporia, you wouldn't be there and I'd be starving to death, probably. See you tonight."

The sales lady got the silver metallic evening purse out of the showcase for Anna - it was perfect for her to carry at the 'ball' - $8 00! - more than the material had cost for the sleek black dress with the silver metallic trim that lay in her suitcase! She was in Salina waiting for the train. Somehow, she just had to have something to carry - she couldn't find evening gloves even if she would have worn or carried them - to a dance...Dad had handed her his last $10 - he knew she was down to her last $2 after she paid her final car payment and the month's gas bill at Philip Miller's garage.

"I'll take it," she said and the sales lady slipped it into a bag for her.

"That will make a wonderful gift for someone," she said as she took the $10 bill and handed Anna back $2 in change.

As Claude Noel would say, 'You gotta' look like a million dollars if you don't lay up a dime,' Anna thought as she drove her car into the storage lot at the depot. With $4 in her everyday purse and a new silver metallic purse - empty, of course, in the suitcase with the formal gown, Anna felt like a million dollars - she'd think about Christmas coming up - on her train ride home.

Ray met her at the depot in Manhattan in his Buddy's car that Friday night. Three of his friends with their dates had planned to go to the Old Dutch Mill, a night spot between Manhattan and Topeka, but a slow leak in one of the tires would abort that plan. She finished the night in the girls' dorm with one of the girls. Ray had made the reservation at the Hotel Wareham for Saturday night.

Anna looked as 'formal' as anyone at the ball when the other girls and their dates had gathered in her room (No. 306). They smuggled in popcorn, cookies, apples and bottles. 'NO FOOD IN THE ROOMS' a sign on the inside of the door said.

"Well, who could know that till he got in here, anyway?" Ray said, and everybody laughed and agreed.

One of Dale's quotes was that 'Anticipation is always greater than Realization' but the Beauty Ball at the Hotel Wareham was the realization of any and all of Anna's dreams of anticipation. Like Cinderella, she had a magical time at the ball. She had been able to dance since she and Norline Heald and Myrtle, Averill and Norris Yonally danced up behind the stage at the Woodman Hall when she was about ten years old - while the musicians played the music on the stage and the grown-ups danced out on the dance-floor.

But that was like comparing the creation of a four-tier wedding cake to baking mud pies when she was small - there just was no comparison.

The ballroom was decorated with royal purple and lavender crepe paper flowers and streamers and white balloons with just enough light to show off the dresses and suits all the dancers were wearing - the twenty-piece orchestra filled the room with music. Anna held her silver evening purse in her left hand resting lightly on the shoulder of her partner as they moved to the music in a dream world of enchantment.

Just after intermission the beauty queens were chosen: Taylor B. Lewis, dressed in a black tuxedo with tails and a black bow tie, stood out plainly as the imported artist and judge most likely to know about female 'personality and pulchritude' as the clipping from the paper had said. His cummerbund-clad waistline and slender hips emphasized his broad shoulders and black 'patent-leather' hair.

This contest, arranged by the yearbook staff would award five queens from the sororities with a full length picture in the yearbook. The crowd looked on, the band played softly as the girls walked across the front of the platform in a group, casually talking and then singly, turning slowly and gracefully while the judge checked points on sheets of paper on his clipboard. They were all lovely!

The contest over, the dancing resumed and, as always, dance enthusiasts stayed on till the music stopped at midnight. The three girls had to get back to the dorm by one o'clock so Ray and Anna's party went back to Room 306 early to finish the snacks that had been left from intermission. Several of the college kids called friends at home. The phone in the room was a luxury they had not had available since school started that fall. They sat on the bed and the chairs, laughing and talking - awaiting their turn.

"I wonder if anyone has the room next to ours," said one of the girls.

"Well, I can tap out Morse code. I'll ask them," said one of Ray's friends, as he tapped on the wall behind the bed. He got a faint but clear response.

"Yep, but he don't know Morse Code," he said, as everybody laughed.

They all left at once - still travelling with the one buddy who had a car, in order to get the girls back to the dorm by one A.M.

"Your train doesn't leave till eight tomorrow night but I'll be here to pick you up when we get that tire fixed. Jim is taking it down to the filling station when he gets up in the morning," Ray said.

"No. You are. Tomorrow's Sunday. I won't be up till noon," Jim said, with a malicious smile.

"Don't worry, Anna, I'll be here before then," Ray assured her as he closed the door.

Turning back into the now quiet room, Anna suddenly felt very much alone and a long way from home. She picked up the stray kernels of popcorn and the empty paper sacks that had held cookies and apples. The NEHI pop bottles would have to be taken out in her suitcase - they wouldn't look good in the wastebasket. Oh, well, she had lots of room in her suitcase, she thought as she wrapped the bottles in a couple of the sacks and set her suitcase on the bed. She was taking out her nightgown when a gentle knock came at the door.

'Was that tire completely flat when her friends went down to the parking lot - maybe they wanted to call their dorms - it was almost one when they left' she thought as she went to the door.

She had to open it wide enough to see the caller who had flattened himself against the wall beside the door.

"Has you boy friend left yet?" The bow tie and the cummerbund was gone, the shirt collar was unbuttoned but the speaker was unmistakably TAYLOR B. LEWIS, the erstwhile larger-than-life judge of female charm from Kansas City!

"Yes, but he's coming right back," Anna lied, "to use the phone again." Anger replaced fear as she looked at the slippery character who had replaced her dream king. "You must be more hard up than I imagined you'd be to pick up strangers in hotel rooms!"

"Why did you tap on my wall if you didn't want to be picked up?" he said angrily, "I called down to the desk and found that your room was booked to a 'Miss' so I assumed when your guests left you'd be ready to party some more."

"Well, you assumed wrong," Anna said as she closed the door and put on the night chain.

She remembered those kids fooling around with the 'Morse Code'-they were just as green as she was at the time, but she had learned not to tap on walls in hotel rooms even if her college friends didn't know any better yet. She was still shaking when she finally took off the glamorous gown and folded it into her suitcase. Some of the glitter was worn off the cummerbund and twinkled on the rug - she noticed as she turned out the light. Cinderella had lost her glass slipper and the coach had turned back into a pumpkin!

But the weekend was not over yet. Ray picked her up before lunch and they stopped at the desk to pay for her night's lodging. No. 306 was registered to Miss Anna Allison.

"Let me pay for my room," she said.

"No. The boys all chipped in - I've got the $2.25 for one night's lodging. But you may have to help me with a tank of gas - I've got the car till after I take you to the depot tonight," Ray explained, "And I'd like to show you around the college campus."

"Take this $2.00 now, then you can fill it up whenever you think it needs gas."

They were at the depot at 7:30 to present Anna's return ticket to the depot agent and found the room was full of black soldiers. They were waiting for the train to take them back to Fort Riley after a weekend pass. Black soldiers had their own barracks, their own mess halls - and their own haunts when they visited Manhattan or Kansas City. There would be room enough to fill a passenger car with them when the train came to take them back to Fort Riley on its way to Salina where Anna's car was waiting. 'And barely room for one small old-maid school teacher' Anna wondered? Ray and Anna spent a long half-hour sitting in the corner of the waiting room at that depot as the black soldiers chattered and danced about the room. They laughed and sang and told stories in a dialect unknown to Ray and Anna, just 'showin' off, she thought.

The depot agent stayed behind his cage as the room became rowdier and noisier. When, at last, the train was arriving, Ray went up to the ticket window and spoke to the depot agent, Anna following close at his heels. She had visions of boarding that train with thirty or more black soldiers for more 'entertainment' all the way to Fort Riley. However, the conductor had room for her in another passenger car and the black soldiers had a car all to themselves. She waved goodbye to Ray and blew him a kiss from the train window. It had been a magical weekend.

The following Monday her little girls were discussing what they wanted for Christmas.

"Emma Jean wants a black dolly," Betty Mae said, "but I don't think anybody is going to get it for her."

226

Anna remembered wanting a doll buggy and getting a little home-made doll bed instead - after she had found out that Santa didn't bring things without help from one's folks. "Emma Jean, maybe Santa will bring you the doll you want," she said.

"Mammy said he wouldn't," Emma Jean said, her big black eyes filling with tears.

As Anna was cutting off that evening gown that evening (she had enough material to make a softly pleated flounce around the bottom of a street-length dress), her eye fell upon the package from the Kress store. The silver metallic purse! It looked new - it even had the sales slip still in the package.

The following Saturday, the weekend before the Christmas program and gift exchange they were having at the Sand Creek School, Anna needed money desperately as she knew she would when she spent her last dollar - almost, on that silver metallic purse! She took it back to Salina and exchanged it for decorations for the school room, four little comb and mirror compacts for the 'big' girls and a little black dolly for Emma Jean!

'Necessity is the mother of invention,' Anna thought with satisfaction as she drove home from Salina that day.

****

The Old Model T

Oh, the old Model T in the junkyard
Lives in my memory,
For my mammy and my pappy
Thought they'd something pretty snappy
When they first got the old Model T.

Tune: The Old Apple Tree - accredited to Annette C. Symmes and printed in The Good Old Days, January 1969)

"Anna, I got a letter from Claude," Dorothy Noel said, as she stood on the doorstep of the Allison house on the Main Street in Wells.

Ed Noel, The section foreman, had been transferred to Cottonwood Falls on the mainline of the Santa Fe that spring. Claude had gone into the CCC's - he was in Seneca, Kansas, Ernie was working for a farmer up near Miltonvale, and Dorothy remained in Wells. The Noel family had gone separate directions and they were all homesick for family.

"Come in, Dorothy," Anna urged her, anxious for news of her friends.

Dorothy sat down to read: "I've bought a 1917 Model T Ford touring car from an old farmer up here. He had it standing in his machine shed. It is almost twenty years old but it looks brand new," Claude wrote. "I'm planning on driving it down by Miltonvale, where I'll pick up Ernie and his girl friend and then I'll be down to Wells. I want to go on down to Cottonwood Falls and see Dad and Muzzy. I'd like to have you and Everett go along. Ask Anna if she'd like to come too..."

Dad had just come in the back door from the tin shed in time to hear Dorothy, "That Ford may look brand new but if it's been standing in a shed for twenty years it won't even get to Wells, let alone go all the way down to Cottonwood Falls; that's at least a hundred miles further," he said.

"You know Claude, he wasn't here when they moved and he's homesick to see the folks," Dorothy said, "I'll ask Everett what he thinks."

Everett was twenty years older than Dorothy. His wife, Florence had died, leaving him with a ten-year old daughter, Vivian. Dorothy had been keeping house for Everett and his daughter. Dorothy weighed more than three hundred and fifty pounds when she was twenty-one, and had often told Anna she had to find a man - she wanted to have a baby before she was twenty-five, she said.

Anna and Dorothy had been friends since Anna was a freshman in high school in Minneapolis. Dorothy was a sophomore then and about five-foot-ten and weighed nearly two-hundred pounds. She was pretty and smart but she was bigger and taller than most of the football players, even then. Anna worried that she would have little chance of fulfilling her dream of motherhood in her early twenties. Now that miracle was about to come true, at least Everett had discovered that Dorothy had a good mind and a heart as big as her body. Anna hoped she'd realize her dream.

Claude arrived in Wells in his 'new' 1917 Model T touring car after noon Saturday. "It will go thirty miles an hour without crowding it," he said, "So, if we can start from here by three, we should be in Cottonwood Falls by ten tonight."

"Claude, does your dad know you're comin?" Charlie Allison asked. Claude was filling the radiator at the town pump by the creamery, and the canvas water-bag that lay in the folds of the laid-back top.

"No, I want to surprise them. Why?" he asked.

"Why, I was thinking he better be ready to come and get you when those old tires blow out," Anna's kill-joy father said. Dad didn't want Anna to go along with them 'on that kind of a wild goose chase' as Mother had already explained to her.

It was a beautiful summer day and there would be a full moon that night - no rain in sight for the whole weekend. Anna decided to go along with the Noel kids, Ernie's girl-friend and Everett Payne. Dad was always over-protective when it came to allowing Anna to go anywhere.

Six people, some heavy enough to make two, filled the touring car. Ernie and Arlene didn't get to take their guitars. Dorothy and Everett and Anna sat in the back seat; Ernie and Arlene sat in the front so Ernie could push up on the 'spark' and the 'gas' levers as soon as Claude pulled up on the crank and the engine 'fired'.

Chorus:

> *"Say goodbye, say goodbye, say*
> *goodbye to the old Model T.*
> *I hope Henry'll make another fit to*
> *be her little brother,*
> *Just as good as the old Model T."*

Arlene sang as they rode along. She had a strong singing voice and often entertained at Community meetings as she was growing up; in fact, that's how Ernie had met her. He had a guitar to pick on before he was old enough to have a girl friend.

"It won't be so rough riding as soon as we hit the Blue Line east of Bennington," Claude hollered back to Anna from the driver's seat in front.

"We hold this back seat down pretty well, Claude," Dorothy said, "Seems like it's settling some on this side."

"There wasn't any broken leaves in the springs. I looked before I paid that old farmer $25 for this 'new' car," Claude said. "It's just these rough roads."

They were nearing Talmage when Everett suggested, "Claude, let's find a garage and see if we can buy a spare tire here - just in case Dorothy and I sit too heavy on this right-hand back tire and it goes flat."

The mechanic just laughed as they drove in to inquire about his stock of tires, "I haven't had a tire to fit that rim for ten years, at least. I doubt if you can get them anymore," he said, " It's low, all right; it's probably got a slow leak in it. I don't think it would help it any to hunt for the leak and patch it. We could vulcanize it but it would probably leak around the patch - old rubber like that."

They drove on after they filled it up with gas and replenished the water in the radiator. Everett and Dorothy had exchanged places with Ernie and Arlene. Dorothy sat in the middle of the front seat where the whole chassis would carry her weight rather than that weak tire. At twenty miles an hour the going was slower so it was dark when they got into Chapman.

"Did you turn on the lights to see if they worked, Claude?" Ernie asked.

"They're on but they aren't very bright. It's not dark enough, I guess," Claude explained. "This car doesn't have a battery so they run off of the magneto."

"Oh, Wow! So when you advance the spark and go real fast they are bright and when you slow down so you can see somethin' they get so dim you can't see anyway. Some engineering!" Ernie sneered.

"You got that right, little brother," Claude snapped, "You want to walk?"

"We should find the fastest way out of town to avoid notice. They probably have a town cop here and they like to pick you up for no lights," Everett suggested. "There's going to be a full moon tonight after while and when we get out in the country away from these Delco lights we won't need headlights."

They were driving along in the darkness when Everett's fears were realized. A city cop pulled up along side of the car. "Pull over!' he said.

Claude and Everett got out and went to talk to him.

When they came back to the car they were both laughing. "Boy, I'm glad you were along with your WPA card, Everett," Claude said," he didn't believe my story about the CCC Camp in Seneca." Claude stopped to crank his Model T and jump in as Everett took up the story:

"There's a Transient Camp here for bums off the railroad and travelers with old jalopies who are hungry and can't get any farther down the road and are lookin' for a job. He wanted to throw us in there till morning. I told him I had a job and showed him my card."

"Why are we following him?" Dorothy asked.

"Oh, he's showing us the way to the nearest garage," Claude said, "That tire is completely flat now, in case you haven't noticed and we do need some light bulbs. Everett told him we had to visit our sick folks and be back in Wells Monday morning to go to work."

The answer was the same at the garage in Chapman. They didn't stock tires or light bulbs for 1917 Model T Fords. The city cop escorted them to the edge of town and wished them 'Bon Voyage'.

One after the other, the remaining tires went flat as they travelled along in the moonlight at about five to ten miles an hour. It was one of those magical Kansas moonlight nights that get cooler and cooler as the moon moves from east to west across the heavens.

'Papa was right,' Anna thought, as the midnight dew settled around the family going home to check on their 'sick' parents. 'If they aren't sick now they will be when we roll in to surprise them - as Claude said.'

All conversation subsided as the old Model T limped along - Claude continued driving - it was too cool and damp, as the early morning fog settled down on the creeping vehicle, for anyone to sleep.

Anna had no idea how they finally got there - she had retired to a state of dormancy when they finally stopped beside the Ed Noel home, three railroad cars, joined together, beside the main line of the Santa Fe - outside Cottonwood Falls.

Claude's folks didn't have the nice four-room house by the railroad track like they had in Wells but it certainly had more activity. A fast freight train or a streamliner whizzed by at least every fifteen minutes.

Claude's mother was truly happy to see her three children and their friends but it seemed to Anna, in her state of exhaustion, that Ed Noel was less than surprised, more like flabbergasted - that his children had arrived at his door at all.

Dorothy helped her mother stir up pancakes - the center car held the kitchen and dining room table and was a good place to sit and visit - when the trains weren't rumbling by - and the two cars, one on either end, had beds or bunks for sleeping.

"It's really too big for two people - the railroad put this place together to accommodate a section gang," Mrs. Noel explained, "but there's plenty of room for you girls to take a nap in one end of the house and the boys to play poker on the bunks in the other end."

"I have to borrow your car, Dad. I want to go see that old guy who collects Model T's to see if he's got tires for them. I have to get back to CCC Camp tomorrow," Claude said.

Ed Noel was nearly as heavy as Dorothy but he was four or five inches taller. Ernie and Claude were more like their mother's side of the family and weighed, maybe one hundred and seventy pounds each. He didn't laugh at his two 'small boys' like Anna's dad would have done. He just said, in a matter-of-fact voice, "Son, you'd better borrow my car and plan to drive it all the way to Seneca. Ernie can go along and bring it back to Wells. I'll see that collector about your Model T."

Claude's dad had a new 1935 Ford Sedan - maybe that's why Dad would have ridiculed Claude and Ernie about attempting to drive that old Model T Ford car two or three hundred miles. Ed Noel was the Section Boss on the train tracks that went from Wells to Barnard and the train ran every day through Wells all during the depression - in spite of many railroad workers losing their jobs. The railroad industry had slowed to a crawl, but Ed Noel had a job and could feed his family. He didn't need the $25 every month that was sent home from Claude's CCC Camp. Anna knew why Dad would laugh at Claude. Poor Papa - he was envious and Anna didn't blame him.

They left after a big Sunday Dinner and Anna was back in Wells by evening.

"Say goodbye, say goodbye, say
goodbye to the old Model T.
I hope Henry'll make another fit to
be her little brother,
Just as good as the old Model T.

****

Geography Song

First Verse:
> *Oh, have you heard geography sung?*
> *For if you've not, it's on my tongue,*
> *About the earth in air that's hung,*
> *All covered with green little islands.*

Chorus:
> *Oceans, gulfs and bays and seas;*
> *Channels and straits, sounds, if you please;*
> *Great Archipelagoes, too, and all these*
> *Are covered with green little islands.*

Second Verse:
> *All o'er the earth are water and land,*
> *Beneath the ships or where we stand,*
> *And far beyond the ocean strand*
> *Are thousands of green little islands.*
> *(Repeat Chorus)*

Third Verse:
> *Continents and capes there are,*
> *Isthmus and then peninsula,*
> *Mountain and valley and shore stretching far*
> *And thousands of green little islands.*
> *(Repeat Chorus)*

from *Songs The Children Love To Sing*
D. Appleton Century Company, 1916

In the second year at Sand Creek, Anna broadened her interest to include the community. Wells and its interests had seemed to stop at the road on the south side of the Ottawa County State Lake - which was just two and one-half miles south of the sidewalk leading across the street from the hardware store to the big general store in the center of Wells.

The people in the Sand Creek community sometimes hauled their wheat to Wells at harvest time but Bennington was really their home town. Anna's second year at Sand Creek had scarcely begun when Darlene Essig, a sixth grader announced, "Mother says we should take a float to the Old Timers' Day in Bennington. They'll be having a parade and all the schools are being asked to come."

"When is it, Darlene?" Anna asked.

"They have the Fall Festival the first weekend in October, and the Old Timers' Parade starts it on the Friday," Darlene paused. "Mama says she knows where we can buy a piano for $20. We need one if we're going to have community meetings - and there'll be prizes for the best float."

232

Anna had a few days to think about a float and what to do to earn $20. They could have a carnival at one of their community meetings - maybe a Halloween carnival, each child could take charge of one booth. She had Vernon Apple, another sixth grader, Betty Mae Lipe, now in the fourth grade, Joan Apple in the third grade, and Emma Jean Lipe, now a big second grader - not a very big group to have a carnival; she'd have to enlist the help of the community to raise funds for a piano. But, first, she'd have to win one of those prizes they were offering the schools to participate in an Old Timers' Parade.

That weekend Anna made the rounds to collect her first paycheck: $60! she was getting for her second year of teaching, "Betsy," she asked, "you're an old timer here, aren't you?"

Anna had called her school board member, 'Betsy' since Margaret Essig had told her last year that no one would have any idea who she was talking about if she continued to refer to their white-headed neighbor as 'Mrs. Constable.'

"Yes, I was born right here in this house in 1874 and I expect to die here," Betsy said as she signed the receipt Anna had picked up from Guy Peck.

"Well, that won't be any time soon since you're only sixty-one," Anna said, doing a rapid calculation in her head.

"You know, I went to a ciphering school when I was sixteen - there was a math professor who taught anyone who wanted to come, how to do sums and subtractions in your head in a hurry." Betsy said, "but most young people have to use a lead pencil."

Anna's attention was immediately caught! "You went to a ciphering school? Where? In Bennington?"

"Yes, I had finished McGuffys' Readers and was helping a woman there in Bennington. I always liked to cipher. You ought to have a ciphering match at one of our community meetings. Or a spelling match, I was good at spelling, too." Betsy talked on, "The most fun was at a singing school one winter in Bennington. For a long time I could recite all the states in the union and their capitals:

> 'Maine, Augusta, on the Kennebec River;
> New Hampshire, Concord on the Merrimack;
> Vermont, Montpelier, on the Winooski;
> Massachusetts, Boston, on the Boston Bay!'

The verses were set to music."

"Wow! I know the capitals but the rivers we didn't learn," Anna said, and then on inspiration, "The old time schools! That's it! We can have a singing school! Wouldn't you like to ask Mrs. Bender and Mrs. Peck and any other ladies you want? We'll need you all to ride on a float. I have to think of something by a week from today for the Old Timers Parade."

"Well, you ask Grace when you go to have Herb write out your check, maybe she could be the teacher. We can find a hayrack and Jim can pull it with the old blue Chalmers," Betsy agreed, "and I'll write out the Geography Song as I remember it and talk to Grace about it tomorrow."

Anna knew at once that she had said the right words, "We'll need you all to ride on the float." Betsy's eyes had gleamed and Grace liked the idea also. She found the old song book with the Geography Song in it. Sand Creek School wasn't just the children now in school - it was all the old timers who wanted to help. And they had a good cause - a piano for the school.

In the parade, a team of milk cows that Willis Darg, Herman Eisenhauer and Harold Buck had managed to harness with an ox yoke to pull an old wagon belonging to one of the earliest settlers, Hiram Crow, took top honors. Cows, like oxen, required all the skill old timers had that day. But in the school division, 'The Singing School,' from Sand Creek got first prize, also. The $5.00 prize started the nest egg for the piano.

The Halloween Carnival held the last Friday in October kept the children busy planning the ring toss and the apple dunking contest. Darlene ran the cake walk - she solicited all the ladies in the district to donate a cake and everyone bought a spot in the circle for a dime. When she had sold fifteen chances for the numbered spots on the floor, Darlene started the music and they started to walk. When the music stopped, they stopped on whatever number they were standing on. Emma Jean drew the winning number out of a hat. The lucky person standing on the number drawn won the cake. There were eight donated cakes so her cake walk netted $12.00.

Vernon had a couple of cork guns and a row of pop bottles and the men and boys bought chances to shoot. Anna and her mother made prizes of some sort nearly every evening in October. With a contest or a cookie sale that each child could manage, everyone contributed and by the time the games were over and cookies and cider was served, the piano was assured. Maurice Stultz, the lone bachelor in the neighborhood, handed Anna $2.00 just as he was ready to go home. He said he hadn't furnished a cake and was carrying one home that had cost him only a dime.

* * * * * * * * *

Since Dad had been working in the Works Progress Administration - the WPA - another one of Roosevelt's plans to put the country back to work and Anna was teaching school at Sand Creek it was possible to save some of those checks for $25 that came from the government for Dale. There were several in the dresser drawer in October of '35 when the shocking news came to the Allison home in Wells:

234

Dear Mother, Dad and Anna,

I'm flat on my back in the hospital. I've been operated on for hernia - so my writing's worse than usual....Write to me c/o Fort Snelling Army Hospital, St. Paul, Minnesota. These are cranky old army nurses from the First World War. One just told me I will not be sitting up for 25 days. The food isn't as good as at camp - Did you ever try to eat lying flat on your back.....?

I was really glad to get your letter. Some of these guys have been lying here flat on their backs for four or five months. They are young CCC guys just like me - I feel so sorry for them - these old army nurses have no sympathy for them. They have broken backs from falling out of those trees - they climb up on those ladders and their safety straps break or something and they fall backward. I guess these old nurses saw lots worse-off soldiers during the war - some of them are still in here, been here for years - paralyzed - they never will walk again.
I guess I'm not so bad off. But I'm just getting weaker and weaker from lying here so long. I was even strapped down for several days. They were afraid I'd get up and tear my stomach open again. One of those poles came loose in a hurry when I was reaching up to unhook the chain - as it rolled off the side of the truck it hit me in the stomach - they brought me into The Cities by ambulance........

The Allison's could do little but send encouraging letters, and hope that Dale would be allowed to come home soon. Meanwhile, life went on. The piano was purchased and in place at the Sand Creek School in time for the Christmas program. Anna loved the programs just as well as the children, but they had to study their lessons early to have time to practice. Grace Essig played the piano for them, and, while she never seemed to mind, Anna felt inadequate as a teacher because she was no pianist, and Grace would come over with her small son, Herbie, who would be in school the next year. They came after the last recess and they'd practice till four.

****

Election Year - Leap Year
1936

February, shortest month of the year receives a lot of attention, including mention in the following memory aids:

Thirty days hath September
April, June, and November.

February has twenty-eight alone,
All the rest have thirty-one;
Excepting Leap Year - that's the time
When February's days are twenty-nine.

Fourth, eleventh, ninth and sixth,
Thirty days to each affix;
Every other thirty-one
Except the second month alone.

"It is February 29, 1936 - Bachelor's Day or Ladies Day. Sometime back in the Middle Ages, women acquired the privilege of proposing marriage during the leap year. In 1288, the Scottish Parliament even codified the tradition with a law." Anna was listening to the radio that morning in Wells. She would be twenty-one before that year was over and so far there was no man in sight with any intention of changing her marital status from single to married and she hadn't been looking for one.

Her world was Wells and it's environs and the world was her oyster that last day in February in 1936:

"Late February days; and now, at last.
Might you have thought that Winter's woe was past;
So fair the sky was and so soft the air." (Morris).

Anna crossed the street to the sidewalk and strolled down to the post office. Frank Goodfellow was there first, visiting with Aunt Cora at the small window through which she presided over all the printed and packaged affairs that came and went from Wells.

Frank Goodfellow was the bachelor of the community - he had always been a man as far as Anna knew. His father had been killed in 1912 while repairing a bridge abutment on a township road. He, and another member of the township board, Fred Harder's father, had been saving the township money by shoring up the crumbling rocks themselves, rather than hiring a stone mason at public expense. The Goodfellows were frugal and conservative Republicans, of course, and conscientious to a fault. Frank's mother, Molly Goodfellow, was left with six children to raise. Since he was the oldest, possibly twenty-one at the time, Frank helped her bring up and send out into the world all his younger brothers and sisters. His baby brother, Earl Goodfellow, had been Anna's fifth - grade school teacher.

"Good morning, Anna," Frank said, "I expect you're busy teaching these days. Almost an old-maid school teacher, aren't you?"

"Well, I'll be twenty-one in November so I guess that's right," Anna agreed, and added, on inspiration, "Frank, I heard on the radio this morning that this is Leap Day- Ladies Day to ask the first eligible

236

bachelor you meet to marry you. If he turns you down he has to get you a new silk dress. Frank, will you marry me?"

Poor Frank! He sputtered and coughed and became too flustered to speak.

Aunt Cora was also shocked, "My goodness, Anna, is that any way to treat Frank?" she asked.

"Well, think about it, Frank," Anna said, laughing, as she opened Box 275 and took out the Allison mail. "I don't think I'd be such a bad catch."

"Now, Anna, you know you're not half my age," Frank gasped.

"But still - almost old enough to be an old maid! You said so yourself," Anna laughed as she left them. "I think you have twenty-four hours to let me know."

About a week later, Laura Goodfellow Comfort, Frank's youngest sister, delivered a wrapped package for Anna at the Allison house in Wells.

Anna unwrapped a little Kewpie doll dressed in silk. Frank had sent his answer.

"Now, Anna. Whatever possessed you to pick on Frank Goodfellow that way?" Mama scolded when she heard the explanation.

"Well, he called me an old maid - and it just came in handy that morning. I don't think it hurt him to think someone considered him eligible...I'll bet it even made him feel younger. Anyway, I got a silk dress out of it," Anna said, as she set the Kewpie doll up on the shelf above the radio.

"Anna, Edith Heald was here yesterday. She is the Democrat Chairman for Grant Township. She wants to put you on the ballot for Township Clerk this fall," Mother said.

"Mother! I won't be twenty-one till Election Day. I won't even be able to vote! Who is the township clerk now?" Anna spluttered.

"Oh, Honey, you wouldn't get the job, anyway. Ocea Copeman has had that job for years. Edith is just trying to fill the slate. You know how few Democrats there are in Grant Township!" Mother dismissed the importance of Anna's party picking her name to appear on the Democrat ballot in the Primary. "I told her to go ahead and put you down. You can't register in time for the election but you can be a registered Democrat by the time you'd have to take office next year so it's legal."

"Ocea Copeman! Oh, Boy! Will I have some fun with him!" Anna said, smiling to herself all the way to Sand Creek that morning. Ocea and Gene Copeman ran the big General Store in Wells though Anna was sure that it was Viola, Ocea's wife and Crystal's mother, who really ran the place. Anna was remembering how Viola lined those two men up and sent them out the door to that secret Ku Klux Klan meeting when they thought a Catholic Democrat was going to get to be President in 1928. They didn't like Roosevelt either. Now he was running for a second term. Yes, 1936 was going to be a fun year!

* * * * * * * * *

237

Dale was given a medical discharge and sent home in March, 1936. But he was no longer the Allison's teen-age son and brother. He had become a man - his twenty first birthday had been in June of '35. He was so weak from lying in that army hospital bed and frustrated at his weakness that he developed a very strong determination to get back to robust health at once. Every night he took the wash tub off the nail on the back porch, set it by his bed and carried a couple of buckets of water to fill it. In the morning he'd leap out of bed at 5:00 a.m., break the ice on the bath water and take a sponge bath - to strengthen his muscles and nerves - he explained.

The kitchen sink where the Allisons washed their faces and combed their hair before breakfast had a bucket of water on the shelf beside the sink - fresh-pumped every morning from the well in the front yard beside the creamery porch. A wash-pan in the sink with warm water from the teakettle on the stove or from the reservoir on the side of the cookstove had served to bring everybody to the table with clean faces and hands and hair combed before. But Dale had learned differently.

"We had showers in those barracks - cold water to wake us up and make us hungry - everybody gained weight," Dale informed them.

"Mother, the sink drain is frozen up again. This wash pan of water won't run out," Anna said from the sink as she finished washing her face and was combing her hair before coming to the table.

"And that's another thing I'm going to fix, Mother," Dale informed them, "and I'm going to start this morning."

"What are you going to start?" Dad asked.

"I'm going to dig a hole about four feet across and six feet deep right out there in the yard for that wash water from the sink to run in," Dale explained. "There's no reason why Mother has to empty the wash water out in the back yard, throw out the dish water or have the wash pan of water freeze in that pipe sticking out the side of the house every morning when it's no colder than twenty degrees. I can fix that."

"That's a good idea, Dale. I'll help you over the weekend. Today I have to work and the ground is frozen, too," Dad agreed, "it's supposed to warm up by tomorrow."

"I've got to do something to strengthen these stomach muscles; I'll quit when I'm tired but I'm starting today!" Anna's stubborn brother informed them all.

When Anna came home from teaching a day of school at Sand Creek that evening the hole was three feet deep and several long pieces of scrap iron and a couple of sheets of old galvanized iron had been gathered and were waiting for the hole to get six feet deep. The pipe from the sink would be changed to run through the floor and out through the basement wall two feet below ground level.

"I'll finish it tomorrow - it was easy after I got below the frost line. It's just pure sand in this country-just like brown sugar." Dale sounded a little weak but apparently no worse for the wear.

238

By the weekend when Dad wanted to help the job was all done and, while it still was a job to carry water in in buckets and fill the boiler on the stove on wash day - it was no longer necessary to carry it out. It was a great help to Mother and Anna. It would be several years later before there was electricity in Wells, a pressure tank in the basement at the Allison house and water at the sink just by turning a faucet.

When Dale went to Miltonvale to pick up his diploma - he found that his last work in the bookkeeping class had not been turned in by the Officer's Orderly at the CCC Camp two years before. He finally had to go to Minneapolis a piece of the last semester in 1936 to get a high school diploma.

Dale regained his strength and had the experience of almost two years in the CCC to broaden his understanding. Stella and Anna were trying to convince him that teaching a rural school was not the worst way for a young man to spend a winter.

The school board offered Anna $70 on the last day of school to return the third year - more than twice what Dale made in the CCC's. A $10 raise per month each year meant that Anna's teaching career was a success. Anna signed the contract and Dale decided, 'Well, why not give teaching a try?' Dale finally got that elusive high school diploma in Minneapolis and signed a contract to teach Concord in the fall of '36.

Dale had to take that Second Grade County Teacher's Exam and Anna would have to take the First Grade County Exam in seventeen subjects to have a certificate to teach. She had passed the Second Grade exam with a percent grade in the 80's in fifteen subjects but the First Grade test was going to be tougher; there would be seventeen subjects with the addition of College Algebra and English History. One also had to make a percent grade of 90 but, once acquired, it could be extended to three years. Dale and Anna decided to go to Cram School in Abilene.

Abilene was only thirty-five miles away but it was in another county and they had to board with some one there and be gone from Wells for six weeks. Abilene had a lot of German Mennonites who had settled there from Pennsylvania after the Civil War so Dale and Anna each found a big house whose owners took in boarders at $2.00 a week. The fee for enrollment was $30 and would-be teachers from all over Kansas gathered there. Anna met Dale's roommates and Dale met Anna's. They each had a date or two; there were about one hundred and fifty students, all cramming for the same reason - to be able to teach in a rural school that fall. They both passed their exams and were home for the blazing summer of '36.

Not only was the summer of 1936 hot, it was also very dry. "Between the grasshoppers and the drought, it looks like little chance for further crops this year, but with the big wheat crop safely cared for, no one seems to be complaining very much," stated an article in the Minneapolis Messenger on July 6, 1936. When the temperature in Minneapolis had hit a high of 116 degrees in 1934, a new record was set. That record only lasted two years as it was broken on August 12th and 13th, 1936, when the thermometer reached a record high of 119 degrees. E. G. Sidener, the official weather observer for Minneapolis recorded that in the 72 days from June 17 through August 27, a total of 56 days saw temperatures over 100 degrees.

Dale finished the summer as a hired hand for various local farmers, wearing his army-drab wool shirts that he brought home with him from CCC Camp. The sweat turned them white by evening. Mother washed clothes with a tub and stomper and had clean work clothes for Dad and Dale every day. Anna helped her carry in buckets of water from the old hand pump by the creamery. It could also be heard filling canvas water jugs almost every hour of the night at the Allison house by the side of the road. Farmers passing through always knew where to stop for water.

Dad worked for the Works Progress Administration (WPA) that summer. Farmers had few cows and separators were used less and less to sell cream. Some farmers worked up milk routes and hauled milk for themselves and their neighbors to market in Concordia or Salina. Mama seldom had cream to test for the Concordia Creamery Company.

Employees had to have a Social Security Number and companies hiring more than four employees had to report the amount of wages they paid to each employee and pay in a percentage in taxes to the federal government. This amount was being matched by taxes being taken out of the wages they had paid the employee. Mother had been thrilled when Roosevelt and the Democrat Congress had enacted the Social Security Act in 1935 which would provide old-age insurance to every one when they were no longer able to work as employees.

However, the Concordia Creamery Company found a way to get around paying any tax to the federal government for any of the cream buyers in all the small towns. They sent Mother a sign to tack on the outside of the creamery that said, "CONTRACTOR." She was no longer an employee of the creamery company. Dad had a Social Security Number but Mother did not. This was a source of much bitterness for her and only served to make her a more 'rabid' Democrat and a stronger supporter of the man or woman who worked for wages. The creamery that had provided an average of $70 a month since Anna was five years old till the depression hit with the 'dirty thirties' no longer was a source of income or pride to Anna's working mother.

Along with Dad's work on the roads for the WPA, he had the job of distributing Commodities for the federal government in Wells. Apples from Washington, corn meal from Iowa, canned beef from Government Canneries in Omaha, surplus foods that had been bought from the producers by the government all over the United States were shipped into the county seats of all the 105 counties in Kansas. All the men who worked on the WPA were eligible to receive food. They were the working poor with many small farmers amongst them. They had sold their dairy herds when the drought dried up their feed crops. Chickens and eggs were not plentiful on the small farms either for the same reason.

240

When the commodities came they were delivered by truck from Minneapolis to the cream station beside the Allison house in Wells. Dad had a chart to show him who had applied for commodities and how many apples each family got, how much flour, how much cornmeal, how many cans of beef, depending on how many children were in each family. Where twenty-four ten-gallon cans of cream had often stood on the floor of the Creamery on Saturday nights - now baskets of apples, boxes of canned beef, tins of lard, small sacks of flour and other foodstuffs covered the floor. There were more than fifty eligible recipients of government commodities.

Most of the people were deserving. WPA wages were small and were supposed to cover the cost of winter shoes and clothing for the children in each family. To get free food was a Godsend, literally, since the drought and dust storms had cleaned out all the pantries of canned foods that diligent housewives had hoarded for years. Winter blankets had worn thin, children's coats had grown threadbare and been handed down several times too often. Dad often saw tears in strong men's eyes as he weighed up the bags of beans or counted out the big red apples, full of juice from far-off Washington where they must have had some rain.

In that election year, Roosevelt was running for a second term and Dad had a sticker on the back of his car that stood in front of the house. The sticker read ROOSEVELT. Dad had been able to negotiate a Home Owners' Loan from the federal government and saved him losing his home to the loan shark from Ada who had surfaced three years after the bank closed in Minneapolis. Dad considered God and Roosevelt to be his saviors and, not necessarily in that order.

There was one WPA worker, a Russian immigrant named Alex Graff who had six children and lived with his family on a poor farm southeast of Wells. It was widely reported that he did not use his wages to feed and clothe his children. Neighbors said they went to school with gunny-sack wrapped around their feet and carried lard sandwiches in their dinner pails. When he got his paycheck he was seen over at the Ruggles Auction where farmers brought their calves and pigs to sell from pens along Fifth Street. He was slowly building a herd of cattle from farmers who had been forced to sell their cows to the government because they had no feed for them and then, finally had to sell their calves, too.

Dad had just finished counting out the largest sack of apples and the most 5-lb sacks of corn meal, etc. for Alex Graff because he had the biggest family - and had come in the house to rest when a knock was heard at the door.

"Mr. Allison," Alex Graff had come back to explain in his broken Russian: "You don't hav to vote for dis Roosevelt in order to get dis food, you can vote for who you vants to and still dey give it to you." He was standing on the porch pointing at the sticker on Dad's car.

That was the first and only time Anna ever saw her dad slam the door in anyone's face. "Damn Russian," he muttered, sitting down heavily in his old leather chair.

****

Third Year at Sand Creek
1936 - 1937

Anna stood in the hall outside the study hall at the Minneapolis High School building. Ottawa County teachers had used it for their week-long Institute - held every year the last week in August by the county superintendent of schools.

She paused on her way down the steps to see what the learned professor from McCook County, Nebraska, had written in her Institute Handbook. All the teachers had been inspired by his lectures and were handing him their handbooks for his autograph. He had filled a whole page as she had waited by his desk...

She read: "I have never met in any Kan. county a prettier, more charming personality than yours. You radiate a sweetness and "freshness of spirit" which is stimulating. I would rather wish to know your background and ambitions. You should go far.
Luck,   R.L. McCann 8 - 28 - 36

Anna blushed as she tucked the little notebook in the side pocket of her purse and hurried down the steps. Such a compliment from a successful educator was not something one could bat her eyes at and dismiss with "I'll bet you tell that to all the girls!" She didn't even know that she would show it to Dale when she got to the car.

Dale would drop her off at Sand Creek and take her car on over to Concord next Monday morning for the First Day of School in those two districts - and pick her up in the evening. They would both board with Mother and Dad through September, at least. Muddy roads later might necessitate making other arrangements but, for now, Dale could drop her off and pick her up and he could see about the car - which had always been an extra hurdle for her.

Five families brought children to school that first Monday in September, 1936. The two grandchildren of Betsy Constable: Clayton and Jeff Campbell, would both be in the first grade. Anna had assured Betsy's daughter, Lou Campbell that she'd love to have both Clayton, who was six, and Jeff, not yet five, in the first grade. Along with Clydie Chrisman and Herbie Essig, she'd have four first graders; James Chrisman and Emma Jean Lipe would be the two third graders; there was one pupil in the fourth grade, Joan Apple; Betty Mae Lipe in the fifth and two seventh graders: Darlene Essig and Vernon Apple. At least Anna would be too busy for boredom.

Lou had married Leo Campbell from up in the Hall community north of Wells when she was just a sophomore in high school. She had gone home with his sister, Maurine, for a weekend. Leo was at home, a young man with a thriving business fixing radios for anyone who brought one that was ailing - to his father's farm. Clayton Campbell had a big farm on the Pipe Creek bottom but Lou and Leo had not been able to move to themselves. They had just enlarged the household of the paternal father and mother.

Now there were two little boys and Lou decided to bring them down to Sand Creek as her mother had volunteered to send them to school that winter. Lou had taken a job caring for an old lady down by Bennington. She and Leo would be at the Constable farm home on the weekends.

Jim Constable, Betsy and John Constable's youngest, was just twenty years old that fall. He had driven Lou and her two little boys up to the school that First Day of School in September and sat waiting in the car while she enrolled them in school. Anna remembered going back to the back of the school room the year before during a community meeting when he was graduating from Bennington High School and congratulating him - she had heard that he was joining the Navy.

As they drove away, Anna remarked to her oldest pupil, Darlene Essig, "I thought Jim was going into the Navy more than a year ago. I wonder what ever happened to that?"

"Oh, Betsy said that John actually cried - he's an old man, you know, and he didn't want his baby son leaving him - so he offered him that north-west forty on the Swanson place to farm for his own - so he's going to be one of our young farmers, I guess," Darlene explained, "Jim's brother, Tom, is seventeen years older than he and his sister, Grace is sixteen years older. Lou is nine years older."

Anna thought, 'girls couldn't join the navy. Dale could go to CCC Camp but if she was going to 'go far' as the educator from Nebraska had said, she'd have to stop teaching each fall and go on to college. And she couldn't save any money at $60 a month last year. Maybe she'd do better with $70 a month this year.' She sighed, "It's tough for young men to get a toehold these days, Darlene."

"Dad says Jim spends all of Betsy's cream and egg money for gasoline to run around - and he changes cars every year. He said if Jim was his kid, he'd get up and milk the cows, too. All he does is keep the farm machinery running." Darlene went on, "He's a good mechanic."

Clyde Crisman drove up with his two sons. James cried and hung back. They were both shy but James didn't want to get out of the car. Clyde said, "He'll get over it in a day or two - he's that way every year at first."

Mrs. Lipe arrived with her two little girls and Mrs. Alva Apple soon after. Vernon and Joan were both thin and small. They would have a mile and a half to walk - they lived just east of the lake.

School was starting - ten children - the year would be exciting.

The fall rains began in September. Dale had a long muddy trip driving to Sand Creek first and on to Concord so Anna decided to board at Wayne Peck's. Thelma charged her $3 a week for Monday through Friday. Dale said they could hardly drive it for that! He could take the car west from Wells on the county road past Doerings and have just a mile and a half of mud - except on Monday mornings and on Friday evenings. Anna had a Model A sedan - dark blue with red wheels.

"If that car is yours, I shouldn't think you'd like to have your brother driving it all week," Wayne said one Friday evening when Dale drove in the yard to pick her up.

"I've got a date to go to the show in Minneapolis tonight with Jim Constable in his Model A, Wayne," Anna explained, "a girl doesn't need a car like a boy does."

"Aaha!" Thelma said, "I was wondering when Jim came over to play cards the other night how soon that would happen."

"I make payments on that car at the Ottawa County State Bank. Dale may buy it from me when he gets a few more months' wages," Anna went on, still thinking how expensive it was for a young man. If Dale got a date he'd have to have money for the show. If he asked a girl to a dance, he'd have to have at least $5 for gasoline, the admission to the dance, and hot dogs and pop. Dale didn't go with anybody. Anna felt sorry for him.

Last winter she had gone to dances on Thursday nights in Minneapolis and Glasco with Carroll Kimmerling from Glasco. He had made arrangements with Johnnie Baker or Jake Fisher from Minneapolis to drive to Wells and pick her up and then he would bring her home. It was thirty-three miles to Glasco from Wells. He ran a dairy for his mother just outside of Glasco. He'd get home from Wells about 3:00 a.m. - just in time to start milking for early morning deliveries. Anna loved to dance - she'd be tired on Fridays but by the next Monday she'd be ready for another week of school.

Her ten smart children were practicing for a Halloween program. Everybody had a part, even little Jeff stood on a step ladder behind a shock of feed and said "T'witt to Wooo" from time to time.

James and Clydie were black cats. Their mother had dyed long underwear black for them and Anna had made long black tails. They were to crawl in and "Meow, Meooow" at intervals. Betty Mae, Emma Jean and Joan were three witches on broom sticks. Vernon was the farmer and Darlene was the housewife. Herbie, though he was only six was a good singer. His mother came over to play the piano.

Anna looked at Jeff up there behind his shock of corn. He was smiling from ear to ear. Clayton was a black bat who was watching Clydie and James with a worried look on his face. Clydie's eyes were swimming with tears.

"Clydie, don't you want to crawl on the floor?" Anna asked with some concern.

Clydie nodded his head and the tears splashed on his black paws.

"James, do you know why Clydie is crying?" Anna asked. She didn't know what Jeff thought was so funny. Shy little James just shook his head.

The witches flew in on their broomsticks. When Anna looked back around for her black cats, a great pool of water had spread about where they were crawling. Jeff, her five year old had known all along what was the matter with Clydie! She kissed him and scolded him at the same time. Why didn't he say he had to leave the room, she asked?

"Miss Allison, a cat can't hold up his hand," Clayton said.

Anna took both black cat suits home to wash and brought them back next morning. Mrs. Crisman was too busy with a new baby to be told about Clydie's accident and, anyway, Anna felt it was her fault for being so preoccupied with practice. Halloween was over and election was coming up.

****

*"It matters not whether you win
Or whether you lose -
It's: How you play the game."*

Clayton Spivey was waiting on Anna in Sparger's Pharmacy in Minneapolis. Anna had known him since they were both freshmen in high school. In fact, they were both born November 8th in 1915. "Clayton," Anna observed, "I have not minded not being able to vote for Roosevelt this year because I've remembered you can't either."

"Why?" asked Clayton as he set her cherry coke down in front of her on the counter.

"Because I know that, if you could vote, and I could too, we'd just cancel each other's vote anyway!" Anna said, taking a long sip on her straw. It was the Saturday morning before the first Tuesday after the first Monday in November, 1936.

"You surely wouldn't vote for Roosevelt when our own Governor Alf Landon of Kansas is running against him, would you?" Clayton asked, as he wiped his hands on the dish towel over his shoulder.

"I would if I thought he was the best man for the job," Anna assured him. "Don't you think Roosevelt deserves a second term?"

"No, I think he's done enough already. I can't keep track of all the 'alphabet agencies'. The WPA, the CCC, the NRA; he's spending us into the poor house!" Clayton and Anna both loved to spar over politics.

"Clayton, what were you going to do with all that money of yours, he's been spending?" Anna laughed as she teased him.

"Laugh if you want to - but money comes out of my pay-check every week to pay for my 'social security' and I won't get it back for fifty years," Clayton complained, "And Guy has to match what he takes from my check to build that up so I'm not going to get any raise in wages any time soon if that free-spending Democrat gets back in there."

"Well, he's going to make it, anyway, Clayton. In fact, I'll bet you a dollar Landon doesn't even carry Kansas!" Anna was feeling flush with money. Her payday had occurred just the week before.

"I'll just call that," Clayton said, "Be sure you save a dollar till next Saturday."

When the votes were counted Roosevelt carried every state in the union except Maine and Vermont. Anna went into Sparger's Pharmacy, collected her winnings and bought a jar of Ponds Cold Cream.

"Now you're getting the idea of how to be a Democrat, Clayton," Anna chided her friend, "You're putting your money back in circulation and you've created some buying power."

"It was fun! Let's do it again four years from now. The result is bound to be different," Clayton agreed.

In Grant Township the result had already been different. When the votes were counted that rock-ribbed Republican precinct around Wells had just handed Roosevelt 93 votes and Governor Alf Landon 369. Anna had been down to the Woodman Hall when the votes were tallied.

Ocea Copeman had also been there with a worried look on his face. "He must have wanted that Township Clerk's job awfully bad," Anna told her mother, "He winced every time they tallied a vote for Anna Allison. I got 153 votes and Roosevelt only got 93!"

"Well, you did pretty good, not even being able to vote for yourself," Dad laughed.

"Yeah, I congratulated Ocea. I told him he ran away ahead of his ticket, nationally. It had come in on the radio that Roosevelt had already swept the eastern states."

"What did he say?" Mother asked.

"Oh, he barely skinned his teeth, "Anna said, "he was probably still wondering who in Grant Township would vote the Republican ticket and cross over and vote for me for Township Clerk?"

"I wonder, too," Mother agreed. "Anyway, this has been one election I wish Pa had lived to see."

* * * * * * * * *

Election over and Christmas on the way - Anna had to be thinking ahead - her students always wanted to make something for their parents for Christmas. There was a Christmas program to plan, Thanksgiving was in between, and, of course, the Course of Study from the Kansas State Department of Education, had to be followed strictly.

They decided on Woodpecker door knockers - and Dachshund Dog spool holders for presents for their parents. Anna had a pattern book for woodworking since she had six boys and four girls to keep busy when it was rainy or snowy and they couldn't go outdoors to play. The noon hours were never long enough when they all got busy with sandpaper, little cans of paint, coping saws and pin cushion dog collars.

Problems arose early - the Dachshund had to be made out of 2 by 6 pine so his back would be wide enough to hold four dowels for spools of thread. He was to sit on mother's sewing machine and keep needles and thread handy. Coping saws in small hands produced only frustration when the boys started sawing out foot-long dogs from 2 by 6 lumber.

Anna was telling Wayne and Thelma about her problems with their chosen projects. Thelma spoke up, "Wayne, couldn't you saw those dogs out in your carpenter shop in the cellar and cut out the heads and bodies for the woodpeckers?"

"Why, I suppose I could, but I don't want to beat those boys out of using the coping saw."

"Oh, Wayne, could you?" Anna was delighted, "They can sandpaper and paint and cut the dowels. Could you drill four holes in the back of each dog? They can put glue in each hole and stick in the sucker-sticks - and paint. That will give them plenty to do - four of those boys are only six years old!"

Wayne and Thelma and Anna became Santa's elves every evening for some time while she stayed at their house and walked up across the field each morning to Sand Creek School. Thelma even made a door knocker for Wayne and a Spool-caddy dog for herself. And, when Jim walked across the field from Constable's they all spent a few evenings in the cellar where Wayne had his wood-working shop.

"Jim, will you bring down the bowl of popcorn and that sack of apples on the kitchen table?" Thelma would holler up to him when they heard him stomping off the snow as he came in upstairs. Thelma had been Jim's teacher in grade school so he always made himself at home at her house.

When Christmas came the school children had made and wrapped presents for mothers and grandmothers and fathers, grandfathers and brothers and sisters. Anna bought the first Christmas tree for the school house and took it home after the program. Mother had always frowned on such luxury when people everywhere needed warm mittens and caps.

"Mother, times are getting better, we can afford this Christmas tree. Besides, I had to have something to put all those presents the children made - around. Not everybody thinks a Christmas tree is a waste!"

"Oh, I know it, Honey. I guess I'm just too much of a Quaker!"

****

When Anna had gone over to Constables' to have her voucher signed just before the Christmas vacation Betsy had asked her if she'd like to go to Saint Louis with her and John and Jim for Christmas.

247

"Since Lou and Leo are here to do the chores, Tom and Queenie have asked us to come to Saint Louis for Christmas," she said. "And when I asked Jim if he'd drive us down there, he said, 'Not unless you can get Anna to come along with us. I'd like her to meet Tom and Queenie.' I think he just doesn't want you going with anybody else while he's gone."

"I'll have to think it over and talk to the folks about it. That will be the longest trip I've ever been on and I've never been away from home for Christmas," Anna had answered. Now she had to decide.

"Mother," Anna said, as she was trimming the tree again that Saturday morning - she had just taken it down after the program the night before at Sand Creek, "Betsy Constable wants Jim to take her and his dad to St. Louis for Christmas. She told me he said he would if she'd ask me to go along."

"Why, Anna, you must be getting serious about that boy to think of taking a trip like that right at Christmas. I don't know what Charlie will say."

"I'm going to have to make up my mind in a day or so, Christmas is next Wednesday. I told Thelma about it and she said Jim was so much younger than his brother, seventeen years, I guess, and he didn't have anybody his age when he took his parents to visit Grace or Tom. She said that once when he was in high school and playing football, he had to miss an important game to take his mother down to Lubbock, Texas, because his sister, Grace, had dust pneumonia. She had three little boys under school age and he got to watch them while Betsy went to the hospital. And when he got home his girl friend had gone to the pep rally with another guy and they had lost the game to Longford. I feel sorry for him. He comes over to Thelma and Wayne's about every evening when I'm down there. If I'm busy grading papers he just reads. But we play cards a lot. I'd like to go..."

"Well, talk to your dad about it and see what he says," Mother said, resignedly. "All the girls your age are already married. There's really not much going on around here. Charlie worries when you go away off up to Glasco to a dance and don't get home till 3:00 a.m. I don't know what he'll say about a trip to St. Louis!"

Dad had little to say, "Anna, you're 21! When I was twenty-one, I was planning on homesteading in western Kansas and all the young women my age were already married and had a couple of children. Times have changed. Do what you want to do."

"I can't, Dad. I can't be two places at once. I've never been out of the State of Kansas and I've never been away from home at Christmas."

Jim and his father and mother picked Anna up on Monday morning. He had a 1934 Plymouth Sedan with a heater and a radio. Jim was an excellent driver. His parents rode in the back seat and had little to say when the speedometer rolled up to sixty-five on the straight stretches across Kansas. When the wooded hills of Missouri took their place, however, Betsy and John, began to complain of being dizzy in the back seat.

"Jim, can't you slow down going around these curves?" Betsy asked.

"Not much, if you want to get there before dark," Jim retorted, "And we'll never find their house after dark. We got to keep rolling right along."

Anna could see that Jim was pretty much in charge. When she suggested that maybe his mother wouldn't feel so dizzy if she rode in front, he said, "No, I need you to watch the map for me."

Betsy agreed. "This is John's and my second honeymoon," she said, "and I don't want to be separated from him back here."

John just said, "Hummph!"

They arrived in Webster Grove, a suburb of St. Louis, before dark.

Queenie was an imposing figure of a lady. Anna had never met anyone like her. She was short and rotund - below the waist. She had flashing black eyes and an aristocratic voice and dominated any room she was in. Anna would always feel 'like two-cents worth of dirty ice' (a popular description for worthless) any time she was around. It was strange that she didn't really dominate Jim's big brother, Tom, but, in the end she usually got her way.

"But, Connie!" would usually end the discussion. Tom would purse his lips and stalk off - to do what she had suggested, (or insisted upon). Although Anna was definitely out of her element, it was a memorable week.

The Queen, as Jim called her, took them shopping the day before Christmas so they could buy gifts for under the big tree by the fireplace. Tom and Peg, as she preferred being called, had one son, Little Tom, who was about a year old at that time. Queenie taught English in the Webster Grove schools while Tom sold Mutual Life of New York Insurance. They had a nice home with oak paneling and murals all around the dining room and solid wood furniture to furnish it. It was, by far, the nicest home Anna had ever been in. Tom and Peg had a young lady who was going to college in St. Louis, living with them, to help with the housework and stay with Little Tom while Queenie was teaching and Tom was gone.

The Christmas feast was sumptuous. Tom cooked the turkey. He and Queenie spent most of Christmas morning in the kitchen, Queenie insisting that Betsy always cooked at home but that she must stay in the living room by the fireplace at her son's house. They cooked enough food to last for a week.

Then came the sight-seeing the day after Christmas. Queenie was determined that 'Connie's' father and Mother see all the cultural landmarks around St. Louis. Jim and Anna would enjoy them also. The Catholic Cathedral of St. Louis, (the largest west of the Mississippi,) the Jeffersonian Institute which rivaled the Smithsonian and houses much of Charles A. Lindbergh's memorabilia from his non-stop flight across the Atlantic Ocean in 1927, was of great interest to Jim - airplanes were his first love. But when it came to the huge zoological gardens and the seventy-five acre Missouri Botanical Garden, also known as Shaw's Garden famous for its twelve thousand species of plants and trees and the Jewel Box, show case for all the hundreds of varieties of poinsettia, Betsy and John both began to tire.

Jim managed to cut the sight-seeing short by discovering that he had lost his billfold which contained all the money for the trip. Betsy became hysterical when Anna admitted that she had given Jim the cash she had brought along, also, to carry for her. When they got home, the billfold was lying on the floor behind the chair where Jim had hung his pants the night before. All the money was intact.

Jim wanted to go to the Golden Skates Extravaganza being held down at the Ice Skating Arena during the Christmas Week. No one else in his family wanted to go. Sonja Henie, fresh from Norway where she had won a gold medal for figure-skating at the Winter Olympics - was the star attraction. She was on her way to Hollywood where she had just signed a contract to star in a movie.

Tom assured Jim that the Skates Arena was just seven miles straight down the road so Anna and Jim set out alone. They discovered that no roads in St. Louis were very straight and they all converged into a bend in the river like the spokes in a wheel. They got to the Skates Arena and enjoyed the skating but the trip home was a different story. They wandered around in St. Louis and found the steel mills. The foundries were powered by coal and the little houses for the mill workers, each about ten by twelve and two stories high, had clothes lines between each one with sooty clothes hanging out. Jim and Anna would both be ready to go back to Kansas where the air was clean if they ever found their way back to Tom's house.

The turkey was gone and the soup was made with the last of the brussel sprouts that no one had liked but Anna, when Betsy decided it was time to go home. It had, indeed, been a memorable trip but they were ready to tackle 1937 in Kansas with more appreciation for the wide-open spaces.

****

At School - Close

Her little realm the teacher leaves
She breaks her wand of power apart,
While, for your love and trust she gives
The warm thanks of a grateful heart.

excerpt from a poem by John G. Whittier.

January, 1937, and Old Man Winter arrived to stay for awhile. Anna walked across the fields from Pecks early to build a coal fire in the furnace so she could ring the half-hour bell with the schoolhouse warm for the children. It was just sixteen degrees above zero that morning and the wind was blowing a gale from the northeast. She wore leather boots to keep out the snow and ice but her feet felt like two chunks of ice when she unlocked the door and crippled down the stairs to shake out the ashes and lay the kindling and nuggets of coal. Anna liked to build fires and feel the schoolhouse grow cozy for the children but this morning she had to do that first and then take off her boots and socks and put her feet in cold water to bring back circulation in her numb feet.

"Thank heaven," she mumbled to herself, "There's still enough water in the bucket to fill the wash basin and I don't have to go out and pump a bucket of water, too."

She sat on the recitation bench by the register with her bare feet in the basin of cold water till she felt a little heat coming up from the furnace fire she had kindled. Then she dried her feet since they were beginning to tingle. She pulled on her socks and laced up those boots. She'd have to go out and pump a fresh pail of water. If their parents could get their cars started, the children would be arriving soon. She hoped the pump wasn't frozen. There would be no way to heat a tea kettle of water and stand out in that wind getting a pump thawed out.

She ran down stairs and put more coal on the fire. The schoolhouse was beginning to warm up and the pump wasn't frozen - a bucket of water should last all day.

The children all arrived with varying stories of whether cars would start or what neighbors helped. They played games in the basement at noon and recess and they were ready to go home when four o'clock came.

As they were all leaving, Lou Campbell walked in to walk home with Clayton and Jeff. She said Leo and Jim were busy playing dominoes and she had grown tired of waiting on them to start the car so she walked across that frozen field to keep those two little boys from starting out in that cold to walk home. She stood by the door, refusing to come up to the register and warm up.

"Hurry up and get your overshoes on, boys. We have to go," she said with some irritation. "Jeff, put on your overshoes, Clayton is all ready to go."

Anna glanced down at her feet and saw, to her horror that one of her shoes was covered with blood!

"Lou, what has happened to you?" she asked. As Anna looked the blood was slowly making a puddle on the floor around Lou's foot.

"Oh, it's nothing. Come on boys. We have to go."

Anna looked at her face and realized that she was in shock. "Lou, you have to sit down and wait till I get Jeff's overshoes on," she said, bringing the chair from behind her desk.

"No! We have to hurry home!" Lou said, emphatically.

Anna weighed less than a hundred pounds and Lou weighed almost twice as much. She wasn't tall but she was plump, and usually jolly. Anna took her by the shoulders and shook her and she crumpled in the chair, her shoulders shaking as she started to cry.

"Darlene, will you turn that waste basket over and bring it for a footstool for Lou," Anna directed as she lifted the bloody hem of Lou's skirt to reveal a six-inch long cut across her fat knee. She had fallen crossing that icy plowed field and had laid that knee open two inches deep - a terrible cut! The children gasped!

Darlene was ready to run home and phone somebody when Jim and Leo had got a car started and come over to bring Lou and the boys home. Instead, with a little help from everyone they wrapped the scarf Anna had worn over her face that morning - around Lou's knee with two rulers for splints to keep the knee straight, and took Lou and the little boys straight on to Bennington to Dr. Hinshaw.

It was two months before Lou could bend her knee - she had to wait for it to heal before the stitches could be removed.

* * * * * * * * *

"There are only eight grades in the public school system but children are all different. No two are alike and what one has to do is see that each child moves ahead in his learning," Anna explained to her mother. "He must be challenged - and the work shouldn't be too hard or too easy for him."

Mother served as a sounding board as Anna deliberated what she should do for her pupils. Mother nodded and Anna went on, "Herbie Essig is a first grader but he is so smart and, being the youngest in the family, June and Margaret and Darlene have all taught him so he knows and understands arithmetic like a third grader, at least, and could read that whole primer and first grade reader before he ever started to school this fall. I just don't know what I'm going to do with him. I'm going to visit with the County Superintendent about him, maybe get him some supplemental readers and arithmetic work books or something."

Frank LaPlant suggested that Anna get a Stanley IQ test for six-year olds before prescribing extra school work for Herbie. He ordered one for her and when it came Anna made a special time for Herbie to take it.

It was a timed test with blocks of small pictures for non-readers. One block had twelve isolated hand or foot pictures, some with clenched fists or walking on the hands or feet with soles up, etc. The student had thirty seconds to put a check mark on all the left hands or feet pictured. Anna read the instructions as she held the stop-watch. "Go," she said.

Anna stood there, stop watch in hand, studying the first small picture of a hand to decide which it was - left or right?

Herbie said, "Done," and Anna, glancing at the watch, realized that only twenty seconds had passed and said "Stop."

She pronounced words like 'callow' and he selected a baby chick out of a dozen small pictures. The word 'venerable' and he found a small picture of an old man walking with a cane.

His score at the end of that test was 137 - just three points short of a genius!

All the left hands or feet were right, according to the scoring sheet!

The County Superintendent looked over the test and allowed Anna to put Herbie in the Second Grade - there were no other second graders and the readers were new to him. He seemed happier but he told her some years later that he wished he had been bigger in high school - he graduated when he was only sixteen.

"I would have been able to do better in athletics," he said.

"Pupils who do not fit the norm always require special attention," she told him. "That's what makes teaching a challenge. And we cannot always do what's best for the body when we have to occupy those bright minds."

That year they took their skit to the county play-off and won 'First' with it. Herbie sang a solo.

* * * * * * * *

District 28 had scored well in their scholastic tests as well as being successful with their ten-minute skit. Every pupil was successful in his own special way and Anna was proud of all of them. March winds were warm over the Kansas prairie. Daisies would be popping up out in the pastures. Spring was on the way. The Normal Instructor had kites on the cover that month and Anna had sent for the special packet of patterns for making kites.

Girls and boys, alike, seemed to enjoy making kites. Dragons, eagles, airplanes, as well as hexagons and trapezoids took shape in the art classes that lasted half the day. The children had to show off their kites!

"Why don't we fly our kites on the Last Day of School?" James suggested, "My dad could help me get mine up."

So they planned something special for their parents for the Last Day Of School. They sent out invitations to the Dinner and Kite-Flying Contest and urged everybody in the district to build a kite and bring it to the school. Prizes would be given to the owner of the kite that flew the highest.

There were no trees and no phone lines or light wires for kites to tangle in and Jack Beverly's pasture offered plenty of space. The blue sky and Kansas wind on that last Friday in April cooperated too. Clyde

Crisman, Leo Campbell, Herb Essig, Jim Constable, Alva Apple and his son, Vernon, Jack Lipe and Wayne Peck all had kites in the sky. Maurice Stultz and Guy Peck were the judges. The oft-heard remark that 'you can tell the age of the boys by the size of their toys' was proven that day. A box-kite six feet long won the competition. One fellow got a pocket knife for the prize but they all had fun.

Anna could have returned to Sand Creek for a fourth term but she had decided to apply in a bit richer district that would hire a special music teacher for one period a week and still give her seventy dollars a month.

She had been asked to apply at Burnham where they would have four pupils in the eighth grade the next year and their teacher, Miss Della Danner was getting married. Her three years at Sand Creek were over. She gave her ten precious pupils a Souvenir Booklet that closed with a poem:

> *"And, when the world shall link your names*
> *With gracious lives and manners fine,*
> *The teacher shall assert her claims*
> *And proudly whisper, "These were mine!"*

> *(last verse of <u>At School-Close</u> by*
> *John Greenleaf Whittier.*

****

254

I wish I was an apple,
A-hangin' in the tree
And ev'ry time my sweetheart passed,
He'd take a bit of me...

Old Folk Song

Anna signed the Teacher's Contract on May 28, 1937 with no misgivings. The fact that a clause had been hand-written in the margin, "You agree to stay single until this year expires" was no threat to her. Burnham was just six miles west of Wells on the County Road into Minneapolis. She could stay at home and catch a ride each morning with Dean Sommers and Le Roy Windhorst. They would be driving into Minneapolis to high school every morning she was teaching. She'd be home in Wells by 5:00 PM - a perfect arrangement. She could sell her car to Dale; he had it most of the time anyway.

It would be an exciting new year. Burnham had four girls who would be in the eighth grade that year. An Englishman, Richard Chappell, was on the school board, along with Matt Davis and Lee Doering. Mr. Chappell had arrived in the United States to work for his uncle on a farm in the Burnham District. His story was an exciting one, in itself.

When Anna signed the contract at his home she met his wife, Clara, and two charming little daughters. A son, Richard Jr. had already graduated. Clara had come over to 'The States' from England much later - when Mr. Chappell went back to claim her older sister as his bride and found her already married. They were a 'pure' English family - undiluted with Irish, German, Swede, French, or other northern European settlers in Ottawa County. They all spoke with a decidedly English accent.

"I should like you to teach my girls their sums so they can work them for themselves," Mr. Chappell explained, "They must be able to understand their problems and explain them to me. We will have four pupils in the eighth grade who must take the County Examinations. They may require extra hours of teaching."

"I'll be pleased to work with children who are willing to 'stay in' after to school to learn," Anna assured him.

'Miss Allison' would have Claudina Davis, Marjorie Bell, Lauretta Pierce and Joan Chappell in the eighth grade; Lorraine Bell in the seventh grade; Audrey La Plant and Max Davis in the fifth grade; Ella Vaughn Davis, Harold Lee Doering and Rosemary Chappell in the fourth grade and Jimmie Davis and Frankie La Plant in the first grade, - twelve pupils in all. There would never be a dull moment that year.

The summer of '37 was a good year and Anna hauled wheat for Jim Constable, using his car with a trailer hitch and a wheat wagon that held sixty bushels. John Constable had two wagons so one could be waiting in the field to be filled with wheat while Anna was gone to the elevator with the other. Wheat harvest was an exciting time and she enjoyed every minute of it. Jim drove the tractor and his father rode on the combine. Anna would get back to the field with one empty wagon in time to position it under the grain spout, unhitch, and hitch the full wagon to the car and get back to the elevator in Wells without losing her place in line with other haulers from other fields in the vicinity. There were always errands to run, too.

"Anna, will you tell the men that dinner is on the table," Betsy said as she came up to the gas barrels where Anna was filling five-gallon cans to take back to the field. She came out to help Anna lift the full five-gallon cans into the trunk.

"Will you have time to eat with us?" Betsy asked.

"No, I'll just take a drumstick with me now. I'll stop at my house in Wells and get some boysenberries. Mother said she had a couple quarts to pick. I like them with sugar and cream on them. Could I bring you a quart?" Anna asked.

"They must ripen right in harvest. Yes, I'd make a pie out of them if you bring them to me," Betsy said as she put a few pieces of chicken in wax paper and a brown paper bag for Anna.

Betsy was sixty-three years old that summer and, though she bragged a lot about how she had always lifted five-gasoline cans of gas, carried five-gallon pails of slop to the hogs, milked the cows all by herself during harvest, baked bread twice a week for John (Jim didn't like his mother's home-baked bread made with a starter), Anna observed that she favored one knee and looked old enough to start taking things a bit easier.

Jim was farming the northwest forty of the Swanson place to wheat for the first time that summer. He had broken it out from pasture and raised watermelons on it in 1936 when John had told him that he could have the proceeds from that forty for himself if he'd stay home from the military. This year he had planted it to wheat and it was making thirty-seven bushels to the acre. It was new ground and was making almost twice as much as the rest of their acreage. They owned only one hundred and twenty acres but had had the Swanson place under lease since Tom was at home helping with the farming. Jim had taken over keeping the tractor running and the combine in repair since he was ten years old. He was a very 'old' young farmer when he turned twenty-one that September.

"I came to settle up with you for hauling our wheat," Jim explained his impromptu call on Anna about a week after harvest was over. "Get your swimming suit and let's go down to the lake."

Anna and her mother were still canning four pints of boysenberries each day. "Go ahead, I'll finish these up," Mother said.

Anna thought Jim's eyes looked a little too bright with excitement for just an afternoon swim. She understood why when he reached in the pocket of his coveralls as soon as she got in the car on the main street of Wells that afternoon. His eyes shone as he opened a small velvet box to reveal a diamond ring!

"I think you'd make a good farmer's wife," he said. "Will you marry me?"

"Not for another year," Anna said, eyeing the beautiful ring in its velvet box. "I have a school to teach."

"Well, let's try it on and see if it fits," Jim said. "We can, at least, be engaged, can't we?

"A Keepsake diamond!" Anna said, as she held out her third finger on her left hand; she admired the sparkling little ring as Jim reached out to lift her chin for a kiss.

Anna had admired Jim for a long time. The first time she could remember noticing him, he was dancing with Claudine Jennings, a girl from the Bennington High School - they were all down at Welsh's Barn Dance just west of the lake. 'All' meaning everybody who liked to dance from all over Ottawa County. Barn dances were common for summertime entertainment and everyone looked forward to dancing at least once a week all summer except the few busy weeks of the harvests. Anna had wished that she knew Jim at that time. He was a neat dancer.

His folks owned a farm. He was a young farmer. 'Maybe security plays a big part in the decision one makes on how to spend the rest of one's life,' Anna thought as she weighed her seventy-dollar-a-month job as an 'old-maid school teacher' against a permanent job as a farmer's wife and decided that Jim's offer had the real appeal.

"Yes, we can be engaged," she said, as she looked at her beautiful ring and glanced up and down Main Street before returning his kiss.

****

At institute in August a music teacher from Delphos had decided to free-lance among the rural school teachers in one-room rural schools with a proposition that she would divide the school day into four periods and drive to fifteen schools each week - giving each school one class period of music each week. Anna had always felt that her musical ability was not adequate and that children needed more exposure to music than she was able to give them. She and Dale had taken tap-dancing lessons from Alfred Hawkins in Minneapolis and had wished they had a pianist when they were planning programs for community meetings. With accompaniment they could teach the children simple tap routines.

The music teacher wanted $15 a month from each school district - $225 a month - she would be making. She'd be driving to three schools each day all winter over muddy township roads - it was probably worth it. Anna called on her school board once more and they liked the idea of enriching their children's school curriculum with music. 1937-1938 became an exciting and successful year.

War clouds were rolling across Europe with the rise of Adolph Hitler, an ambitious and ruthless dictator in Germany. The First World War was still vivid in everyone's mind and the theme for the Fall Festival in Minneapolis was World Peace. Rural schools were invited to compete with floats in the parade. Anna decided to make a world out of blue oil-cloth and ask the men of the district to make a round frame out of wire or lathe to fit it on. Each of the twelve children would be dressed in the costumes of a different country and would be holding hands in friendship around the world.

It would be a learning experience for the children to paint the countries of the world on the oil cloth while the four foot by twelve foot strip of oil-cloth was laid flat on the stage in front of the desks. Anna had cut it out at home in sections and sewed it together, except for one seam so it would lie out flat for painting.

The learning experience extended to everyone in the district when the men tried to bend lathe and nail it together to hold up oil-cloth in a round shape to look like a world. When that didn't work they tried to wire - with no more success. Matt Davis and Jim La Plant finally took the oil-cloth world to the nearest straw stack and stuffed it with straw the morning of the parade and Anna sewed it together with a big darning needle, while the mothers dressed their little 'children of the world'.

Burnham captured First Place with that somewhat pumpkin-shaped world and Anna was sure that everyone in that school district heaved a sigh as they fell asleep that night to the tune of the song: 'Let there be peace on earth - and let it begin with me.'

* * * * * * * * *

Anna ran out the door of the Allison house one morning and jumped in the back seat of Dean Sommer's car. He and Le Roy Windhorst were ten minutes late to pick her up that morning but so was she - she had slept too late and was carrying an apple for her breakfast as well as her books and her lunch in a brown paper bag.

"ZZZZZZZ" was the inaudible sensation experienced by the backs of her legs and her shoulder blades as she landed on the back seat. She slid her grade book, with its papers she had graded at home, under her bottom and leaned down to put her sack lunch on the floor boards. Anna was five years older than Deane and Le Roy - an 'old-maid school teacher' to them - and she registered no surprise for their enjoyment. She continued to sit forward in the seat - after all, it was only six miles! She continued eating her apple.

"Dad, I think you should speak to Deane and Le Roy about wiring the back seat of their car. I got a real shock this morning when I sat down on the back seat, I could feel the places where it stung me all day," Anna complained to her dad that evening.

Charlie Allison just laughed. He had several stories that Anna had heard before about wiring chairs and one particularly shocking one about

258

wiring a corner in a blacksmith shop so that when a visitor went back there behind the blower to relieve himself the electricity would follow up the stream and shock him in a very tender spot.

"Well, Dad, after all, I am paying them $6 a month for my ride. You'd think I might be entitled to a little respect," Anna said.

Dad continued laughing.

Some years afterward the boys confessed that since Anna had registered no shock at being zapped, they increased the voltage a little and asked one of their girl friends if she'd like a ride home at noon. She made a terrible fuss and they were called into the office. Her mother was there demanding their punishment. They decided that pranks like that were funnier in Wells than anywhere else.

* * * * * * * *

Anna was sitting alone at her desk with her back to the door, grading papers one afternoon about four-thirty. The children had all gone home and the country schoolhouse was quiet. Dean and Le Roy would not be by to pick her up till about five. She had swept the schoolhouse with compound, dusted the piano, tidied up the activity table and had thirty minutes to plan lessons for tomorrow.

"Should we have knocked?" she heard a male voice say.

Anna whirled around in her chair to see two tall men dressed in Kansas State Highway Patrol uniforms. They were young and handsome and would have made a wonderful impression on her pupils if they had come in school hours.

"Little off the beaten path, aren't you?" Anna asked, refusing to be flustered by their sudden and gorgeous appearance. Having read the monthly news bulletin from the Kansas State Board of Education she had been made aware of effort being made by the State Highway Department to call on grade school children to deliver safety bulletins about riding bicycles or horses on the state highways, with the laws concerning the legal age for driving and the qualifications to become a Highway Patrolman (over six feet tall and less than two hundred pounds). "Highway 81 is a mile west of here." she said.

"Oh, we're just doing our duty, spreading pamphlets to rural school children on highway safety," one handsome fellow said.

"Well, you are an hour late," the 'old-maid school teacher' replied, "And I'm so sorry, as I have four boys who would be so impressed and anxious to grow six feet tall so they could wear one of those uniforms - not to mention the eight little girls who need to see handsome men in uniform doing something other than writing speeding tickets."

"We came to see you. You can hand out these pamphlets tomorrow. Play us a tune on the piano," one said, while the other lounged on the recitation bench.

"You play the piano, I have to finish grading these papers before my ride gets here," Anna said.

"I've never learned to play on anything but the linoleum," he said, with a suggestive smile.

"We'd best be going before all the schools are locked up and the teachers are gone," the other one said, rising from the recitation bench.

"Thank you for stopping but, next time, remember that school hours are from nine to four. The children would be so excited to see you," Anna smiled and added, "And I'm sure I would be more impressed."

'Really a tough job,' she thought as she watched them folding their long legs into the clearly marked Highway Patrol Car, 'But women just couldn't handle anything that complicated even if they could qualify.'

****

While not all twelve Burnham pupils were intent on learning they were all willing and suggestive to leadership. The two Chappell girls had that quality of leadership so important to teachers of one-room rural schools with differing levels of learning. Anna could spend extra time in the classroom at recess or part of the noon hour with the five upper class pupils who must take county exams that spring and send the two six-year-olds, three fourth-graders and two fifth-graders out to play since Rosemary Chappell was among them. She mothered the two little boys, saw to it that Harold Lee Doering treated them fairly, that nobody was out without mittens and cap as well as keeping a game going that everyone liked to play.

Meanwhile Joan Chappell, one of the eighth graders who must take county exams was so willing to 'stay in' to study that the attitude was catching. They all passed - one or two had to take Geography and Physiology tests over along with the seventh graders because they had failed the previous year. Joan was in the top-ten eighth graders in the entire county when the County graduation exercises were held in the Minneapolis High School Auditorium that spring.

The music teacher came once a week, and as winter kept the children inside, Anna had ordered pasteboard in sheets four feet by eight feet from the Jayhawk Paper Company in Lawrence. The theme for the County Competition in those ten-minute lyceum skits had been announced so she had decided upon a 'Living Album' with pasteboard pages laced together with bathrobe cord, complete with tassels. The book was titled 'Through the Years.' The children were hidden in the pages and traced the United States History in Music and Dance. With powdered wigs and knee britches and hoop skirts, they danced the Minuet - the Revolutionary War days, did 'Tenting Tonight on the Old Campground' for Civil War days; did 'Don't Sit Under the Apple Tree - With Anyone Else But Me' for the first World War years and tap danced to 'The Sidewalks of New York' for the Roaring Twenties.

The children painted the pasteboard pages with Prang Paints - tents in the moonlight, a spreading apple tree, skyscrapers for New York etc. - a wonderful outlet for their artistic abilities. The only problem was in transporting the book. Anna had worn the diamond ring all winter and it was well-known that the 'queer-fellow' as Mrs. Chappell called him - who came over to the community meetings and programs - was planning to end Anna's teaching career at the end of the year and would be pressed into service to haul the big pasteboard book.

Jim tied it on the back of his car, resting it on the rear bumper and obscuring his rear window, and patiently went to all the programs they were asked to participate in that spring. It was a 'never-to-be forgotten' success and took second in the County-wide Competition in Minneapolis.

****

> "We need a bell' the preacher said,
> But taxes must be paid.
> I guess we'll have to call upon
> The members of the Aid."

The social life around Wells was built around the two churches, The Methodist Episcopal and the Spiritualist Camp. Wells Union 2 and the Woodman Hall united the two factions for school programs, town plays and community meetings.

No one missed the community meetings. They were held once a month at the Woodman Hall all through the winter, starting the first Friday in October and ending the first Friday evening in April, when everyone got too busy with farming and spring and summer activities.

The Methodist Church was bursting at the seams during the thirties. Regular church services and Sunday School classes were held winter and summer, whereas, the Spiritualists had a three-week-long camp meeting each summer and met in the homes for seances or prayer when one of their ranks was very sick.

The Children's Day activities were held at the Methodist Church and everyone was welcome. School was out for the summer, dances at the Woodman Hall were over till fall, the Community Meetings wouldn't resume till October and children in every household wanted to go to Sunday School - all their friends would be there.

The City Dads, as all the respected older men were called, met at the grocery store or the hardware store on Sunday morning while their wives and mothers went to Sunday School and Church and, of course, the farmers came to town to bring the wife and children to Sunday School, sell their cream and eggs, buy groceries, fill their tanks with gas, pick up chicken feed or block salt for the cattle at the elevator. It was called 'killing all the birds with one stone.' 'Saturday night' moved up to 'Sunday morning' for the summer.

As the economy slowly came back to life after the dust storms and drought and depression, the women of the church began to complain of the need for more room in the Methodist Church. All the Sunday School classes were crowded. There was no room for the teachers to have their own studies without the babies in the nursery, with their names on the cradle roll, disrupting serious study in the pew behind.

Anna had an old poem that kept running through her mind as she listened to her friends, Dolly Comfort and Marnece Schur talk about what their mothers-in-law had tried to discuss in Sunday School Class, and couldn't hear themselves think, they said. They gave up till they could meet for Ladies Aid:

> *"We need a bell, the preacher said,*
> *But taxes must be paid*
> *I guess we'll have to call upon*
> *The members of the Aid!".........*

More than a bell was needed, it seemed. "Mom said that Aunt Cora and Darrel's mother have a plan in mind to build an addition on the church with a basement underneath it to have some room for Sunday School classes and even a place to serve coffee and have Ladies Aid meetings and bazaars," Marnece Schur said.

"Oh, yes," Doll agreed. "Mother came home all excited about their plans."

"Reverend Flowers came in to pick up Mrs. Flowers and he's all excited about the plans, too. Mom volunteered Johnnie to dig the basement; he and Darrel can bring their slips, they've both got tractors and can dig it in one day," Marnece sounded excited, and it was catching.

Soon everybody was volunteering something - Anna's fourth-grade teacher, Glenna Windhorst, had married Harry Heald. They had built a new filling station on the corner north of Miller's Garage and had tile left over that could be used to lay up the inside walls of the basement.

Dad and Mother had quit going to Sunday School as soon as Dale and Anna had been able to walk there themselves. Dad had belonged to the Hall Methodist Church when he was a boy and Mother had been baptized in the Solomon River up by Delphos when she was a girl in a Christian Church group. Dad didn't feel it necessary to belong to either the Spiritualists or the Methodists and Mother had been raised a Quaker.

"I know George Miller thinks I shouldn't be testing cream on Sunday morning but I'm right here by the creamery and, if someone wants to sell me cream so they can get a few groceries, I'm here to buy it," Mother said to Anna many times.

And Dad would say, "That hypocrite! He's got his hired help over here pumping gas and putting in spark plugs up there at that garage right along with the rest of us 'back- sliders' on Sunday morning."

But George Miller had moved to Minneapolis and his son Philip Miller was running the garage and filling station; times had changed.

"Stella, they're going to dig a basement on the north side of the church," Dad said one day in the fall of '37, "And build an annex on the north side of the church right above it. I'm going over and help them when they get ready to lay up the basement walls. Preacher Flowers seems to be a builder, too. At least he has the plans."

"That church is too small when there's a funeral, I know...," Mother said.

"Well, they want to build a basement room about twenty by forty and an annex to the chapel right above it - that will seat fifty people. Clarence and Howard Comfort, Chet Siler, Daniel Crow and Leonard Kuhlmann, the Hanes boys, there's a lot of jack-knife carpenters who can put up that annex in a hurry," Dad said. He loved to see things go up in a hurry.

"Philip and Ruth have been having the Sunday School class in their house for the young married couples," Anna laughed. "They've got all new furniture since they got married and moved into his dad's house, and he was telling Charlotte Crow that nobody weighed less than he and Ruth and when they come in, they don't just sit down on Ruth's new couch - they collapse!"

Charlie Allison was working on the WPA at that time. He had been the master mason when the Shelter house at the lake was built. That had been a state and federal project to provide work for the unemployed. He also spent long hours on a croquet ground just north of the lumber yard and men came to town evenings to have croquet tournaments. He worked his hours on the WPA and spent his evenings laying up the sidewalls and leveling the floor of the basement for the church so he got the praise and blame for the cement floor not being quite level - water always stood on the floor. A sand point was driven down for water and a pitcher pump installed to provide water for the kitchen when they had dinners. Wells was slowly coming out of the Great Depression.

Fund raising for the church became a major preoccupation in the town during the fall and winter. Wolf hunts were held over in Bowen's four sections, as a large area of grassland was called out east of the Hanes' pastures. The ladies of the church made hundreds of bologna sandwiches and doughnuts, furnished apples and coffee to the hunters and charged for everything that was donated. Chicken dinners, ice cream socials, oyster suppers and watermelon feeds took the place of any other entertainment.

Marnece and Johnnie Schur, who lived with John and Cora Schur on the hill three miles west of Wells, worked tirelessly on the project. When the old grade school in Minneapolis was torn down and the materials sold, they used money from the fund of money made and donated for the church to buy the tin ceiling for the basement. They also bought fifty wooden folding chairs for $1.00 each at the Jilka Furniture sale when it went out of business in Salina. Marnece and Nettie Hemming, Harry Kinsey's mother, solicited funds from local farmers and business people who couldn't otherwise help.

The annex was built with one paid carpenter, Fred Trow, from Minneapolis. All the rest of the work was done by volunteers so the total expense came to less than $2,500. Marnece and Johnnie invited the young peoples' Sunday School class to a party at their home to celebrate the completion of the annex. There were fifty people who came.

Reverend and Mrs. Flowers had increased the size of the congregation and filled the pews to overflowing by the time they left their flock the next fall. The Ladies Aid made a Friendship Quilt for Rev. and Mrs. Flowers* and presented it to them as a remembrance of the congregation who loved and appreciated their tireless enthusiasm that had made their expanded church possible.

****

It's time to think of wedding things
Like sweet bouquets and golden rings.
Delightful dreams this spring of springs -
With all the joy that true love brings.

"But Anna! You can't get married on Friday! That's Execution Day!" Mother was walking the floor, her eyes wild, wringing her hands. Anna had never seen her mother so agitated.

"That may have been back in the Middle Ages, Mama, but this is the Twentieth Century. Jim and I are not getting hung, just hitched. And next Friday fit Rev. Flowers schedule," Anna tried to explain to her mother.

"Well, you'll just have to change it," Mother declared, "You can't get married on Friday. It's bad luck!"

"It's bad luck to postpone a wedding, too," Anna lamented, "and it won't be easy. I can't even call Jim on that party line. We went up to Lamar to see Rev. Flowers. The second week in May looked full for him on his calendar."

"You'll just have to move the date up to Thursday then, Anna. What's the matter with May 5th?" Mother asked.

Anna had had to enlist Marnece's help to make the wedding dress over on the hill three miles west of Wells to keep from having scraps of rust lace and peach satin lying about the living room on the main street of Wells. This had to be kept a secret. They were getting married at the church, though none of the young people had attempted that in years.

---

* Many years later at a United Methodist Women's meeting at the home of Mrs. Glenna Heald ("Miss Glenna"), Anna learned that Glenna's daughter, Carolyn, had discovered a friendship quilt at a "Bread and Breakfast" high in the San Juan Mountains in Colorado. When she recognized names of people she knew from Wells, she asked the Manager where he got the quilt. He explained that it was bequeathed to him by his grandmother, Mrs. Reverend Flowers. Carolyn took pictures of it. Mr. and Mrs. C. F. Allison and Mr. and Mrs. J. S. Constable were among the many names embroidered on the quilt.

They all sneaked away to a parsonage of some church in a neighboring county and tied the knot before all the friends around Wells knew about it. Charivaris were planned to disrupt honeymoons and discommode weddings by all the local pranksters. Anna wasn't even sure that Dad could be trusted to not think of something for her friends to do to keep Jim and her from getting out of Wells if they went public with their wedding plans. And privacy was almost an impossibility.

The wedding party was small and all sworn to secrecy: Doris and Earl Markley from Bennington, (Earl was Jim's Best Man and Doris was chosen as Anna's Matron of Honor because she couldn't play favorites between Avis, Norline, Myrtle, Dolly, etc., all friends from childhood). Anna's mother and dad; Jim's mother and dad; Anna's brother, Dale and his current girl friend, Maxine Sheffler, from McPherson, John and Marnece Schur to serve the small reception in the new church basement; and, of course, Rev. and Mrs. Flowers completed the wedding party.

Jim had the most trouble with the change to a day earlier. Anna called him on the phone and left a message with his mother, "Just tell him that party that was planned for Friday has been moved up a day to Thursday, May 5th."

He called that evening and asked, "What party? I didn't know we had a party to go to this week, too."

"You know - the party that we invited Doris and Earl to," Anna answered evasively. "Why can't you run up here for a little while this evening and we can call them again?"

"I guess I've forgotten all about any party this week, too much on my mind. I'll be up in a little bit if I don't get stuck - these roads are a son-of-a-gun - mud holes between here and there no matter which way I come," Jim sounded doubtful.

It had rained all the last week of April, the road over Beaver Dam Hill was impossible, the one up past Jerry Barta's was no better and the one over past Guy Peck's took one over the county road which had been cut in so deep with traffic that the mud was a real loblolly. Wells was sandy and Anna hadn't thought about how terrible the roads had been getting out in the country. When Jim finally arrived with mud all over his car from hitting the mud holes in high gear, the 'bad luck' of a Friday wedding seemed unimportant.

"I would never have thought," he told Mother, "That you'd be so anxious to marry your daughter off that you'd set it up a day earlier." He laughed at her. Poor Mother. She didn't think it was funny.

The wedding went on without a hitch though afterward all their friends assured them that they knew something was afoot for various reasons: Charlotte Crow said, "I heard Jim talking to his mother on the party line something about Jim not having time to get to Salina for a new white shirt and she was having to do up a white shirt for John and him both in one week - I just knew it had to be some big occasion!"

* * * * * * * * *

Jim and Anna spent their wedding night in the Sunflower Hotel in Abilene, Kansas, going on to Topeka on their honeymoon. Lela Allison, Uncle Roy's daughter, had a small apartment there. They had planned to go on to Kansas City, but Lela urged them to stay with her, meet her current boy friend, and go with them to a big dance on Saturday night. She was working as a waitress in a big Chinese restaurant across from the Capitol building. Many of the State Senators and Representatives came in there so her pockets were full of coins at the end of the day.

"See my new sewing machine," Lela said, "I'm making payments on it from my tips."

Anna hadn't heard of tipping before, "Wow, that's a great place to work!" she exclaimed, "Do you like to work for the Chinese manager?"

"Well,...It's different - I'll show you tomorrow when you come in to eat dinner," Lela said. "Ask me to go to the restroom and I'll take you back through the kitchen."

The trip through the kitchen was an eye-opener. Chinese coolies worked in there. The bowls where they mixed the Chinese noodles were made from big mounds of flour dumped on the counters, water poured in and kneaded with the hands, then run through an antique noodle-making machine. They bowed and smiled at Lela but they couldn't speak a word of English.

"Don't try to talk to them," Lela advised. "The manager doesn't want them to learn to speak English. He is the only one who speaks English. He imports these Chinese and pays them pennies to cook. They live in here. I suppose their living conditions are better than they had in China, but sometimes he comes back here and shouts at them in Chinese. Then his face changes and when he comes back through the swinging doors to the cash register, he's all smiles, bowing and scraping to the customers."

They went to the dance on Saturday night. In the lobby there was a fellow reading handwriting, so Jim and Anna had their handwriting read and found out that they both procrastinated, both had fine powers of concentration, both were good natured and peace loving and their Heart Barometer showed they were very compatible. Anna discounted the whole process when she discovered that her handwriting showed that she was musical!

That night they got back to Lela's apartment too late for her boyfriend to go home, so they, all four, finished the night sleeping crosswise of her double bed.

The next day was Sunday. Jim and Anna turned west when they got out to the highway and got back to Ottawa County that evening. The honeymoon was over and they still had a new mattress to put on his double bed upstairs in the Constable house. The old feather-tick was relegated to the west bedroom. John and Betsy's house had been built about 1880 and very little had been done to improve it. The staircase was too small to get a double bed mattress upstairs that way so they had to take out an upstairs window, lean a ladder against the house and pull the mattress up with ropes. Leo and Lou Campbell, Jim's sister, were there so they got that done with their help that evening.

They had bought fifty candy bars and popcorn to pop and lemons at ten for a dollar - enough to make gallons of lemonade - just in case the charivari crowd from Wells had been alerted by someone who might have seen them come through Bennington that Sunday afternoon - on their way home. The crowd didn't arrive till the following night, however.

"Listen!" said Jim as they were finishing supper, "What kind of a screeching noise is that?"

It was eight o'clock, just getting dark. They were in for a long evening.

Fred and Grace Windhorst had replaced the Copemans in the Grocery Store by that time, and Le Roy and Bonnie had furnished everyone with two-foot long balloons. No tin pans and spoons were needed for noise-makers. Those balloons made the most awful screeching noise just by blowing them up, tying them and dragging one's hands up and down the sides of them.

A whole new layer of Wells rascals had taken over also. Dave and Eileen Comfort, Rex Comfort. Bonnie Windhorst, Dorothy Lois, Clayton and Weston Comfort, Kenneth, Allan and Myrna Miller, Jimmy, Logan and Lloyd Luther, Rex and Carolyn Heald, Malcolm, Vernon and Gloria Comfort, and, it seemed like a hundred others, had found their way down to the John Constable home, a half mile south of Daniel Crow's farm home and off the road to the west, a quarter mile, in the timber. Doll, Avis and Marnece helped Anna make lemonade and Jim handed out candy bars till they were gone. The twenty-four foot kitchen and smaller living room ceiling was covered with two-foot long balloons that had escaped their owners and floated overhead.

With so many people around, it was impossible to keep track of all the charivari crowd at once so when they all went home and a very tired newly-married couple went upstairs to bed, they found that some gremlins had stood their new mattress over against the wall, dismantled their bed and removed it - down the ladder they had left conveniently leaning against the outside of the house. The slats were found in the haymow, the springs were behind the chicken house and the bedstead, reassembled, was standing out in the maple grove the next morning. They slept on the new mattress on the floor that night.

"I intended to remind you to put that ladder away yesterday," Anna said to Jim at the breakfast table the next morning.

"He wouldn't have known where to put it if you had," John said, "Jim always leaves things wherever he last uses them."

Jim just smiled.

"The handwriting expert was right about the procrastination, wasn't he?" Anna laughed. "Maybe I am musical, after all."

****

267

The Little Old Sod Shanty

Yet, I rather like the novelty of living in this way,
Though my bill of fare is always rather tame,
But I'm happy as a clam in the land of Uncle Sam
In the little old sod shanty on my claim....

(excerpt from __The American Songbag__)

"Jim! Pancakes are on!" Anna awoke with a start and glanced over at her new husband. That was his mother calling him to breakfast.

"Jim! Jim!" There it was again but he gave no sign of waking up. Anna raised up on one elbow and punched him. He snuffled a little in his sleep and turned over.

"Casper Milquetoast, time to rise and shine," Jim's mother called again.

Anna set her feet out on the bare wooden floor of the upstairs and hastily dressed. Jim still had not stirred. She slipped down the rickety stairs and into the corner of the kitchen. A warm fire was going in the Home Comfort Range and the smell of pancakes told what was cooking. Pails of milk stood on the floor around the separator by the door.

"Is Jim gettin' up?" Betsy asked.

"I'm not sure," Anna said, "Have you already milked the cows?"

"Oh, yes, John and I always do that first. He's out slopping the hogs right now while I fry the pancakes," Betsy explained, and stepping over to the staircase door, she called again, "Jim, pancakes are on!"

"I want to feed my chickens. I'll go do that while Jim is getting up," Anna said. She had bought fertile eggs from Betsy early in March and took them to the Hatchery in Minneapolis. Jim and Anna had plans to get married as soon as school was out but that would be late to start baby chicks. She wanted a cash crop of baby pullets so she would have eggs to sell the next winter. She had made a deal with Betsy, she thought. She'd keep her baby chicks in Betsy's brooder house and they'd build a new hen house after harvest.

Anna bought five hundred eggs and paid Betsy for them. Anna would have them culled so that she would have three hundred pullets who would be laying hens by fall. They hatched out the first of April. Anna had given Jim the money to pay the hatchery and Betsy had gone along with him to pick up the baby chicks when they were ready to be brought home from the hatchery. Those baby chicks were hers to own and care for. However, Betsy had bought a hundred Leghorn rooster chicks to eat this summer.

"Oh, I already fed them while John was going after the cows," Betsy said. "John and I always get the chores done before breakfast."

"Betsy, you've taken care of my baby chicks for a whole month while I finished teaching but I want to take care of them now," Anna said.

"Tsch, tsch, that no chore, besides we're going to eat the roosters as soon as they're big enough, and I like to watch them grow," Betsy retorted.

Anna went to the sink to wash her face. She took the pitcher and dipped warm water out of the reservoir. The reservoir was low and the bucket was, also. 'Well, at least she could get a bucket and fill the reservoir,' she thought to herself, 'I need to earn my breakfast around here, some way.'

Jim stumbled down the stairs, washed his face, combed his hair, and sat up to the table as John came in from feeding the calves. Betsy brought a plate of pancakes from the warming oven, and butter and syrup to the table. Anna set the table.

"Do you want to pour the coffee, Anna?" Betsy asked, "There's hot water in the tea kettle for your tea, I didn't know how strong to make it."

Anna had a nice brown teapot that she had brought from home. She didn't drink coffee. She and Mother had always drunk tea while the men drank coffee. She poured the coffee and fixed the tea.

"They are having a bridal shower for us in the schoolhouse basement in Wells," Anna said. "Doll told me last night."

"Yes, Myrtle Hanes called Grace Essig and told her. She has invited me and Esther and Thelma and Irene Peck and Charlotte Crow, everybody who wants to come is invited," Betsy said. "They called the Burnham people, too."

"You know, they had a shower for me on the Last Day of School over there. Audry and Frankie La PLant gave me a rolling pin and Joan and Rosemary Chappell gave me a linen tablecloth. They all gave me something, I hope they come anyway, they don't have to bring anything," Anna worried.

"Well, Grace is going to come and get me and I know what I'm giving you - I'm keeping those new sheets I bought for the new mattress till I give them to you at the shower," Betsy said.

"I think you've done enough," Anna said, "I'm going to feel like a star boarder here if you don't stay in bed tomorrow morning and let Jim and me get up and do the chores."

John said, "Hummph." He was English, and given to little conversation. Betsy, the pure Irish person in the family, always interpreted his thoughts for him.

"Tsch! That's the only time John and me have for lovemaking, the days are so long and the nights are so short in the summer."

John said, "Hummph," again.

"Jim, I have to pick up a pasteboard clothes closet that I ordered at Montgomery Ward. Mother said it had come in the mail. We have to have someplace to hang our clothes when I bring mine down here."

"Since Grace is bringing Mom up to the shower, why don't you take the car and run up and get it?" Jim asked. "You said you had to help your mother wash your clothes before you bring them down."

Betsy seemed relieved when Anna gathered up the towels and dishtowels and all their clothes that they had worn on the wedding trip and took them to Wells to wash with Mother's weekly wash. Betsy had no clothes line - she just hung Jim's and John's work clothes on the corral fence and put her dresses on hangers and hung them in the doorway. Betsy built a fire under an old iron kettle in the back yard and washed Jim's work coveralls out there, she had earlier explained to Anna.

To make a long story short, she had no way to wash, really, and had not done too much of it since Lou, Jim's older sister had married and moved up to Campbell's farm to live.

"I'll make some changes around that place," Anna explained to her mother, "If I ever do any washing down there."

"Well, honey, it'll take time. Jim and John are too busy farming to put up clotheslines. We're still stomping clothes since the old washer gave out. I always dreaded dragging it out of Dale's bedroom anyway. I like to have you have a reason to bring your wash up here - that way you can help me - carrying in wash water and filling the boiler on the stove is more than I can do alone, anyway," Mother looked tired as she spoke of patience with her daughter.

"Jim has a lot to do, keeping machinery running, planting feed for the cattle for this winter, and getting the tractor and combine overhauled before harvest next month; it's fine with me if you always bring up the wash - I'll get to visit with you once a week that way."

"Mother, do you know Jim doesn't even get up in the morning and help with the milking or any of the morning chores. John and Betsy get up early and have everything done before they call him to breakfast. She even had my chickens fed before I woke up."

"Charlie said that wasn't going to work. You know, we drove down there while you kids were on your wedding trip last Sunday, and Betsy took us up to the brooder house to see the baby chicks," Mother talked as she and Anna finished the pot of tea, "Betsy said,' I bought these Leghorn roosters from the hatchery to eat this summer and the rest of these baby chicks were hatched from my eggs'."

"Oh, wow!" Anna exclaimed.

"Then when we were on our way home," Mother went on, "Charlie said, 'Anna's not going to have anything of her own down there, and she's not going to be too happy, just taking Betsy after groceries and hauling her to the Ladies Aid."

Anna became more of an errand boy than that - she went to Salina for parts to fix the machinery, went after chicken feed, went after the cows in the evenings, carried the butter to the spring after each meal, and went to fetch it as well as the cream that was being kept cold till they got enough to churn butter; made the early morning trips to the garden to pull the radishes and cut the lettuce, pick the tomatoes, dig the potatoes and harvest the peas, string beans, onions and carrots - and hoed the crab grass out of the strawberries. There was no end to the things

270

Anna could do. Being a farmer's wife was a never-ending chore with little respite.

"Betsy, we should can the string beans today," Anna said, one morning after coming in from the garden, "I've picked away too many beans to eat today. Where do you keep your fruit jars?"

"Oh, I don't do much canning," Betsy answered, "I'll just take a few sacks full to the Ladies Aid this afternoon - those town women don't plant much garden and they're always glad to get fresh string beans."

"Well, if you're going to give them away, I'll just take them to Wells and Mother and I will can them. Mother will let me borrow a few dozen jars and we'll have string beans to eat this winter. Maybe I can take jars from here?" Anna said.

"I just don't have any, Lou borrowed all mine," Betsy explained. "I just never laid up much for the winter. I was always scared that I'd die and John's second wife would get to eat up all my summer's work."

Anna mimicked her father-in-law and said,"Hummph!"

* * * * * * * *

When memory recalls the past and moves to smiles or tears,
A weather beaten object looms right through the mist of years;
Behind the house and barn it stood, a hundred yards or more,
And hurrying feet a path had made, straight to it's swinging door.
from "The Passing of the Outhouse," by James Whitcomb Riley

Anna took her mother-in-law to the Ladies Aid that afternoon but she took the string beans to Wells, snapped and started them processing, before she went back to Bennington to pick Betsy up at the Methodist Church when the Ladies Aid was over.

Mother had a small two-burner oilstove that the copper boiler fit on and Anna could can twenty-four jars of beans at the same time. She water-bath canned them by boiling the jars three hours.

"Will you take them off the fire and seal the jars for me, Mother? I have to get Betsy," Anna said, hugging her Mother and hurrying away.

"You'll have to store them in your mother's basement," Betsy said when Anna told her how many cans of beans they'd have for the winter, "Those glass jars will freeze anywhere in the house this winter."

"Ah Ha! It finally comes out! She wasn't really concerned that she'd be canning up stuff for your second wife, John. She just doesn't have any place to keep canned food," Anna said.

"Well, we used to when my dad lived here. We had a smoke house out in the back yard and it had a pit under it, but one day it caught on fire and burned down," Betsy explained, "And we eat enough vegetables when they are in season, anyway."

"Don't you eat vegetables in winter?" Anna queried.

"Not many, we have chicken and dumplings and salt pork, mostly," Betsy retorted. Sometimes Anna thought she said everything for shock-effect, mostly, too.

Changing the subject, Anna asked, "Is there a pit out there in the back yard where the pile of tin cans and other junk is?"

"Yes, that's where the old smokehouse burned down," Betsy said and went on to tell about her father and homesteading. "This wasn't the first place they built when they came to this section and decided to stay for the winter. That old house that Maurice Stultz lives in to this day was where Tom Patterson and Dorcas, my dad and mother, (Mother was his second wife) and their children and hired hands and Mother's brother, Uncle Bill Blake with his wife and family spent their first winter in Kansas. There were thirteen people lived in that little one-room cabin that winter."

"Dad said they had brought a cook stove with them, thinking they could buy stovepipe in Solomon. The railroad didn't come through till '87 so they were still hauling settler's supplies into Solomon in freighter wagons and stove-pipe was in such short supply in Solomon that they had to sell each settler one length of stove pipe - just enough to get the smoke out of the house. That might have worked for dugouts but Dad and Uncle Bill had hauled timbers from down on the Solomon River and built a house for their families to live in. They put that cook stove up on packing boxes so that the thirty-inch length of pipe would reach through the ceiling. The women had to walk up on boxes for steps to cook."

"There were two babies born there that winter and two women to do the cooking. One woman died and one lived. Uncle Bill Blake's wife died and he took his family back to Missouri to her people and Dad came over here and built this house. I was born in the bedroom John and I sleep in - in 1874."

"Betsy, how old was your father when you were born?" Anna asked.

"He was sixty years old. Dad left home when he was sixteen and we never knew his folks. We were part of Tom Patterson's second family.

"I'll bet he had a lot of interesting stories to tell about the early years. My Grandad Jordan wasn't even born till 1850," Anna spoke with undisguised interest and Betsy went on.

"Yes, he told about being a hostler on a caravan of freighter wagons that made a trip to Santa Fe in 1835 when it was still a part of Old Mexico. They were hauling furs from St Joseph, Missouri. They had traded those furs for bolts of silk that had been brought from the Orient by Spanish traders who freighted them up from the gulf coast of Old Mexico," Betsy paused.

"Yes, yes, go on...," Anna urged.

"On their way back to Missouri they were surrounded by Indians who wanted to trade, and, of course the Indians had nothing to trade except their saddles. Dad said those saddles had been made from slabs of buffalo meat that had been cured by the sweat of the ponies' backs and the sweat from their own backsides." Betsy went on, "They had to trade and Dad said the last they saw of their beautiful bolts of silk the Indians had tied the silk to their ponies' tails, the bolts were unrolling and the silk was billowing out in the wind as they disappeared over the hills."

"What a fascinating story! Too bad you never knew him, Jim," Anna said.

"That's right," Betsy agreed, "Dad would have been 103 years old when Jim was born. Dad went back to Missouri after my mother died. He spent his last years with his first family and died just the year before Tom was born - so we named our son for his grandad."

"Betsy, where was Jim born?" Anna broke in.

"Oh, he was born right here, too, when I was forty-three. I expect to die here. I always say: 'I never expect to get beyond the quacking of the geese.' When Jim was born, August 31, 1916, we had a flock of geese and John was so set-up over having a son when he was forty-six that, when the wheat was threshed, he went out and bought a new Apperson car. Everyone but me went for rides in that car but I had to lay right there in that bed and listen to that flock of geese quacking. Lou was nine years old and she fed those geese shelled corn right under my window."

"What brought this on?" John finally broke in.

"Well, I was asking about the pile of tin cans out there in the back yard..." Anna said.

"Why did you want to know about them?" Jim asked.

"Jim, do you remember when you were building those fancy new stanchions out in the barn before we were married, and you promised you'd build an outhouse with a door on it closer to the house - not way out there in the corral with the opening facing the spring lot - well, you didn't do it and I married you any way," Anna paused for breath.

"So?"

"Well, I was thinking. Tom and Queenie are coming from St. Louis with their little boy. Why couldn't we haul off that pile of trash and dig the pit a bit deeper and bring that outhouse up into the yard and put a door on it before they get here?" Anna was talking rapidly.

"Tssch! It doesn't need a door on it," Betsy said, "It's ventilated better that way - it faces the spring lot anyway."

"But the little guy can't learn to use it - out there in the corral ..." Anna argued.

"Well, it can't be out there in the corner of the yard," Jim said, " The drainage isn't right and it's too close to the well."

"Queenie won't be out here too often, anyway," Betsy explained, "She always stays with some of her high-falutin' friends in Minneapolis, and just drops out here to eat chicken."

"That reminds me - " Jim spoke up, "I told Charlie Smith when I was up to the lake delivering fish worms to old Kubach, that you would dress him a couple of fryers to take back to Salina, Anna. You can get a dollar apiece for them, dressed."

Betsy and Anna had been dressing at least two chickens to fry every day for a month or so. It would be no problem to add a couple more.

"That's great, Marnece sells stuff to the lake front people all the time so I've been wanting to get a business started selling dressed chickens to them when they come up to the lake on weekends," Anna forgot to continue fussing about the need for a new outhouse as she planned for her new cash crop.

When she went up to Wells to do the weekly wash for the Constable household, she told her mother, "I'm looking for a place to move to - Jim and I are never going to have that place on our own. Betsy said today that she was born there and she was going to die there. I thought maybe she might someday decide to move to Bennington but she's not going to."

* * * * * * * * *

Anna sat in the car reading the <u>Saturday Evening Post</u>. She and Jim always had a continued story going in the magazine and she had come along with Jim while he measured wheat ground.

"Could you come along with me and carry the clipboard, Anna? And enter the widths of this old river bed as I cross it in a dozen places?" Jim asked as he returned to the car after rolling a big wheel the length of the dry river bed - a piece of farm land down west and south of Bennington.

"I'd like to finish this section of our continued story before next week's chapter comes. I came along with you so I could sit and read...," Anna complained.

"You can read when we get home," Jim said, "Has Betsy read it?"

" Yes, she read it yesterday while I dug the potatoes and dressed a couple of chickens. She does all the chores that we should be doing every morning while we're lying abed. I think she's entitled to sit down after I finally get up," Anna complained. "Have you noticed how her knee bends out when she carries that five-gallon pail of slop up to the pig pen for your sow?"

"Betsy's knee has always looked like that and she wants to carry that full five-gallon pail or she wouldn't do it," Jim retorted. "You'll just have to take time out to read and quit worrying about what gets done while you're doing it; but come and help me now."

Anna continued talking as she walked beside him, carrying the clipboard and recording the widths at intervals across the dry river bed. Jim rolled a wheel that had a sixteen and a half foot circumference measuring a rod with each revolution of the wheel. It had sixteen spokes and gave an accurate measurement of acres for farmers.

Anna remembered how proud she was of Jim when she was visiting with Wayne and Thelma Peck several years earlier.

"How did Jim get a job like that?" Wayne had asked.

Since Roosevelt's plan to lift the farmers out of the Great Depression had brought about the refinancing of farm loans and a plan for raising prices through crop control through the Agricultural Adjustment Act of 1933, farmers in Ottawa County had been in farm programs. Jim had started working for the AAA Office in Minneapolis in 1935.

"Why, didn't you know my boy friend is the smartest man in Richland Township?" Anna had retorted, laughing.

"I taught him my last year at Sand Creek," Thelma had said, "He was a smart little boy then."

"Lou's husband, Leo Campbell, has taught Jim a lot about radios and electricity. He made a radio when he was eight years old," Wayne said. "He ran an aerial wire over the telephone line and he could get reception from all over the world."

"Yes, but no one else could call out on that party line," Thelma interrupted. "Mac Sheppard looked for several days for the reason no one was able to use the telephone but Betsy. She could call out but no one could call her."

Yes, Anna remembered how proud she was of Jim's ability to get a government job just out of high school. She was still proud and happy when he got a check for his work from the federal government but there was never time to even read a magazine any more.

"Jim, I'm not going to bring the Post up to you in the field so you can read the continued story first, anymore," she said, "Last week, you were sitting there in the car reading and I was embroidering and Marnece came driving across the field to tell us about the Ice Cream Social to buy those chairs for the church."

"So what?" he asked as he clicked off another revolution of the wheel.

"I heard in Wells yesterday that Marnece is calling you the 'Saturday Evening Post Farmer' now." Anna explained.

"I wonder if Marnece ever lets Johnnie sleep, or read a magazine," Jim mused, "She's a real go-getter, isn't she?"

"Well, the next time I come up to the corner to get the mail and the Saturday Evening Post comes, I'll just stop down by the driveway and take time to read the story first," Anna asserted, "Who wants to be a go-getter anyway."

"By the way, I got a letter from Lela today - she quit her job at that Chinese restaurant in Topeka. Lela said she had finished paying for her sewing machine and not long after as she was carrying the platters of Chow Mein back through the swinging doors, the manager ran past her and a big meat cleaver whistled past her ear and sank itself in the floor beside her."

"Lela just set the order of food down at the customer's table and went up to the cash register and asked for her wages," Anna continued, "She never went back for her tips - she decided she'd had enough of Chinese food."

"Well, even if you have a hard time finding time to read your stories, you'll have to admit, it's not nearly so dangerous to be a farmer's wife," said Jim with a grin.

****

This, my love, is my Autumn rug
I made it in the Fall,
When nature with a vengeance
Back to earth her loves doth call.
A funeral dirge for flowers,
When birdlings fly away,
To spend their winter hours
In southern gardens gay.

Jim and Anna sat beside the kerosene lamp at the kitchen table playing Chinese checkers. The wind was singing a bitter song even through the dense timber that protected the Constable farm from winter winds...The fire burned low in the kitchen range.

Betsy spoke from the living room door, "I'm going on to bed, Jim. Now, don't sit up and burn all my kindling to get breakfast with. And be sure there's a full pail of water and the reservoir is full before you go to bed. The pump will be froze in the morning."

"That old sow of mine is going to pick tonight to have her pigs, I think. She was hurrying around building her nest when I came down from the barn," Jim told her, "I'll have to go out and see about her and I'll bring in more wood before we go to bed..." The phone rang.

"That was Queenie," Betsy reported again from the living room door. "She's in Minneapolis - her father is dying and the whole Hart family have arrived from everywhere. She wanted to know if she could sleep on our living room couch tomorrow night. I told her 'Sure,' if the snow doesn't block all the roads so she can't get out here."

"It's too cold to snow much," Anna said, "But it's really a blizzardy night. I suppose the west bedroom upstairs is too cold for Queenie to sleep there? I'm so sorry about her father. How old is he?"

"Oh, he's a lot older than her mother - John Hart was a wealthy bachelor when he married Queenie's mother. He's in his eighties. Queenie has five sisters and one brother, and they're all home, I guess."

Queenie had driven out from Minneapolis the next afternoon but, in the meantime the Constable farmstead had grown by six new residents. Jim had gone out the next morning to find that the first of his three sows had farrowed and her piglets had frozen.

Little white frozen piglets, six of them, lying stretched out in a grape basket on the oven door, greeted Anna when she came down the stairs.

"They're dead, aren't they, Betsy?" she asked, horrified.

"Oh, I've seen them come back to life as soon as they thaw out. We'll have to see," she said.

Amazingly, they began to stir and squeal as Jim and John came in from the hog pen.

"If that old fool sow had ever settled down, she could have kept them from freezing," John said.

"I borrowed the money from McMichael to go into the hog business," Jim said, "The Ottawa County State Bank may never get paid at this rate."

"Oh, you can't tell, they may live," Betsy said, But they'll have to be hand fed for a few days."

"Then will their mother take them back?" Anna asked.

"It's hard to say, some will and some won't," was all the encouragement Betsy or John could give about the little half-alive creatures in the grape basket on the oven door.

Anna always had trouble eating those sour-dough pancakes that were the regular bill of fare around Betsy's breakfast table - she finished her cup of hot tea and embarked on the project of keeping those six little pigs alive till the weather cleared and the old sow would settle down and raise them.

She heated cow's milk just to scalding and added warm water. "No sugar," Betsy said, "That would give them scours."

One by one she picked them up and spooned a few drops in each little mouth. They were all alive!

"How often should they be fed?" she wondered aloud.

"Oh, they'll let you know," John assured her, "Those bloody little rascals will squeal and the only way you can get them to shut up is to spoon 'em some more milk."

"John, they aren't bloody. Did you ever see such fine pink skin? They're beautiful! Just look, they have long white eyelashes." Anna had fallen in love with the helpless little creatures.

All of that cold, windy day with the snow that had fallen the night before blowing outside, Anna cleaned the living room, brought down the feather tick from upstairs to make the old spring cot warmer and more comfortable for Queenie when she arrived, stopping every little while to spoon the warm milk into the little pink mouths. As the baby pigs got stronger, their voices grew, too. Soon they were rousing at intervals to squeal. They had to be fed every hour!

Anna transferred them to a bushel basket and took them into the living room, setting the basket on top of the pile of wood behind the stove - the warmest place in the house. She was crocheting a rag rug out of worn out shirts, old ragged dresses and work pants. It would make something warmer to step their feet out on by the new bed upstairs.

Betsy was baking bread. She had a starter sitting on the back of the kitchen counter that she kept working by adding sour milk, a bit of flour and sugar every few days as she took some of the bubbly stuff out to set a new batch of bread. Today she would bake an extra three loaves for Queenie to take back to Minneapolis where the big Hart family would be gathering for her father's funeral.

Betsy loved to cook. She was also making noodles to go in the pot of chicken that was boiling in the black iron kettle on the Home Comfort Range. She had cut up a pumpkin and cooked it the day before. She was ready to bake a few pumpkin pies when the bread came out of the oven.

"Jim, will you be trying to get to Wells today?" she asked as Jim came in from building a better shelter for the old sow who was still having pigs - seven more were still alive in the pig pen!

"Why?" he asked. "Do you need something? I've got to get a sack of chicken feed for Anna's pullets, we're about out."

"You are out of bread and I'll need a pound of lard before I can bake bread for John again," Betsy said. Jim didn't like his mother's sour dough bread. He had somehow developed a taste for 'store-bought' bread and Betsy could always get him to go to town for groceries if she mentioned that he was out of bread.

Anna spoke up, "I'll call Mother and have her get a few cans of the string beans I canned and some of Dad's sweet potatoes and some onions out of the basement if you can stop at the house."

"Come and go with me, can't you?" Jim asked her.

"EEEEEE! EEEEEE!" was the piercing squeal coming from behind the living room stove.

"No. I'm confined to the living room for today. Mother will understand. Isn't thirteen piggies an awful lot for one litter?" Anna asked as she picked up the tiny pigs, one at a time; 'Jim could be the go-getter for today,' she thought.

"She probably won't raise them all but, yes, she can be a proud mama if she can settle down and raise even ten of this litter," Jim agreed, as he watched Anna spoon the warm milk in each little mouth. "Looks like the ears are going to turn black on the tips on a couple of these."

"Well, I'll be a proud mama if they all stay alive till you can get her to take them back," Anna said, finishing the last little squealer, and tucking them under the torn square of worn-out flannel sheeting that had been lying on top of the heater in an old tin pan. "Would you carry in some more wood for us before you leave?"

"And chop some kindling size for the kitchen stove," Betsy added, "I'm going to keep the fire going most all day with all this baking."

Anna went back to her crocheting, tearing the clean rags and rolling them in balls. She would finish with the throw rug by evening and have it lying in front of the couch. Betsy scrubbed the chamber pot and set it under the end of the bed out of sight.

"Queenie never has used the outhouse when they visit," Betsy explained, "Tom always carried this pot in and out for her but I guess I will this time. She said 'Connie' couldn't get away so she made the trip back from St. Louis alone."

Queenie arrived late in the afternoon, too tired to take much interest in the baby pigs behind the stove in the bushel basket. However, Anna spent the night, sleeping by 'fits and starts,' hurrying down the stairs with her flashlight to feed the little pigs before they could start squealing, and replenishing the wood in the parlor stove as quietly a possible.

But Queenie did manage to say one thing that 'stuck in Anna's craw' as Betsy said, long after she had returned to Minneapolis with a big box of 'farm fresh' food for the gathering Hart clan.

As they were eating supper she had said, "Jim, when are you and Anna going to move out and start making a living for yourselves like Connie and I did?"

No one answered her; they all just went on eating.

When Anna was in Minneapolis the next week she went in to see Frank La Plant and asked him to put her name on the extra board as a substitute teacher for the next year. 'I guess I can make a living for myself,' she thought, 'if that's the way they feel about me.' Maybe someone who had signed a contract to teach in one of the rural schools wouldn't be able to teach and they would need a teacher - married or single, it wouldn't matter in that case.

On the way to Wells on the east side of the road was a rock house, a barn, a chicken house and an outhouse. Lew Sheffler rented the ground around it but there was no one living in the house. It had a tall windmill but, for some reason, there was no water there - so it had stood empty for a long time.

"Jim, let's go see Lew Sheffler and see if he will rent that house to us. You can fix up the barn and corral for your hogs and I can fix up the chicken house, and we can 'start making a living for ourselves,' as Queenie says." Anna was excited as she began to plan.

"That old farmstead has no water, I already asked Lew Sheffler about it. He wants $7.00 a month rent and we'd have to haul water," Jim said.

"But it does have an outhouse with a door on it! And we can borrow a couple of ten-gallon cream cans from the folks and haul water from home! I want to see inside the house." Anna could turn into a 'go-getter,' herself, when she was given an opening.

There were three rooms downstairs, two rooms upstairs and a full basement with a dirt floor. Mother helped Anna paper the kitchen and living room. Two orange crates with a curtain in front that matched the window curtains, served as a washstand. Mother's two-burner oil stove sat on another orange crate and cooked their first meal in their new home. They moved that bed with the new mattress down the ladder one more time and, with the pasteboard clothes closet, their bedroom was complete. A new white metal kitchen cabinet, a small kitchen table, a living room couch that the back folded down on to make a spare bed - and a new linoleum in the kitchen made the old rock house into a honeymoon cottage. Anna had her own 'four walls' before their First Anniversary!

****

279

"Mr. and Mrs. James Constable's first wedding anniversary was celebrated Thursday evening, May 4, 1939. Mr. and Mrs. Wendell Hanes, Mr. & Mrs. Ernest Geist, Mr and Mrs Forest Hanes and Mr. and Mrs. Ward Comfort, Davy and Eileen surprised them with wieners and the trimmings for a first class wiener roast, followed by a ride in Wendell's pick-up, to the picture show, "Dodge City". Some time was also spent at the skating rink and the Markley Grove in Minneapolis."

A clipping from the "Wells News" column in the Minneapolis Messenger the next week announced the beginning of celebrations held each year for the above named couples which provided most of their social activities throughout the year. Beth and Ernest Geist's Anniversary was August twelfth; Swede and Lene, (Wendall and Norline Hanes' nicknames) were married December ninth; Toy and Myrt, (Forrest and Myrtle Hanes' nicknames) celebrated their anniversary March seventh, while Ward and Avis Comfort celebrated January first of each year. Five celebrations of such magnitude satisfied most appetites for entertainment and created never-to-be-forgotten occasions spaced at sufficient intervals so they could follow their serious pursuits of making a living.

In August there was swimming at the lake, picnics at the shelter house, watermelon feeds, ice cream feeds, and picture shows. Sit-down dinners, New Year's Eve parties and other original plans were devised to mark the passage of each year of wedded bliss for these couples.

Betsy would often refer to the 'Wells Click' that took up so much time and was, she implied, so exclusive that no time was left for 'Benningtonites'.

Doris and Earl Markley were an exception. They were farmers and lived south of Bennington. Doris and Jim had danced together at public dances when Jim was in high school in Bennington. When Anna and Jim became a couple they visited Doris and Earl, ate meals at their home and since Earl was one of Jim's friends from Bennington and was Jim's best man when Anna and Jim were married, Doris was asked to be Anna's Matron of Honor at their wedding.

They were often invited for Sunday Dinners with Doris and Earl so Anna was excited about having them up for Sunday Dinner, May 7th, 1939. They had their own home now!

"Doris, Jim and I have moved to ourselves," Anna said when she called from her mother's house in Wells. "We'd like you to come for Sunday Dinner. We live a half-mile south, a half mile east and another half-mile south of Wells. Can you come?"

"That sounds great," Doris agreed, "It's just a year ago we had that big wedding. Time to celebrate?"

"That's right!" Anna said. "I was wondering if you'd wear your blue floor-length dress and I'll wear my wedding dress and the boys can wear the suits they wore at the wedding? You know, no one took any pictures when we were married and I want some pictures before we all grow out of our clothes. Jim has gained twenty pounds since last year!"

"Well, so have I," Doris said, "I suppose you still weigh 110 pounds?"

Doris had been very small the year before but she had problems with her teeth and had had all of them pulled and a complete set of dentures made in the meantime. The doctors had said her teeth were poisoning her system. That must have been the problem.

However, the day was sunny and they went out west of the house on a windy hill and took pictures with Anna's box camera - the sooner, the better. Doris and Earl's son, Lonnie, was born the next May. Time was marching on.

The year spent in the rock house was a year of 'making do' with what one had. Jim lined the chicken house with those sheets of cardboard from the ~Through the Years' book Anna had used at Burnham. There was enough to line the barn and make it a snug place to keep Jim's hogs.

That old barn hadn't been used for a few years and had a lot of trash and old boards inside it. Jim was busy tearing out stanchions and getting it ready to be a hog-house with the corral out back for his young pigs.

Anna looked in on his work as she was going into Wells to do her washing with her mother. There he was sitting on the floor tugging at an old board that was fastened to the sole of his shoe.

"Come in here and pull this board loose," Jim said, looking a little 'green around the gills,' she thought.

"Mercy! What have you done?" Anna asked, horrified, as she bent over to discover that the board was 'nailed' to his foot with a long rusty nail!

He had stepped on a nail and it had run through his shoe and almost through the ball of his foot!

With a very queasy stomach she had pulled the board away from this shoe; he looked faint. "I'll help you to the car. We'll have to go to the doctor right now, Jim," Anna said.

"Oh, no, I don't need to rush off to the doctor. It'll quit hurting by evening. I want to get this hog shed done today. Herb Essig said he could help move my hogs up so Betsy won't have to be carrying slop to them any longer," Jim said.

Anna remembered how Margaret Essig had said that her Dad was always worrying about how Jim laid in bed till five minutes till eight, let his mother and dad do the morning chores and 'drove like a bat out of Hell' to make it to high school on time. 'I guess Herb Essig will find out that Jim has grown up now,' she thought.

"I hope you'll be able to step on that foot by morning," she said, going on into Wells to wash clothes with her mother.

"Mother, Jim stepped on a nail out there in the barn he's making into a hogshed. He just went right on working after I helped him pull the board off of his shoe. It was nailed right to his foot," Anna reported as she carried in the dirty clothes and set up the wash tubs.

"You should have made him take off that shoe and soak that foot in Lysol water, Anna; it'll be a wonder if he doesn't get blood poisoning in that foot," Mother asserted.

"I'll have to run down to the store and get a bottle before I go home," Anna said. "He wants to move his hogs up tomorrow while Herb Essig has time to help him."

"I've got the barn ready," Jim said, as he hobbled in that evening and removed his shoe for the first time.

His foot was swollen but the little hole in the bottom of his foot hadn't bled much at all. Anna mixed a solution of Lysol with hot water in the wash pan and set it on the floor, "Mother said you'd have to soak this foot till that hole opened up or you will get blood poisoning in it," she said.

For eight days Jim hobbled about on that foot, soaking it whenever he sat down and moaning in his sleep. Anna fixed a pasteboard box under the covers for him to keep the swollen foot in because he couldn't stand to have even a sheet rest on his toes. At last she had had enough of worrying and mixing Lysol solutions and sleeping on the couch with one eye open to play Florence Nightingale! His foot was still swollen and a bright red streak was beginning to show up on the top of his instep!

Anna burst into tears, "I've had it with you," she sobbed. "If you don't go down to Dr. Boyle right now - you can just go back down and let your mother take care of you. She said yesterday that all you needed was some of her good chicken noodle soup and that foot would heal right up. Well, I've worried long enough!"

When they went to the doctor that day he said that they had done the right thing, he could do no more. "It will gradually get better," he said, "It just takes time."

"Dr. Boyle, what good would chicken noodle soup do?" Anna asked, still rankling at Betsy's suggestion about how she always cured her children when they were in her care.

"Well, don't soak his foot in it," he laughed. "You look as if you could use some and a good night's sleep, Anna. And, if you have any left I could use some, too."

Dr Boyle lived in Bennington as well as Dr. Hinshaw and both men were busy; Anna looked at his tired face and thought, 'eight days of doctoring is all I could stand, I surely couldn't make a career of it.'

* * * * * * * * *

Jim and Anna lived in the rock house that winter. Anna's hens laid a thirty-dozen case of eggs a week. Fred and Grace Windhorst bought eggs and sold groceries on the east side of Main street in Wells. Ward And Avis Comfort ran the hardware Store on the west side of the street.

Eggs were nine cents a dozen at their lowest price but Anna could buy enough groceries to feed just the two of them on their egg money. Jim and his dad continued to rent the Swanson place and farm it to wheat. The economy was gradually pulling itself out of the Great Depression. The shelter belts were growing that the Forest Service had planted and the threat of dust storms each spring subsided.

Jim sold his pigs when they reached two hundred pounds and paid off his banker, "McMichael told me he'd lend me money to buy calves this fall," he announced that evening.

Anna had been waiting to tell him the news that Frank La Plant, the County School Superintendent had called his mother, he had a school for Anna to teach that fall!

Union Grove School District, five miles east of Bennington on the Blue Line, had been closed for several years - their school board members had children, high school age, to haul to Longford, also, as well as three grade school-age children, between them. They had been collecting money from the district for transportation as long as there were less than four children of grade school age. A big wheat farmer in that district felt he was paying school taxes in that district to haul his neighbor's children to Longford so he moved his hired man, a Mr. Brown, into one of the vacant houses on his wheat land. Mr. Brown had four sons, grade school age, who had to be educated. That forced Union Grove to hire a teacher and have school in that district.

Anna explained all that to Jim with some excitement.

"That's a good twelve miles from here, Anna. What kind of wages will you get?" Jim asked.

"Sixty-five dollars per month, Frank LaPlant said," Anna explained, "I want to run into Wells and see Dale if he's home. I'd like to buy my car back so I'll have something to drive."

"Dad's going to have to buy a new tractor. I have an idea to buy a hammermill, too, so I can cut the feed and dig a trench silo so I can have ensilage to feed the cattle with all winter," Jim said, with no more discussion of Anna's new job - it was as if she had been doing nothing about the farming which might conflict that teaching school five days a week all winter.

"What has John been feeding his cows all winter with - up till now?" Anna asked with some disgust.

"If I go to the sale ring and buy a bunch of yearling calves I'll be feeding them every day down there; and John won't have to hitch up the team every day all winter and feed his cows bundle feed. I'll feed his cattle right along with mine with the tractor."

"Well, let's finish supper and run into Wells, I have to talk to the folks about taking a job, teaching, away down there on the Blue Line," Anna said, "And I'll have to do something about the washing, I can't just dump your mother's and my wash in her lap every Sunday night all winter, and Betsy isn't able to wash your clothes, her own and John's either."

Kansas Power and Light had brought Rural Electrification to Wells through the REA as one of Roosevelt's efforts to modernize farms and make rural living easier. Anna had a plan.

"Let's stop here," she said, as they drove into Wells, coming to the Hardware Store. "I want to talk to Ward before we go on up home."

Ward had bought Avis a new electric washer and had a used washing machine for sale.

"Ward, what was wrong with this old Dexter that you had to get a new one for Avis?" Anna asked.

"Nothing, except the new one has a soak cycle and I convinced Avis she could do without that extra tub for soaking the kid's clothes. There just isn't room in the back room for a kitchen and living room on wash day," Ward explained, "Why? Are you getting electricity?"

"No, I'm just thinking; what would it cost to wire Mother's house for electricity?"

"I wired this building for about twenty-five dollars worth of wiring. Of course, an electrician to do the job would cost you more. I could sell you this washer for forty dollars," Ward bargained.

Adelbert Leslie, a young man from Arkansas, a cousin of Philip Miller's, had come to work up at Miller's Garage and now had 'board and room' with the Allisons. Mother and Anna had been doing his washing and ironing, also - every week. He had Anna's room since she had married and left home. He was close to his work and his church, being a quiet religious young man and ate whatever food was prepared without complaint. Mother got twelve dollars a week 'board and room.' It was just that those washings, coupled with the Constable wash was too much for a wash board and stomper if Mother had to do it all alone.

Anna paid for the wiring and the 'new to them' electric washing machine. Dad and Dale wired the house for electricity, and Mother paid for it all eventually by washing for Anna and Jim as well as the rest of her enlarged family.

The winter of '39-'40 was a busy one. Jim drove down to the farm to feed cattle every day as well as hauling water and feeding hogs at the rock house; Anna taught school at Union Grove and gathered the eggs every evening when she got home. Dad had invented a saw-rig and he and Jim sawed wood to keep the three houses warm that winter. There was little time for sin.

****

284

Union Grove -- 1939-1940

Four little boys - all from one family - what could be so tough about that? The school house had a basement that was little more than a coal bin and a big stove in the middle of the desks. It had a jacket around it - brown enamel and a big fire box - Anna could build a good coal fire each morning. It was only a one-room schoolhouse, well-lighted with seven windows on the north.

"You'll have trouble heating this place when the wind gets in the north," the school board member said, "That's why we quit having school here, really, the kids complained every winter and were sick half the time with colds from sitting around in this building."

"It's nice and clean but there aren't many books in the library," Anna hesitated...

"Well, you won't need many with those four boys," laughed the school board member's wife, "I understand they aren't much on books."

"Oh? What grades are they in?" Anna asked.

"Well, there's one who isn't quite all buttoned up, he's fifteen - they say he fell on the ice when he was little and has a steel plate in his head; there's a pair of twins in the third grade who still can't read. We didn't hear much about the fifth grader, did we?" One lady spoke to the other.

"Their folks didn't send them to school enough for the teachers to really get acquainted, I guess," laughed the other, "Except the oldest one - they really wanted him out of the house."

The three school board members and their wives were a congenial group. They had cleaned the schoolhouse and filled the coal bin and kindling box, and mowed the weeds. The outhouses had been swept - 'and both had doors on them' Anna thought, 'and she'd get sixty-five dollars a month for teaching that winter - more than she got for running errands last winter.'

"They sound like quite a challenge," Anna said, noncommittally.

Frank La Plant had already told her she'd get no complaint from the parents or the school board either about anything. It sounded almost boring - but she had wanted to teach so this was the opportunity.

Anna always felt that she learned more than she taught that winter. The twins looked alike. They were healthy little third grade boys. One was more aggressive than the other, however. LaVerne was seated ahead of Vernon so, in the classroom Anna could tell them apart, assuming each sat in his assigned seat. LaVerne's personality was more pleasant than Vernon's. He smiled a lot. Vernon often had a rebellious look on his face, as though he'd rather be out playing than sitting in the schoolhouse at an assigned desk.

They didn't talk in complete sentences. They had their own way of speaking to one another but their skills of communicating with others were sadly lacking. Anna laid simple first grade books on each desk and asked each, in turn, to read, only to be greeted with a grin from LaVerne and a stare from Vernon.

George, the fifth grader, was also pleasant and spoke in whole sentences but wasn't interested in reading anything and read in a halting fashion, even first grade books.

Lewis was fifteen. His statement was: "I don't like "Nited States. When I get sixteen I'm goin' to Californy!"

At recess the three younger boys liked to toss the basketball to one another. Lewis had to be forced to leave the schoolhouse, even to go to the outhouse. Anna had to stand at the door to the basement and order him outside after she discovered that, left alone in the schoolhouse, he would go downstairs and relieve himself on the coal.

"Lewis, this is recess. We will go outside and play basketball. Now!" Anna would repeat, and finally enforce by advancing down the aisle with fist clenched. She never touched him, she just bullied him around.

"I must teach him something," Anna said, to her mother, to Jim and finally to Frank La Plant.

"I doubt that you ever will feel the satisfaction of having done so," he said, on her first visit to Minneapolis to the County Superintendent's office, "Others have tried it and have long ago given up. We're just complying with the law in opening a school in that district for four children. It is a long legal process to put him in an institution and, so far, his parents have resisted. Next year it will be a different story. He will be sixteen and his parents will have to keep him at home."

As Fall advanced and the weather was cold and windy, Anna brought patterns, a coping saw and wood to make gifts for parents and sisters. The Brown boys had five sisters who were older and already grown and gone from home.

Woodworking was done at recess and noon after sack lunches were eaten. Vernon, LaVerne and George liked to saw and sand, glue and paint and would have spent the day that way, had not the teacher called them to take their seat and study when 1:00 p.m. came.

One day, when it was time for the last recess, Anna said, "LaVerne, it's your turn to use the coping saw. Vernon used it last."

LaVerne, sitting ahead of Vernon, just smiled - but made no move to get the coping saw and start on his project.

Vernon jumped up and proceeded to do his sawing. Anna interposed, "LaVerne, it was your turn. Didn't you want to saw today?"

LaVerne continued to smile.

George spoke up and explained to Anna, "LaVerne always lets Vernon go first."

"Always?" she asked.

"Yes, he always has," was George's reply, "We try to get them to take turns but LaVerne don't want to."

"Doesn't want to." Anna corrected.

"No, he don't," George assured her.

"Even when we are playing 'Toss the Basketball?'" Anna asked.

"Yes," explained George, "Vernon will toss the ball to me and, if I throw it to LaVerne and, if Vernon is anywhere, close, LaVerne will step sideways and let Vernon catch it."

George had taught Anna something about the psychology of twins. At least she could tell those two apart on the playground as well as in the schoolroom and it wasn't yet Christmas! If only they could express themselves in sentences!

Some years later she was to read in The Minneapolis Messenger that the small town of Ada had a winning basketball team. They had gone all the way to State. They boasted a pair of twins, Vernon and LaVerne Brown, who seemed to confound any and all competition under the hoop.

George had explained something about his brothers that other basketball players wouldn't grasp easily in competition. "I'd like to see if they each express whole thoughts yet," Anna told Jim, "or if Vernon says one and LaVerne smiles."

In January the temperature fell to fifteen above zero and the wind blew from the north, a few inches of snow fell but the roads were fine. Anna came to school early to build a fire. The water bucket was half full and frozen solid. She built the fire, wearing her coat, gloves and scarf, and never removed them that day. The Brown children didn't come to school at all.

The meager library had a book, 'Sergeant York', that she wished, years later, she had swiped from that school. She read it that day as she hung over that jacketed heater, sitting on a stepladder that was used to reach the curtains when they rolled to the top on those seven tall windows. The movie that was later made about Sergeant York didn't begin to touch on the austerity of the life that old book described in the West Virginia hills. It said that one could 'throw a cat through the walls' of the houses there. Anna wondered if she would live to be a hero like Alvin York, at least she had the same humble beginnings!

About 2:30 in the afternoon she 'closed up shop' and drove up to the home of the closest school board member and was invited in to warm up.

"We will close that school for two weeks," he said, "You shouldn't have stayed over there this long."

"I put in one more day," Anna answered, "Of the one hundred and sixty that constitutes a school term."

"Well, don't worry about that! You'll draw your pay and please us better if you just stay home. After all we are the ones who hired you!" he grumbled, as his wife hurried around fixing hot tea.

"Here, drink this. You'll be sick, getting so cold for so long. We wondered why you were still there?" She spluttered.

Anna drove into the farmyard to tell the Browns that school had been closed for two weeks due to the cold.

Mrs. Brown opened the door a crack and said, "Well, we don't have a clock and by the time we started thinking about sending the boys, it was too cold and they didn't want to get out, anyway."

Union Grove had a Last Day of School Dinner in April. The boys came to get their grade cards, but their parents didn't. All three school board members and their wives were there. Anna brought her box camera and took pictures of the Brown boys and the friends she had made in District 68. The men tossed the basketball with the boys.

"We should have put up a hoop last fall," one of them observed, "You didn't have much to play with out of doors, did you?"

"Well, anyway, we complied with the law, didn't we?" one of the ladies observed, and they all agreed.

****

Spring of 1940

School at Union Grove was over - May fifth was coming up and their Wells circle of friends would be showing up at the rock house for Jim and Anna's Second Anniversary.

"Jim, we'll simply have to get those three hundred baby chicks out of the upstairs and out to a brooder house - I imagine I can smell them down stairs," Anna said at breakfast.

They had got their baby chicks the first of March and set up the brooder stove upstairs. There were two nice bedrooms up there that had no furniture and tall windows on the east, west and south - an ideal place to start baby chicks - but now they were two months old and needed to be out on the ground. Jim had laid down a thick layer of newspapers and covered them with peat moss in the east room up there. There was good ventilation and the chicks were growing like weeds.

"Betsy wants us to bring them down there - she says she can feed them and the roosters will be handy when they are ready to fry," Jim said between bites of pancake.

"Handy for her, maybe," Anna retorted, "But I feel that I should be the one chasing those roosters and dressing those fryers this summer."

"Oh, she likes to do that, Anna," Jim explained, "Betsy wouldn't have it any different."

"Jim, when are you going to start calling her "Mother" and realizing that she has limitations? Betsy was sixty-five last fall," Anna nagged Jim constantly - it seemed to her that he treated his mother like a reliable hired hand.

John and Jim had hired Gwynn Lassey from Miltonvale to come down and dig a well east of the house and put in an electric pump in the fall of '39. Betsy now had running water in the house but so far, no electricity. She was still using the kerosene lamps. Jim and Anna had given them an Aladdin Lamp with a mantle for the Christmas of '38.

"All the light we'll ever need," she had declared.

* * * * * * * * * *

"We're still hauling water and packing it up these stairs, Anna, and when we get a brooder house with a chicken pen fixed up here we'll still be packing water; the hogs are a big enough job," Jim argued, "And Mom has a spicket right across the driveway from the brooder house, now. And we won't need a pen. They can run out and catch grasshoppers."

Anna stopped arguing. "I will get Dad to help me if he's not busy and I'll borrow enough chicken crates of him to bring the chicks down there today. I've got to scoop that peat moss and chicken manure into tubs, burn those newspapers and clean this house," Anna said, outlining her own busy day.

"Better bring the chicken manure and peat moss down to the farm too, and I'll scatter it on the strawberries. Betsy's garden is looking fine," Jim agreed, "Getting that stuff down those stairs won't be nearly as big a job as it was - hauling it up there."

The day didn't go at all as planned, however. Jim had announced as he drank coffee at his mother's table that Charlie and Anna would be bringing down the young chickens later that morning.

"We'll have to clean out that chicken house this morning then, and whitewash it to kill the mites," Betsy had said, starting to leap up and get at it at her usual speed when she discovered that she couldn't lift her right arm or make her right leg carry her. The next sentence was slurred and she couldn't swallow. Betsy had had a stroke!

Jim and John had picked her up and put her in the back seat of John's big old Hudson and rushed her down to Dr. Hinshaw in Bennington.

"Dr. Hinshaw said that a blood vessel had burst near the left temple, crossing over to her right side near her throat, affecting her swallowing and her speech, and the use of her right arm and her right leg," Jim explained.

"Why didn't he take her on to the hospital in Salina?" Anna asked when she and her dad arrived with some of the young chickens.

Betsy was lying on the old spring cot in the living room and John was sitting beside her stroking her work-worn hand, slow tears coursing down his cheeks unheeded.

"John said he could take care of her," Jim went on to say to Anna as he motioned her out to the kitchen where the breakfast dishes still sat on the table, "Dr. Hinshaw said there was nothing to do for a stroke except rest and let nature route the blood flow to other blood vessels."

"But she can't rest with all this work to be done around here!" Anna exploded, "And John sitting there patting her hand!"

"I know, but John didn't want to put her in the hospital - he wanted to bring her back home," Jim spoke softly, "And Dr. Hinshaw said she'd rest for awhile, at least, because she couldn't do anything else with a paralyzed arm and leg."

Anna's dad went out to the chicken house and scooped out last year's manure. Jim whitewashed the interior. Then Dad went back to the rock house and scooped up the peat moss and chicken manure. He brought Mother down to clean up the papers to burn and 'set Anna's rock house to rights' as she said.

Anna and Jim moved back down to the farm by slow degrees as spring turned into summer and the dizzying round of farm work picked up. Betsy was soon sliding a chair around the kitchen with the paralyzed knee resting on it, and her right arm hanging, lifeless, at her side.

Anna still took the washing to Wells and she and her mother washed canned the harvest from Dad's big garden or Betsy's big garden. Fried chicken, the mainstay of everyone's meal, was always in the process of being prepared wherever Anna was. Four chickens a day fell under Anna's wicked knife, lost their feathers and wound up in the skillet, either at Mother's house, Betsy's house or Anna's rock house on the hill.

Harvest came with it's usual round of hauling wheat to Wells, picking up groceries and chicken feed for the growing chickens and the hogs that still had their pen at the barn at the rock house. Jim was just as busy - keeping machinery running, planting row crops so he'd have feed for the calf crop and young heifers and John's cows, running to Salina for repair parts, axle grease, veterinary supplies, etc. When Anna took time to think, she wondered if farming would ever slow down so one could look back and say, "Well! We did it." It seemed to her that there would always be something more that should be done!

One hot summer day when the wind was in the west, Anna stopped at the Rock House to strip the sheets from their bed - they still slept there - when they slept. Running up to the screen door - she stopped short of flinging it open. The screen seemed to be alive - she couldn't see through it. She moved to a window and peered into the kitchen. Her curtains were covered with flying ants! Knots of them were clinging to the curtains inside and crawling on the window! Running around to the west door she tried to open it. No one ever used it - the road led to the back door so Jim had inserted a case knife between the woodwork and the casing. She couldn't get in her house without opening that screen door! Mammma!!!! Anna turned and fled to Wells.

Dad was gone but she and Mother, wash day forgotten, gathered brooms and fly spray, and hurried back to Anna's precious 'honeymoon cottage' that was being invaded!

With Mother beside her to sweep off the ants if they attacked her, Anna flung open the screen door! The ants - wings included - were about one-half inch across but there were thousands of them - piled up on one another from the top to the bottom of the screen.

Peering into the kitchen, Mother announced, "Anna they're coming from around that flue cap on the chimney. When a colony of flying ants migrate, they sometimes attach themselves to the cupola on a barn - the tallest thing they come to in their flight. Pa told one time about a colony settling on his team when he was cultivating out in the field."

The ants had hit that tall rock chimney on top of the roof and came on down the chimney, continuing to the nearest light which was only a

290

crack where the stove pipe had been removed when Anna took out the kitchen stove in the spring and put up a flue cap to cover the hole. The ants didn't seem to want to bite or sting - they just seemed to want to get on their way, so Anna and her mother swept and, using dish towels, wiped the curtains and shook them out the door. At last there seemed to be no more ants coming down the chimney. They left the screen propped open, stripped the bed, and went back to Mother's house on Main Street to do the weekly wash.

With harvest over, Jim finally fixed the pig pen up and moved his hogs back to his folk's farm so Anna had to give up and move back to the farm, too. The attempt to 'make a living for themselves' as Queenie had said, was over.

****

My candle burns at both ends;
It will not last the night;
But ah, my foes and oh, my friends--
It gives a lovely light!
Edna St. Vincent Millay

1940 - another Election Year - and no one loomed on the scene who even compared with Roosevelt. The people, laughing at jokes about his 'alphabet agencies,' continued to vote for him. Election to a third term behind him, Roosevelt tried to position the United States with a powerful navy, even as Congress adopted a position of neutrality as Japan invaded Manchuria and Hitler dominated Europe.

Dad read the papers and listened to the radio and worried for his son. Dale was still not married and continued to work for Fred Windhorst, Johnnie Schur, Uncle Frank Jordan on his farm up by Glasco, Philip Miller with his garage and gasoline tank wagon service out of Wells, but still Dad worried. "Dale, I wish I could afford to send you down to Wichita for some schooling in building airplanes, you're not getting ahead very fast - going to Kansas Wesleyan in Salina winters and working for all these farmers in the summer."

After Dale's one year at the job of being a rural school teacher, he knew for sure that teaching was a 'dead-end' street for him without more education. He had enrolled in Roosevelt's National Youth Association (NYA), a program that gave colleges money to hire young people to work on college campuses and pay their tuition.

"One of these days all Hell is going to break loose, Dale. That damned Hitler intends to dominate the world,"
Dad fretted.

Le Roy Windhorst and Dean Sommers had gone up to Lincoln, Nebraska to an Aeronautics school. Dad was wishing he could tell Dale to quit working for fifty dollars a month and get started in a real career before war broke out and his son would be drafted as a foot-soldier.

Anna could read her father's mind as she sat at their table on one of those wash days when she brought up the Constable's washing and helped her mother carry in water and wood, sort and hang clothes and cook for Dale and Dad. Dale would drop in often when he was working for farmers right around Wells and came to town on errands.

Mother washed and ironed Dale's shirts and work pants and Dale paid for the groceries at the Allison household. Dad's work was sporadic on the WPA and he planned to grub timber down on Hohensee's land by the river again that winter.

"Tell Jim I've built a new saw table on that saw rig of mine and he can saw wood for the whole county this winter if he wants to," Dad changed the subject as he focused on his daughter and her problems with her busy husband. "What's he doing today?"

"Dad, I can't keep up with him from minute to minute. He's either buying a new binder to cut feed for the cattle he's buying at the sale ring or measuring wheat ground for the Triple A, or stahlyting plow shears so he can plow night and day for Chet Siler after he gets ours done or building a portable welding rig up at Leo Campbell's. Take your pick," Anna's eyes looked tired as she spoke and Dad immediately frowned.

"That guy is smart enough if he's just channel it in one field."

Immediately on the defensive, Anna retorted, "Dad, you are a blacksmith who could be an inventor, a stone mason who could be a master craftsman, a butcher for all your neighbors, a really good mechanic, a carpenter who could build houses...," She paused for breath.

"And I'd build you one if you'd just decide where you want it and come up with the money," Dad said.

Anna sighed, "Jim doesn't even know one is necessary."

* * * * * * * * *

Anna got the scarlet fever that winter, she had no idea from where - but she gave it to a young neighbor in the Sand Creek community, she thought. Anna visited the Essig's when she was coming down with what she thought was a cold and three weeks later Darlene had it also.

Dr. Boyle confirmed the diagnosis when she became so ill she was chilling and aching all over while visiting with her mother in Wells. Mother had called him and Jim and put her to bed in her own room at the Allison house in Wells. Quarantined again! For a month Dad and Jim batched in the basement so they could come and go as they pleased so long as they had no contact with the women upstairs.

Jim had to feed his cattle and measure wheat ground - he couldn't be quarantined with a sick wife and Dad went down to the river and grubbed timber with neighbors who needed to replenish their wood piles for winter. Dad sold wood for 'five dollars a rank' as he said. Job-training was being provided by the government in Wichita and Dale had quit working for farmers around Wells and had gone down to work and learn aeronautics.

Jim was standing at the window visiting with Anna one day as Philip Miller walked by on the way down to the grocery store from his garage.

"Jim, you'll never be a papa that way," he taunted.

They were all glad when the month's quarantine was lifted and Anna could go back down to the Constable farm and Dad could come back upstairs and enjoy Mother's cooking.

"Dad, your birthday is coming up next Sunday, March 28 and we're coming up with fried chicken and an angel food cake," Anna said. "Mother says you're going to be sixty years old, so I'm bringing up the camera to take your picture."

"I haven't had my picture taken for twenty-five years," Charlie Allison said, "You'd better not try that - I might break the camera.'

"Be sure to remember to bring up that camera Sunday," Mother reminded Anna - in a phone call next day. Charlie has gone to Minneapolis to get a hair-cut and he said, 'I've got to dress up, Sunday - Anna's going to take my picture.'"

Dad's sixtieth birthday was celebrated, complete with pictures. He was happy and full of plans for a big garden and had ordered sweet potato plants from Henry Field's.

It was a rainy, chilly April day when Swede Hanes came to see Dad, "Charlie, could you build me a sink cabinet for the kitchen. Lene just won't let me alone about our old wash stand," he explained.

"What size do you want it and have you got the sink?" Dad was always ready to embark on a new project for his neighbors.

Dad built the sink cabinet on the scales under the eaves of the lumberyard across the street from the house. Swede was to tell Anna later that he always felt bad when he looked at that new sink cabinet because he came to town to check on Charlie's progress and he was standing there under the eaves chilling, the cold wind blowing around him. It was Dad's last project for his neighbors. He got the flu and he never recovered. Dr. Boyle came to see him several times when Dad had chills and there was no way to stop them.

The doctor finally gave up on the seventeenth of May and took Dad over to Asbury Hospital. Doctors Eaton and Sheldon, resident doctors, in Salina took charge and, though they visited him daily and took numerous X-rays they could find no tumor.

Mother never came home while Dad was in Salina. Hazel and Frank Sommers opened their home to her. She could come and go as she wished. She slept on their couch, called a taxi and spent much of her daytime hours at the hospital.

Harvest came and went and Papa got no better. Dale came to see him from Wichita every weekend. Anna picked and canned the boysenberries and raspberries and watered their garden in Wells. She drove over to Salina between hauling loads of wheat to Bennington.

"Dad, do you know that Hitler is taking his troops into Russia - he's overrun Poland and all the eastern European countries and now he's moving toward Moscow," Anna told him one day.

"Good," Dad said, "They'll never get to Moscow but a lot of them will die trying. Maybe that will keep them occupied and keep them away from England and out of the Atlantic."

After harvest, Jim bought a used 1939 Club Coupe with a deck behind the front seat. It was in good repair and Anna and Jim drove it over to the Asbury Hospital and parked it outside Dad's window where he could look out and see it.

"Now, Jim," he said, "You should get Charlie Houdek to pound you some irons to fix a good rack just ahead of the back bumper to carry that measuring wheel so you don't tear up your spare tire rack. Let me show you," he went on, and reaching for a pencil he drew a picture to show what he meant. Dad had designed his last invention.

The middle of July, Dr. Sheldon talked about sending him home so Jim and Anna went on a trip to Colorado. Toy and Myrtle Hanes went along. They were gone five days, climbing Pikes Peak with their new 'to them' Chevrolet, visiting Buffalo Bill's Grave on Lookout Mountain, going over Loveland Pass, staying in cabins in the Gunnison River Gorge, back to the Swinging Bridge over the Royal Gorge, and finally up through the cherry country on the Front Range to Cheyenne, Wyoming, in time for the Cheyenne Rodeo.

When Anna got home Mother had been trying to call her, Dr. Sheldon had told her that Dad wasn't going to get well. In fact, he had said that he had very few days left and had moved him to a private room. Anna rushed over to the hospital and met Mother in the hall outside Papa's room.

"Anna, I had the strangest experience last night. I couldn't sleep, I was so sad as I lay there on Hazel's couch. Shirley had been out for the evening and came in and went to bed for the night. The screen door let in the night breeze and the street light lighted up the room with a soft glow. I know I wasn't dreaming, I saw two little boys come through the screen door and walk by my couch back into the dining room area. I thought, 'What nice shaped heads they have.' I sat up, wondering why I heard no footsteps, and spoke out in the dark to Shirley; 'Did you hook the screen, Shirley?' I asked. She hadn't fallen asleep yet and she got up and went to the screen door."

"'Yes, it's hooked,' she said, 'I was sure I'd hooked the screen.'" Mother paused with a deep sigh.

"Mother," Anna said, "That was your two little boys who died at birth. They came to tell you that they would be in Heaven to greet Papa when he gets there."

"Oh, Anna, do you think so? They'd be twenty-eight and twenty nine years old by now," Mother said in wonderment.

"But they grow slower in Heaven," Anna said with conviction and a tender smile.

In the few days of Dad's life that followed, Mother told him about the two little sons they'd lost and all the other friends who had passed on and they talked of the reunion he's have in Heaven with his mother.

294

"You know, Anna, Hazel is such a strong Spiritualist and when I told her about seeing the little boys, she assured me that you were exactly right," Mother said later.

"And it does no harm to think so, does it?" Anna said, kissing the tired cheek.

Papa was too sick to take any interest in the cards that kept arriving from all the places Anna had mailed him cards, but his stout heart beat on for two weeks. Papa passed away August 8, 1941, at the age of just sixty years.

* * * * * * * *

The funeral was held on Sunday at the Wells Methodist Church and crowds came from everywhere. Charlie Allison had many friends who knew him for his whimsical humor and great kindness, so, even though the addition made the church bigger, it still did not hold the congregation and many had to stand outside.

Uncle Hank Allison, Dad's beloved brother who was just two years younger than he, was coming by bus from Pasadena, California. He called the mortuary almost at the time for the funeral and asked that they postpone the burial till the following morning. The bus had been delayed due a hot brake on one of the wheels. They were still in Hays, Kansas.

At the close of services there in the crowded church, the mortician (undertaker, he was called in those days) walked to the front of the church and announced, after talking to Dale and Anna, that Charlie Allison's burial would be delayed until Monday morning at the Hall Cemetery at ten o'clock.

This change in schedule set off a whole chain of happenings that would be unforgettable. Dad's body was brought back to the Allison house on Main Street in Wells to spend one last night in the house he had built for Stella. Uncle Hank arrived about six o'clock that Sunday evening.

Meanwhile up at the Hall Cemetery, the undertaker had driven by after the funeral and placed the rough box that covers the coffin - down in the grave to keep the open pit from caving in - leaving the large mound of dirt beside the grave. Late on Sunday evening, Melvin and Roland Allison, having been elsewhere on Sunday afternoon, noticed that their Dad, who tended the graves in the Hall Cemetery, had not yet closed that grave. They stopped, and taking shovels from their car trunks, scooped that great mound of dirt over the rough box in the bottom of the grave and neatly closed the grave.

When they got home they phoned their father to tell him that they had finished the work for him at the cemetery. All Allisons, living or dead, around the Hall Cemetery chuckled as those two young men got up early on Monday morning and dug that grave again before the long procession arrived from Wells with the body of their friend.

And no one would have smiled wider than Charlie! He had his one last joke.

****

The Exodus

Mother had always loved Uncle Hank because Dad had loved him - he was her favorite of all the Allison clan. Of course, Charlie was her husband, and, to her, head and shoulders above any of the rest of his family, in intelligence, manual skills, sensitivity; in short - he was her love of a lifetime - and now he was gone. She was like a small boat without a paddle, wallowing in a sea of confusion that Monday morning after Dad's burial.

"Come and go back to California with me, Stella," Uncle Hank said, "You and Charlie never did get to Montana while we lived up there. Francis told me to bring you back."

"Oh, Hank, I'm fifty-eight years old and so far, I've never been out of the State of Kansas." Mother looked as though she wasn't qualified to travel anywhere else.

"All the more reason to come with me," he insisted, "What have you got to do here?"

Mother looked around at Anna and asked uncertainly, "What do I have to do here, Anna?"

"Nothing that I can't do for you," Anna assured her, "Why don't you go with Uncle Hank?"

Jim and Anna had been sending in those Home Owner's Loan payments every month all summer. That $600 mortgage was set up with the Federal Government to be paid at $2 a month to save their home in 1934 and that note could be refinanced.

"Mother, Jim and I will move in here and rent your house. I'll make your loan payment every month and send you $5, so you'll get $7 a month rent for your house," Anna said, "Stay as long as you like."

"Stella, you can make all the pocket change you need helping Francis dress rabbits. Anna, you can send in all $7. We'll take care of Stella," Uncle Hank said.

"Well, Dale's gone back to Wichita, so he's not here to cook for and I don't have his shirts to iron. With Charlie gone, there's nothing here for me," Mother sighed as she spoke, tears threatening her blue eyes.

"Mother, you deserve a trip. Dale and I will do fine. I'll help you pack," Anna assured her.

Stella Allison left with Uncle Hank just five days later. Her sister, Belva Coughlin, had lived in California since 1923 and came to Pasadena to take her on down to San Diego after about two weeks with Uncle Hank and Aunt Francis.

California seemed like Utopia to Mother. "I wish Charlie and I had moved to California a long time ago. Maybe he wouldn't have had to work so hard and he'd be with us yet," she wrote to Anna, "Your Uncle Dave and Aunt Belva are living in a house that Belva built up the Jamul Valley from San Diego. Dave was very sick after the crash came - his heart was bad and several of his friends committed suicide. They lost everything in San Diego but, as a developer and real estate agent, he had acquired about ten acres up this valley that nobody wanted. When the dust all cleared away from their shattered dreams, Belva persuaded him to come up here. This soil is pulverized granite and it grows avocados. They require lots of water but they've dug a well in the bottom of the canyon, terraced the hillside and have the most beautiful avocado orchard you ever saw."

Mother's letters were also glowing to Dale, too. "Your cousin, Kerry, is married to the cutest little lady you ever saw. She's a school teacher. Right now they are looking for their first baby. It's to be born in January. Kerry has a job as a navigator. He works for Consolidated Vultee Aircraft Factory. His job is navigating new planes all over the world when they get orders from other countries. Kerry says there are hundreds of jobs out here and they are crying for people like you who have some training in building aircraft. Dale, you should come to San Diego."

* * * * * * * *

Meanwhile, back in Wells, Jim and Anna moved into Mother's house from the parsonage where they'd lived after moving from the rock house and Betsy's house. They didn't have a lot of furniture to move - a living room couch that laid out flat for a bed - a double bed mattress, a kitchen cupboard - but Mother had the accumulation of furniture from thirty years of marriage, so they didn't need a lot.

Lloyd Baker, who lived just northwest of Wells, came to Anna's door late that August. "Anna," he said, "We've lost our teacher for this fall. They are paying more for women to work in aircraft factories in Wichita and we got a resignation from that woman this morning - before she ever started. Could you teach for us this winter?"

Pleasant Valley was about four miles from Wells and she'd have ten pupils, Claude Baker's children, Fred Harder's children and Morris Heald's three daughters, a lovely group of children. They offered her sixty-five dollars a month.

There was one little problem, though. All Europe was at war In September, 1940 Congress passed a Selective Service Act, authorizing a general registration and the training of eight hundred thousand drafted men. So all that summer of 1941 various friends of Jim's, farmers' sons from around Bennington, were being drafted into the armed services.

"Anna, you won't be a dependent of Jim's if you teach school this fall," Betsy said.

Jim had tried to enlist in the Navy just out of high school in 1935, Anna remembered, but his parents found a way to keep him from going;

John had allowed him to break the northwest forty on the Swanson place, for his very own to farm. Now, they had bought a new tractor, Jim had cattle and they had dug a trench silo. They had also bought a hammermill that run from a power-take-off on the a new Allis Chalmer's tractor which they bought in 1940.

In short, what Betsy was trying to tell Anna was that, for sixty-five dollars a month, she'd be removing their son's marital status with a dependent wife. Jim could be drafted!

There were not many young farmers left, and though Jim was only twenty-five, one year under the exempt age, he'd been farming for ten years, at least. Anna felt that she didn't want to be responsible for Jim being drafted so she told Chris Livengood, Fred Harder, and Lloyd Baker, the three school board members, the problem and they prepared a statement to go in Jim's Selective Service file stating that Anna had not solicited the job of teaching and had been drafted into that position due to the resignation of the teacher they'd hired in the spring.

Jim was once more, saved from doing something 'for himself' as Queenie had said at the Constable table several years before - and Anna taught Pleasant Valley that winter.

* * * * * * * * *

Anna had been teaching about a week when Dale came home from Wichita to prepare to move to California. He had completed his aeronautics training and could have gone to work for Beech in Wichita but Mother's letters had been so glowing about the climate and the opportunities in San Diego so he felt he should go out there. Dale had promised his father that he'd look after his mother so he was leaving Kansas.

Just at four o'clock, as the children were leaving the schoolhouse, Marnece Schur drove in the school yard, "We're having a surprise farewell for Dale this evening at your house," she said, "And since you're not leaving, I thought you'd want to know!"

Anna thanked her for the early warning, "How many people know about this?" she asked.

"Oh, about thirty-five, I suppose," Marnece explained, "It's such short notice but he's going in the morning, isn't he? "We're letting everybody know that we see."

"What shall I fix to serve, Marnece," Anna asked, thinking about Dale's washing and ironing process that would be in full swing in the middle of the kitchen when she got home. She'd have to mop and prepare something in great quantity without arousing Dale's suspicion - a surprise would not be easy!

"Oh, pop some corn - just anything - Mom's baking some cookies; we want to surprise him. We hate to see him leaving. Isn't your mother ever coming back?" Marnece worried.

"Oh, she's helping Aunt Belva. That's the way it always was when they were girls. When Aunt Belva taught for thirteen years, Mother ironed her seven petticoats every week and dozens of blouses - she finally taught one term herself and met Dad. Now Dad's gone and Aunt Belva has got her back."

"What's she doing?" Marnece asked.

"Aunt Belva sells dressed chickens by the dozen and delivers them on a weekly route," Anna explained, "Dale says he's going out and rescue Mama; he's having to do his own shirts right now."

"Well, we'll see you about seven," Marnece said, driving away.

****

This bright new day is given me
To live each day with zest...
To daily grow and try to be
My highest and my best!
(excerpt from "A New Year" by
William Arthur Ward)

"Wheeee!" A long low whistle disturbed the quiet classroom at the Pleasant Valley school that morning. All eyes were drawn to Janet Heald's bright face. She had been working a problem that Anna had written on the blackboard:

"Jim and Anna Constable and Forrest and Myrtle Hanes had left Salina at 1:00 p.m.- travelling west on 40 Highway to Colorado Springs. They arrived in Colorado Springs at 8:00 p.m. Their speedometer showed that they had traveled 420 miles. How fast did they travel?'

"You went sixty miles an hour all the way," Janet exclaimed, her eyes bright with excitement.

Warren Harder, a serious fourth grader, also, smiled at her and asked, 'Didn't you think a '39 Chevy could go that fast?"

Anna really appreciated that school room full of bright children - Alice Harder, her seventh grader, was good at scrabble, so she, Hollis and Marilyn Heald learned to play in self defence when the weather was bad and they couldn't go outside...the smaller ones played "I Spy." Every day was exciting! Her home in Wells was exciting, too! Though Dad had died, she felt he knew that she and Jim were living there and he was happy that he'd built a house that his daughter could call 'home' when Dale and Mother had left Kansas.

Jim had seen Earl and Doris Markley and their baby son, Lonnie, in Bennington and asked them up to Sunday Dinner the 7th of December, 1941. Anna had a pot roast, cooked in her new Wearever Roaster on top of the stove. (She had bought a whole set of Wearever Aluminum in 1936 and Mother had been using it until Anna had a kitchen of her own). She had baked an angel food cake in that roaster on top of the stove the day before, too. Sunday Dinner had been a success - Lonnie was down for his afternoon nap - Jim, Anna, Doris and Earl were all four lying across the couch that Jim had laid out flat in the living room (the only piece of living room furniture they had as yet - except for Dad's radio and big old black leather chair). Jim reached out and turned on that radio - expecting some quiet music....

EXCITED VOICES! SHORTWAVE MESSAGES! They all four sat up to listen! OUR NATION WAS AT WAR! THE JAPS HAD BOMBED PEARL HARBOR! With that one little turn of a switch their lives had changed forever!

Every phone line and every radio station was jammed all at once it seemed. How dare that little country come sneaking across the Pacific ocean all the way to Hawaii to bomb the United States' naval base!

Japanese envoys had come to Washington D.C. in late November, supposedly to settle disputes over the freezing of Japanese assets. And, while the envoys were supposedly considering United States proposals, the Japanese war fleet was sailing in attack formation. They also attacked the Philippines, Guam, Midway and Wake Island, Hong Kong, British Malaya and Thailand.

The United States, Great Britain, the Netherlands, Australia, Canada, New Zealand, and some Latin American countries declared war on Japan. Germany, Italy, and the Axis satellites with the exception of Finland, declared war on the United States, which then declared war on them, all in a matter of hours. "December 7, 1941," President Roosevelt declared, "A day that will live in infamy."

The whole west coast, California, Washington and Oregon, was on war alert - the whole country was mobilized, trains, planes, telegraph lines, all ways of transportation or communication were all commandeered by the government - the American people were at war!

Mother and Dale were in San Diego; Dale was building amphibious planes for Consolidated Vultee Aircraft Company. Consolidated was employing over twenty thousand skilled workers at that time and would be a prime target for the wily Japanese.

"Consolidated has a contract with the Netherlands to build amphibious planes for island hopping for the Dutch East Indies. Aunt Belva's son, Kerry, is a navigator for Consolidated and is delivering those planes in fleets of six at a time out across the Pacific - they are equipped with Dutch instruments which he has been trained to operate," Mother had written earlier.

Every home in Wells was affected in this same way. Every one had someone somewhere in a dangerous position and the Allison's were partially responsible. Dale had told George Comfort, who had married Louise Stilwell, that if he and Junior Kay could find work in San Diego, he'd drop him a postcard, which he had done. So a farewell party had been held in Wells for the Comfort-Stilwell family: George, Louise, and her two children, Junior and Marjorie, in October.

300

Anna was to think often of the old quote: 'They also serve who only stand and wait' as she rushed to the post office to get word from Mother. Word came slowly - mail service was also in high gear as every person in the country who hadn't been drafted did his best to stay at his post of duty - be it farming, teaching, postman, repairman or housewife - and still lend support to his loved ones in the armed services or working at strategic jobs in the States.

At last, five days later, Anna got a letter from Mother:

"Black-out curtains are being installed in every window up and down the west coast and a camouflage tent is being built which will stretch for miles up and down 101 Highway so that, should the Japanese try to destroy Consolidated some night, looking down, they will see only trees, not roads, not city lights, not factory roofs and not parking lots filled with the cars of thousands of workers gathered there to build weapons of war."

"Air raid sirens can be heard up this canyon every night. Dale and Junior Kay have found a little cabin a couple miles closer to San Diego. They have forty miles to drive to work but it's safer up here. George and Louise are right down in San Diego. An Aid Raid Siren went off last night and all those workers were plunged into darkness. Loud speakers told them to vacate the premises - go to their cars and drive without lights to their homes. Dale thought he was not even going to get out of that parking lot where two thousand cars are parked. He could hear fenders grinding against fenders as people struggled to get away from the bombs they felt would soon be dropping."

"Dale made it to George and Louise's apartment - it's just two blocks up from 101 Highway and about a mile from the factory. He said he went up to the door and knocked. There were no lights in any windows - no street lights - he carried a little pen light. He said Louise's hand reached out and grabbed his collar and yanked him inside. Her eyes were as big as saucers and she lit in on him, "Dale Allison," she said, "You got us into this - writing that post card telling us what big wages George would get. Well, he got the job but what good will it do us if we're all dead! I wish we were back in Wells right now without a dime!"

"Dale said those camouflage curtains are being built out of inch-mesh chicken wire and sprayed with glue and then chicken feathers are being blown into them. The feathers are dyed green and brown and will stick there and let the rain through - it's going to take a lot of chicken feathers, glue and wire to stretch over the naval base, marine installations and aircraft factories down there along the water-front."

"I feel so sorry for Clarabella - her baby is due in January and Kerry hasn't been heard from since Pearl Harbor - he was navigating a fleet of amphibian planes out over the South Pacific toward the Dutch East Indies. They think the military commandeered the planes and pressed them into service but they weren't equipped with weapons and the pilots were civilians. Belva and Dave are so worried and so am I, of course. Sometimes I feel like Louise - I wish I were back in Wells."

"I want you kids to come out for Christmas. Dale and Junior work the night shift and I go down the road from Belva's and cook a meal for them every day. You'll have two weeks vacation from your teaching, won't you? Please come. I have to stay here and cook for Dale - I urged him to come out here and he's doing so well at his work. It's so beautiful here - geraniums are blooming. Belva picks a case of avocados every day. They make me sick - I wish I could eat them - they are supposed to have all eight vitamins in them. Please write and tell me you're coming. Dale and I would be so pleased to see you both. Love, Mother."

It was a long letter and one Anna related to every one who asked. It was like news from the battle front.

Everyone stood around in the grocery store and listened to Anna read about the friends on the west coast. Wells folks were just like one big family when they were scattered across the Unites States.

Grace Windhorst spoke up, "We talked to Le Roy. He and Dean had been looking into starting a used-car lot in Wichita - they had grown a little tired of working for Beech. Sunday, they were on their way to Great Bend to buy a few used cars and they turned on the radio - I guess they went on out to the sale but didn't buy any - they decided they should go back and stay with their jobs - building airplanes."

Jim was afraid the tires on their '39 Chevy wouldn't stand a trip to San Diego. When Anna mentioned this at school, word traveled fast. Chris Livengood came down to the schoolhouse next day.

"You can't buy tires right now, Anna," he said. "The government has put a freeze on new tires - they are all being shipped from the tire shops to fill government orders."

"I guess I'm homesick to see my mother," Anna said. "You know she left with Uncle Hank when Dad died and Dale is out there, too..."

"Well, don't cancel you trip. I've got almost new tires on that wheat wagon we used last summer. Tell Jim to come out and get them, and go. And be sure you come back! And tell us all about what it's like on the west coast!"

"You can't travel across state lines toward either coast without your birth certificate," Toy Hanes told Anna that evening in the grocery store, "I heard on the radio that State Militia have guards posted at every state line on the major highways to keep track of spies who have infiltrated the country."

"Oh, Wow! Everybody around here knows I was born over there behind the lumberyard in the house Ernest Baker lives in now, Toy! - But how will I prove it to someone who has never heard of Wells?"

Aunt Cora Comfort, at the post office told her how to send to the Bureau of Vital Statistics in Topeka for a copy of her birth certificate. "But you won't get it in time," Cora explained, "It might take a month to come."

Jim had a Social Security number because he worked out of the Triple A Office, measuring wheat ground and money was taken from his pay to match what they sent in to build up his social security for his old age, but local school boards only contracted school teachers so Anna had no need for a number. Jim also had his draft card that showed he had been deferred from serving in the army for six months and Anna took along her big certificate that had been issued by the Kansas State Board of Education that showed she had been neither absent nor tardy for eight years from Wells Union II School, Ottawa County, Kansas from 1921 through 1929. 'That should impress 'em!' she thought.

Doll and Darrel Comfort agreed to look after their house while they were gone. The whole gang: Beth and Ernest, Toy and Myrt, Swede and Lene, as well as Ward and Avis, Davey and Eileen from across the street in the grocery store gathered the evening before they left - to see them off and tell them what to tell Peanuts and Louise, Dale and Mother, Junior Kay, and anybody from Wells that they might see. "We'll feed Pup (Jim and Anna had inherited Dad's dog when he died - Pup wouldn't leave Dad's home) and have the house warm and your house plants all back in place when you get home," Doll and Darrel assured them.

They felt like pioneers must have felt, setting out into the great unknown but were not stopped till they crossed the Colorado River at Yuma, Arizona. Their car was searched but the four extra tires in the trunk of the car caused no problem - Jim just explained they were borrowed from a local farmer to assure a safe trip, after all, it was Christmas, even if the whole world was at war!

Christmas Dinner was a traditional affair up the Jamul Canyon at Aunt Belva's. Dale had worked the graveyard shift at Consolidated and was still asleep down at his cabin. Clarabella, Cousin Kerry's wife, was so pretty and so pregnant. They were all still waiting for word from Kerry. Two or three of the pilots from the fleet of amphibious planes they had been delivering out across the Pacific when the war broke out had arrived back in San Diego. However, Kerry, being the only one who could navigate the planes with those Dutch instruments, had been pressed into service in Guam.

"The last I saw of him," Mitch, one of his crew who called Clarabella, said, "He was running for cover like all the rest of us - the Japs were strafing the beach and we were told to turn back - our planes had been pressed into service by the U.S. Government."

Uncle Dave, always a large and pompous man, referred to his son as "The Commodore" and left no doubt that the Christmas Feast was being held in his honor.

Jim and Anna went down into San Diego and drove onto the Naval Base - as far as they could go without being stopped. It was raining -

the guard who should have been at the gate, came out of the canteen and demanded to know what their business was there. "Just sight-seeing," Jim explained.

"Well, get out of here!" he barked, rain water dripping off his tin hat onto his nose.

"Where can I turn around?" Jim asked, anxious to comply.

"You can't! Drive right out here," the guard said, pointing to a foot-high curb separating the yard from main road.

"Here?" Jim said, studying the face of the surly young guard.

"Yes, Sir!"

Jim drove over the curb.

They went down to Tijuana, Old Mexico, about twenty miles south of San Diego, driving right through the gate manned with Immigration Officers who waved them on. A group of young army recruits were being drilled on a grassy knoll outside the hovels and mud huts of the Mexican town. They were in a foreign country! The Mexicans were mobilizing, too. A half-dozen World War I planes were being readied for action, should there be an attack. No one stopped their aimless sightseeing and they bought presents for all their friends back home.

The hitch came when they attempted to go back through the gate and Immigration Officers asked them to open the trunk of their car. Chris Livengood's stack of four tires plus Jim's spare filled the trunk! Then they got to show all the evidence that they weren't international pirates bootlegging tires into a country that had frozen all tires for civilian use! Their total innocence finally convinced the authorities and they were released with their tires intact. Anna was convinced that her production of the Certificate of Attendance in the Wells Union II Grade School for eight years was the deciding factor!

The trip home was just as exciting. It had rained most of the week they had spent in California and Anna developed a cold, to Mother's consternation. She had always been on hand to make chicken soup and nurse her daughter back to health. She felt that the climate was on trial, too. She wanted Anna and Jim to like San Diego County with its geraniums in bloom and its lush green avocado trees heavy with fruit.

Anna would have liked to bring Mother back to Kansas but Dale had applied for housing in Linda Vista because he had a mother to care for and she had him - and they constituted a family. Consolidated was building hundreds of homes for their workers with families. They would soon move into one of those lovely little homes -with hot and cold running water, an inside bath room and gas heat! Anna couldn't deprive her mother of that!

Jim drove and Anna lay on a pallet behind the front seat in the club coupe - all the way from San Diego across California and Arizona into Texas. The rain in California was a first-class blizzard across the Great Plains so they were traveling the southern route. She awoke from her congested stupor. "Where are we?"

"North of Amarillo," Jim answered, "Feeling any better?"

Anna raised up and looked out into the darkness. She had slept all day - now it was night - the car lights caught a glittering flag of ice that had blown straight out from a water tower and was congealed into a horizontal icicle at least six feet straight out...an unforgettable sight! She scrambled up into the front seat, "Shouldn't we stop somewhere?" she asked. "What time is it?"

"Just after eight - we could be home by morning. Hardly any place is open - the last place I gassed up it was ten below zero," Jim answered.

"Well, the old heater's puttin' out - it's warm in here. Do you want me to drive? I'm feeling better," Anna agreed as she opened the sack with the mince-meat filled cookies Mother had sent along.

They drove on into the night, crossing the state line into Kansas at Liberal. The blizzard had blown itself out, leaving drifts that had fallen victim to snow plows - the road was clear. Jim finally turned the driving over to Anna at Pratt. He snored as Anna hunched over the steering wheel and drove on through the darkness - ever nearer home.

Feeling a bit closed in - she glanced up from the road to understand why. Her path had been cleared through drifts of snow higher than the car! 'We aren't expected home till sometime in the afternoon,' she thought. 'Ah, well, we can build our own fire if we ever get there.'

They slid in the front door over a drift of snow four feet deep. Ice crystals twinkled in the air and the inside thermometer registered eleven below zero. They built a hasty fire with kindling and a log and crawled under the covers of their bed at five o'clock in the morning.

Darrel came up the street at ten to build a fire and saw their car and the tracks through the drift and left them to sleep. A wisp of smoke curled up from the chimney. Jim and Anna had made it home.

Stepping out of their bed in their bare feet into ice water, they woke hastily to discover that they had left the north window open a crack for fresh air when they left and the storm had blown snow in to fill the springs under the mattress on their bed and the heat from their bodies had melted it to give them a rude awakening about three that afternoon.

All their friends came to town and the house was filled with laughter as they welcomed Jim and Anna home and listened to the travelers recount their experiences. They had been out in the dangerous world - where the action was, and they had got home a day earlier to check on the cattle and shovel the drifts and get ready for the new year.

****

"Never before have we had so little time in which to do so much."

President Roosevelt, 1942

"I don't see why we had to get up an hour early this morning - in the dark to get ready to come to school?" Six-year-old Stanley Harder was attacking the abstraction known as Daylight Saving Time, adopted nation-wide during the war years from February 9, 1942 till September of 1945.

Anna didn't know why either. In the Mid-west the sun governed the time of speeding up farming activities and oft-times slowed down and cut off school time entirely in order to have time for farming but all kinds of Spring activities wouldn't begin till April when school would be out for the summer.

"The President has decreed that this will help the war effort by saving fuel and light - especially in the East and Far West." Anna explained.

"I don't see how," complained Alice. "The only way one could save electricity or kerosene is by staying in bed till it gets daylight."

"But the sun is up an hour earlier on the East Coast, remember," Anna reminded them, "So, for children in New York, it's daylight already when it's still dark here. That's why Central Standard Time is one hour behind Eastern Standard Time."

"But the sun is standing still, Grandma said," Hollis Heald spoke up.

"It is," Anna explained, "The earth is rotating on it's axis toward the east so our part of the earth is tipping toward the sun and the sun shows up on the horizon an hour after children have seen the sun on the East Coast."

Anna was drawing pictures and making circles on the blackboard, trying to explain to herself as much as to the mystified children why it was necessary to come to school in the dark that morning in February when a streak of light showed through a crack in the door.

"There comes the sun now," Stanley Harder said.

Anna put down the chalk and led the children to the door of the cloakroom and out onto the porch to see the sun come up as the Baker children, Junior, Betty, Gwynn and Victor arrived an hour late that morning. Claude Baker was working in Wichita and his family were all living on the farm a mile and a half south and a quarter west of Pleasant Valley School - a long way for small children to walk to school even in daylight.

"Dad was home over the weekend and he said maybe he'd make enough money so we could all move down to Wichita next year. There's lots of work in Wichita," Junior Baker explained.

Claude Baker had stayed with Anna's parents before she was born so he could go to school. Now he was going to move away so his family could go to school easier. Anna didn't blame them for thinking of moving away - it just seemed sad that more and more people had to move off the farms and into the cities in order to provide for their families.

"Time marches on!" It was time to make some changes. Soon there would be no children in these rural schools. Anna heaved a sigh. She would be twenty-seven years old next fall. A sense that she was just marking time while it was passing her by caused her a certain unrest.

She could remember when all these children were born. There were children in most of the homes of her friends: Charlotte and Daniel Crow had two little girls, Connie and Doris, Avis and Ward Comfort had Eileen and Davey; Doll and Darrel Comfort's little boy, Rex, would be nine years old in June. Earl and Doris Markley's little Lonnie was no longer a baby. A baby! That's what they should have - she and Jim - a baby of their own.

Of course, there was Swede and Norline Hanes, Toy and Myrtle Hanes, Beth and Ernest Giest, John and Marnece Schur, all young couples in their age group, who still had not started their families. All of them were living on the home place of their parents or farming with them. Well, Anna knew the feeling of living in someone else's home but now Anna had a home in Wells! Dad and Mother had vacated the premises and left it to her! She and Jim should grasp time by the forelock! There would probably be no better time!

School was out in April. The cream station was no longer in use as a business and it stood there beside the Allison house with the town pump beside it. They had drilled a new well behind the house on the back porch of the house and, since they had electricity, Jim had installed a pressure tank in the basement and Anna had running water in the house. She no longer had to carry buckets of water for washing - through the front door - she had a spigot right in the kitchen. The house had been wired since the fall of '39 when Anna had bought Ward and Avis's electric washing machine - an old Dexter with an electric wringer. - she had a handy way to wash diapers - so the summer of '42 Anna was pregnant.

Jim still farmed with his parents on the Constable place a mile south of the State Lake but Anna did her part as a farmer's wife by starting the baby chicks right at home in Wells. Jim cleaned out the cream station, put peat moss down on the cement floor and had about two hundred baby chicks around the brooder stove to be watered, fed, and cared for by the time school was out for the summer - and water right beside the brooder house.

Memorial Day dawned bright and clear - it would be a hot day and there would be no need for the brooder stove to be running that day. It would get too hot in that cream station for baby chicks anyway, so Anna turned out the brooder stove under the canopy. There would be a parade in Bennington from the Methodist Church up to the Cemetery and Betsy had baked pies for the "Graveyard Dinner" - as she called it, that was always held at one of the churches on Memorial Day. So Jim and Anna took the folks to Bennington for the celebration.

It was a hot day! Betsy sat in the car by the parade route and reminisced: "Jim always wanted to march in the parade - Bobby Dale would be leading the band and Jim always wanted to come to town and march with all the town kids behind the band - up to the graveyard. So every year we had to get him a new pair of shoes the last of May - school shoes were always worn out by the time school was out in April so he always marched in new shoes and wore a blister on his heel. He wouldn't put those shoes on again till fall and by that time his feet had spread out from going barefoot and so we always had a new pair of shoes setting around to give away."

The "Graveyard Dinner" was bountiful - with chicken and noodles, potato salad, creamed asparagus, deviled eggs, pies of all kinds, cakes, strawberries, home-made ice cream, green onions and radishes - the heat in the church basement wasn't as oppressive as it was in the car but Anna had a sick headache by the time the dinner was over. Betsy and John were enjoying the visit with all their old friends when a clap of thunder broke over their heads and every one hurried home. Country roads would get too slick to travel on in a rainstorm.

By the time Jim and Anna got their folks home on the farm and hurried on up to Wells, a violent thunderstorm was in progress. Claps of lightning with deafening rolls of thunder had the baby chicks all crowded under the canopy of the brooder stove. Sheets of rain had cooled the air and the little chickens were cold.

Fred and Grace Windhorst had closed the big grocery store on the east side of Main Street and, since it was Sunday and Memorial Day, Jim and Anna felt pretty much alone there on the street - trying to light that kerosene stove under the canopy for the little chicks huddled about them chirping softly with the cold. The sky outside had taken on a dark yellowish-gray look as the wind, claps of thunder and streaks of lightning pounded the main street of Wells.

Rovena McGavern suddenly appeared in the doorway, "Do you have anymore of that kerosene I could borrow? I thought we wouldn't need a brooder stove anymore," she said.

Rovena and Carl had moved into the back of the grocery store and had three-hundred baby chicks in a little shack behind it.

As Anna started to answer a crash of thunder and a ball of lightning in the street bounced on the Kansas Power and Light wires running up their street.

"Boy, that was close," Jim spoke from under the canopy Anna was holding aside so he could work, "I guess we should never turn these brooder stoves out. They're so hard to get started again."

Rovena was a couple of years younger than Anna. They had been friends since they were little. She was Fred and Grace Windhorst's oldest daughter. They had swam together in the stock tank on their farm north of Wells, primped in front of the mirror in Anna's bedroom on the Main street of Wells on Saturday nights - 'dolling up for the dance in the Woodman Hall.' Now, her folks had moved closer to town, closed the grocery store down the street and Rovena and Carl McGavern were living in the back of it. Rovena had two little daughters and was plainly expecting a third baby.

'Time really has passed me by,' Anna thought, 'While I've been teaching other people's children - but I'm going to be catching up.' That would be her secret for a few months yet, however. She had only just

308

missed that first period and she knew that hope was a long way from reality - eight months at least. The storm raged on.

The brooder stove lighted, they stepped out on the porch of the old cream station and looked north. A great gray blanket stretched from high in the heavens down to the horizon. Sheets of rain drove Anna inside the house. Jim came in after helping Rovena start her brooder stove, wet to the skin.

"Boy, this is the worst storm I was ever out in!" he said, shedding his wet clothes. "You know, it was almost clear in the west and black as night in the northeast, funniest looking sky I ever saw."

They were soon to hear that a tornado had struck down at Bud and Irene Hanes's farm just four miles north of Wells, scattering their home and all it's contents all over the countryside east of Wells, as it continued it's path of destruction. They jumped in their car and went up there to help them save whatever might be left.

"When you see those funnel clouds in the sky they must be further than four miles away," Anna said, as they drove through the sheets of rain. "That cloud covered the whole northeast sky from high in the heavens all the way down to the ground when I came in the house. I didn't see any funnel."

"Well, Viola Whitley called them on the phone and told them it was coming and they had time to get their twelve-year old daughter and get in the car and drive down this road. They even drove across the road and told Darrel and Edna Lott that a tornado was coming - they had no phone. They went back home and picked up a few thing and, picking up Darrel and Edna, drove down this road and looked back to see it tearing up their house," Jim said, as they drove in the yard.

It appeared that the whole Wells community was there - some hurrying about gathering up what they could while others just stood about in a daze. Bud Hanes had the township motor grader job of working the roads north of Wells so the motor grader was still standing there. It was a big one and the wind had turned it around and moved it a few yards. One small wall where the kitchen had been was all that remained of their home - a propane gas bottle stood outside it with the stove still hooked to it on the inside of the wall.

The rain had subsided after dumping seven inches of water in the wake of the tornado. Men were wandering out in the field to the southeast of the farm site, picking up clothing. Anna noticed them bringing in quilts and taking them down into the arch cave - one of the monuments to her Dad which he had built all over the county for people to go down into when tornadoes "cyclones," as Kansans called them then, were coming.

Jim went with a group of men to follow the tornado's path in hopes of finding more possessions so Anna went down in the cave and picked up six of those beautiful quilts. Piled together, sopping-wet, they were rapidly leaching colors and all the patterns would be ruined if they were allowed to dry that way.

'Maybe I can save some of them' she thought, as she piled them in her car. 'I have running water and can borrow wash tubs from Ward and Avis, across the street, I'll need six tubs to put them to soak - they'll have to be washed anyway.'

Her thirty-gallon pressure tank was soon depleted and it was only then that she realized that lightning had struck the transformer on that Kansas Power and Light line at the end of the street and she had no electricity to pump any more water from that new well on the back porch till some electrician came and fixed it. Once again the old hand pump out by the 'cream station-turned-brooder house' was pressed into service. Jim arrived back in Wells with more stories of the freak things done by the Memorial Day Tornado that had hit one of their own in the Wells community, before Anna got the six quilts and two feather sofa pillows out on the line.

"You know, that storm carried a roll of fifty pennies three miles and the wrapper never came undone till they hit the ground. They were lying in a pool of water and just the end had broken open and two pennies had fallen out and were right there at the end of the roll," Jim talked as he helped Anna hang the quilts on the line. "Irene had won that roll of pennies at an IGA banquet for being the most helpful, capable and charming grocery clerk in the whole chain of stores."

"Poor Irene! These beautiful heirloom quilts will never be the same. The colors still ran some more when I washed them but at least they're clean," Anna said.

"Let's hurry. I want to drive up by Lamar where that tornado tore up the old Walmsley rock house before it hit Bud's place," Jim said, "I guess several families saw it coming and drove down there to get in their arch cave and it took fourteen men hanging onto a rope around the door to keep from sucking those people right out of the cave."

"Well, Dad built them for everybody else but he always said he'd rather be up where he could watch them coming and lie down in a ditch," Anna sighed, "And he'd take his chances of being hit by Grandma's trunk or a roll of pennies."

"Grandma's trunk?" Jim asked.

"Yes, when Grandpa and Grandma Jordan had their first baby, Uncle Frank, and he was only five months old, Grandpa was digging a well by their new two-room house. He had it down about five feet when he looked up to see that a 'cyclone' was coming - he dropped his spade and ran to the house. 'Elizabeth,' he said, 'Hurry, grab the baby and come to the well, there's a cyclone coming.' He just had time to help her and the baby down into the well and went back to shut the door when the tornado hit. He dropped to the ground and rolled about six feet over to the well and fell in beside Grandma."

"They watched as the house was blown to bits. They only found the trunk, caught in the corner of a fence - it had burst open and Grandma's book, The Life of Christ, was there. It was water soaked, but it's leather bound. She gave it to me - I'll show it to you when we get home," Anna paused. "Tornadoes seem to follow a path. Delphos gets hit every so often but I've never heard of one this close to Wells."

The devastation of that big red rock house was so complete that only a pile of rocks remained. A little rag doll was caught in the light wires running along the road nearby. Some shiny wire circles hung there also, the remains of an innerspring mattress that had been airborne and hit the power line wires. Neighbors who had driven down there because they had an arch cave found their cars strung about the countryside but no one lost his life. The population of Ottawa County was grateful. Those missed by the tornadoes could help their neighbors pick their lives back up and go on.

****

All the world's a stage,
And all the men and women merely players:
They have their exits and their entrances;
And one man in his time plays many parts.
                    William Shakespeare

The stage was set on the main street of Wells. Anna was washing, Jim had gone down to the Constable farm to begin his day's work. They were using the old cream station for a wash house sine Jim and Anna were liming in the Allison house just two doors south of Philip Miller's Garage. Mother's old Dexter Washer was washing a load of clothes and Anna had gone back in the house to make a pan of starch for Jim's shirts when a terrible explosion shook the house. She thought the washer or the oil heater that heated the boiler of water out in the wash house may had exploded. Anna looked out the windows toward the south. No flames! The wash house seemed intact. She looked out the north bedroom windows and could see no smoke or flames, just the long tin shed. But something was hitting the roof of the house!

Anna stepped out on the back porch; sticks and chunks of splintered wood were bouncing off the roof. Stepping off the porch to look up on top of the roof so she could see where all the debris was coming from, she lifted her hands over her head to protect it from the flying kindling...

A feeling of impact air caused her to close her eyes for a moment. A crash caused them to fly open and she stared at the twisted hunk of metal six feet long which lay in front of her. It had crushed the wooden porch and the rock step where she had been standing just a split-second before!

Even in her shaken condition, Anna recognized that hunk of twisted metal as nothing that could have come from anywhere in her house or yard. It had to have come from Miller's garage.

The scene inside the garage is best described in the letter Philip Miller wrote to Anna years later when she asked him to describe events in Wells as he remembered them:

"Sometime in, probably 1942, at the Garage in Wells a careless Philip Miller was putting a set of points on Chet Piersee's Model A Ford truck."

"An old 1924 Chevrolet Engine was racing merrily away turning a line shaft half the length of the garage. This one inch line shaft drove a very old air compressor pumping air into a vertical one and one half foot by six foot steel tank with an obsolete gauge and no pop-off valve. A twelve inch rack of paper-wrapped (government - frozen) new tires was suspended over five-gallon cans & half-bushels of grease for the summer's tank wagon service for farmers near there.. The oil burning stove for the office was near there too.- all a few inches or feet from the air compressor.."

"Suddenly there was a terrific explosion. Daylight appeared above the now-racing line shaft - bent in a 90 degree curve over the place where the compressor once stood. The air was full of dust and the building shook. Fifty years of dust was filtering down from the open rafters. No window glass was left in the two sides of the garage. The tire rack of new tires and the white-washed walls of the garage were covered with yellow grease. There were no more whole grease buckets and the oil heater was heap of tin."

"So much for inside. Philip groped his way to shut off the engine and rushed out to see where the air compressor had gone."

"About that time a very ashen Anna Constable who lived just south of the big machine shed next door appeared at the door of the office..."

Dave Comfort said later that he and his cousin Weston, who were hunting out east of Wells, heard the explosion, and looked up to see what looked like a length of stove pipe high in the air over their once peaceful village. They hurried back to town in time to see Philip dragging away the six-foot heap of twisted metal. They marvelled at the wonderful luck that it had so narrowly missed the Allison house, demolishing only the wooden porch and the big flat rock.

Philip had insurance and promptly built a wooden back porch comparable to the one that was there, but the big flat rock that Dad had always loved for a step could never be duplicated. The lumber and labor cost Philip's insurance company $27.

Anna observed that evening, "You know, Jim, if all the world's a stage, as Shakespeare said, and all the men and women merely players, it just wasn't my time to exit this morning. We should thank God I still have a bigger part to play."

"Yeah, well, God couldn't do much about that old compressor of Phil's. That's been an accident waiting to happen for a long time," Jim said. "But, if God had a hand in you getting off that porch, we can thank Him for that."

****

312

To everything there is a season
and a time to every purpose under
the heavens:

A time to be born, and a time to die;
...Ecclesiastes: 3-1-2.

Summer of '42 - Anna was pregnant, gaining weight and feeling so happy. She went to see Dr. Boyle.

"Should I be gaining weight this early, Doctor?" she worried aloud.

"Oh, you are not too heavy. You have always been too light. You can afford to gain twenty-five pounds or so. We'll watch your blood pressure. Just be sure you drink plenty of milk..." He was interrupted by Anna's negative complaint.

"I can't drink milk - and milk on cereal gives me stomach cramps. It has to be cooked in soup or something," she explained.

"Well, you can start taking calcium - you'll just have to have it," he made a note of that and continued, "What about ice cream? Does that cause stomach cramps too?" he teased.

"Dr. Boyle, I cook the eggs and sugar with the milk to make a custard and stir in the cream and then add milk to fill the gallon. Mother thought cooking helped that sugar and milk problem when she was growing up. I don't eat much of it," Anna said, still thinking she might get too heavy.

"Don't worry about getting too heavy yet awhile, anyway. Anna, how old are you?" Dr. Boyle asked.

"I'll be twenty-seven before this baby arrives," she admitted, "According to your calculations. My birthday is November the eighth.- and you estimated December 15th, didn't you?"

"Yes, give a week or two either way. You waited long enough but you'll get along fine. I'll want to see you once a month, at least. You know I am not allowed to deliver babies in the hospital, don't you?" he asked.

"Oh, sure, I want to have my baby at home, anyway," Anna assured him. "Doris Markley liked your nurse so well too. Sadie Lott will be coming along with you, won't she?"

"Yes, she goes along with me on all my deliveries, and I charge an extra $25 for her - and $50 for myself, in case Jim wants to know." he answered.

"That's what Earl and Doris said you charged for Lonnie so you haven't raised your fees in two years, Dr. Boyle. We should be able to save something by December," Anna spoke with pride, "Jim gets all the wheat off of forty acres and he's getting quite a herd of milk cows He buys yearling calves every spring and sells the steers in the fall," she paused and added, "You know we live in Mother's house in Wells, don't you?"

"I didn't, but I'm glad to hear it. Speak to Bea for the same time next month on your way out," he spoke with assurance, "And get started on that calcium now."

Both Dr. Boyle and Dr. Hinshaw were practicing doctors in Bennington. Dr. Boyle was younger than Dr. Hinshaw. He practiced osteopathy, so the American Medical Association, having control of hospitals, could prevent him from doing surgery, delivering babies, or practicing medicine in Kansas hospitals. He was a general practitioner with a huge practice and was busy with office calls and house calls night and day. Anna had known Dr. Boyle since she had developed 'sick headaches' during her second year of teaching, almost ten years before.

"Anna," he had said to her one time, "Why don't you let me help you go to the School of Osteopathy and become a doctor. It wouldn't be any harder work than teaching rural schools. Tension is causing those headaches and there would be no more tension doing back-rubs than trying to explain Arithmetic to some of the pupils I've seen."

Dr. Boyle's only child, Vesta Lee, had sickened and died of a rare heart disease when she was a high school freshman, the same year Jim started to high school in Bennington. Anna remembered her dad telling about Dr. Boyle's beautiful young daughter lying abed. They lived on the Main street of Bennington, not far from his office. As Dad drove through Bennington on his way home to Wells in his truck, he said he would notice her fellow students bringing her lessons to her every day - hoping for the recovery that never came.

Dr. Boyle continued, "I need an assistant here in the office - right now I have three people desperately sick in three different directions out in the country; I promised I'd get out there some time today and the office is full of patients. Don't get married and start raising children...." He had looked so tired as he spoke that Anna felt guilty taking up his time with a few cords in her neck that drew up in knots. That had been at least eight years before. He was still trying to be in two places at once and he was still a good doctor.

'All the young men are going into the armed service out of medical school and off the farms, out of the tire shops; the blacksmith shops, anywhere where young strong boys and men were needed. And Dr. Boyle is still practicing medicine alone in his office in Bennington,' Anna thought. She was glad her doctor was too old for the military. She was glad her husband was married and his father was past seventy years of age, and that Jim also measured wheat ground for the Triple A and custom-cut feed for cattle for other farmers. He did custom-plowing for farmers whose sons had been drafted into the armed forces, they would work in shifts and his tractor and plow worked twenty-four hours a day.

'Jim won't be taken into the military,' she assured herself, 'He is a married man and a busy farmer - and his wife was going to have a baby.'

314

"It will be a boy," Marnece said. "There's always more boys born in war time to replace all the ones that are being killed."

Anna shivered, remembering being in the Farrell's Grocery in Bennington a few months before when Bob Reh's young wife, Margaret, who worked there, was called from her work to be told that Bob had been killed in the Philippines. 'War is taking it's toll on everyone,' she thought, 'I hope I'm not raising a son to grow up and fight in the next one. We fought World War I to make the world safe for democracy. Now, what are we fighting this one for?'

Anna hauled wheat in the harvest, the long lines of cars with sixty-bushel trailers attached - waiting at the Wells or the Bennington Elevator, providing an air of excitement missing from the daily work in the kitchen. Women were everywhere, filling in for the missing men. Ruth Miller worked in the Garage in Wells. She and Philip had two small sons, Kenneth and Allen, who ran errands and helped out as did Eileen and Dave, Ward and Avis Comfort's children, who ran the grocery store in Wells. Philip Miller and Ward Comfort were out delivering gasoline to the harvest fields or helping in the Elevator. No hands were idle throughout the land.

Anna served on the Sugar Board at the Woodman Hall early in the summer of '42. Everyone in Grant Township had to come and declare how many people were in their households. Sugar was strictly rationed, and much laughter was enjoyed about the ones who hoarded sugar ahead of the rationing.

Ward was allowed perhaps a dozen ten-pound sacks of sugar for all his customers each week when he went to the wholesale houses in Salina to pick up groceries for the Wells Grocery. Coffee, chocolate syrup, and many other grocery items were in short supply also. Since he couldn't remember who had bought those twelve sacks of sugar from week to week, he had put out a sign "Limit - Only One Bag per Customer" quite some time before.

"I get the impression that one of our diligent housewives has canned about a tanker full of fruit juice without sugar and is now making jelly for an army this summer," he observed to Anna.

"Ward, I heard that one lady had a terrible accident. She had been hoarding sacks of sugar, coffee beans, coconut and chocolate back under her bed," Anna, the story-teller, related. "And when she started to push a gallon can of gasoline back under the bed she tipped it over and spilled it all over her supply for the winter."

Ward laughed, "I suppose some sugar will still be around when all the Nazis are wiped from the face of the earth, but it's funny what just mentioning that you can only get one case at a time from the wholesale houses - will do to your sales of that item. But don't worry - when you need Karo syrup this winter for your baby's formula, I'll have it in the back room for you."

"But, today I need lemons and sugar, and Pork and Beans; Jim and Wimp Wallace are plowing for Chet Siler - around the clock. I've got the potato salad made and the chicken fried.   Now, all I need is a few gallons of lemonade and I've got to frost a chocolate cake. I've baked rolls, and I'm over here staying away from those hot rolls till they've cooled off so I'm not tempted to eat any more of them," Anna explained, "Good thing I live just across the street from a grocery store."

"Jim was lucky to get Wimp to help him again this year," Ward said as he counted out a dozen lemons. "Isn't he about ready for the draft?"

"Yeah, he's enlisting in the Air Force. We won't get him again. He sings all night as he goes around and around that field, and then, when Jim gets up there in the morning with the second set of plow shares and takes the morning shift, he crawls off that tractor and goes to sleep on a canvas cot with his nose pointed right up to the sun," Anna agreed. "Jim knows he's lucky to still have Wimp."

Farm work was laid by for the winter, except for the daily job of hammermilling feed for the livestock, milking cows, slopping hogs and feeding chickens night and morning. Jim liked living in Wells and driving down to the Constable farm, four miles south of Wells to help with chores. Anna was feeling fine and getting more ponderous by the day. Her check-ups each month were always encouraging. She was fine.

"Dr. Boyle, I read in the Look magazine the other day that for an easy delivery, a woman needed an eleven-inch spread between the pelvic bones. I measured mine and I'm only nine inches across - between these bones," Anna told him.

"Oh, you can read anything in magazines. Women have been having babies long before anyone had learned to read, you know," Dr. Boyle reassured her.

"But, you know my mother lost two little boys before Dale and I were born. She said the doctors told her that she had a cylindrical pelvis," Anna worried further.

"You are not going to be just like your mother," Dr. Boyle reassured her. "However, I think you'd better quit baking hot rolls for Jim and ease up on table salt though for these last two months; you don't need to get any heavier."

Pinochle parties were in full swing at the Woodman Hall. Everyone was welcome. Two couples would take turns getting there early to build the fire and put on the coffee - a pound of coffee in a cloth bag in a five-gallon lard can on a two-burner oil stove. They would set up the tables and buy the prizes - a high, a low, and a prize for the most pinochles. There were usually sixteen tables that winter. Everyone brought his own sack lunch. They met every week but with so many couples one's turn to serve didn't come often.

Anna seemed to be the only one there who was pregnant so she and Jim took a lot of good-natured razzing from all their friends. "I'll bet you won't be here next week!" or "Maybe it's just something you ate!" They took it all in fun. By Christmas they'd have a baby to show for all their patience.

Mother and Dale were both working for Consolidated in San Diego but Mother had got a leave of absence and was coming on the fourteenth of December. She hadn't been home since August of '41, just after Dad died. Anna was so excited - that was just one day before the baby was expected.

"Is your mother going to get here before the baby's due?" Edith Heald asked.

"It is due on the fifteenth. Dr. Boyle says that first babies are more often late than early. Mother is coming into Salina on the train. Hazel and Frank Sommers are going to get her and she'll be at their house when we go over to pick her up," Anna replied.

"That stork will be flying right down the street in Wells before then," Ralph Woolverton said, "I'll bet you a coke on it."

Anna and Jim had just stopped in front of Hazel's house in Salina when 'the bag of waters' broke. Jim had to go in to Sommers' house and bring Mother and her suitcase to the car - and a towel for Anna to sit on, going home. They stopped in Bennington long enough to tell Dr. Boyle what had happened.

"Go home and call me when the pains get five minutes apart," he said. He had an office full of patients but he'd pick up Sadie and be up there promptly, he assured Jim.

The pains did not start that day. Dr. Boyle called and told them to have patience, get some sleep, they'd start in earnest soon. He brought Sadie up the next morning and gave Anna something to induce labor. The baby was kicking strongly but what pains asserted themselves seemed to take the baby up instead of down. At last he chose to use high forceps and assured Jim that they'd have his baby soon. What happened after that was too painful for either Jim, Anna or her mother to describe. The forceps kept slipping off the baby's head - at last Dr. Boyle gave up and said he'd take them to the hospital in Salina.

"What about the baby?" Anna asked as they hustled her into a robe.

"We'd better be worrying about you now," came the answer.

Ralph Woolverton came into Wells and, seeing Dr. Boyle's car in front of the Allison house, stopped and bought a bottle of coke and knocked on the door just as Mother and Sadie were getting Anna into her robe. Jim went to the door and told him there was no baby and they were going to the hospital.

So the folk in Wells, collectively held their breath and collectively sighed when they heard the news - Anna and Jim's baby had died.

Dr. Boyle turned Anna's case over Dr. Sheldon - Chief of Staff at Asbury Hospital. A little boy, they named him Eric James, was born - seventeen hours after his death.

As Anna was being wheeled back to her room, two nurses brought him out of the delivery room, "Do you want to see your baby?" one of them asked.

"Oh, cover up the top of his head so she can't see the cuts...there," the other said, softly.

Post mortems are never very helpful but when Anna talked to Dr. Boyle, he advised her, "You had better let women have babies who can. You have a cylindrical pelvis and your baby had an oval head. He would have weighed seven pounds had he been alive when he was born. You're twenty-seven years old. Your bones didn't give like a seventeen-year-old."

One of the nurses said when Anna repeated that conversation with her doctor to her, "Oh, that's rubbish. I saw your baby born - I thought they'd have to take it out in pieces but he slid right out without a hitch. He was a beautiful baby."

It fell to Jim's lot to take the baby to his mother to be dressed for burial. Anna gave instructions about the dress he should wear, the lot to be bought next to Dad's burial plot in the Hall Cemetery, flowers, the casket from Fout's Funeral Home in Minneapolis, all the arrangements. Jim manfully carried them out alone. Mother stayed in the hospital with Anna. Jim's sister, Lou Campbell and her husband, Leo, and Jim's parents went to the grave side services as well as a number of their friends from in and around Wells.

Poinsettias poured into Anna's hospital room. Some were delivered in Wells and Dolly Comfort took them home to keep them from freezing.

"Doll wanted to take the baby's crib home with her but I told her I didn't know. I'd ask you what to do with it," Jim said.

"No! He tried so hard to be born - I want to look at that crib awhile yet," Anna cried. "And lay his things away in it. Please?"

"Now, Honey, it's whatever you want to do. I just want you home," Jim said, as he carried out the suitcase and the flowers, his chin quivering.

"Anna, Jim has done awfully well through all this. Think about him a little. We just wants you well now," Mother said. "You know, I lost two little boys before Dale was born, and I know Charlie suffered, too. You'll just have to give yourself time."

* * * * * * * * *

Dale had stayed on the job of building bombers in San Diego while Mother came back to welcome Anna's baby. He and Mother had a two-bedroom semi-detached house in a housing area provided by Consolidated for it's workers. Travel at best was hectic and Mother had a long lay-over in the Denver depot in December of '42. She had met a handsome Marine and his young bride from Iowa. He was being sent to San Diego and would be sent to the South Pacific.

Hearing that Mother had been living in San Diego, the lovely young lady asked eagerly, "Do you know of an apartment that I might rent in San Diego? I just wouldn't stay home - I insisted on going with my new husband as far as I could. He has to report directly to his Marine Base and I have nowhere to go."

318

Mother knew that there was not a hotel room, motel or apartment in San Diego available so she gave the girl her address. "My son will be there mornings. He'll be asleep as he works the graveyard shift. Tell him I said you could use my room, you two. He'll feel the same way I do about denying young love when there's an empty bed at hand."

Mother had written Dale several times, that she had arrived in Kansas; the sad news about his first nephew, etc. and asked each time about the young couple she had sent to him in her absence. And still she had heard not a word from him.

"Anna, I just know Dale's sick. It's not like him not to write a word to me or a sympathetic word to you? And, what about that nice young couple I met in the Denver Depot? I couldn't stand not to give them Dale's address. I just know something has happened to him," Mother continued to worry.

At last she got an explanation:

"Dear Mother, Anna and Jim, I was so sorry to hear your sad news but was too sick to write at the time I received it. And now I'm wondering if you'll ever have any grandchildren at all, Mother. I came down with the mumps the day you left, if you remember I was feeling rough when I took you to the train. When the young Marine and his bride came to my door I carried an ice bag to answer it. I told them I had the mumps, but they could tell - I looked like a poisoned pup. They both assured me they had had the mumps so I gave them your room. I needed a couple of nurses, anyway. I kept that ice bag wrapped around my neck."

"The company doctor said I could come back to work as soon as the swelling went down. They were in too big a hurry for me to get back on the job. After one night's work that swelling had gone down in a big way. The doctor tried to get me into a quarantine wing in the hospital but the beds were all full so he sent me home."

"You know, I could put that ice bag between my legs and chase that swelling right back up to my neck - I just kept it traveling back and forth and my nurses kept the ice in the ice bag for me. I don't know what I would have done without them - when that Marine had to report in to the base he had no worries about leaving his bride with me! She cooked my meals, kept the ice bag full of ice, he drove my car and brought in the groceries. I don't know how you could have found any two people better able to take your place, Mother. He's been shipped out and she has gone back to Iowa."

The swelling went down in the most strategic places but my right leg keeps swelling - edema, the doctor calls it - says it will last a long while but I should keep working and resting in between. Believe me, I haven't felt like doing much else."

"Keep a stiff upper lip, Anna. There's got to be happier times. When are you coming back, Mother?"

Your loving son and brother, Dale.

319

Mother went back to work in the big airplane factory the week after New Years - her leave of absence was up and the war raged on. Anna made a scrap book of all the cards, letters, tags from gifts and flowers and kept most of the baby things.

"Dr. Boyle, how soon can we start planning for our next baby?" She asked when she went in for her a check-up.

"Anna, I see you're not going to take my advice and let well-enough alone. You must wait for a year or so, and you know I'm not delivering babies anymore. I'll take care of your check-ups some of the time but Dr. Sheldon over at Asbury has told me he'll work with me on deliveries," Dr. Boyle said. "You never give up, do you?"

"If I had been in the hospital, would Dr. Sheldon have tried a Caesarean section after my water broke and those pains seemed to move the baby up rather than down?" Anna asked.

"The statistics are not good in Kansas yet on C-Sections but everyone's case is different and I'll not second-guess Dr. Sheldon on that," Dr. Boyle said with a pained look on his face. So Anna decided to discuss that with Dr. Sheldon when the time came.

****

A time to weep and a time to laugh,
A time to mourn and a time to dance.

Summer came and with it the wheat harvest. No one slept after the wheat was ripe till it was cut and hauled to the elevators. Factories were not making any farm machinery so when a tractor or combine or car or truck broke down - it just had to be welded, a part found to replace what was broken, the tire patched, the junk pile searched for a missing part.

Sudden storms, hot winds, pounding rains and hail could reduce a quarter section of forty bushel to-the-acre wheat to five bushel to-the-acre hog pasture, almost in the twinkling of an eye. The wheat harvest was always a feverish race with the elements.

During the Harvest of '43 there came a furious rain storm with sheets of lightning and loud claps of thunder. Combines quit running, empty buckets were hung over exhaust stacks and everyone took cover. There would be no more cutting that day.

When Jim and Anna got into Wells with the last sixty bushel wagon load of wheat, the electricity was off in the entire town. Lightning had blown a transformer. The elevator shut down since they couldn't start the hydraulic lifts, Philip Miller couldn't pump gas from his electric pumps, refrigerators had quit running in the stores and houses, and, when darkness fell, there would be no lights except for the old discarded kerosene lamps and candles. The only thing that could not be shut off with a bolt of lightning was the exuberance of the people.

The sun had come out, the wind had died down and the wheat was still standing. Tomorrow would be another day and every man, woman and child would be back at the same feverish pace. However, the human dynamo did not idle down.

Jim and Anna came out on the porch after a bath in the last clean clothes they could find (Anna had not had time to wash). They were both barefoot - their muddy shoes were still on the back porch. Main Street in Wells was sandy and rain water stood in small lakes all up and down the road. Jim got up and strode across the street to a long lake in front of the Comfort Grocery. Anna followed. She had always loved to make 'mud butter' as she called it, by stomping in the wet sand till it was the consistency of brown sugar syrup.

"That looks like a good idea to me," Ward said, as he peeled off his socks and shoes. Eileen and Dave followed suit. Avis came out on the porch, removed her shoes, and joined the group.

"Let's walk over to Miller's house," Jim said, "Old Phil isn't going to get away with closing up shop just because he can't pump gas." Soon the crowd swelled to Philip and Ruth, Kenny and Allen Miller, Si and Lois Van Meter, and little Jimmy, the elevator operators, Doll, Darrel and Rex Comfort, Dorothy Lois, Clayton, and Weston Comfort, ... The crowd continued to grow till there were twenty-two barefooted children of all ages churning up mud puddles, throwing water and sand, laughing and chasing one another with handfuls of wet sand and cans of water. It was a first- class mud fight.

Leonard Kuhlmann came driving into town with his hired hand. They had been down to some pond and swam, putting on overalls, only. They stopped in front of the bank building in wonderment. There were no lights, just people chasing one another in the darkness. Dolly Comfort jumped up on the running board of Leonard's pickup with a handful of wet sand and rubbed it on Leonard's chest. She jumped down to run and Leonard came out of the pickup, caught her, and sat her down in a puddle, almost in one motion.

The Allison pump had been pumped dry. Jim got the hose and tried to wash off various ones but Anna stopped him to save some water for coffee. She went inside and found the kerosene lamp. It had a hole in the chimney with a playing card to protect the flame from drafts but - like bugs who come to a light, the 'children' gradually found their way inside - Ward brought over cookies and the party finally simmered down.

Darrel said the next day that his stock tank was half full of sand since everyone went to his place south of town to wash off, but Anna found that a good bit of 'dry-cleaning' had been done inside her house in the half-darkness of a glorious evening.

That was how the war was fought and the farmers let off steam on the home front.

****

The Big Fire

Philip and Ruth Miller were part of the Wells scene for many years, and because of the close proximity to the Allison produce business and their home, their affairs often became their neighbors' too. Philip's letter to Anna also contained the story of the big fire in Wells:

"It must have been the Spring of 1943. I was loading the 100 gallon compartment of my gasoline tank at the meter pump in front of the station."

"Eugene Whitley had been drafted and Lee Siler had gone to school to be a bomber pilot. Ruth was over at the house preparing to come over and run the station when I took out on the truck. It was about seven in the morning. When checking the oil I noticed the radiator hold-down strap had come unsoldered. Those were hectic days and time was important so I killed two birds with one stone - got my presto light gas soldering flame and very efficiently soldered the strap while the tank was loading. The job was done but the patient died."

"The tank overflowed. As I jumped to shut off the pump I kicked the lighted torch and all was in flames."

"Besides the meter pump I had two old Visable pumps full of ten gallons of gas each which boiled and bubbled with the heat. The interior of the truck cab was instantly in flames and the wood window frame of the office was blazing. I phoned Ruth to bring over the water hose and Jim Constable from next door played it on the garage roof. Anna brought over a hose from next door - hooked to their pressure tank and, standing at the corner of their tin shed, (all the farther that hose would reach), played the hose on the porch and those two boiling gas pumps and kept them from exploding."

"I had a new coil of galvanized wire hanging at the back of the garage. Not bothering to untangle it, I tied it to the front bumper of the truck. Herb Kay was living in the bank building at the time and his old car was standing in the street. He backed it up as close as he dared and I hooked the wire to his back bumper but his old car had so little compression he couldn't budge that truck. I was frantic, to say the least and persuaded several of the onlookers to help me push that truck away from the front of the garage."

The truck was in gear and loaded so it really took a lot of effort and some mighty leery men and Herb Kay with his old car in low gear to move it away. We finally moved about three truck-lengths when the tires on the truck blew."

"Since the burning gasoline was removed from the building front, the two water hoses were effective in dousing the burning building. Anna continued to play the hose on the boiling gasoline in the visable pumps till their pressure tank ran out of water. Those pumps miraculously had not exploded. I came along and let the gas down from the glass bowls and they immediately cracked and broke into a million pieces."

"Quite a crowd had, of course, gathered for the early morning fireworks. The Minneapolis Fire Department got there but the show was over."

"Clyde Comfort replaced the front windows. The meter pump still functioned. I had deliveries scheduled and John Schur loaned me his old flat-bed truck. I borrowed an old 300 gallon tank from Al Powell in Bennington, set it cross-wise on the flat-bed truck and used it for some time."

"You couldn't buy a new truck and even used ones were frozen as to price. I eventually paid $800 for a used Ford truck and gave $2000 under the table - much, much more than I could afford or it was worth."

"I bought a used tank wagon from Derby Oil Co. in Concordia and used it the rest of my stay in Wells. Leonard Kuhlman continued to use it. I was able to buy a new Ford truck in late 1945 - went to Beloit to pick it up."

"Those were hectic days. We all tried to do too much and made too many mistakes."

"I hadn't read the fine print on my insurance policy. I was insured for actual cash value. They paid me $125. My new tank wagon of which I was so proud went for junk as there was no insurance on it."

"So that's how we fought the war in Wells and sometimes, though we weren't on the front lines, it felt that way."

****

Thank you, pretty cow that made
Pleasant milk to soak my bread
Every day and every night
Warm and fresh, and sweet, and white.
                    Jane Taylor

"One of my young heifers dropped her calf today," Jim said one evening in the Spring of '43.

Anna's attention was immediate! "Dropped her calf! You weren't to begin calving for another month, were you?"

"It didn't live. I called Doc Briney - he said he'd be out in the morning."

Anna had studied Normal Training Agriculture in order to teach in the rural schools of Kansas. One chapter was on Diseases of Livestock. "Jim that sounds like Bang's Disease; that's a terrible thing to deal with. In some states the government comes in and destroys valuable herds of cattle because it spreads across whole counties...."

"Now, don't get all shook up till we find out. Jim Cherry lost a calf or two last year - just across the fence to the south of us...," Jim's voice trailed off.

Anna worried all night. She could see the page in the Agricultural Book that she studied in Mr. Kerr's Ag Class - 'In humans, it is called undulant fever - usually affects farmers, veterinarians, and workers in stockyards and slaughterhouses. By leading to abortions or untimely births, the disease ruins valuable herds...'

"Jim, promise me you'll let Doc Briney do whatever has to be done for that heifer," Anna said, as Jim hurried through breakfast, "I know that Bang's Disease is infectious to man..."

"Now Honey, I'm not likely to lose a baby - I'm not carrying any! Stop worrying!" Jim said as he swallowed the last of his coffee. "I'll drive your dad's old car. Why don't you come down after awhile and take Betsy to town after groceries so she'll quit bugging me."

"Don't be flippant, please, Sweetheart," Anna pleaded, tears welling up in her eyes, "I don't want you getting undulant fever just when Dr. Boyle has said we could start trying for another baby."

"Oh, so you want me for a stud!" Jim said, his eyes gleaming, "Now, that's different! Maybe I can come back home for a 'Nooner' but right now I've got to get down there. Doc said he'd be out first thing this morning."

Anna went down to the farm that morning to take Jim's mother to Bennington when Doc Briney had confirmed that they did, indeed, have brucellosis in their cattle.

"Betsy, I'm worried about Jim. You can heat milk to 140 degrees and pasteurize it as a protection against infection from the milk of diseased cows but Doc Briney is teaching Jim to grease his arm so he can reach up into the heifer's wombs and pull those buttons loose from the walls so the afterbirth will come away. The cows have a fever and he could catch it," Anna said.

"Aw, that's just hear-say," Betsy assured her. "If he gets a little fever I'll fix him some chicken and noodles and it won't last long."

Chicken and noodles was always Betsy's solution for Jim's ailments. Anna knew it would do no good to talk to her, anyway. "My Agriculture book says that veterinarians often get the disease. I'll have Jim ask Doc Briney about that."

Jim lost eight calves that spring from brucellosis. Doc Briney came out and vaccinated his whole herd of Milking Shorthorns. The calves were to be vaccinated at six months.

"Jim, did Doc Briney say anything about undulant fever?" Anna asked him as they lay in their bed at home in Wells.

"Yeah, he said he's had it several times. He says you get a headache and a fever every afternoon till it runs its course. He didn't sound like it amounts to much," Jim spoke casually.

"Several times! Won't he ever get over it?" Anna continued to worry.

"No, he said it was like malaria, it comes back from time to time. He said most veterinarians have it. He sweats a lot with it and loses some weight." Jim smiled at her, "Maybe I can cut this two-twenty down to a hundred and ninety if I get it."

"Jim! Don't joke, when you had chicken pox your fever went up to 104 degrees," Anna wailed. "Don't you remember how sick you were? And one gets an immunity to that!"

"Well, don't worry about it, honey. I guess I proved that I'm healthy enough right now, didn't I?" Jim spoke with a slight smirk.

Anna had gone to Dr. Boyle to confirm her pregnancy that day. They calculated that March 6, 1944, would be the estimated birthday of their second baby!

* * * * * * * *

Anna was happy. Harvest was over and she was feeling fine. She had hauled wheat to the elevators again. Ruth Miller had Clayton Comfort* to help her patch tires at the Miller Garage while Philip was out on the tank wagon hauling gasoline to the wheat fields.

All the women were working - in the fields, grocery stores, the elevators, trying to take the places of all the young men at war. Clayton kept the old tires patched up so Anna didn't have to change tires on the wheat wagons - she'd leave a set in the morning and change to a freshly patched set before the day was over. Everyone was travelling on worn out tires. The old ten-foot-cut Holt combine was still holding together with the help of baling wire and hand-crafted hickory poles to replace worn-out steel. No one could get parts or buy new implements - the war effort was taking all the rubber and steel as well as sugar, coffee and cocoa. But still Anna was happy - she was pregnant that harvest.

She walked across a freshly-plowed field to where Jim was working that afternoon in late summer. They had been invited to a picnic at the lake and she wanted him to come home early.

"Come up here and ride back around the field with me," Jim implored," extending a strong, dirty arm down from the tractor seat and removing his cap to wipe the sweat from his forehead. A white line just below his hairline made sharp contrast with the thick film of dirt over the rest of his face, "This soil is plowing just perfect right now, just the right amount of moisture in it. I want you to see how the plow shares are scouring."

She rode, leaning on the fender of their orange Allis Chalmers tractor; new in '40, it was one piece of farm machinery that hadn't required a new part that wasn't available, so far. Jim loved his tractor.

---

* Clayton Comfort was about fourteen years old at the time. He later reached the rank of Major General in the United States Marine Corps, served his country in the Korean War and in Vietnam - he gave the Keynote Address at the Wells Centennial in 1987.

Many women drove tractors and took their turn with the plowing but Anna never had. She weighed about one hundred and fifteen pounds and did well to keep her footing and just 'ride along.' It was a rough ride.

"I carried a couple of buckets of water up to the barrel for your shower and put a teakettle on to heat so you can shower as soon as you get down to the house. I brought your clean clothes along."

"Should you be carrying buckets of water up a ladder?" Jim worried. "I wish I had time to run up to the lake for a swim. Two buckets and a teakettle full isn't going to get all this fine dirt off of me."

"You should get a hose coupling for that pump and pump a barrel full each morning and let the sun heat it for you," Anna advised, knowing that should have been her job if she had been content to live with his mother and dad and be a real farmer's wife. She felt guilty, and a little uncomfortable, bracing herself to keep from leaning on the dusty fender or being thrown from her perch on the tractor.

That night, after the picnic, as Anna was undressing for bed she noticed blood on her undergarments. Calling for an appointment, she went to see Dr. Boyle.

"Jim's herd of heifers are being treated for Bang's Disease but I haven't been near the corral," she told him.

"I'm treating a case or two of undulant fever," he told her. "You'd better take calcium for now and stay away from milk unless it's made into soup. You're not having a miscarriage - yet, but you'd better stay off of tractors. There's surely enough work that you can do around that farm without that. Meanwhile, I'll order Mayo Clinic's research from Rochester on what they know about brucellosis, and undulant fever and it's cure and you quit worrying."

Jim came home early from the farm the next day. "I've got a hell of a headache. And I'm not done plowing. I just couldn't stay on that tractor," he said, as he washed his face and hands at the sink. "I feel like I'm coming down with something."

'Uh Oh!,' thought Anna. She was canning blue plums. They were so easy to can; she just pricked them with a fork and packed them in sterilized jars. After filling them to the rim with light sugar syrup they were boiled in a water bath for twenty minutes.

"I've got a couple more jars to fill and I'll have put up twenty jars. Maybe I'll just cook these in the rest of the syrup I've made and get you some supper. What do you feel you can eat?" Anna asked, hoping it was just an upset stomach and he'd be fine in the morning.

He was! He was feeling fine the next morning and went down to the farm. "A couple more good days and we'll be done plowing the stubble and ready for a rain," Jim told Anna that morning. He was home again with a fever that afternoon.

"Jim, I have to go into Bennington to see Dr. Boyle. He told me he was sending to Mayo's Clinic for research they've done on undulant fever and how it might affect pregnant women. Do you feel like going along with me?" Anna asked.

"No, but I will. You haven't had any more signs of bleeding, have you?" Jim looked ready to cry as he spoke.

"No, just that one day but if he's getting the latest information available on brucellosis in cattle and undulant fever in humans I want to know about it. I visited with Doris Markley the other day and she said her brother was doctoring with Dr. Hinshaw for undulant fever and his face is getting paralyzed," Anna explained as casually as she could.

Dr. Boyle drew a vial of Jim's blood and sent it away for analysis. The test was supposed to show by a series of + 's - conclusive proof that he had or did not have undulant fever, tularemia (or rabbit fever) and several other diseases. When the test came back there were four + 's in the column marked undulant fever - there could be no mistake, Jim had the disease.

Dr. Boyle showed them the results of the research that he had received from Mayo's and explained that, should he have an outbreak of undulant fever to treat, Mayo Brothers would send him experimental shots to use if he would keep a record of their success or failure and take part in the research. They decided to become part of the experiment

Dr. Boyle handed Anna a book they had mailed him - much of it unintelligible to the untrained, but one sentence at the bottom had been underlined by some reader before her. It read, simply: "Pregnant women often miscarry".

Jim and Anna were born and grew up in a time-slot in history when antibiotics were not yet in use. The shots proposed by Mayos' Clinic merely forced higher fevers to burn the infection out of Jim's system. Anna took Vitamin E shots, known at that time to help reproduction.

****

"Where did you come from baby dear?
Out of the everywhere into here."

"John is on the tractor. I guess we'd better go to the doctor and get started on those shots," Jim said, coming through the door of their house in Wells. "Boy, it's hot out there. Soon as we get the harrowing done, I want it to rain."

"I expect your fever is coming up again," Anna said. "And, anyway, that's what the shot is supposed to do."

"Yeah, that's what he said, isn't it?" Jim agreed. "Burn out the bugs if it doesn't burn me up first. I hope they know what they're doin'."

"Well, if they don't, nobody does. Mayo Brothers of Rochester, Minnesota, is as far as we can go toward the latest word on a cure for undulant fever," Anna said, defensively. She knew that his mother and dad had told him he should have gone to Dr. Hinshaw.

They had just returned home and settled down to rest when the phone rang it's familiar 'One-long and four shorts.'

His father was on the other end of the wire, "Tell Jim he'd better get down here. There's a plane crashed just east of the gate on the Swanson place. It's on our place! What shall I do?"

"I'll let Jim talk to you," Anna told him.

"It was flying real low right over my head," John told him. "I could see the Army Insignia on the side of it. The prop wasn't even turning. When it crossed the road it got about fifty yards up into that corn field and nosedived right into the rocky hill."

"You'd better call the operator and tell her you want to report the crash of an Army plane and she'll put you through to Smoky Hill Air Base in Salina. We'll be there in a minute," Jim assured him.

At sixty miles an hour, hitting only the high spots on the dirt roads, it was closer to ten minutes before Jim and Anna arrived at the scene. People were coming from every direction and John had walked up, arriving just as they were turning into the field.

"The Dispatch Officer told me to keep people away from the crash site, but they're already here," John complained.

"Well, I'll tell them to keep hands off till the Army gets here," Jim assured him.

It was a little single-engine trainer plane. It had plowed into the rocky hillside, digging a hole about two feet deep, with it's engine; the body of the plane was a heap of plywood scrap. Its wings were broken from the body of the plane and the cockpit torn open to expose the pilot, a small, dark little fellow, his flight suit torn, bones protruding from the arms and legs, a large hole in the side of his head where some blunt instrument had punctured it. He had plainly died on impact.

The cornfield was hot and as dry as tinder but no fire had been ignited. When the military men got there with their big flat-bed truck, they had only to zip the dead pilot in an oilcloth body-bag, pick up the wings and engine and all the small kindling-like pieces of the rest of the plane. The altimeter was never found. One of the twenty-or-so people who got to the scene first, had it in his pocket, probably. No one ever admitted it, however.

The following week, a five-line notice appeared in the Salina Journal stating that an army pilot. Pvt. Pius Davis from Honda, Texas, had been killed in the crash of a small plane in Richland Township, Ottawa County, Kansas.

Hear-say reports were circulated that the small plane had been spotted, hedge-hopping at a very low elevation, and flying in a very erratic fashion in several places. Military buddies also reported that the pilot was angry and took off in the plane without clearance from the tower. Anna could not forget his small figure slumped in the cockpit. She wondered about his family down in Honda, Texas. 'Would he be missed and mourned as she mourned for her baby son who had not lived to be drafted into war?' She hoped she had a daughter this time.

Christmas came and went. Jim and Anna made their weekly trips to the doctor for his serum shots and Anna's vitamin E shots. Jim continued to have 103 degree fevers every day. Anna went to Salina once a month to Dr. Sheldon. He would deliver her baby March 6th in the Asbury Hospital, according to Dr. Boyle's calculations.

Jim arose every morning, feeling good enough to go down to the farm and run the hammermill, making chopped feed for his milk cows. During the harvest, Anna had helped John and Betsy learn how to run Jim's milking machine which was on an overhead track in the barn. Jim had built eight stanchions. There were twenty-eight cows and they would come up to the barn morning and evening to be milked.

By harvest time the cows were trained to go in the barn, eight at a time, and just four in the last group. Buckets of hammered sorghum were placed in the stall - a long trough behind the stanchions. As each cow came in and stuck her head through the stanchion to eat her allotment of feed, John would hook the stanchion so she couldn't get back out till she was milked and had eaten her chopped feed. Betsy would hook the rubber cups onto the cow's teats. Hoses ran from the suction cups to three-gallon milk jugs hanging under the machine. Two cows could be milked at a time. Betsy could lift the glass milk jugs down off of the overhead track and pour the milk into the ten-gallon milk cans that stood by the track.

Four of the cows belonged to John and Betsy. The rest were Jim and Anna's cows. The milking machine was Jim's. Betsy's work was simpler now that Jim had that milking machine. No more carrying buckets of milk down to the house and running it through the cream separator. Milk trucks pulled up beside the barn and the ten-gallon cans were loaded onto the truck to be hauled to the creameries in Salina or Concordia each day.

Ensilage (chopped feed from the field cutter) was hauled with the tractor and hayrack to and from the trench silo out south of the house. John's work had become simpler, also. Jim fed bundle feed with his tractor so John didn't have to hitch up his team and worry with harness - his horses were turned out to pasture.

John and Betsy's work should have been easier by that time - they were both past seventy years old. Anna felt that she should have been living on that farm if Jim was going to be a farmer. Other farmers past seventy years of age moved into Bennington or Minneapolis or Wells and their sons took care of the farming operation.

Anna had gone down to the farm each morning and fed the calves in the spring with teat-buckets. Jim had built a big calf-pen south of the house in the maple trees. It had seven stout posts along the north side, closest to the house. Each calf had a collar and each of those posts had a harness snap attached to it, and a hook so that the buckets, seven of them, could be attached there.

The calves were taught to come up to the teat-buckets, just above their heads with the rubber teats sticking out at the proper angle so that the milk went into the proper stomach (cattle have four stomachs, Anna learned). She could feed the calves in four hitches and they, like the cows, soon learned to take their turns, seven at a time, to be snapped to the post and milk poured into the buckets. When the rubber teat yielded no more milk the calf butted the bucket with his head and Anna knew to unsnap his collar from the post and another seven were there to be fed.

It seemed to Anna that no matter how much was done to simplify the task, she would always feel unable to get it all done. or to hold up her end of the load, especially since she lived in Wells. John and Betsy lived on the farm and she was like the hired hand, working there through harvest or canning. She brought the washing home with her and the canning was done at her house but the garden that yielded the corn or peas or beans or strawberries or peaches was down at the farm. The boysenberries, raspberries, asparagus, rhubarb and some of the vegetables were raised in her back yard. The chickens were down to the farm. She was the Sewing Leader for the Rockhill 4-H Club, which had been since it started in 1937. She was a busy lady but never seemed to get organized and was frustrated a great deal of the time.

Jim continued to have a high fever every afternoon. It would rage on through the evening so that blue plum juice was all he could eat for supper. His fever would break about two in the morning and Anna would roll him in a flannel blanket as he began to shake with chills. When he quit sweating, she would unroll him out of the wet sheet and heap more covers on the bed. This had been going on for more than four months as well as the weekly shots at Dr. Boyle's office.

"The idea of these shots is to cause his fever to run higher than usual so that it will burn the disease out of his system," the doctor explained to Anna.

"Isn't such fever apt to damage his heart?" she asked.

"I'm reporting his progress to Mayo's and, so far they feel they can safely strengthen the dosage some more. Trying to digest food when he has a fever is not recommended. The blue plum juice is as good as anything, and good for you, too. Plums are rich in iron," Dr. Boyle advised Anna. You're still having this baby in March, aren't you?"

"That's what you said originally and you told me I didn't miscarry it," Anna retorted.

"Now, Anna, you should know that, though a two month's pregnancy might not cause too much bleeding, some women lose a baby in an outdoor toilet without knowing it," Dr. Boyle said. "Anyway, Dr. Sheldon is keeping track of you on that, isn't he?"

"Yes, once a month," Anna agreed. "Mother is getting a six-weeks leave from the aircraft factory in San Diego, beginning March 15th. If the baby comes the 6th as figured, we'll be getting home from the hospital the day she arrives from California."

"Perfect timing, I'd say," Jim said. "I hope I'm over these fevers by then."

"Any time, now, won't be too soon on that," Dr. Boyle agreed.

Winter dragged on and the ruts in the country roads grew deeper where the milk trucks made their daily rounds. Jim went down to the farm every morning and worked about eight hours before the high fever drove him home at three or four every afternoon. He came home early the 9th of March. It was snowing hard.

"Betsy and John sent me home early. They're afraid I'll get caught down there, the roads are so bad. How are you feeling. Any signs of the baby?" Jim asked, sitting down heavily at the table.

"None, so far. How are you after that stronger shot Doc gave you?" Anna asked.

"I've got a pounding headache. I hope our baby holds off till this snow storm is over, anyway. I'm going to bed," Jim answered as someone knocked on the door.

"Why, say, you two, if you need anyone to run Anna to the hospital during the night, just call," Darrel Comfort said, stepping inside the door.

"I'm fine, so far, Darrel. It's Jim and this snow storm I'm worried about tonight," Anna said, as she glanced out before she closed the door behind him. "Sit down a minute while I take his temperature, can't you?"

"Oh, sure, Doll sent me up here to check on you kids," Darrel assured her. "When's your mother getting here?"

"The fifteenth," Jim mumbled, the thermometer protruding from the side of his mouth.

"I should be in the hospital by then," Anna said. "She's coming into Salina so that's no problem."

"It's no problem, anyway," Darrel said. "Rex is hoping we'll get to go after her and he can go along. She baby-sat him as long as she was around here and he misses your mother, Anna."

"She took six weeks off from work so she'll get to visit some - she always asks about Rex," Anna said, reaching out to remove the thermometer from Jim's mouth.

"Jim, your temperature has already climbed to past 104 degrees. You've got to drink some juice and lie down," Anna added after studying the thermometer.

"Shouldn't you call the doctor?" Darrel asked. "Isn't that dangerously high?"

"No, he's giving me stronger shots by Mayo's prescription," Jim said. "But I've got a pounding headache. I don't think I can swallow a thing. I had a hell of a time driving home, the snow is six inches deep on the level and I couldn't see those ruts. If I'd ever got stuck I'd have died right there."

Jim crawled into bed as Darrel looked at Anna with that shocked look still on his face, "Can't you get somebody to help your folks with the chores, Anna?"

"Oh, yes. Herb Essig will go down if we call him but Jim has been working on his income tax and his folks's, too, and only he can read their records. They have to be filed by the fifteenth, you know," Anna explained.

Darrel went on home with several admonitions that Anna should call if she needed them to come up or Jim got any worse. "And call that doctor so he'll know he may have to come up here tonight - talk to him, at least," he ordered.

Anna called Dr. Boyle's home, 'just to talk to him,' she assured Jim. Bea answered.

"Anna, the doctor had an emergency, a patient about fifteen miles west of Bennington that he's been watching closely, had another attack of appendicitis and he has gone to take her to the hospital in Salina."

"Bea, isn't 104.6 an awfully high fever? It's only eight o'clock and his fever doesn't usually break till midnight or after. I can't even count his pulse rate," Anna spoke softly into the phone. She didn't want Jim to know how scared she was.

"Honey, Charley will call and I'll tell him. He'll check with you at his first opportunity. Have you noticed this snow storm?" Bea sounded worried, too. 'The life of a doctor's wife was not one to envy, either,' Anna thought.

She lay down beside Jim on the bed but the whole bed was so hot she went out to the couch in the living room, walking the floor most of the time as the clock slowly crawled to midnight. When his fever didn't break, she took his temperature again. 105.8!!!! Her thermometer wouldn't register much higher! Anna sponged off his face and dribbled water in his mouth. Jim didn't seem to be able to swallow; he was breathing in short gasps.

Anna called Bea, again.

"Honey, hasn't he called you? He was taking his patient's husband home. They had left their children alone. He said he'd call me from there to see if he should go on to Wells. They must be stuck somewhere!" Bea was near hysterics.

The night wore on. Anna sat by her husband's bed and wrung out washcloths and sponged his arms and legs. He made no sound except for his labored breathing. 'People hallucinate with high fevers,' Anna thought. 'Maybe he can't talk - he doesn't seem able to swallow. I shouldn't have urged him to take these awful shots - we should have gone to Dr. Hinshaw or done as his mother suggested - just let her feed him chicken and noodles.' The night dragged on. Anna put more coal in the Warm Morning stove. She climbed up on a chair with the full coal bucket beside her, then lift it up to pour coal in the top. Jim added coal every morning. Since it needed coal, it must be near morning.

She switched on the light in the living room - after 4:00 A.M. Dr. Boyle must surely be lost.

The whole bedroom was hot - Jim's fever had kept it warm all night. She brought a wash basin of cool water from the kitchen and continued softly mopping his fevered brow. The door opened and Dr. Boyle was there.

He gave Jim a shot "to bring that fever down - but not too rapidly," he said. They sat on the couch and waited: "If he lives through this, he'll likely not have any more undulant fever," the doctor said, as he heaved a sigh and went back to Jim's bedside to check his pulse rate.

The fever broke and Jim began to chill. They rolled him in a blanket, removed it, sopping wet and rolled him in another. 'Sweat soaked flannel sheets had been in the wash every day for six months at least,' Anna thought.

"Well, Jim, I believe we've got it licked," Dr. Boyle assured him. "But I'm not going to recommend Mayo's treatment for anyone with a weak heart. Only a strong specimen could have stood what you've been through."

Anna had looked out as daylight was approaching, "Dr Boyle, your car is covered with snow and there's snow packed in the wheels and under the fenders. Did you get stuck?"

"I got lost! There's fourteen inches of snow on the level out there and I thought I could find my way to Wells without going back into Bennington...Nothing looked the same - I don't know where I was - I'll never know, I guess. I kept going east and north and was I happy when I recognized John Schur's house on the hill over west! I couldn't see for the snow coming straight into the headlights and I couldn't travel over five miles an hour and I didn't dare stop...," Dr. Boyle paused.

And Jim spoke, "And all we needed was for Anna's baby to decide tonight was the night."

Anna's baby didn't put in her appearance for two months, however. Jim went down to the farm and gathered up the rest of the income tax papers for that March 15th deadline. Darrel, Doll and Rex went to Salina and picked up Mother and they all waited for Baby's arrival.

Jim's temperature went down into the eighties and stayed there, and Anna worried about that. "Dr. Boyle, should Jim be feeding cattle out in the cold every day with his temperature in the eighties?" she asked in a phone call to him.

"Isn't his temperature normal yet?" the doctor sounded surprised.

"No. And he says he's fine. I think he's afraid Mayo's might have a shot to bring it up again," Anna explained. "He doesn't much want to see you again."

"And what about you? That baby's due date, March 6th, has come and gone and you're still waiting?"

"That's right, Doctor," Anna agreed.

"Well, tell Jim I need one more sample of blood to send to Mayo's but there's no more shots to my knowledge for anyone without a fever, and you'd better go see Dr. Sheldon, Anna," Dr. Boyle said.

Dr. Sheldon found that Anna should watch her salt intake and weight and have patience. And the blood sample Dr. Boyle sent to Mayos seemed clear of undulant fever.

March ended and April came. Jim, Mother and Anna played rummy every evening; and every night it snowed a few inches before morning. The road to the farm became more impassable by the day and everyone's nerves became more frayed as they awaited The Baby.

"The gestation for an elephant is two years," Ernest Geist assured her, "But take heart, you're not that big."

Living on the Main Street of Wells, with Mother home from California, as well, they had lots of company. All the Anniversary Club couples dropped in from time to time. They had all been married longer than Jim and Anna, except Beth and Ernest; they had waited three more months.

"A lot you would know about gestation periods," Anna retorted. "What effort have you and Beth made, Ernest?"

"Oh, we've been studying up on it," Beth laughed.*

Ward and Avis, their two children: Eileen and Davey; Toy and Myrtle; Swede and Norline and Beth and Ernest; all had dropped in that evening.

"Had you thought you might be in the hospital on your Anniversary, Anna?" Myrtle asked.

"Oh, yes, we've had a lot of time to think of everything," Jim answered for her.

"Well, that's what we've come for. May 5th is only ten days away," Avis announced, "So. tonight we're celebrating."

After two false starts, it became apparent on May 3rd that the baby's arrival was imminent. Jim and Anna stopped down at the Constable farm on their way to the hospital in Salina. Betsy had a grocery list that she wanted Jim to get for her.

John came out to the car and said to Anna, "Now, say, Anna, if this baby is fine and healthy and is a girl, I'm going to pay for it. Lou had three boys; Grace had three boys, Tom has just had one son, and you had one that didn't make it - Now I think it's time I had a granddaughter and I'm willing to pay for it."

Anna raged at Jim all the way to Salina, "We can pay for our own baby. 'If it's fine and healthy' he says! If it's a sickly boy - he won't pay. What a bargain! No matter what we have - dead or alive - girl or boy, whatever, we will pay the hospital bill ourselves. Jim, do you hear me!"

"Now, Honey," Jim tried to pacify her. "He didn't mean to hurt your feelings, he just wanted to encourage you."

"Encourage me! What can I do about it. No matter who pays for it, it will belong only to itself, and be its own person. It will be ours to care for till it's grown but even we won't own it," Anna paused for breath as a pain emphasized her words.

"Now, Now, Honey.." Jim consoled her.

"Asbury Hospital is the place to be to have a baby," Anna complained to Jim, after the student nurses had got her established in her room - ready for their long awaited infant. "But I'm wishing for the expert care of Sadie Lott or my mother to decide when to call the doctor.

---

* Beth and Ernest's first born, Douglas, arrived seven months later.

334

The little nurses in here don't know as much as my mother - and they won't call the doctor till the pains are five minutes apart or the head nurse says I've dilated enough. Do you think we'll have Dr. Sheldon?"

Dr. Sheldon had been having attacks of kidney stones at that time, and Dr. Greer, a new, young doctor who had recently joined the staff, had been standing in for him from time to time.

"I don't know. He's Chief of Staff in this hospital, and head-surgeon down on the second floor. Maybe we picked too busy a doctor."

"We didn't pick him, Dr. Boyle did," Anna reminded him.

"Well, we're lucky to have a room," Jim assured her. "They just admitted two more expectant mothers and they've set them up out in the hall. Military wives are pouring in here too fast for the hospital to take care of them. I saw one of my old girl-friends down the hall. She's head nurse down on the second floor in surgery. She said she was night-nurse down there all this week."

"You stay right in this room with Mother and me, Jim, and don't be bothering the busy nurses," Anna teased him.

Exhaustion and worry caused the nurses to decide Anna needed a night's rest and these delaying actions became more frustrating as time wore on. Jim, Anna, and her mother became more acquainted with the staff of Asbury Hospital than they needed to be and Anna lost patience. "My pains are more severe but still six minutes apart and this baby must be getting tired," Anna complained to the nurse. "Can't the doctor give me something to speed things up?"

"Dr. Greer is on the floor tonight, I'll ask him," the nurse replied.

"But my doctor is Dr. Sheldon. Can't you reach him?" Anna asked in alarm.

"Dr. Sheldon has gone home with another of those kidney stone attacks. They are so painful," the nurse explained.

Anna burst into tears as another pain racked her body. Jim had gone home to help John and Betsy with the chores and came back up the hall at about that time and found a couple of the student nurses crying in the hall. They told him they didn't know what to do and the head nurse was in the delivery room with another mother.

Jim went down to the second floor and found his old girl-friend, 'the head-nurse in surgery all this week.'

She came in Anna's room and felt her tummy, "This baby's head is lodged against her pelvic bone," she said.

She stepped to the foot of the bed and changed the position of the mattress with a couple of cranks and stepped back to push down just above those bones in Anna's lower abdomen.

"When the next pain comes, push!" she said.

She stepped back from the bed and spoke to the student nurses, "Call the doctor - NOW. This baby's coming!"

As Anna was being wheeled back to her room after delivery, her baby girl was being wheeled in her little basket from the delivery room over to the nursery.

"Do you want to see what you're in for, Mrs. Constable? Your baby has found her thumb already and she's starving!" a relieved and delighted little nurse said.

Anna looked into the most determined black eyes she would ever see. Her baby was sucking on that tiny thumb as though she would dare it not to produce milk!

She had a deep dent in her forehead. The nurse said, "Don't worry about the shape of her head, that dent will come out in a few days. She was lodged in the pelvis."

Anna's trials were not yet over, however. The placenta (afterbirth) had not come away while she was in the delivery room and every few minutes for another six hours a nurse would come in and knead her stomach. Dr. Greer came in the room and gave orders that she should be taken up to surgery to have it removed but as she was being moved to the surgery cart, it came away with a swish! No one seemed to mind the bloody mess, and Anna was vastly relieved. The sentence at the bottom of Dr. Boyle's research book on undulant fever came back to her mind's eye: "Pregnant women often miscarry." 'The vitamin E shots had done their work almost too well,' she thought.

Judy Charleen and her mother went home on the tenth day. There was a new baby on the Main Street in Wells and every one came to call.

Anna had a 4-H sewing class who had been counting the days till they could come to see the new baby. Gloria Comfort, whose mother had sewed for Anna when she was a girl, Eileen Comfort, Martha Adee and Norline Windhorst were four of the dozen who planned to be first to call.

Rex Comfort was determined to beat Eileen and Davey Comfort and get to see the new baby first. Rex's house was south of Wells, across the railroad tracks. He waited, that morning till he saw them drive into town.

"Come on, Mother," he called, grabbing the gift, "It's time to go."

Eileen and Dave lived just across the street from Anna's house and didn't see their arrival for five more minutes, but Judy's Fan Club was forming. Rex brought the cutest pair of pink booties with lace-up strings and pom-pom ties, the first of many gifts.

****

...A time to build up

Anna had her perfect baby and Mother left for California when Judy was twelve days old. Judy slept through the night - from 10:00 p.m. to 6:00 a.m. She weighed six pounds and four ounces at birth and gained eight ounces a week - tripling her birth weight in six months. She spoke her first sentence when she was five months old: When Anna laid her down on the counter at the Wells grocery store, across the street, Judy smiled up at Davey Comfort and said: "Hi, Dave."

336

She had been named 'Charleen' in memory of her maternal grandfather, Charlie Allison. She had his same smile which he had not lived to see. But she had an adoring Grandpa John and Grandma Betsy Constable and they got to see her and care for her during harvest when Anna hauled the wheat and ran the errands at the farm.

When Judy was six months old a new dimension was added to her life. Her mother found out she was pregnant again! Could life be more perfect? Anna thought so - after the first initial shock. In nine more months, Jim and Anna would have the perfect family.

But much happened before that day came. Jim had always been the baby of the family. His brother and his sisters had helped with the farming, married, and established homes of their own. Now, it was Jim's turn. The Constable farm was only one hundred twenty acres. Betsy had inherited it as her one-fifth share of her father, Tom Patterson's Kansas land. It was the homestead and had the original house, barn and out-buildings that Tom and Dorcas Patterson had built there. However, since one-hundred twenty acres had not been sufficient acreage to support the growing family for a long time, Tom and then later - Jim had urged John to rent more ground. To give Tom his start, the Swanson place and the Fender place, each one hundred and sixty acres (a quarter section) was rented just across the road and south of the home place.

Tom and John had bought a ten-foot-cut Holt combine and planted wheat during the years that Tom was in college. In 1925, when Jim was eight years old and Tom had graduated from college, they had a crop failure. Their wheat only made about five bushels to the acre. Tom had married and he and Queenie each had a job teaching at the high school level in Missouri. As they were leaving they swung by the elevator in Bennington and picked up the check for the sale of the wheat, leaving John to pay all the harvest bills.

"Do you see that screen-door handle there on the kitchen door?" John would say each time the subject was brought up about whether a farmer's son needed a college degree. "Well, that door handle was what Tom brought home from college. It is iron and has the letters 'KSAC' on it. Stands for Kansas State Agriculture College."

"Times must have been better in the twenties, John," Anna said to him on one of those occasions. "When Jim and I got out of high school, the drought and depression had wiped out everybody's livelihood. No one could afford college."

"Well, we couldn't afford Tom's college, either. It got him a job in Missouri and us a mortgage on the farm," John argued.

John was proud of Jim's interest in farming and his ability to keep machinery running. 'Constable and Son' had a good ring to it. He could go to the Bennington Methodist Church to Sunday School and argue 'Bible' in the Men's Class with the best of the landed gentry.

But the machinery was wearing out, especially the old Holt combine. It was old when the war started in '41. They had bought a new tractor in '40 and a hammermill so they could feed cattle all winter. Jim had found a good used binder with a power-take-off and did custom-cutting to pay for it.

One Sunday when Betsy's two sisters, Mary Torpey and Ona Rehberg, had come out from church in Bennington for Sunday dinner and brought their families, the subject of the wartime farm picture, the shortage of machinery, manpower, and the draft was the topic for conversation.

Guy and Mary Torpey's son, Mike had been drafted early in '42. He was just a year younger than Jim but had not married and had no interest in farming. If he had, Guy would have bought him a farm and could have afforded machinery before there was an embargo on it. His father had left him money and farms.

"Jim, if I was to buy that Winsett place just east of Wells, would you farm it for me?" Guy asked.

"How much wheat ground is there on it?" Jim asked with great interest.

"There's a long hundred and sixty on the south side of the road with the railroad out and the southwest quarter where the house is. I don't know the size of the pasture but it has a good barn and windmill," Uncle Guy replied. "Of course I'd have to fix up the house so you could live in it."

"I'll run out and look at it in the morning and let you know," Jim said, his excitement growing.

When the Torpeys and the Rehbergs had left that Sunday afternoon, John said, "That Torpey never did a day's work in his life and couldn't get his own son to take any interest in farming. I'd like to know why he thinks Jim don't have enough to do right here."

"Aw, Dad," Jim said, overhearing his father as he came in the back door, "We could handle another hundred and sixty acres of wheat. And maybe I could apply for a permit to buy a combine of some kind. That old Holt won't make it another year."

Jim, Anna, and their baby daughter went home that evening full of dreams of their own farm where Jim could have his own cattle, Anna could have her own garden, her own kitchen...She could cook noon meals right at home for her farmer husband...the more they thought of a farm of their own the more excited they got!

Guy Torpey was up to Wells very early the next morning to go out to the 'Winsett place' with Jim to look it over. They came back full of plans for things to be done, and in what order, to give Jim and Anna Constable a farm home of their own. Guy bought the farm that very week - in time for Jim to do the fall plowing and planting of the wheat.

"I'll have to keep feeding my cattle down to Johns' this winter but by next spring I can have the barn ready and move the milking machine up here. You and I can milk those cows with the milking machine... Can't we?" Jim said, his plans coming so fast he scarcely had time to think of them before he thought of something more...

338

Anna had plans in her head to put in a bathroom in Mother's house. With one baby to potty-train and another baby on the way, she h d been dreaming that when the war was over, maybe they could build on a back porch and a bath room; but the war was still going on - and Jim's Uncle Guy was willing to fix up that house in the country - maybe it might have a bathroom in it if Jim could raise a couple good wheat crops...

"How are John and Betsy taking your plans to move the cattle feeding and milking up to our new farm next winter after the house is made liveable and we move out there?" Anna asked Jim one night when the roads were bad and getting worse as the winter of '44 approached.

"Oh, John has already said they'd just go back to hand milking their four cows, and separating the cream," Jim said with some disgust. "You can't argue with him!"

"But nobody's testing cream anymore. We'd have to take their cream to Minneapolis - I don't know if anyone is buying cream up there, even!" Anna went on. "Are you going to get to bring the tractor up here to run the hammermill so we can feed the thirty cows you're planning on for next year?"

"Betsy keeps shaking her head every time I mention bringing his cows up here with mine and feeding all the cattle in my pasture - she says, "Don't say anything to John - I'll talk to him!"

"Jim, he'll be seventy-five years old next spring. He can't go back to feeding cattle all by himself with a team of horses hitched to a bundle-wagon, can he?" Anna snorted.

"Oh, he'll come around when he sees I"m really going to do it. ... I think," Jim said. "Anyway, don't worry about it. We've got the rest of this winter and next summer before we have to think about that. I want to get that house so that you and I can move into it by the first of April. You can worry about that."

So Anna worried to herself. Jim and his father had never had a business arrangement - Jim had taken the cream and eggs to town, sold them and bought his mother the groceries she had on her list - and kept the rest of the money, Anna thought. At least, he always had money to take her to a show or a dance and he always said that his mother was never without a little bit of money, even in the depression. Of course, there was that mortgage that they paid some on every year after harvest.

Anna had her own bank account during the years when she taught school and when she and Jim were married, they opened a joint account. His checks from the government for measuring wheat ground, custom plowing, welding or other mechanical work he did for others went into that account. When Anna took Betsy to town to buy groceries or go to the Ladies Aid, Betsy sold the cream and eggs. She bought the chicken feed. The car was Jim's. Anna bought gasoline at Miller's Garage. If she drove John's big old Hudson, the gas came out of the barrel on the farm and was paid for after harvest.

Anna continued to worry about how Jim was going to get his farming separated from his parents. She was sure that when Judy was born 'a fine healthy girl' as John specified, Jim had allowed John to pay the hospital bill. 'John was never going to realize that he didn't own Jim,' Anna thought to herself as she lay awake at night turning over and over in her mind how Jim was going to be able to take over the farming operation that he had down at his folk's place and still move his wife and family onto a place of their own. 'John Constable owns us all,' she concluded.

* * * * * * * * *

That fall, Tom Yonally brought a cavvy of horses back from Colorado. He said they were wild and had been caught out in the Douglas Pass area and he had them for sale for the guy who had rounded them up. So far as they knew, they had never been ridden.

"I'm going up and pick me out a saddle horse," Jim said one morning. "Toy and Swede and Darrel are going to be up there and I'd like to get my pick first."

"I've never seen you ride a horse, Jim - and those are supposed to be wild horses. Who is going to break him for you?" Anna asked.

"I want a mare, and I'll break her myself." Jim said, confidently.

Anna was used to the boys and young men around Wells being cowboys. They all wore cowboy boots and had saddles and spurs but Jim had been a plain dirt farmer since she had known him.

"Are you sure you can break a horse, Jim? You'll need a whole new wardrobe, too - jeans and a cowboy hat and spurs," she argued.

"I won't need spurs and I have a saddle up in the granary. I used to ride a horse to high school when I was a freshman," Jim just smiled at her concern. "I don't need any of that stuff to pick out a horse."

Anna was over in Ward and Avis' grocery store the next morning and heard Toy Hanes describe Jim's selection of his horse: "I was never so surprised in my life as I was when ole' Jim threw a lasso around that big horse's neck. Tom helped him get a halter on her. They got her over against the fence and Tom slipped the lasso off of her as Jim crawled on her back. She pranced sideways a little bit and settled down to some real fancy traveling around that corral fence."

"What color is she?" asked Ward.

"She's a big dapple gray, but Jim couldn't pick out a smaller horse since he weighs over two-hundred," Toy explained, and turning to Anna, he asked, "What do you think of Jim's horse?"

"I haven't seen her yet but I got to name her. Her name is Belle Starr. Jim says she's a single-foot pacer and what they call a five-gaited horse. He says that if she was amongst a bunch of wild horses she got away from somebody. There weren't any more there like her," Anna told him.

"Well, he fell in love with her at first sight," Toy laughed at her. "You may have just lost your farmer to the first cattle-drive that comes along."

340

And she did. Jim bought all the trappings and volunteered every time anyone was shipping cattle out of Wells. Anna couldn't see why he needed that horse but decided that 'All work an no play made Jack a dull boy,' and it was probably safer and maybe cheaper than the other hobby he had taken up earlier.

He had been taking flying lessons also, which was something Anna thought he should have taken up before he married, not after he had married and started his family. He got his student's license and would have flown every day if something else hadn't occupied his time that day. Flying lessons were expensive.

He had told Anna to tell 'Torpey,' as he called him, what she wanted to have done to that house so that she could move out of her mother's house by next spring.

"Jim," Anna said, "Torpey said he'd pay for whatever was needed, but you'll have to make out a list and go get it and either get a carpenter or do the work yourself. There needs to be screens made for all the windows and closets made between those two small bedrooms with a door between them if I'm to put Judy in one bedroom and have the new baby's basket in our bedroom. Don't you agree?"

"That's your territory. Talk to Torpey about it," Jim dismissed the problem without action.

However, they did get a door between the two bedrooms so that Anna could take care of the needs of two babies without walking through the dining room and living room to get to the second bedroom. And Jim made a really nice sink cabinet with counter space and drawers and shelves for pots and pans. But no screens were ordered or made to fit the windows. There were four windows on the west, one in each bedroom and two in the kitchen that could not be opened for air in the summer till screens were provided.

Mother was still in California but her work at the airplane factory was winding down. Her employment would be terminated and she was coming home for Easter. The war was drawing to a close - and none too soon for a war-weary world. Jim relaxed immediately as far as worrying about where his wife and family would hang their hats - he trusted Anna and her mother to see to that. He did more flying and riding his beloved Belle Baby.

Jim also planted a big garden at the foot of the hill where there had been a corral on the Torpey place. Someone had drilled a new well close to the house on the hill above it, moved the windmill up there, and piped the water down the hill to a tank on the north side of the barn in a new corral. The old corral had grown up to weeds for several years but it was a wonderful garden-spot, Jim assured Anna.

Jim applied for a permit to buy a Combine. The only thing available was an Allis Chalmers five-foot cut. The United States Department of Agriculture (USDA) only issued five permits for combines that year for Ottawa County. Allis Chalmers had been allowed to make a very small number to be distributed across the United States since the production of wheat was essential to the war effort. Jim bought new farm machinery at every opportunity so his dad would have a string of machinery also. The tractor was Jim's but his dad had none so he continued planting spring crops down at their farm as well as plowing, discing and planting his new half-section - the Torpey place.

Corn did not do too well some years because it usually turned off too hot and dry, but Jim studied the new kinds of seed on the market and planted corn west of the house - a new kind that was a hybrid and would mature early, he said. He had planted feed that would be cut with a field cutter and run through the hammermill for the cattle next winter. He had more than three hundred acres of growing wheat on three different farms, also. He was a busy farmer.

Anna needed help with packing and moving so she hired June Essig Babcock. She was Herb and Grace's oldest child, had rode to high school with Jim, graduated, worked in the telephone office, met a soldier from Camp Phillips in Salina and married early. She was home with a two-year-old son, Dee; her husband was overseas. Dee and Judy in her walker played underfoot. In four more months Anna was expecting another 'bundle of joy.' Her pregnancy was going well this time.

They moved from Mother's house in Wells - out to their home in the country - in March. The move went smoothly, however, Anna scarcely saw Jim. His folks were planting garden also and he was helping them plant spring crops and get a flock of chickens started.

Jim and Anna were still in the process of moving, had no telephone or radio when the news came from Wells that President Roosevelt had died. The war was not yet over; President Harry S. Truman would have to carry on. So would they all.

****

Franklin Delano Roosevelt 1882-1945

When Death Came - April Twelve 1945

Can a bell ring in the heart
telling the time, telling the moment
telling of a stillness come,
in the afternoon a stillness come
and now never come morning?

A bell rings in the heart telling it
and the bell rings again and again
remembering what the first bell told,
the going away, the great heart still-
and they will go on remembering
and they is you and you and me and me.

*And there will be roses and spring blooms
flung on the moving oblong box, emblems
flung from near-by, from faraway earth
corners, from front line tanks nearing
Berlin, unseen flowers of regard to The
Commander, from battle stations over the
South Pacific silent tokens saluting
    The Commander.*

*Can a bell ring in the heart
in time with the tall headlines,
the high fidelity transmitters,
the somber consoles rolling sorrow.
the choirs in ancient laments - chanting:
    "Dreamer, sleep deep
    Toiler, sleep long,
    Fighter, be rested now,
    Commander, sweet good night."*

Excerpts from a moving tribute written especially for the <u>Woman's Home Companion</u> by one of America's greatest poets, Carl Sandburg - and a quote from The Editors:

"Appropriately, Mr. Sandburg is a leading authority on another great wartime President who died as his tasks were coming to a close - Abraham Lincoln. We are publishing this poem as an expression of the sorrow in millions of hearts throughout the world."

Avis Comfort, left the grocery store in Wells that morning to come out and tell Anna that the President had died. He was thought of as her family's friend since he was first elected in 1932. Elected for four terms, he had lived but a few months into his fourth term.

Even those who had never supported him knew that the nation and the world had lost a great man. The Roosevelt years had marked a time when more Americans than ever before were unemployed; at another, more Americans than ever before were enlisted in the armed services. It was an age of battle, in which the people fought the longest and most serious depression the country had ever experienced and took part in the greatest war in the history of humankind.

Social Security was enacted as a system that gave hope for the future. Though many said it would bankrupt the nation, no one was willing to give it up, once it was in place.

Nature had taken a hand and drought struck the Great Plains. The Dust Bowl years had been overcome with social programs and conservation and reclamation projects. The Home Owner's Loan Corporation (HOLC), the Work's Progress Administration (WPA), the

343

Civilian Conservation Corps (CCC) and the American Agricultural Adjustment Act (AAA) had all contributed to Anna's family livelihood.

Mother would be coming home in a few days, having contributed to the war effort and paid off the government loan against the house that Dad had built, and thanks to Social Security that she had earned, she would not be penniless in her old age.

Anna went back to her washing after thanking Avis for bringing the sad news - with a profound sense of loss, thankful, however, that she had lived in the Roosevelt years and learned from him, first hand, that 'you have nothing to fear but fear itself.'

****

Do You Fear The Force of the Wind?

Do you fear the force of the wind,
The slash of the rain?
Go face them and fight them,
Be savage again.
                                    Hamlin Garland

Mother arrived from California just before Easter. Judy was eleven months old. She and Anna were baptized and Anna joined the Wells Methodist Church that Easter Sunday in 1945. It was a beautiful Spring morning. God was in his heaven and all was truly right with the world for the Constable family.

Jim had been a Methodist since he was a child but Anna had been going to church and Sunday School all her life without being baptized or joining a church. Mother had held the old Quaker view that her children would make their own religious decision when they were ready. On that day Anna did. When they came home from church, Jim took Mother, Judy and Anna's picture in the front yard at the Torpey place, and Anna took Jim's picture, holding his baby daughter. They had a Sunday Dinner of roast beef, potatoes, onions and carrots that had been roasting in Anna's Wearever pan on top of the propane gas stove while they went to church.

"Anna, what are you doing with my house in Wells when you kids have moved to the country?" Mother asked over Sunday Dinner.

"So far, nothing, Mother, I thought maybe you might want to live there. Helen Mangel wants to rent it. She has been living there in that big old Copeman Store building with old C.B. and Minnie. Her husband, Claude, is working away somewhere. She wants a place of her own. She says her little girls are getting so spoiled...." Anna hesitated.

"Why don't you rent it to her, Mom, and stay right here with us?" Jim interrupted. "Anna needs you, especially, this summer. And you could help me milk. The calves are coming on and as soon as they're weaned Betsy can feed them with tit-buckets. We'll have twenty-four milk cows, twenty are mine..."

"Whoa! Whoa, Jim. Did you see Mother's certificate? She has just been discharged from 'meritorious service as a member of the Aircraft Industrial Army of Consolidated Vultee Aircraft Corporation.' She's entitled to a vacation and Uncle Ney is coming down from Miltonvale to take her home with him for a visit..." Anna wanted her to stay with them, too. But that had been the story of Mother's life, helping someone else.

"I can help Jim with his milking, Anna, while he's making this move. And you can stay out of the cow barn - somebody has to stay with Judy," Mother agreed with Jim! She was always just too helpful.

"I'm not moving the cows up till they're all done calving. Go do your visiting - Anna's going to need you more later," Jim explained. "Right now I'm going to slip over to Salina and do a little flying today. Since I've been able to solo, I've been wanting to fly over our farm. So, if you're looking up in about an hour or so, you may see a small plane banking right over the house. That will be me."

"My goodness, Anna!" her mother said after Jim had gone to do his flying. "How did you come to let Jim start that? What if something happened to him?"

"Let him?" Anna retorted. "Just try to stop him!"

"Well, I hope he's got insurance to protect his family if he does crack that thing up while he's 'banking right over the house,'" Mother said, caustically.

"Now, Mother," Anna said, defensively, "Jim didn't get to play much when he was little; he started keeping the tractor running when he was eight, you know."

"But aren't airplanes rather expensive toys?" Mother argued.

"Oh, we manage to keep our heads above water, selling milk all winter and the yearling steers in the spring," Anna said, casually, thinking to herself that all the new machinery Jim was buying would take up all the wheat harvest money. They'd have to pay off the bank. McMichael was always too ready to lend Jim money for machinery.

"Anna, what do you do for recreation?" Mother persisted.

"Oh, I still belong to club and we still celebrate anniversaries, five couples of us. And, now that you're home, I'll be able to sew. Maybe you can keep Judy out of mischief. You know, I always loved to sew," Anna sought to divert her mother from complaining about Jim.

Judy weighed twenty-two pounds at a year, May fifth. On her first birthday, John and Betsy had bought her a little rocking chair. She climbed into it and stood up - she would tip over backward if someone didn't catch her. Anna borrowed a playpen of Helen Mangel and hid the rocking chair. But Judy stood at the edge of the pen and hollered. She wanted to be put back in her walker.

Judy could roll that walker everywhere and reach things on the dresser.

"Your Grandpa John says you'll never learn to walk as long as you have wheels," Anna explained to her.

Judy learned to walk one Sunday down at the Shelter House at the State Lake. Excitement of a picnic made her forget her walker. She was thirteen months old.

The wheat was getting ripe and the garden down at the bottom of the hill was really producing - peas and beans to be canned. Mother would be home from visiting her brothers in another week. Anna was busy washing jars and getting ready to can beans.

"Judy, it's time for your nap," Anna said, as she fixed a tub of water for her bath on the porch.

By the end of July Anna would have two babies: one new-born and one fifteen months old, and the tomatoes would be ripe. But Mother would be home. Anna straightened her back. Judy was getting too big for Anna to lift out of the tub. Anna put her in her crib and opened the door to the clothes closet that swung back at the foot, shutting off the afternoon sun from the west window.

Anna wished she could open those west windows but Jim still hadn't done anything about screens. It was a bright, hot summer afternoon as Anna went back to the kitchen to scald jars and get ready to can beans. She noticed a gray cloud coming up in the west. Jim was down to the barn working on stanchions, she thought. The new combine had been delivered the afternoon before; 'it was nice too have him working right at home,' she thought.

Anna looked up from snapping beans. 'What was that dull roar she was hearing? No train this time of day,' she thought. Suddenly it hit the west side of the house and instantly the house filled with bouncing hailstones and showers of glass. Some of the stones were an inch across. Sheets of rain pelted the west side of the house. No screens! The unprotected windows were no more!

What a hailstorm! And the sun was shining through it! Anna rushed through the dining room and living room to look in the bedroom where Judy was sleeping. Bits of fine glass and hailstones covered the double bed and beyond that was the crib. Anna had opened the closet door making a solid screen to protect the crib from the hot sun. That door had protected the crib from the flying glass and hailstones. Sheets of rain and hail soaked the double bed beside it but the crib had only a hailstone or two and no glass - only Judy standing up, looking at Anna her black eyes as big as saucers! The mirror on the dresser, unbroken, showed Anna that her eyes also were as big as saucers.

"It's all right, Honey," Anna said, "Mama will be back in a minute."

'She had to go see what had happened to Jim? He'd surely be up here by now if he hadn't been hurt,' she thought. Anna rushed back to the kitchen and looked down the slippery clay hill toward the barn. There was Belle Baby, bucking and tugging at her bridle, the hailstones bouncing off her back. She was snubbed to a post by the barn door. There was no sign of Jim! Had Belle thrown him? Where was he???

346

Anna made a tent of his big raincoat, left hanging on the porch, and slipped and slid over the hailstones, the sheets of rain washing the slippery clay under her feet. Anna reached the south barn door and looked in. No sign of Jim! Stepping into the hallway between the stall and the granary on the west side of the barn she glanced in the granary door. There was Jim - trying to replace a wooden window that had been knocked out by the force of the hail!

"It's raining in on my new combine canvass," he said. "Could you hand me a board and that hammer?"

"No!" Anna exploded, "It's raining in all over my house. I thought your new combine canvass was rubberized!"

She turned and fled, anger and fright lending wings to her heavy body as she made her way back up the hill.

The rain was subsiding as Jim followed her. Surveying the damage, he grabbed the broom to clean up the mess. Anna sat on the couch, holding her baby daughter. It was the only protected corner in the house that hadn't been hit with hail, rain and flying glass.

Finally she asked, "How come Belle was snubbed up to the barn, bucking and pitching, when I looked down there?"

Jim had brought up half his cattle the day before after fixing the pasture fence. "Honey," he explained, "I heard that hailstorm coming and Belle was in the corral. I threw a bridle on her and went out to the end of the pasture. I knew those cattle would bolt when that hailstorm hit. I had them headed for the corral when it hit but they turned and scattered. We made it back to the barn and I tied Belle there to keep her from following the cattle."

* * * * * * * *

Eight panes of glass and a box of glazer points later, Judy and Anna were back canning beans and tomatoes - the kitchen was hot but screens would have to wait till harvest was over. Torpey had said he'd get somebody to make window screen to fit the windows.

Anna had picked a peck of tomatoes, pushing Judy down the hill in her stroller to watch at the end of the patch. Several trips were taken to bring baby, stroller and, finally, tomatoes up to the house to be canned.

"Judy, where are you?" Anna asked, as she came in from the porch where she had been sorting fruit jars. The stroller was there but Judy was nowhere about.

"Judy, where are you?" she said again, "Are you playing hide and seek with Mamma?" The table was covered with ripe tomatoes - waiting to be sorted, washed, the slicers saved, the smaller ones, scalded, peeled and canned.

"Where is my big girl?"

"Eehh," came a small sound from somewhere.

The refrigerator was about eight inches out from the wall so Anna went over to peek beside it - no sign of Judy: a thirteen month old baby might be able to squeeze herself around behind the refrigerator but Anna had to move the refrigerator out to look there. There she was, a big ripe tomato in her tiny fist - juice dripping off her elbow.

Anna had told her, "No, no, Judy," as she piled the tomatoes on the table, and "Mind me, Judy," as she continued to reach for the tomatoes. Too many tomatoes had already upset her digestive machinery so "No, no, Judy," and, "Mind me, Judy," it had to be - if she was to stay well.

Anna's perfect baby was now growing into a determined little girl whose vocabulary now included "No,no, Judy," and "Mind me, Judy," as she stamped her little foot and ran around behind the table to reach for another tomato.

There was nothing to do but stop and put her in the high chair. 'Divert her attention' was the rule. Anna knew she was to have a full time job with two babies with differing needs and desires. But she wished for a bathroom instead of a potty chair and an electric washing machine like she had in town. The stomper, tub, hand wringer and washboard were poor substitutes, when it came to washing diapers and training panties.

'Big families had been raised on farms before' - Anna reasoned. 'Mother managed to cope with she and Dale only sixteen months apart. Once harvest is over, Jim will be able to help more,' she told herself.

But harvesting that year was a long drawn out task. Jim had about three-hundred acres to cut with a five-foot swath on his new Allis Chalmers combine and the rains came intermittently, causing delays while the ripe wheat grew weedy. He finished cutting wheat on the July 29, the day their baby was to be born. It was the first year since Anna had been married that she hadn't hauled the wheat to market. 'Next year will be different' she assured herself.

Mother was at home now and would be on hand to care for Judy and the house while Anna was in the hospital for ten days - that's how long the doctor insisted on - they were ready for the new baby to arrive.

Doll and Darrel Comfort came out to assure Mother that they would keep Judy whenever she wanted to go to Salina to be with Anna in the hospital. "Rex is impatiently waiting till we can have Judy," Doll said. "He thinks we should keep her all ten days you're gone, Anna."

"Don't let Jim hear you offer that, Dolly. Jim has found out that Mother can milk cows and I've told him that someone has to stay in the house with Judy. He's used to Betsy milking cows but I want him to stay home and milk his own cows. I guess he's bringing up half the milkers today," Anna told her.

"Now don't worry about a thing," Darrel said. "If Jim needs some help with the milking when he has to be in Salina, just let me know."

Anna was sitting out on the well curb in the shade one hot afternoon the first week in August when Philip Miller came out to deliver gasoline from his tank wagon. As he drove out of the yard he leaned out of the cab, grinned and her and said, "Cheer up, Anna. Maybe you just swallowed a watermelon seed."

What could she do but laugh?

****

The wind sang to the windmill
A merry little tune.
The windmill answered gaily
"The harvest's coming soon."
Excerpt from "August"
by Eunice Fallon

The baby came August twelfth, after seventeen hours of labor. He was a beautiful baby boy. His had been an easy birth in comparison to the other two deliveries. He had a small round head and presented no problem for Anna's cylindrical pelvis. He weighed four ounces more than Judy had at birth and was three and one-half inches taller - another perfect baby.

They named him Terry Patrick. Constable was such an English name. The Comic Section of the Wichita Beacon had a macho strip called "Terry and the Pirates." Patrick Ryan was one of its heroes. They flew fighter planes so the name was Jim's suggestion. Anna thought her dad with his Irish good humor would have liked Terry Patrick's name. Jim flew every day from the Salina airport when he came over to visit Anna in the hospital.

The Masonic Lodge Building in Salina was just across the street from the Asbury Hospital and Anna could hear celebrations going on in the street as she was in the delivery room. The USO had a Canteen there, and soldiers from Camp Phillips and Smoky Hill Air Base were dancing in the street. The war was over! Anna would still have to get a ration book for Terry, even so, as many foods would still be in short supply for a long time, and the Nation's fighting forces would still be eating first.

"The war is not over yet for me," said one of the nurses in the delivery room, "My husband won't be home from overseas for another seven months."

"The war will never be over for me," said another bitter voice, "I still have a son to raise without a father."

'A son to replace the ones lost,' Anna thought. 'Surely this has been the war to end all wars.' A United States bomber had dropped an atomic bomb on Hiroshima (August 6) killing 160,000 people in Japan. The next day another was dropped and leveled Nagasaki. Japan had sued for peace and accepted the Allied terms for unconditional surrender. At least the fighting and killing was over.

When Terry was twelve days old, Jim went with Toy Hanes to Kansas City on the train with a carload of cattle. Several farmers were selling a few cattle, enough to make a carload, but they didn't all need to go along.

"Jim, Mother is sick with the flu. Can't someone else take your place and bring your check for the sale of your six head home to you? Someone who doesn't have a new-born son!?" Anna asked.

"Now, that's what he gets for taking so long to get here. When we ordered that railroad car, he was supposed to have arrived in July," Jim blithely explained. "I'll only be gone one evening at milking time. Get somebody to help you."

That evening Mother said, "Anna, I can't possibly walk out and bring in those cows. If they'd just come in, maybe I could milk them. I'm feeling better, just pretty weak yet."

Anna knew that her mother was exhausted from coping with a fifteen-month old baby for ten days and Jim had left her to milk those cows, too, Anna knew. She said she had taken the stroller down by the barn - on a few occasions - so she could help with the milking. Anna couldn't milk cows without the milking machine - which was still down to the folks' farm.

"Mother, I'll walk out and get the cows," Anna said. 'I'd rather do that than call anybody and ask them to come and milk our cows and try to explain why Jim needed to go gallivanting off to Kansas City right at this time,' she thought to herself.

Anna had gained no excess weight during her pregnancy and weighed only 109 pounds when she came home from the hospital. The walk to the end of the pasture after those cows showed her that her mother wasn't the only one who was 'pretty weak.' She squared her shoulders: 'If I'm going to be a farmers wife...'

Jim came home with a pair of red silk panties for her, a bathrobe for each of the babies - a seventy-nine dollar Bulova watch for himself - and nothing for Mother!

****

...a time to tear down

August had turned off hot and dry after raining all through July. The fields were dry and weedy and even Jim's new spring-tooth harrow would only scratch the ground.

"I'll never get any wheat in the ground next month if I can't plow," Jim complained, "And I've got feed to cut down on the folks' place - John wants me to put it in the trench silo down there - and, if I'm to move my cattle up here - I want the hammer-mill up here. He can't run it without my tractor anyway." He continued to stew.

"Jim, you'll have to decide on some course of action, and then do it, even if it's wrong," Anna said.

"That's easy for you to say," Jim retorted. "John needs a hired hand all the time - and I guess that's me. And I can't be down there and up here at the same time!"

"Well, while you're making up your mind about that, will you pick up a putty-knife in town and a can of putty?" Anna outlined. "We need to get these panes of glass puttied in the windows so they'll be ready for screens or storm windows before fall. It's fast approaching."

Dale came home from San Diego. Jim envied him - he made enough money during the war, helping build bombers, to buy a lovely big home up Spring Valley from San Diego, Dale had met a beautiful girl from Minnesota who came out to California to see her brothers off to war and stayed to work for Consolidated. Evelyn had gone back to Clarkfield, Minnesota, to get ready for their wedding. Now Dale had stopped to pick up Mother. She was invited to accompany her son to his wedding.

Dale sat at the kitchen table, drinking coffee, listening to Jim tell about all the problems he was having, and all the money he'd been spending for new or used machinery to get started farming on his own

Dale said, "I bought my house for $9,000. It's on the side of a hill facing west - has plate glass windows from floor to ceiling facing Mt Helix. There's a cross up there and people from all over San Diego County come out there for Easter Sunrise Services every year."

Do they have hail out there? " Jim asked.

"Not that I've ever heard of," Dale answered, swatting at a fly. "They don't have flies either, I don't know why."

Jim continued to list all his problems with wartime shortages, the low price of wheat and the way the weather worked against him. Finally Dale said, "I'll tell you, Jim, I'd rather take what little I could scrape together after paying my bills and go up to Santa Anita and play the horses than to try to farm in Kansas. There is just no bigger gamble."

Anna was to hear her brother quoted on farming and gambling as many times as they had visitors that fall. Jim became more discouraged and got less done as the days went by. The milking machine was still in the barn at his folk's place but Betsy and John weren't using it.

"I like to go up to the barn, just John and me, and milk those cows, it reminds me of when the kids were young. It was the only time we had for love-making!" Betsy said with the perversity of the Irish.

Anna tried to talk to her mother-in-law about how Jim was just spinning his wheels and worrying instead of going ahead, moving the rest of his milk cows and the milking machine. "I went out and lined the chicken house with pasteboard boxes, Betsy. Could I take up that wire chicken crate of Dad's with a couple dozen young pullets in it so we could gather a few eggs right at home for cooking and eating?"

"Oh, you don't have to tend chickens while the babies are so little. I'll send you up a dozen or so every week when Jim is down here," Betsy said. "I'll have to buy chicken feed this winter anyway.

"I don't want to bother Jim with bringing eggs to me. That's one thing I can do and I've already lined the chicken house..."

"Why don't you just let Jim come down here of a morning and help John feed and eat chicken and noodles at noon this winter," Betsy suggested. "It'd save you a lot of trouble."

"Betsy, I'm not letting Jim do anything. He wanted me to move out to Torpey's farm. And he's got a lot of winterizing to do on that house. You know, it has a half dug basement under it - half full of water. It will be bitter cold this winter. Torpey told him he was ready, anytime to send up anybody Jim wanted to pump that water out and lay up basement walls and get storm windows on it," Anna paused...

"Tschh, I knew just how much he'd get done about that, all along."

'No wonder Jim can't concentrate on one single thing to do. A simple thing like having a few chickens in one's own yard wound up exactly nowhere,' thought Anna, in disgust.

* * * * * * * * *

Dale and Evelyn, her new sister-in-law, arrived from Minnesota, bringing Mother back on their way to San Diego to live in that new house. They would visit the Grand Canyon on their honeymoon. The grapevine was working and the first night they were there the gang from around Wells gave them a noisy charivari. It was the first social event they had held in Jim and Anna's farm home.

When they had left on their honeymoon, Jim's mood was very depressed. "Well, I wish it were us going south for the winter. Judy and Terry will both freeze this winter - they'll probably get pneumonia," Jim worried aloud.

Mother had sold her home in Wells to Thayne and Moyne Siler before she left for Minnesota. Neither she nor Anna suspected that Jim would care.

"If your mother hadn't sold your house in Wells we could have moved back in there. We know we can keep the children warm in there," Jim lamented.

"Jim, I had no idea that you would even consider backing out on what we've set out to do; we just have to take this month to get this house ready for winter," Anna was shocked!

Jim put his head down on his forearms, his elbows on the table and began to cry.

Where was Anna's enthusiastic husband who could take flying lessons, buy a riding horse and break her to ride, plant and harvest crops, buy new machinery and keep all those 'balls in the air' with seeming ease? Here he was - crying - like a child!

Terry had developed a cold at three weeks and, with a baby so tiny, there was no way to blow his nose. Anna had spent the night with him lying across her chest where she had rubbed mentholatum. By breathing the fumes, he seemed to be able to breathe. His skin was too tender to rub mentholatum on his chest. He had slept some with much snuffling but Anna had lain awake, worrying, and had discovered that Jim was quivering all over instead of relaxing to sleep as he usually did!

Mother was home to take care of Judy so Anna took Terry to the doctor and talked to him about Jim. "Dr. Boyle, what is the matter with Jim?" Anna asked, describing his failure to relax and sleep and his tears.

"Anna, it sounds like he's building up to a nervous break-down. Why don't you bring him in and I'll see what can be done," Dr. Boyle advised.

Anna went home with a heavy heart.

When Dr. Boyle checked Jim over and discovered that he had no reflexes and visited with him for awhile, he recommended that Jim go down to Halstead, "They have a good nerve specialist down there and you know you ran a very high fever with that undulant fever."

"But he passed an Airman's Physical six month's ago and they found no problems," Anna said.

"Oh, do you like to fly airplanes?" Dr. Boyle asked.

"Not any more! I've lost all interest in it," Jim told him. "But I did get my private license. I don't know why. It costs too much to fly."

'A complete reversal in his thinking,' Anna thought, 'But he doesn't want to go ahead with fixing up the house for winter either!'

Andy Shriver came up and helped him plow. They had often worked together on John's place, the Swanson place and Andy's farm. Bessie came along to see Judy and Terry and visit with Anna and her mother.

"Andy says that Jim isn't like himself these days," Bessie said, bluntly, "What's the matter with him?"

"I wish I knew," Anna answered, thinking desperately that, with a pair of babies, both in diapers, a house that needed a month's work before winter, she could hardly have time to put her mind to all the farm work that Jim had started on three places and would have had done by now if his heart was in it!

Mother was on hand to care for the children when Anna had to go down to the Constable place with Jim to move machinery.

On one such occasion, Betsy complained, "We never get to see those babies. Why didn't you bring them along?"

"Betsy, Jim is sick. He wouldn't have come himself if I hadn't insisted. He has feed to shuck in both places, he says. I guess he needs help. Dr Boyle wants to send him down to Halstead to a nerve specialist...," Anna paused.

"Tschh!" Betsy replied. "Jim always did hate to work alone. Send him down here to work a few days and I'll feed him chicken and dumplings. That will cure him."

"Well, we have to do something, even if it's wrong. I wish you'd talk to him," Anna pleaded.

Chicken and dumplings did not appeal to Jim. In fact, nothing did. At last, Anna took him down to Halstead. He was to remain for a week and then they would evaluate his case. Mother stayed home with Judy and Terry.

Anna was only able to nurse Terry for two months. He was always hungry and took a six ounce bottle of milk every three hours. He wasn't gaining as fast as Judy did, either. When Anna took him to Dr. Boyle for his six-weeks check-up he had said, "Now, Anna he's not going to gain at the speed his sister did. All babies aren't alike. He's fine."

"Mother, these babies are not going to know me, as often as I have to keep leaving them with you," Anna complained. "But I don't know what I would do without you."

"I'm just glad I'm here when you need me, Anna. Doll and Darrel come out and help with the milking - Doll stays at the house with Judy and Terry. We're getting along fine," Mother assured her.

When Anna went down to Halstead for the consultation, Jim's doctor assured her that Jim's having had such high fevers with undulant fever had nothing to do with his attitude now.

"He has a type of nerve disorder that is characterized by mood swings," he advised her."

"What has caused it?" Anna queried. "It's his attitude that causes his unhappiness, he's so depressed."

"Mrs. Constable, attitude is a state of mind. This young man had too many people depending on him. In my visits with him, he mentions a father and mother, an uncle and aunt, a wife and two very small children, not to mention a mother-in-law, who, by the way, he's depending on to take his place while he's gone," the doctor explained.

"It was his idea to have Mother live with us - not mine. I tried living with his folks the first several years of our marriage but I had to have a place of our own before we could start a family," Anna admitted.

"Well, don't have any more children. They are a threat to your husband's well-being," the doctor asserted.

"Is too much pressure what caused this?" Anna asked.

"No one knows what causes this condition," he said. "However, it is known that last children or only children are more apt to have it. When you go in to see him, don't talk about all the problems at home. Tell him you're getting along fine. I'll have to keep him another week at least."

"Then do you think he'll approach that thirty head of milk cows with the vigor he had when he was building the stanchions and getting the milking machine? He won't even move it up from his folks' place. They are milking half of his herd by hand and Mother is milking the other half and the milking machine just stands idle," Anna explained with eloquence.

"I know you've had a lot to worry about, Little Mother," the doctor spoke patronizingly, patting her on the shoulder. "But he'll soon be functioning again as a husband and father. Just don't mention milk cows yet. At present he wants nothing to do with a farm ever again."

Jim seemed anxious to be home after one more week but resumed crying and complaining as soon as he faced the mountain of small jobs that had to be done at home.

Torpey wanted Jim to tell him what needed to be done to the house - he didn't ask Anna. His dad and mother wanted him to come down there and help with what they needed done that fall, etc. and he couldn't make any decisions. He wanted to go back to the hospital. Anna took him back, agreeing to call the doctor at the end of a week. Jim was also worried about the brakes on their 1939 Chevy business coupe that they had driven all through the war.

"Anna, I want you to take this car into Minneapolis and get the brake drums replaced before you come after me again," he insisted.

Anna felt she was imposing altogether too often on all their neighbors. The wonderful field of hybrid corn was ready to shuck and Toy and Swede Hanes were organizing a crew of farmers with teams to come in and shuck it all in one day. Joe Grubham, Frank Comfort, Lysle Alderson and Darrel Comfort all had teams and wagons. There would be a dozen to feed. Doll was going to come out and help Mother. Anna wanted to be home to help serve them dinner that noon, not sitting up there in Minneapolis waiting for whatever had to be done on those brakes or getting somebody to bring her home. Poor Mother with two babies! 'And they were a threat to Jim!!!'

"Mrs. Constable, your husband doesn't want to be a farmer ever again at this point. He tells me that his sister in Texas has asked him to bring his family down to Texas for a visit and your brother in San Diego has room in his big home to keep you until he can find a home for you. Is this true?" the doctor queried at the end of a week when Anna called.

"Well, yes, our relatives have offered their homes but if we go for any length of time we'll have to sell our cattle. Can't Jim come home and sell them?" Anna couldn't take thirty head of milk cows to the sale ring in Salina!

"I don't think it would be wise for Jim to go home at this time. He needs a complete change of scenery. He may look at things in a different light in a couple of months, but right now - no, he couldn't sell his cows," the doctor advised. Surely some of your neighbors can help you."

****

The day is done, and the darkness
Falls from the wings of night
As a feather is wafted downward
From an eagle in its flight.

Come, read to me some poem,
Some simple and heartfelt lay,
That shall soothe this restless feeling,
And banish the thoughts of the day.

355

And the night shall be filled with music,
And the cares, that infest the day,
Shall fold their tents, like the Arabs,
And silently steal away.
- Henry Wadsworth Longfellow

Anna was in a pensive mood as she drove back to Wells that afternoon. She was just thirty years old that day in November in 1945. And what had she made of her life, thus far? Papa had always wanted her to marry some farmer and have the security that he felt came from owning a piece of the Kansas land. That might have come if they could have held the course but how had they come to this impasse?

Fred Windhorst and Darrel Comfort had hired the trucks and rounded up their cows and calves and hauled them to Salina to sell at Jack Beverley's sale ring that day. Jim had been so proud of his thirty head of Milking Shorthorn cattle - acquired over eight years of borrowing money at the Ottawa County State Bank, buying hogs first and then calves, selling some and paying off the note, building his credit, month by month, then year by year, till those cattle were free and clear. They'd have money in the bank. So what? What future?

Her farmer didn't want to face the problems in Ottawa County ever again, so his doctor in Halstead said - but he might change his mind in a couple of months. It was as if he was saying, "Stop the world, I want to get off." And Anna had no choice but to stop it for him, did she?

They'd be heading south for the winter: Mother, sixty-three, Judy, seventeen months, Terry, three months, and herself, a woman, thirty years old, in a car that, according to Jim was 'just a bucket of bolts.'

'Well, I've spent five hundred dollars on tires and brakes and the universal joint (whatever that is),' she told herself, 'and I can tell Jim that the mechanic said he wouldn't be afraid to drive it to California.'

All their friends, or thirty-five of them, at least, gathered at the Woodman Hall for a Farewell Dinner for them that bright Sunday in November. They snapped pictures with their box cameras of the whole group on the south side of the hall and one group that Anna was most proud of: the twin daughters of her eighth grade teacher, 'Miss Edith' (Yonally), now Mrs. George Lyne; Beth and Ernest Geist's son, Douglas Geist, and Judy, holding her baby brother, all sitting in their war-model wooden baby buggies and stroller. It would cause a lump in her throat when she looked at it as long as she lived.

The day of departure came. Anna had made a three-foot square playpen for Judy and still had room for Terry in his basket on the deck behind the front seat with room for his diaper bag and bottles of milk, with cookies, carrot and pineapple salad and milk for Judy. Terry's diapers, blankets and clothing were stored under his mattress in the basket. It had been a trick to get all their suitcases in that club coupe with room for Jim's suitcase when they picked him up in Halstead on their way south. It would be a long trip from Wells to College Station, Texas.

Now Anna could relax. Her strong husband was at the wheel and he seemed happy to see them all tucked in and waiting for him to take over. She was relieved she could tend the children.

Jim was nervous and eager to be on his way when they left Halstead. He would drive without stopping to rest until they reached his sister Grace's house at the end of the journey.

"I always said I'd never leave home for more than a week without my sewing machine, but I couldn't fit it in," Anna joked by way of excusing the cramped conditions with Jim under the wheel, Mother on the passenger side, and herself in the middle and two babies with all their paraphernalia behind the front seat.

Judy had developed a liking for big words and as they drove along she stood up behind the front seat and practiced, magpie fashion, the latest acquisitions to her vocabulary, "Hospital, hospital," she chirped.

"That will do," said Anna, noticing the tightening of Jim's jawline. At least, Terry was sleeping.

"Sewing machine, sewing machine," Judy said with a smile.

The End

CPSIA information can be obtained
at www.ICGtesting.com
Printed in the USA
LVHW040908050222
710354LV00014B/1177